SUPER HOROSCOPES'
Compatibility
Guide

by
**The Astrologers of
Super Horoscopes**

GROSSET & DUNLAP
A FILMWAYS COMPANY
Publishers • New York

TABLE OF CONTENTS

FOREWORD

The fault, dear Brutus, is not in our stars,
But in ourselves . . .

If you open this book expecting easy and ready-made solutions to all your problems you will be sorely disappointed. And what is true of this book—even though it is the most complete, candid, and detailed guide available—is equally true of all horoscopes, including personal ones.

The "fault is not in our stars" for they are always true and point out the many paths that open before you. Only you can act on the guidance the stars provide. If there are days when caution is called for and you act rashly, the fault then is clearly in yourself—not in the stars.

From ancient times mankind has known that the key to life for every individual was provided in two simple words: "Know thyself." This COMPATIBILITY GUIDE offers you that opportunity. Indeed, it does more than that. It provides an understanding of others around you, people you meet, love, work with, live with; it examines your relationships and the influences and interactions of all characters with each other.

You have in your hands the means to a fuller, happier life in every area of human activity. How you use it to guide your every day activity is up to you. Miracles do not come neatly wrapped and cheaply. Success and happiness must be worked for, fought for.

It is for this reason THE COMPATIBILITY GUIDE was created. The rest is up to you.

The Editor

ARIES
March 21 — April 20

CHARACTER ANALYSIS

People born under the astrological sign of Aries are often strong-willed and energetic. Ariens are seldom afraid of taking a risk, provided that it is well-calculated. They are people who dare; they are sometimes impulsive but almost never irrational. The Aries man or woman likes to keep busy. They are not a people who like to while away the time in an aimless fashion. Ariens are known for their drive and their boldness. They generally know how to make proper use of their energies; they are positive and productive people who seldom doubt themselves. They know what they want out of life and they go after it. They generally have a pioneering sort of spirit and are always anxious to begin something new. They know how to make use of opportunity when it appears. Many Ariens have no trouble in achieving success.

The strong and positive sort of Arien knows how to channel his energies properly so that he will get the most out of what life has to offer. He is a sensible, practical person, who does not only think about himself but does what he can to help those in less fortunate positions than himself. If a plan goes awry, he does not hesitate to see what he can do to fix it. The Arien is usually quick to initiate a change if it seems necessary to do so. He is an activist, generally, and does not believe in sitting about, waiting for good things to tumble into his lap. If good fortune does not appear, the positive Arien will go out and look for it; his search does not end until he has it. Obstacles do not frighten the Aries man or woman. In fact, contrary situations or people seem to spur him on. The Arien often thrives on adversity. He knows how to turn a disadvantage to an advantage in short order. Not easily discouraged, he will forge ahead on a plan or idea until it is exactly the way he wants it. The

Arien knows how to shift for himself. He won't wait for others to lend a helping hand, but starts himself, without assistance. Some find the Aries person a little too ruthless in his manner for getting what he wants. Patience is a virtue some Ariens lack; they are people who are usually interested in fast results. They want to see the fruits of their investments as quickly as possible.

The average Arien is a person who has many ideas; he is never at a loss for a new approach to an old or familiar situation. He is ever adaptable and knows how to make a profit out of a loss. In emergency situations, the Arien is always quick to act. When an accident occurs, he often knows the proper remedy. Decision-making does not frighten the strong Aries man or woman. They have the ability to think clearly and to direct their interests and energies toward their ultimate goal. Aries people are easily attracted to anything that is new and interesting. They have naturally inquiring minds.

Although Ariens are often alert and quick to act, they are sometimes easily distracted by side issues. Almost everything interests them and this can have its disadvantages, especially when a one-track mind is needed in order to solve a problem. Ariens can sometimes make a mess of things in their eagerness to get things done as soon as possible.

The weak or poorly directed Arien sometimes has a problem trying to put all of his eggs in one basket. He is easily distracted and often argumentative. He sometimes finds it difficult to see the forest for the trees. In trying to get many things accomplished at one time, he achieves nothing. In spite of his short-comings, he is apt to be quite caught up with what he fancies to be his virtues. He will underestimate the intelligence and abilities of others, especially if they seem to threaten his position in one way or another. The confused Arien is always ready for a quarrel. He will often refuse to see the other person's point of view and dismiss their opinions as so much poppy-cock. The Aries man or woman who does not know how to concentrate his or her energies effectively, easily jumps from one mistake to another, leaving things in an incomplete and jumbled state. The weak Arien will seldom admit his faults, although he will eagerly point out those of others . . . or what he imagines to be those of others.

The misdirected Arien more often than not misses his mark. He is too anxious to succeed. He wants success fast and is in too much of a hurry to prepare himself adequately. The weak Aries man or woman can be as stubborn as a mule. When intent on some illusory goal they will seldom take the time to listen to others. Not afraid of taking a risk, the ill-prepared Arien often finds himself leaping from one unsuccessful plan to the other. His optimism often makes a fool of him. He is the type of person who leaps before looking. Although he is easy to anger, his temper quickly cools off. When hurt, he can rant and rave for an hour but once he has defended himself, he will drop the matter altogether and move on to something else. The Arien seldom carries a grudge. In love, too, the Aries man or woman who has not learned how to curb impulsiveness, often finds him- or her- self in a pot of hot water. Love at first sight is not uncommon to this sort of Aries person; he is romantic for as long as the impulse carries him. He is not averse to fly-by-night romances, and is liable to throw caution to the winds when in love.

Because the Aries person has an enterprising nature, he never finds it difficult to keep busy. He is an extremely independent person —sometimes to a fault. Others sometimes find him rather haughty and arrogant. This weak sort of Aries finds it difficult to be objective in anything. He resents criticism even when it is due, yet he will not find it difficult to criticize others. He is the kind of person who takes any dare as an opportunity to prove his worth. Others are often annoyed by the manner in which he presses an issue. He is capable of becoming quite aggressive when the situation calls for tact and understanding. If the weak Arien made an attempt to see or understand both sides of one story, he could improve his own insight into problems. He should do what he can to develop a balanced sense of judgment. It is important for this sort of Aries person to prepare himself adequately before taking on a new project. He should avoid overdoing as that only ends in total exhaustion and very little actual progress is made.

Health

People born under the sign of Aries are generally quite healthy. Their physical condition tends to be good. Still, it is necessary that they take steps not to abuse their health by overdoing. The Arien is sometimes accident-prone because he is careless in his actions, particularly when intent on achieving a particular goal. The head and the face are areas of the body that are often injured. It is important that Ariens learn to relax. The Aries man or woman usually does fairly well in sports. Their bodies are generally well-developed and lithe. The Arien's constitution is almost always good. He is capable of great physical strength for short periods of time. This, or course, has its disadvantages as well as advantages. The Arien can achieve more if he learns how to apply his spurts of strength correctly. Sports where staying power is important are not likely to be ones in which he can excel. The sign of Aries governs the head; nerves, head, and stomach are apt to be the weak points under this sign.

Headaches and fevers are not uncommon complaints. As was mentioned before, it is essential that the person born under this first sign of the Zodiac learn how to relax. It is often the case that they wear out easily because they are impulsive and headstrong; they do not know how to channel their energies in a consistent manner. This can sometimes lead to a breakdown. The Arien is so intent on achieving his goal that he allows himself to overwork. Self-control must also be learned. Sometimes the Arien is too free in expressing himself—this can lead to emotional bankruptcy. He is a person who is quick to anger; he worries. Controlling negative emotions is vitally important as bad moods can often affect his health. People born under this sign should always get their proper rest. Adequate sleep can help an exhausted Arien to regain his strength. A sensible, well-balanced diet is also important. Overeating or immoderate drinking habits can, to some extent, incorrectly influence the general disposition of the Aries man or woman. The Arien does not like to be ill. Sickness makes him restless and impatient. He does not like to spend too much time recuperating from an illness. Because of his drive and enthusiasm, the Arien often recovers more quickly than others. An illness may strike him hard, but he is soon on his feet again. The person born under this sign is almost lively and enterprising. Ariens generally lead long and active lives; to some, they never seem to grow old. The Aries person who learns how to conserve his energies as well as to correctly channel them, can add years to his life-span. Good health habits should be continually observed.

Occupation

The Arien is an active, industrious person. He should find a career in which he can best put his talents to use. Although an Arien is apt to have many interests, he should try to find out which interest is the most suited to his actual means and abilities. He is a person who is sincerely interested in getting on in the world and making a success of himself.

The sign of Aries governs the head and the intellect. The person born during the period, March 21 to April 20, is usually quite ambitious and enterprising. He is not a person who can sit still when there is something to do. Some Ariens have an artistic bent and do well in creative work. Others have some trouble in making up their minds about what kind of work they should do because they are interested in so many things and can handle them all reasonably well. Generally speaking, whatever profession the Arien chooses to enter, he makes a good job of it. The Aries man or woman is never lacking in personality and charm. Quite often they do well in work that requires them to come in direct contact with the public. Quite often they are clever conversationalists. They know how to deal with people—how to amuse them, how to convince them. Others often turn to Aries for advice or counsel when in difficulty. The Aries person can usually handle a position that requires authoritative behavior without any problem at all. They make good leaders and advisors. Ariens are inventive and forward-looking. They have plenty of energy and drive; many have a talent for successfully realizing their plans and dreams.

Aries is a person of action. Quite often he does well in the military or in organized sports. Some Ariens make excellent doctors and nurses. Other do remarkably well as dentists and draftsmen. They are a resourceful people—men and women who often know what they want to achieve in life.

The person born under the sign of Aries is more often than not an individualist. He prefers giving orders to taking them. He is not a "group" sort of person. He enjoys working by himself more than working in a team. A modern person, he usually sees to it that he keeps abreast of the new developments in his field.

One fault often found in the underdeveloped Arien is that he will undertake a project with much enthusiasm, then as his interest flags he will readily give it up for something new. In such cases, he will often pass the unfinished chore or project on to someone else. Some Ariens make a habit of starting things, then turning them over to others. The sort of Arien who falls into this habit often does it unknowingly. New plans and ideas attract people of this sign quickly. They are always off for new fields to conquer. The strong Arien, however, seldom has difficulties of this sort; he knows how to stick with one job until it is done. He will do his utmost to direct his efforts and energies toward one goal. This sort of Ram makes a success of his life without much effort.

The Aries man or woman is seldom a person who is only interested in work and material gain. He or she knows how to go about having a good time. Some are quite happy when they are able to combine business with pleasure. Ariens usually are not hard materialists, but they know well what money can do. They busy themselves earning money, but they sometimes spend it as soon as it comes into their pockets. The Aries man or woman is generally honest when it comes to money matters. If he or she directs him or her self to one goal, there is a good chance that it will be attained without too much effort. The Arien has a driving and courageous personality. In work, this often stands him in good stead.

People born under the sign of Aries generally like to be surrounded by fashionable furnishings and the like. Luxury makes them feel comfortable and successful and often has an important influence in making them positive and enterprising. Shabby or old surroundings are apt to depress the Aries person. He is modern and forward-looking; he must live in an environment that is suited to his general disposition.

Some Ariens tend to be rather careless with their money. Saving is something of a problem for them. They would rather spend what they earn instead of putting something aside for a rainy day. They know how to live for the moment. The weak Arien often invests unwisely or mismanages his joint finances without regard for his partner or mate. The wise Arien avoids impulsive spending and thinks of the future. He sees to it that he learns how to budget his expenses in an effective manner.

Home and Family

The Aries man or woman is a home-loving person by nature. Home means a lot to the Ram. Here he can relax at the end of a hard day and enjoy the comfort of his surroundings. Aries woman are generally excellent home-makers. They have a way with furnishings and color arrangement. They know how to make a home radiate harmony and comfort. Invariably, they have good taste. They can beautify a room or a home without much difficulty. The Aries home usually gives one the feeling of freedom and roominess. A guest is not apt to feel himself confined or uncomfortable.

The Arien enjoys entertaining his friends and family. Nothing pleases him more than people dropping in. He knows how to make the best of a social situation even if it occurs on the spur of the moment. They know how to please visitors and enjoy company. Friends generally respect them and their homes.

In family matters, the Aries man or woman is very emotional—in the good sense of the word. Affection and love between members of his or her immediate family are essential for getting along. The Arien is keenly interested in keeping his home peaceful and harmonious. If possible, the Aries husband or wife tries to exert a strong influence in household matters. The Arien feels that his guidance is important to others.

The person born under this sign of the Zodiac is usually quite fond of children. They understand children and children usually feel close to them. The Arien himself usually has something youthful about his nature. Children have no difficulty in getting along with them and generally enjoy having them join them in some of their activities. Ariens know the value of a good joke and children love them for this. A sense of humor that is rich and well-balanced makes them a favorite with children. Aries people seldom forget the joys of their own youth and enjoy living somewhat vicariously through the adventures and games of their own children.

Although the Aries man or woman is not much of a disciplinarian, they do become rather disappointed if their children do not live up to their expectations in later life. Aries generally thinks he knows what is best for his children and can become rather overbearing if his children are not inclined to agree. The Arien is a person who enjoys being popular and respected and he can be a proud parent.

Social Relationships

The Aries person usually has no trouble in making new friends. He is generally outgoing and generous. He enjoys having many friends. People are easily attracted to the Arien because of his bright and pleasant personality. He knows how to make people feel at ease and encourages them in their self-expression. People often turn to an Arien when they are in trouble. The Aries man or woman knows how to counsel a friend in trouble; he or she is sometimes willing to share the burden or responsibilities of a good friend.

On the other hand, Aries people often make a habit of jumping from one friend to another. As long as a person remains new, interesting, and somewhat mysterious, he remains a friend. As soon as an Arien becomes aware of this friend's limitations, he is apt to try to find someone new to replace him. This is the pattern an uncultivated Arien follows in work. As long as the project is new, it absorbs his interest. As soon as it becomes old hat, he turns it over to someone else and starts something new.

Ariens make friends quickly. If they are really impressed, they will place the new friend on a very high pedestal. Some Ariens become very possessive of their friends and if someone else shows an interest in them, they become rather jealous and resentful. If a friend becomes tiresome or dull, the tactless Arien will not hesitate to handle him in an inconsiderate manner.

Although Ariens generally have a talent for making friends quickly, they also are apt to lose them rather fast if they are not careful. Some Ariens tend to neglect their friends and acquaintances as soon as something new catches their fancies. The weak Arien is sometimes a bit of a gossip and finds it hard not to supply others with the secrets of their friends. This sort of Aries person generally takes people for what they appear to be and not for what they actually are.

LOVE AND MARRIAGE

Romance and the Aries Woman

The Aries woman is more often than not charming. The opposite sex generally find her attractive, even glamorous. She is a woman who is very interested in love and romance. The female Arien has plenty of affection to give to the right man—when she meets him. Women born under this sign are usually very active and vigorous; their intelligence and strong character are also qualities which make them attractive to men. The Aries woman has no trouble in communicating with a man on an intellectual plane; she can easily hold her own in any conversation. She should, however, try to curb her eagerness to talk; quite often she winds up dominating the conversation. The Arien who has cultivated the talent of being a good listener generally does not have any trouble in attracting the sort of man who might propose to her.

The Aries woman is not the sort to sit back and wait for the right man to come along. If she sees someone who interests her, she will more than likely take the lead. She can usually do this in such a charming fashion, that the object of her affection hardly notices that he is being coaxed into a romance.

The Aries woman has no trouble in being true to the man she loves. She is true to herself and believes in remaining faithful to the man she has chosen. She usually makes a thoughtful and considerate companion. When her man is in need of advice she is often able to give him wise counsel. Aries women are generally able to voice an intelligent opinion on just about any subject. Their range of knowledge—just as their range of interests—is quite broad. They are imaginative and know how to keep a relationship alive and interesting.

The woman born under the sign of the Ram makes an excellent wife. It is seldom that she will bother her mate or partner with matters that she can easily handle herself. She has a way of transforming almost any house or apartment into a very comfortable home. With household budgeting, she often turns out to be a mastermind. All in all, the Aries woman is very considerate and dependable; she has all the qualities it takes to make an excellent wife or partner. She knows how to bring up children correctly. She is fond of children and affectionate. She is often the kind of mother who enjoys a large family.

Romance and the Aries Man

The Aries man is often quite romantic and charming when courting the opposite sex. He knows how to win the heart of the woman he loves. The Arien in love is as persuasive and energetic as he is in anything else that interests him. He makes an attentive and considerate lover. A direct and positive person, he has no trouble in attracting women. They are often taken by his charming and dashing manner. The opposite sex feels very safe and confident when with an Aries man—for he knows how to make a woman feel wanted and appreciated. However, the Aries man is sometimes so sure of himself that he frightens the more sensitive woman away.

Although the man born under the sign of the Ram, is usually quite faithful when married, he does not mind "playing the field" as long as he remains single. He can be quite a flirt; sometimes the Aries man goes from one romance to the other until he finds the right girl. Making conquests on the battlefield of love is apt to give his ego quite a boost. The Aries man never has very much trouble with rivals. When he is intent on love he knows how to do away with all opposition—and in short order. The Arien is a man who is very much in need of love and affection; he is quite open about this and goes about attaining it in a very open way.

He may be quite adventurous in love while he is single, but once he settles down, he becomes a very reliable and responsible mate. The Aries man is really a family-type man. He enjoys the company of his immediate family; he appreciates the comforts of home. A well-furnished and inviting home is important to a man born under this sign. Some of the furnishings may be a little on the luxurious side; the Arien feels often inspired to do better if he is surrounded by a show of material comfort. Success-oriented, he likes his home to radiate success.

The Aries man often likes to putter around the house, making minor repairs and installing new household utensils. He is a man who does not mind being tied down as long as he does not really feel it. He will be the head of the house; he does not like the woman to wear the pants in the family. He wants to be the one who keeps things in order. He remains romantic, even after marriage. He is tremendously fond of children and is quite apt to spoil them a bit. He makes an affectionate father. Children make him happy when they make him feel proud of them.

Woman—Man

ARIES WOMAN
ARIES MAN

The mating of Aries with Aries could lead to some pretty frantic fireworks, but it does not necessarily have to. As strong in her ways as he is in his, the Aries woman will make her Aries man happiest by supplementing his drives and dreams. An Aries woman can understand and respect a man born under the same sign if she puts her mind to it. He could be that knight in shining armor that Aries women are often in search of. Women born under the sign of the Ram are hard to please and are not interested in just getting a man. They know just what kind of a man he should be and usually do not settle for anything less than their ideal. They are particular. As far as love goes, neither of them shilly-shally with passion. They play for keeps. An Aries-Aries union could be something strong, secure, and romantic. If both of them have their sights fixed in the same direction and have mutual appreciation for each other, there is almost nothing they could not accomplish. It is a block-buster of a combination.

However, if the Aries wife chooses to place her own interests before those of her husband, she can be sure of rocking the boat . . . and perhaps eventually torpedoing it. The career-minded Aries woman, out to do better than her Aries husband, generally winds up doing herself in. He won't stand for it and your relationship won't stand the strain it will bring about. The Aries wife who devotes herself to teas and evenings of bridge will find that she's burned the one bridge she didn't intend to. The homeloving Aries man finds hastily scribbled notes on the dining-room table and TV dinners in the freezer equally indigestible. When you get home from that night out with the girls, he'll take his heartburn out on you instead of reaching for the Alka-Seltzer. If you want to avoid burps and bumps in your marriage, be on hand with his favorite meals, snacks, plus a generous amount of affection. The way to an Arien's stomach is through his heart.

Homemaking, though, should present no problems to the Aries wife. With her, it's second nature. With a pot of paint and some paper, she can transform the dreariest domicile into a place of beauty and snug comfort. The perfect hostess—even when friends just happen by—she knows how to make guests feel at home and this is what makes her Arien man beam with pride. Home is where some people hang their hat; for an Arien, it's where you hang your heart. It's his castle. Marriage can coast along royally for the Aries couple if the little woman keeps the home fires burning and wholeheartedly stands behind her man. This is no problem for the sensitive Aries wife.

ARIES WOMAN
TAURUS MAN

It is the Aries woman who has more than a pinch of patience and reserve who can find her dream-come-true in a man born under the sign of the Bull.

The steady and deliberate Taurean is a little slow on the draw; it may take him quite a while before he gets around to popping that question. For the Arien women who has learned the art of twiddling her thumbs and who doesn't care if her love life seems like a parody of "Waiting for Godot," the waiting and anticipating almost always pays off in the end. Taurus men take their time. Every slow step they take is a sure one—they see to that, especially when they feel that the path they're on could lead them to the alter.

Any Aries woman looking for a whirlwind romance had better cast her net in shallower waters. Moreover, most Taureans prefer to do the angling themselves. They're not keen on women taking the lead—once she does, he's liable to drop her like a dead fish. Once the Aries woman lets herself get caught on his terms, she'll find that her Taurean has fallen for her: hook, line, and sinker.

The Taurus man is fond of comfortable homelife. It's as important to him as it is to the Aries woman. The Arien who centers her main activities on keeping those home fires burning will have no worries about keeping that flame in her hubby's heart aglow. The Aries woman, with her talent for homemaking and harmony, is sometimes the perfect match for the strong, steady, and protective bull. He can be the anchor for her dreams and plans, and can help her acquire a more balanced outlook and approach to her life and her goals. Not one for wild schemes, himself, the Taurean can constructively help her to curb her impulsiveness. He's the man who is always there when you need him. Taureans are rather fond of staying put, especially when it's near someone they love and cherish. When tying her knot with a Taurean, the Aries woman can put away all fears about creditors pounding on the front door. Taureans are practical about everything including bill-paying. When he carries you over that threshold, you can be certain that the entire house is paid for.

As a housewife, the Arien married to a Taurus man, need not worry about having to put aside her many interests for the sake of back-breaking house chores. He'll see to it that you have all the latest time-saving appliances and comforts.

The Aries mother can forget about acquiring premature gray hairs due to unruly, ruckus-raising children under her feet. Papa Taurus is a master at keeping offspring in line. He's crazy about his kids, but he also knows what's good for them. And although he may never resort to the rod, he'll never allow himself to spoil his child, either. Children respect Taurean authority and will usually do their best to make papa proud of them.

The Taurus spouse or lover is generous, patient, and easy-going. He's no slouch and it can lead to disaster if the ambitious Aries wife misinterprets his plodding ways for plain laziness. He knows where he's going. Make no bones about that. Stick with him even if sometimes he seems as slow as molasses on a cold day, and your marital life will be all sweetness and light.

The Taurus man is a steady-Eddy—the kind of man the Aries woman often needs. He appreciates her interest in his work, and pays heed to her helpful suggestions because they pay off. Taureans are faithful and never flirt. All his love and attention are riveted to the woman of his choice, as long as she shows that she's deserving.

ARIES WOMAN
GEMINI MAN

The Aries woman and the Gemini man are a twosome that can make beautiful music together. Perhaps that is due to the fact that they are alike in certain respects. Both are intelligent, witty, outgoing, and tend to be rather versatile. An Aries woman can be the Miss Right that Mr. Gemini has been looking for—his prospective better half, as it were. One thing that causes a Twin's mind and affection to wander is a bore, and it's highly unlikely that an Arien would ever be accused of that. He'll admire the Ram for her ideas and intellect—perhaps even more than her good cooking and flawless talent for homemaking. She needn't feel that once she's made that vow that she'll have to store her interests and ambition in the attic somewhere. He'll admire her for her zeal and liveliness. He's the kind of guy who won't pout and scowl if he has to shift for himself in the kitchen once in a while. In fact, he'll enjoy the challenge of wrestling with pots and pans himself for a change. Chances are, too, that he might turn out to be a better cook than his Mrs., that is, if he isn't already.

The man born under the sign of the Twins is like an intellectual mountain goat leaping from crag to crag. There aren't many women who have pep enought to keep up with him. But this doesn't fluster the spry Ram. In fact, she probably knows before he does which crag he's going to spring onto next. In many cases, she's always a couple of jumps ahead of him—and if she's the helpful wife Ariens usually are, she won't mind telling him when and how to jump. They're both dreamers, planners, and idealists. The woman born under the sign of the Ram, though, is more thorough and possesses more stick-to-it-iveness. She can easily fill the role of rudder for her Gemini's ship-without-a-sail. He won't mind it too much, either. If he's an intelligent Twin, he'll be well aware of his shortcomings and won't mind it if somebody gives him a shove in the right direction—when it's needed. The average Gemini does not have serious ego hangups and will even accept a well-deserved chewing out from his mate quite gracefully.

You'll probably always have a houseful of interesting people to entertain. Geminis find it hard to tolerate sluggish minds and dispositions. You'll never be at a loss for finding new faces in your living room. Geminis are great friend-collectors and sometimes go about it the same way kids go about collecting marbles—the more they sparkle and dazzle, the greater their value to him. But then in a day or two, it's not unusual to find that he has traded yesterday's favorites for still brighter and newer ones. The diplomatic Arien can bring her willy-nilly Gemini to reason and point out his folly in friendships in such a way that he'll think twice before considering an exchange of old lamps for new.

As far as children are concerned, it's quite likely that the Aries wife will have to fill the role of house disciplinarian. Geminis are pushovers for children, perhaps because they understand them so well and have that childlike side to their nature which keeps them youthful and optimistic. They have no interest in keeping a child's vigor in check.

Gemini men are always attractive to the opposite sex and vice-versa. The Aries woman with her proud nature will have to bend a little and allow her Gemini man an occassional harmless flirtation—it will seldom amount to more than that if she's a proper mate. It will help to keep his spirits up. An out-of-sorts Twin is capable of brewing up a whirlwind of trouble. Better to let him hanky-pank—within eyeshot, of course—than to lose your cool; it might cause you to lose your man.

ARIES WOMAN
CANCER MAN

It's quite possible that a man born under this sign of the Crab may be a little too crabby for the average Aries woman; but then, Cupid has been known to perform some pretty unlikely feats with his wayward bow and arrow. Again, it's the Arien with her wits about her who can make the most out of a relationship with the sensitive and occassionally moody Cancerian. He may not be altogether her cup of tea, but when it comes to security and faithfulness—qualities Aries women often value highly—she couldn't have made a better choice.

It's the perceptive Arien who will not mistake the Crab's quietness for sullenness, or his thriftiness for pennypinching. In some respects he can be like the wise old owl out on a limb; he may look like he's dozing but actually he hasn't missed a thing. Cancers often possess a storehouse of knowledge about human behavior; they can come across with some pretty helpful advice for those troubled and in need of an understanding shoulder to cry on. The Aries girl about to rush off for new fields to conquer had better turn to her Cancerian first. Chances are he can save her from making unwise investments in time and—especially—money. He may not say much, but he's capable of being on his toes even while his feet are flat on the ground.

The Crab may not be the match or catch for many a Ram; in fact, he might seem downright dull to the ambitious, on-the-move Arien. True to his sign, he can be fairly cranky and crabby when handled in the wrong way. He's sensitive, perhaps more sensitive than is good for him. The talkative Arien who has a habit of saying what is on her mind had better think twice before letting loose with a personal criticism of any kind, particularly if she's got her heart set on a Cancerian. If she's smart as a whip, she'd better be careful that she never in any way conveys the idea that she considers her Crab a little short on brain power. Browbeating is a sure-fire way of sending the Crab angrily scurrying back to his shell, and it's quite possible that all of that ground lost might never be recovered.

Home is an area where the Aries woman and the Cancer man are in safe territory. Both have serious respect and deep interest in home life, and do their best to keep things running smoothly and harmoniously there. The Crab is most comfortable at home. Once settled in for the night or the weekend, wild horses couldn't drag him any further than the gate post—that is, unless those wild horses were dispatched by his mother. Cancerians are often Momma's boys. If his mate doesn't put her foot down, the Crab will see to it that his mother always comes first whenever possible. No self-respecting Arien would ever allow herself to play second fiddle, even if it is to her old gray-haired mother-in-law. If she's a tactful Ram, she may find that slipping into number-one position can be as easy as pie (that legendary apple pie that his mother used to make). She should agree with her Cancerian when he praises his mother's way with meat loaf, then go on to prove herself a master at making a super-delicious chocolate souffle. All Ariens are pretty much at home in the kitchen; no recipe is too complicated for them to handle to perfection. If she takes enough time to pamper her Cancerian with good-cooking and comfort, she'll find that "mother" turns up less often, both at the front door and in daily conversations.

Crabs make grand daddies. They're protective, patient, and proud of their children. They'll do everything to see that their upbringing is as it should be.

ARIES WOMAN
LEO MAN

For the Arien who doesn't mind being swept off her feet in a royal, head-over-heels, fashion, Leo is the sign of love. When the Lion puts his mind to romancing, he doesn't stint. It's all wining, dining, and dancing till the wee hours of the morning—or all poetry and flowers, if you prefer a more conservative kind of wooing. The Lion is all heart and knows how to make his woman feel like a woman. The Aries lass in constant search of a man whom she can admire, need go no farther: Leo's ten-feet tall—if not in stature, then in spirit. He's a man not only in full control of his faculties but of just about every situation he may find himself in, including of course, affairs of the heart. He may not look like Tarzan, but he knows how to roar and beat his chest if he has to. The Aries woman who has had her fill of weak-kneed men, at last finds in a Leo someone she can lean upon. He can support you not only physically, but also as far as your ideas and plans are concerned. Leos are direct and don't believe in wasting time or effort. They see to it that they seldom make poor investments; something that an Arien is not apt to always do. Many Leos often rise to the top of their profession and through their example, are a great inspiration to others.

Although he's a ladies' man, he's very particular about his ladies, just as the Arien is particular about her men. His standards are high when it comes to love interests. The idealistic Arien should have no trouble keeping her balance on the pedestal the Lion sets her on, so long as he keeps his balance on hers. Romance between these two signs is fair give-and-take. Neither stands for monkey business when involved in a love relationship. It's all or nothing. Aries and Leo are both frank, off-the-shoulder people. They generally say what is on their hearts and minds.

The Aries woman who does decide upon a Leo mate, must be prepared to stand behind her man with all her energies. He expects it, and usually deserves it. He's the head of the house and can handle that position without a hitch. He knows how to go about breadwinning and, if he has his way (and most Leos do have their way), he'll see to it that you'll have all the luxuries you crave and the comforts you need.

It's unlikely that the romance will ever die out of your marriage. Lions need love like flowers need sunshine. They're amorous and generally expect similar amounts of attention and affection from their mates. Fond of going out occasionally, and party-giving, the Lion is a very sociable being and will expect you to share his interest in this direction. Your home will be something to be proud of. The Joneses will have to worry about keeping up with you.

Leos are fond of their children but sometimes are a little too strict in handling them. The tactful Aries spouse, though, can step in and sooth her children's roughed-up feelings if need be.

ARIES WOMAN
VIRGO MAN

Quite often the Virgo man will seem like too much of a fuss-budget to wake up deep romantic interests in an Arien. Generally, he's cool, calm and very collected. Torrid romancing to him is just so much sentimental mush. He can do without it and can make that quite evident in short order. He's keen on chastity and if necessary can lead a sedentary, sexless life without caring too much about the fun others think he's missing. In short, the average Aries woman is quite likely to find him a first-class dud. His lack of imagination and dislike for flights of fancy can grate on an Arien's nerves no end. He's correct and likes to be handled correctly. Most things about him will be orderly. "There's a place for everything and everything in its place," is likely an adage he'll fall on quite regularly.

He does have a heart, however, and the Aries woman who finds herself attracted to his cool, feet-flat-on-the-ground ways, will find that his is a constant heart, not one that cares for flings or sordid affairs. Virgos take an awfully long time before they start trying to rhyme moon with spoon and June, but when and if they get around to it, they know what they're talking about.

The impulsive Arien had better not make the mistake of kissing her Virgo friend on the street—even if it's only a peck on the cheek. He's not at all demonstrative and hates public displays of affection. Love, according to him, should be kept within the confines of one's home, with the curtains drawn. Once he believes that you're on the level with him, as far as your love is concerned, you'll see how fast he can lose his cool. Virgos are considerate, gentle lovers. He'll spend a long time, though, getting to know you. He'll like you before he loves you.

An Aries-Virgo romance can be a life-time thing. If the bottom ever falls out, don't bother to reach for the Scotch tape. Nine times out of ten, he won't care about patching up. He's a once-burnt-twice-shy guy. When he crosses your telephone number out of his address book, he's crossing you out of his life for good.

Neat as a pin, he's thumbs-down on what he considers "sloppy" housekeeping. An ashtray with just one stubbed-out cigarette in it can be annoying to him, even if it's just two-seconds old. Glassware should always sparkle and shine. No smudges please.

If you marry a Virgo, keep your kids spic-and-span, at least by the time he gets home from work. Chocolate-coated kisses from Daddy's little girl go over like a lead balloon. He'll expect his children to observe their "thank yous" and "pleases."

ARIES WOMAN
LIBRA MAN

Although the Libran in your life may be very compatible, you may find this relationship lacking in some of the things you highly value.

You, who look for constancy in romance, may find him a puzzlement as a lover. One moment he comes on hard and strong with "I love you," the next moment you find that he's left you like yesterday's mashed potatoes. It does no good to wonder "What did I do now?" You most likely haven't done anything. It's just one of Libra's ways.

On the other hand, you'll appreciate his admiration of harmony and beauty. If you're all decked out in your fanciest gown or have a tastefully arranged bouquet on the dining-room table, you'll get a ready compliment—and one that's really deserved. Librans don't pass out compliments indiscriminately and generally they're tactful enough to remain silent if they find something is distasteful or disagreeable.

Where you're a straight-off-the-shoulder, let's-put-our-cards-on-the-table person, Librans generally hate arguing. They'll go to great lengths just to maintain peace and harmony—even lie if necessary. The frank Aries woman is all for getting it off her chest and into the open, even if it does come out all wrong. To the Libran, making a clean breast of everything sometimes seems like sheer folly.

The Aries woman may find it difficult to understand a Libran's frequent indecisiveness—he weighs both sides carefully before committing himself to anything. To you, this may seem like just plain stalling.

Although you, too, greatly respect order and beauty, you would never let it stand in the way of "getting ahead." Not one who dilly-dallies, the Aries may find it difficult to accept a Libran's hestiation to act on what may seem like a very simple matter.

The Libra father is most always gentle and patient. They allow their children to develop naturally, still they see to it that they never become spoiled.

Money burns a hole in many a Libran's pocket; his Aries spouse will have to manage the budgeting and bookkeeping. You don't have to worry about him throwing his money around all over the place; most likely he'll spend it all on you—and lavishly.

Because he's quite interested in getting along harmoniously chances are he won't mind an Aries wife taking over the reins once in a while—so long as she doesn't make a habit of it.

ARIES WOMAN
SCORPIO MAN

Many find the Scorpio's sting a fate worse than death. The Aries woman quite often is no acception. When he comes on like "gangbusters," the average Aries woman had better clear out of the vicinity.

The Scorpio man may strike the Aries woman as being a brute and a fiend. It's quite likely he'll ignore your respect for colorful arrangements and harmonious order. If you do anything to irritate him—just anything—you'll wish you hadn't. He'll give you a sounding out that would make you pack your bags and go back to mother —if you were that kind of a girl. Your deep interest in your home and the activities that take place there will most likely affect him indifferently. The Scorpio man hates being tied down to a home— no matter how comfortable his Aries wife has made it. He'd rather be out on the battlefield of life, belting away at what he feels is a just and worthy cause. Don't try to keep those homefires burning too brightly too long—you may just run out of firewood.

As passionate as he is in business affairs and politics, he's got plenty of pep and ginger stored away for romance. Most women are easily attracted to him, and the Aries woman is no acception. That is, at least before she knows what she might be getting into. Those who allow a man of this sign to sweep them off their feet, shortly find that they're dealing with a cauldron of seething excitement. He's passion with a capital P, make no bones about that. And he's capable of dishing out as much pain as pleasure. Damsels with fluttering hearts who, when in the embrace of a Scorpio, think "This is it," had better be in a position to realize "This isn't it," some moments later. Scorpios are blunt. If there's not enough powder on your nose or you have just goofed with a sure-fire recipe for Beef Stroganoff (which is unlikely, you being an old hand with pots and pans) he'll let you know and in no uncertain terms. He might say that your *big* nose is shiny and that he wouldn't serve your Stroganoff to his worst enemy—even your mother. She might be sitting right beside him when he says this, too.

The Scorpio's love of power may cause you to be at his constant beck-and-call.

Scorpios often father large families and generally love their children even though they may not seem to give them the attention they should.

ARIES WOMAN
SAGITTARIUS MAN

The Aries woman who's set her cap for a man born under this sign of Sagittarius, may have to apply an awful amount of strategy before being able to make him say "I do." Although Sagittarians may be marriage-shy, they're not ones to shy away from romance. An Aries woman may find a relationship with a Sagittarian—whether a fling or "the real thing"—a very enjoyable experience. As a rule, Sagittarians are bright, happy, and healthy people and they can be a source of inspiration to the busy, bustling Aries woman. Their deep sense of fair play will please you, too. They're full of ideas and drive. You'll be taken by the Sagittarian's infectious grin and his light-hearted friendly attitude. If you do choose to be the woman in his life, you'll find that he's apt to treat you more like a buddy than like the woman he deeply loves. But it is not intentional; it's just the way he is. You'll admire his broadmindedness in most matters—including that of the heart. If, while you're dating, he claims he still wants to play the field, he'll expect you to do the same. The same holds true when you're both playing for keeps. However, once he's promised to love, honor, and obey, he does just that. Marriage for him, once he's taken that big step, is very serious business. The Aries woman with her keen imagination and love of freedom will not be disappointed if she does tie up with a Sagittarian. They're quick-witted, generally, and they have a genuine interest in equality. If he insists on a night out with the boys once a week, he won't scowl if you decide to let him shift for himself in the kitchen once a week while you go out with the girls.

You'll find he's not much of a homebody. Quite often he's occupied with far away places either in daydreams or reality. He enjoys —just as you do—being on the go or on the move. He's got ants in his pants and refuses to sit still for long stretches at a time. Humdrum routine—especially at home—bores him. At the drop of a hat, he may ask you to whip off your apron and dine out for a change instead. He'll take great pride in showing you off to his friends; he'll always be a considerate mate and never embarrass or disappoint you intentionally. His friendly, sun-shiny nature is capable of attracting many people. Like you, he's very tolerant when it comes to friends and you'll most likely spend a great deal of time entertaining people. He'll expect his friends to be your friends, too, and vice-versa. The Aries woman who often prefers male company to that of her own sex, will not be shunted aside when the fellows are deep in "man talk." Her Sagittarian will see to it that she's made to feel like one of the gang and treated equally.

When it comes to children, you may find that you've been left to handle that area of your marriage single-handedly. Sagittarians are all thumbs when it comes to tots.

ARIES WOMAN
CAPRICORN MAN

Chances are the Aries woman will find a relationship with a Capricorn man a bit of a drag. He can be quite opposite to the things you stand for and value. Where you are generally frank and open, you'll find the man born under the sign of the Goat, closed or difficult to get to know—or not very interesting once you've gotten to know him. He may be quite rusty in the romance department, too, and may take quite a bit of drawing out. You may find his seemingly plodding manner irritating, and his conservative, traditional ways downright maddening. He's not one to take chances on anything. "If it was good enough for my father, it's good enough for me" may be his motto. He follows a way that is tried and true.

Whenever adventure rears its tantalizing head, the Goat will ring up a No Sale sign; he's just not interested. He may be just as ambitious as you are—perhaps even more so—but his ways of accomplishing his aims are more subterranean or at least, seem so. He operates from the background a good deal of the time. At a gathering you may never even notice him, but he's there taking everything in and sizing everyone up, planning his next careful move. Although Capricorns may be intellectual, it is generally not the kind of intelligence an Arien appreciates. You may find they're not quick-witted and are a little slow to understand a simple joke. The Aries woman who finds herself involved with a Capricorn may find that she has to be pretty good in the "cheering up" department, as the man in her love life may act as though he's constantly being followed by a cloud of gloom. If the Arien and the Capricorn do decide to tie the knot, the area of their greatest compatibility will most likely be in the home and decisions centered around the home. You'll find that your spouse is most himself when under the roof of home sweet home.

Just being there, comfortable and secure, will make him a happy man. He'll spend as much time there as he can and if he finds he has to work overtime, he'll bring his work home rather than stay in the office.

You'll most likely find yourself frequently confronted by his relatives—family is very important to the Capricorn, *his* family, that is—and they had better take a pretty important place in your life, too, if you want to keep your home a happy one.

Although his caution in most matters may all but drive you up the wall, you'll find his concerned way with money justified most of the time. He is no squanderer. Everything is planned right down to the last red penny. He'll see to it that you never want.

As far as children are concerned, you may find that you have to step in from time to time when he scolds. Although he generally knows what is good for his children, he can overdo somewhat when it comes to taking them to the woodshed.

ARIES WOMAN
AQUARIUS MAN

The Arien is likely to find the man born under Aquarius dazzling. As a rule, Aquarians are extremely friendly and open; of all the signs, they are perhaps the most tolerant. In the thinking department they are often miles ahead of others, and with very little effort, it seems. The Aries woman will most likely not only find her Aquarian friend intriguing and interesting, but will find the relationship challenging as well. Your high respect for intelligence and fair play may be reason enough for you to settle your heart on a Water Bearer. There's an awful lot to be learned from him, if you're quick enough. Aquarians love everybody—even their worst enemies, sometimes. Through your relationship with the Aquarian you'll find yourself running into all sorts of people, ranging from near-genius to downright insane—and they're all friends of his.

In the holding hands stage of your romance you may find that your Water Bearing friend has cold feet that may take quite a bit of warming up before he gets around to that first goodnight kiss. More than likely he'll just want to be your pal in the beginning. For him, that's an important step in any relationship—even love. The "poetry and flowers" stage will come later, perhaps many years later. The Aquarian is all heart, still when it comes to tying himself down to one person and for keeps, he is liable to hesitate. He may even try to get out of it if you breathe too hard down his neck. He's no Valentino and wouldn't want to be. The Aries woman is likely to be more attracted by his broadmindedness and high moral standards than by his abilities to romance. She won't find it difficult to look up to a man born under the sign of the Water Bearer —but she may find the challenge of trying to keep up with him dizzying. He can pierce through the most complicated problem as if it were a matter of $2 + 2$. You may find him a little too lofty and high-minded, however. But don't judge him too harshly if that's the case; he's way ahead of his time; your time, too, most likely.

In marriage you need never be afraid that his affection will wander. It stays put once he's hitched. He'll certainly admire you for your intelligence and drive; don't think that once you're in the kitchen you have to stay there. He'll want you to go on and pursue whatever you want in your quest for knowledge. He's understanding on that point. You'll most likely have a minor squabble with him now and again, but never anything serious.

You may find his forgetfulness a little bothersome. His head is so full of ideas and plans that sometimes he seems like the Absent-Minded Professor incarnate. Kids love him and vice-versa. He's tolerant and open-minded with everybody, from the very young to the very old.

ARIES WOMAN
PISCES MAN

The man born under the sign of Pisces, may be a little too sluggish for the average Aries woman. He's often wrapped up in his dreams and difficult to reach at times. He's an idealist like you, but unlike you, he will not jump up on a soapbox and champion a cause he feels is just. Difficult for you to understand at times, he may seem like a weakling to you. He'll entertain all kinds of views and opinions from just about anyone, nodding or smiling vaguely, giving the impression that he's with them one hundred percent. In reality, that may not be the case at all. His attitude may be "why bother" to tell someone he's wrong when he so strongly believes that he's right. This kind of attitude can make an Arien furious. You speak your mind; he'll seldom speak his unless he thinks there'll be no opposition. He's oversensitive at times—rather afraid of getting his feelings hurt. He'll sometimes imagine a personal injury when none is intended. Chances are you'll find this sort of behavior maddening and may feel like giving your Pisces friend a swift kick where it hurts the most. It won't do any good, though. It may just add fire to his persecution complex.

One thing you'll admire about this man is his concern and understanding of people who are sickly or who have serious (often emotional) problems. It's his nature to make his shoulder available to anyone in the mood for a good cry. He can listen to one hard-luck story after another without seeming to tire and if his advice is asked he's capable of coming across with some very well-balanced common sense. He often knows what is bugging a person before that person knows it himself. It's amost intuitive with a Pisces, it seems. Still, at the end of the day, he'll want some peace and quiet and if his Aries friend has some problem or project on her mind that she would like to unload in his lap, she's liable to find him rather short-tempered. He's a good listener but he can only take so much.

Pisces are not aimless, although they may often appear to be when viewed through Arien eyes. The positive sort of Pisces man is quite often successful in his profession and is likely to wind up rich and influential—even though material gain is never a direct goal for a man born under this sign.

The weaker Pisces are usually content to stay put on the level they find themselves. They won't complain too much if the roof leaks and the fence is in need of repair. He's capable of shrugging his shoulders and sighing "that's life."

Because of their seemingly free-and-easy manner, people under this sign, needless to say, are immensely popular with children. For tots they play the double role of confidant and playmate.

Man—Woman

ARIES MAN
ARIES WOMAN

The Aries man will be contented with the Aries woman so long as she reflects his qualities and interests without trying to outshine him. Although he may be progressive and modern in many things, when it comes to pants-wearing, he's downright conventional: it's strictly male attire. The best position an Aries woman can take in the relationship is a supporting one. He's the boss and that's that. Once that is settled and thoroughly accepted by his Aries spouse, then it's clear sailing.

The Aries man, with his seemingly endless drive and energy, likes to relax in the comfort of his home at the end of an action-packed day, and the Aries wife who is a good homemaker can be sure of his undying affection. He's a lover of slippers and pipe and a comfortable armchair. The Aries wife who sees to it that everything in the house is where her man expects to find it—including herself—will have no difficulty keeping the relationship ship-shape.

When it comes to love, the Aries man is serious and constant, and the object of his affection should be likewise. He is generally not interested in a clinging-vine kind of wife; he justs wants someone who is there when he needs her; someone who listens and understands what he says; someone who can give advice if he should ever have to ask for it—which is not likely to be often. Although he can appreciate a woman who can intelligently discuss things that matter to him, he is not interested in a ranting chatterbox who, through her fondness for earbending, is liable to let the apple pie burn up in the oven.

The Aries man wants a woman who is a good companion and a good sport; someone who will look good on his arm without hanging on it too heavily. He is looking for a woman who has both feet on the ground and yet is mysterious and enticing . . . a kind of domestic Helen of Troy whose face or fine dinner can launch a thousand business deals if need be. The cultivated Aries woman should have no difficulty in filling such a role.

The Aries man and woman have similar tastes when it comes to family style: they both like large ones. The Aries woman is crazy about kids and the more she has, the more she feels like a wife. Children love and admire the affectionate Aries mother. She knows how to play with them and how to understand them. She's very anxious that they do well in life and reflect their good homelife and upbringing. However, both Aries parents should try not to smother their offspring with too much love. They should be urged to make their own decisions—especially as they grow older—and not rely unnecessarily on the advice of their parents.

ARIES MAN
TAURUS WOMAN

The woman born under Taurus may lack the sparkle or dazzle you often like your women to have. In many respects, she's very basic—never flighty—and puts great store in keeping her feet flat on the ground. She may fail to appreciate your willingness to jump here, then there, especially if she's under the impression that there's no profit in it. On the other hand, if you do manage to hit it off with a Taurus woman you won't be disappointed at all in the romance area. The Taurus woman is all woman and proud of it, too. She can be very devoted and loving once she decides that her relationship with you is no fly-by-night romance. She's pretty rugged, too, or can be, when the situation calls for a stiff upper lip. It's almost certain that if the going ever gets too rough she won't go running home to mother. She'll stick by you, talk it out, fight it out, or whatever. When bent on a particular point of view, she can be as hard as nails

—without having it adversely affect her femininity. She'll stick by you through thick and thin. She can adjust to hard times just as graciously as she can to good times. You may lose your patience with her, though, if when trying to explain some new project or plan to her, she doesn't seem to want to understand or appreciate your enthusiasm and ambition. With your quick wit and itchy feet, you may find yourself miles ahead of your Taurus woman. At times, you are likely to find this distressing. But if you've developed a talent for patience, you won't mind waiting for her to catch up. Never try grabbing her hand and pulling her along at your normal speed—it is likely not to work. It could lead to flying pots and pans and a fireworks display that would put the Fourth of July to shame. The Taurus woman doesn't anger readily but when prodded often enough, she's capable of letting loose with a cyclone of illwill. If you treat her correctly, you'll have no cause for complaint. The Taurus woman loves doing things for her man. She's a whiz in the kitchen and can whip up feasts fit for a king if she thinks they will be royally appreciated. She may not fully understand you but she'll adore you and be faithful to you if she feels you're worthy of it. She won't see green, either, if you compliment another woman in her presence. When you come home late occasionally and claim that there were a lot of last-minute things to attend to at the office, she won't insinuate that one of those last-minute things was most likely your new, shapely secretary. Her mind doesn't run like that. She's not gullible, but she won't doubt your every word if she feels there is no reason to. The woman born under Taurus will make a wonderful mother for your children. She's a master at keeping children cuddled, well-loved, and warm. You may find, however, that when your offspring reach the adolescent stage you'll have to intervene: Taureans are not very sympathetic to the whims of ever-changing teenagers.

ARIES MAN
GEMINI WOMAN

You may find a romance with a woman born under the sign of the Twins, a many-splendored thing. In her you can find the intellectual companionship you often crave and so seldom find. A Gemini girlfriend can appreciate your aims and desires because she travels pretty much the same route as you do, intellectually . . . that is, at least part of the way. She may share your interests, but she will lack your stick-to-it-iveness. Her feet are much itchier than yours, and as a result, she can be here, there—all over the place, and all at the same time; or so it seems. It may make you dizzy. However, you'll enjoy and appreciate her liveliness and mental agility.

Geminians often have sparkling personalities; you'll be attracted by her warmth and grace. While she's on your arm, you'll probably notice that many male eyes are drawn to her—she may even return a gaze or two, but don't let that worry you. All women born under this sign have nothing against a harmless flirtation; they enjoy this sort of attention and, if they feel they're already spoken for, they'll never let it get out of hand.

Although she·may not be as handy in the kitchen as you'd like, you'll never go hungry for a filling and tasty meal. She's in as much a hurry as you and won't feel like she's cheating by breaking out the instant mashed potatoes or the frozen vegetables. She may not be handy at the kitchen range but she can be clever—and with a dash of this and a suggestion of that, she can make an uninteresting TV dinner taste like something out of a Jim Beard cookbook. Then again, maybe you've struck it rich with your Gemini and have one who finds complicated recipes a challenge to her intellect. If so, you'll find every meal a tantalizing and mouth-watering surprise.

When you're exercizing your brain over the Sunday crossword puzzle and find yourself bamboozled over 23 Down and 11 Across, just ask your Gemini friend; she'll give you the right answers with-.out batting an eye. Chances are she probably went through the crossword phase herself years ago and gave them up because she found them too easy.

She loves all kinds of people—just like you do. Still, you're apt to find that you're more particular than she. Often, all that a Gemini requires is that her friends be interesting—and stay interesting. One thing she's not able to abide is a dullard.

Leave the party-organizing to your Gemini sweetheart or mate and you'll never know what a dull moment is. She'll bring the swinger out in you if you give her half a chance.

With kids, woman born under Gemini seem to work wonders. Perhaps this is because they are like children themselves in a way: restless, adventurous, and easily bored. At any rate, the Gemini mother is loving, gentle, and affectionate with her children.

ARIES MAN
CANCER WOMAN

Romancing a girl born under the sign of the Crab may occasionally give you a case of the jitters. It may leave you with one of those "Oh, brother . . . what did I get into now" feelings. In one hour she can unravel a whole gamut of emotions that will leave you in a tizzy. If you do fall in love with a Cancerian, be prepared for anything. She'll keep you guessing, that's for sure. You may find her a little too uncertain and sensitive for your tastes. You'll most likely have to spend a good deal of your time encouraging her, helping her to erase her foolish fears. Tell her she's a living doll a dozen times a day and you'll be well-loved in return. Be careful of the jokes you make when you are with her—and for heaven's sake don't let any of them revolve around her, her personal interests, or her relatives. Chances are if you do, you'll reduce her to tears. She can't stand being made fun of. It will take bushels of roses and tons of chocolates, not to mention the "I'm sorrys", to get you back in her good graces again.

In matters of money-managing, she may not easily come around to your way of thinking. Ariens are often apt to let money burn a hole in their pockets. Cancerians are just the opposite. You may think your Cancerian sweetheart or mate is a direct descendant of Scrooge. If she has it her way, she'll hang onto that first dollar you ever earned. She's not only that way with money, but with everything from bakery string right on to jelly jars. She's a saver and never discards anything no matter how trivial.

Once she returns your "I love you", you'll find that you have a very loving, self-sacrificing and devoted friend on your hands. Her love for you will never alter unless you want it to. She'll put you high up on a pedestal and will do everything—even if it's against your will—to see that you stay up there.

Cancer women make reputedly the best mothers of all the signs of the Zodiac. She'll consider every minor complaint of her child a major catastrophe. She's not the kind of mother who will do anything to get her children off her hands; with her, kids come first. You'll run a close second. You'll perhaps see her as too devoted and you may have a hard time convincing her that the length of her apron-strings is a little too long. When Junior or Sis is ready for that first date, you may have to lock your Cancer wife in the broom closet to keep her from going along. As an Arien you are apt to understand your children more as individuals than your wife. No matter how many times your Cancer wife insists that no man is good enough for your daughter, you'll know it's all nonsense. If you don't help her to curb her super-maternal tendencies, your Cancer wife may have a good chance of turning into a formidable mother-in-law.

ARIES MAN
LEO WOMAN

If you can manage a girl who likes to kick up her heels every once in a while, the Leo woman's your mate. You'll have to learn how to put away your jealous fears—or at least forget about them—when you take up with a woman born under this sign, because she's often the sort that makes heads turn and sometimes tongues wag. You don't necessarily have to believe any of what you hear; it's most likely just jealous gossip or wishful thinking. She's usually got more than a good share of grace and glamor. She knows it, generally, and knows how to put it to good use. Needless to say, other women in her vicinity turn green with envy and will try anything short of shoving her into the nearest lake in order to put her out of commission, especially if she appears to be cramping their style.

If she has captured your heart and fancy, woo her full-force if your intention is to eventually win her. Shower her with expensive gifts, take her regularly to Ciro's, and promise her the moon—if you're in a position to go that far—and you'll find that Miss Leo's resistance will begin to weaken. It's not that she's so difficult—she'll probably make a lot over you once she's decided you're the man for her—but she does enjoy a lot of attention. What's more, she feels she's entitled to it. Her mild arrogance, though, is becoming. The Leo woman knows how to transform the crime of excessive pride into a very charming misdemeanor. It sweeps most men right off their feet . . . in fact, all men. Those that do not succumb to her leonine charm are few and far between.

If you've got an important business deal to clinch and you have doubts as to whether it will go over well or not, bring your Leo wife along to that business luncheon or cocktail party and it will be a cinch that you'll have that contract in your pocket before the meeting is over. She won't have to say or do anything . . . just be there at your side. The grouchiest oil magnate can be transformed into a gushing, dutiful schoolboy if there's a Leo woman in the room.

If you're a rich Arien, you may have to see to it that your Leo wife doesn't become to heavy-handed with the charge accounts and credit cards. When it comes to spending, Leos tend to overdo. If you're a poor Arien, then you have nothing to fear—for Miss Leo, with her love of luxury, will most likely never give you the time of day, let alone exchange vows.

As a mother, she can be strict and easy-going at the same time. She can pal around with her children and still see to it that they know their places.

ARIES MAN
VIRGO WOMAN

The Virgo woman may be a little too difficult for you to understand at first. Her waters run deep. Even when you think that you do know her, don't take any bets on it: she's capable of keeping things hidden in the deep recesses of her womanly soul—things she'll only reveal when she is sure that you're the one she's been looking for. It may take her some time to come around to this decision. Virgo women are finicky about almost everything; everything has to be letter-perfect before they're satisfied. Many of them have the idea that the only people who can do things correctly are other Virgos. Nothing offends a Virgo woman more than sloppy dress, character, or careless display of affection. Make sure your tie's not crooked and your shoes sport a bright shine before you go calling on this lady. Keep your off-color jokes for the locker room; she'll have none of that. Take her arm when crossing the street. Don't rush the romance. Trying to corner her in the back of a cab may be one way of striking out. Never criticize the way she looks—in fact, the best policy would be to agree with her as much as possible. The Arien, however, with his outspoken, direct, and sensible nature, may find a Virgo relationship too trying. All those Do's and Don't's you'll have to observe if you want to get to first base with a Virgo may be just a little too much to ask of you. After a few dates, you may come to the conclusion that she just isn't worth all that trouble. However, the Virgo woman is mysterious enough, generally, to keep her men running back for more. Chances are you'll be intrigued by her airs and graces.

Love means a lot to you and you may be disappointed at first in Virgo's cool ways. However, underneath that glacial facade lies a hot cauldron of seething excitement. If you're patient and artful in your romantic approach, you'll find that all that caution was well worth the trouble. When Virgos love, they don't stint. It's all or nothing as far as they're concerned. Once they're convinced that they love you, they go all the way right off the bat, tossing all cares to the wind. One thing a Virgo can't stand in love is hypocrisy. They don't give a hoot about what the neighbors might say as long as their hearts tell them "go ahead." They're very concerned with human truths. So much so that if their hearts stumble upon another fancy, they're liable to take up with that new heart-throb and leave you standing in the rain. She's that honest—to her own heart, at any rate. But if you are earnest about your interests in her, she'll know, and will respect and reciprocate your love. Do her wrong once, however, and you can be sure she'll come up with a pair of sharp scissors and cut the soiled ribbon of your relationship.

As a housewife, she'll be neat and orderly. With children, she can be tender and strict at the same time. She can be a devoted and loving wife—it all depends on you.

ARIES MAN
LIBRA WOMAN

That girl born under the sign of Libra is worth more than her weight in gold. She's a woman after your own heart. With her, you'll always come first, make no mistake about that. She'll always be behind you, no matter what you do. And when you ask her for advice about almost anything, you'll most likely get a very balanced and realistic opinion. She's good at thinking things out and never lets her emotions run away with her when clear logic is called for. As a homemaker, she's hard to beat. She is very concerned with harmony and balance; your home will be tastefully furnished and decorated. A Libran cannot stand filth or disarray—it gives her goose bumps. Anything that does not radiate harmony, in fact, runs against her orderly grain.

She's chock-full of charm and womanly ways; she can sweep just about any man off his feet with one winning smile. When it comes to using her brains, she can out-think anyone and sometimes with half the effort. She's diplomatic enough, though, never to let this become glaringly apparent. She may even turn the conversation so that you think that you were the one who did all the brain work. She couldn't care less, really, just as long as you wind up doing what is right. She's got you up there on a pretty high pedestal. You're her man and she's happy if you make all the decisions, big and small—with a little help from her if necessary. In spite of her masculine approach to reason, she remains all woman in her approach to love and affection. You'll literally be showered with hugs and kisses during your romance with a Libra woman. She doesn't believe in holding out. You shouldn't, either, if you want to hang on to her. She's the kind of girl who likes to snuggle up to you in front of the fire on chilly autumn nights. She'll bring you breakfast in bed Sundays then cuddle beside you and tuck a napkin under your chin so you won't get any crumbs on the blankets.

She's very thoughtful about anything that concerns you. If anyone dares suggest that you're not the grandest guy in the world, your Libran is bound to defend you. She'll defend you with her dying breath. When she makes those marriage vows she means every word. As an Arien who also has a tendency to place people you like on a pedestal, you won't be let down by a girl born under the sign of Libra. She'll be everything you believe she is . . . even more. As a mother of your children, she'll be very attentive and loving. However, you won't have to take the backseat when Junior comes along. You'll always come first with her—no matter if it's the kids, the dog, or her maiden aunt from Keokuk. Your children will be well-mannered and respectful. She'll do everything in her power to see that you're treated like a prince.

ARIES MAN
SCORPIO WOMAN

The Scorpio woman can be a whirlwind of passion—perhaps too much passion to suit you. When her temper flies, better lock up the family heirlooms and take cover. When she chooses to be sweet, you're apt to think that butter wouldn't melt in her mouth . . . but of course, it would. She can be as hot as a *tamale* or as cool as a cucumber, but whatever mood she is in, it's no pose. She doesn't believe in putting on airs.

Scorpio women are often quite seductive and sultry—their charm can pierce through the hardest of hearts like a laser ray. She doesn't have to look like Mata Hari (quite often Scorpio women resemble the tomboy next door) but once you've looked into those tantalizing eyes, you're a goner. Life with her won't be all smiles and smooth-sailing; when prompted she can unleash a gale of venom. Generally, she will have the good grace to keep family battles within the walls of your home; when company visits she's apt to give the impression that married life with you is one great big joy-ride. It's just one of her ways of expressing her loyalty to you—at least in front of others. She may fight you tooth and nail in the confines of your living room but at a ball or during an evening out, she'll hang on your arm and have stars in her eyes. She doesn't consider this hypocrisy; she just firmly believes that family quarrels should stay a private matter.

She's pretty good at keeping secrets. She may even keep a few hidden from you if she feels like it. This sort of attitude, of course, goes against the Arien's grain; you believe in being open and straight-from-the-shoulder.

Never cross her up, not even in little things; when it comes to revenge, she's an eye-for-an-eye woman. She's not keen on forgiveness if she feels she's been done wrong. You'd be well-advised not to give her cause to be jealous, either. When she sees green, your life will be made far from rosy. Once she's put you in the dog-house, you can be sure that you're going to stay there an awfully long time.

There's a good possibility that you may find your relationship with a Scorpio too draining. Although she may be full of the old paprika and bursting with dynamite, she still is not the girl you'd exactly like to spend the rest of your natural life with. You'd prefer someone gentler and more direct; someone who won't go throwing pots and pans at the mention of your secretary's name; someone who's flexible and understanding; someone who can take the highs along with the lows and not bellyache; someone who can ride with the punches. If you've got your sights set on a shapely Scorpio, you'd better forget that sweet girl of your dreams. True: a woman born under Scorpio can be heavenly, but she can also be the very devil when she chooses.

ARIES MAN
SAGITTARIUS WOMAN

You most likely won't come across a more good-natured girl than the one born under the sign of Sagittarius. Generally, they're full of bounce and good cheer. Their sunny dispositions seem almost permanent and can be relied upon even on the rainiest of days. No matter what she'll ever say or do, you'll know that she always means well. Women born under this sign are almost never malicious. If ever they seem to be, it is only superficial. Sagittarians are quite often a little short on tact and say literally anything that comes into their pretty little heads, no matter what the occasion. Sometimes the words that tumble out of their mouths seem downright cutting and cruel. They're quite capable of losing their friends—and perhaps even yours—through a careless slip of the lip. On the other hand, you're liable to appreciate their honesty and good intentions. To you, qualities of this sort play an important part in life. With a little patience and practice, you can probably help cure your Sagittarian of her loose tongue; in most cases, it will be worth the effort.

Chances are she'll be the outdoors-type of girlfriend; long hikes, fishing trips, and water skiing will most likely appeal to her. She's a busy person; she could never be called a slouch. She sets great store in being able to move about. She's like you in that respect: she has itchy feet. You won't mind taking her along on camping or hunting trips. She is great company most of the time and generally a lot of fun. Even if your buddies drop by for an evening of poker and beer, she'll manage to fit right in. In fact, they'll probably resent it if she doesn't join in the game. On the whole, she is a very kind and sympathetic woman. If she feels she's made a mistake she'll be the first to call your attention to it. She's not afraid of taking the blame for a foolish deed.

You might lose your patience with her once or twice, but after she's seen how upset you get over her short-sightedness, and her tendency to talk too much, chances are she'll do everything in her power not to do it again. She is not the kind of wife who will pry into your business affairs. But she'll always be there, ready to offer advice if you ask for it. If you come home from a night out with the boys and tell your Sagittarius wife that the red stains on your collar came from cranberry sauce, she'll believe you. She'll seldom be suspicious; your word will almost always be good enough for her.

Although she can be a good housewife, her interests are generally too far-reaching and broad to allow her to confine her activities to just taking care of the house. She's interested in what is going on everywhere.

As a mother, she'll be a wonderful and loving friend to her children. She's apt to spoil them if she is not careful.

ARIES MAN
CAPRICORN WOMAN

If you're not a successful businessman or at least on your way to success, it's quite possible that a Capricorn woman will have no interest in entering your life. She's generally a very security-minded female and will see to it that she only invests her time and interests in sure things. Men who whittle away their time and energy on one unsuccessful scheme or another, seldom attract a Capricorn. Men who are interested in getting somewhere in life and keep their noses close to the grindstone quite often have a Capricorn woman behind them, helping them to get ahead. Although she is a climber herself, she is not what one could call cruel or hard-hearted. Beneath that cool, seemingly calculating exterior there's a warm and desirable woman. She just happens to feel that it's just as easy to fall in love with a rich or ambitious man as it is with a poor or lazy one. She's practical. Although she is keenly interested in rising to the top, she's not aggressive about it. She'll seldom step on someone's feet or nudge competitors away with her elbows. She's quiet about her wishes. She sits, waits, and watches. When an opening or an opportunity does appear, she'll latch on to it, lickety-split. For an on-the-go Arien, an ambitious Capricorn wife or girlfriend can be quite an asset. She can probably give you some very good advice about your business affairs and when you invite the boss and his wife to dinner, she'll charm them both right off the ground. She's generally thorough in whatever she undertakes. She'll see to it that she is second to none in good housekeeping.

Capricorn women make excellent hostesses as well as guests. Generally, they are very well-mannered and gracious, no matter what their background is. They seem to have a built-in sense of what is right and proper. Crude behavior or a careless comment can offend them no end.

If you should marry a woman born under Capricorn you need never worry about her going on a wild shopping spree. Capricorns are very careful about every cent that comes into their hands. They understand the value of money better than most women and have no room in their lives for careless spending. If you turn over your paycheck to her at the end of the week, you can be sure that a good hunk of it will wind up in the bank.

Capricorn girls are generally very fond of family—their own, that is. With them, family ties run very deep. Never say a cross or sarcastic word about her mother. She won't stand for that sort of nonsense and will let you know by not speaking to you for days. In fact, you'd better check her family out before you decide to get down on bended knee, because after you've taken that trip down the aisle, you'll undoubtedly be seeing an awful lot of them.

With children, she's loving and correct. They'll be well brought up and polite.

ARIES MAN
AQUARIUS WOMAN

If you find that you've fallen head over heels for the woman born under the sign of the Water Bearer, better fasten your safety belt. It may take a while before you actually discover what she's like and even then you may have nothing to go on but a string of vague hunches. This girl is like the rainbow—full of all bright and shining hues; she's like no other girl you've known. There's something elusive about her, something delightfully mysterious—you'll most likely never be able to put your finger on it. It's nothing calculated, either; Aquarians don't believe in phoney charm. There will never be a dull moment in your romance with the Water Bearing woman. She seems to radiate adventure, magic, and without even half trying. She'll most likely be the most open-minded woman you've ever met. She—like you—has a strong dislike of injustice and prejudice. Narrow-mindedness runs against her grain.

She is very independent by nature and is quite capable of shifting for herself if necessary. She may receive many proposals for marriage and from all sorts of people. Marriage is one heck of a big step for her; she wants to be sure she knows what she's getting into. If she thinks that it will seriously curb her independence and her love of freedom, she's liable to shake her head and give you back your engagement ring—if she's let the romance get that far.

The line between friendship and romance is a pretty fuzzy one for an Aquarian. It's not difficult for her to remain buddy-buddy with someone with whom she's just broken off. She's tolerant, remember? So, if you should ever see her on the arm of an ex-lover, don't jump to any hasty conclusions.

She's not a jealous person, and doesn't expect you to be, either. You'll find her pretty much of a free spirit most of the time. Just when you think you know her inside-out, you'll discover that you don't really know her at all.

Very sympathetic and warm, she can be helpful to people in need of assistance and advice.

She's often like a chameleon and can fit in anywhere without looking like she doesn't belong.

She'll seldom be suspicious even if she has every right to be. If the man she loves slips and allows himself a little fling, chances are she'll just turn her head the other way and pretend not to notice that the gleam in his eyes is not meant for her. That's pretty understanding. Still, a man married to a woman born under Aquarius should never press his luck in hanky-panky. After all, she is a woman—and a very sensitive one at that.

She makes a fine mother, of course, and can easily transmit her positive and big-hearted qualities to her offspring.

ARIES MAN
PISCES WOMAN

Many a man dreams of a Piscean kind of a girl—and an Arien is no exception. She's soft and cuddly, and very domestic. She'll let you be the brains of the family; she's content to just lean on your shoulder and let you be master of the household. She can be very lady-like and proper; your business associates and friends will be dazzled by her warmth and femininity. She's a charmer, though, and there's much more to her, generally, than just her pretty exterior. There's a brain ticking away in that soft, womanly body. You may never become aware of it, that is, until you're married to her. It's no cause for alarm, however; she'll most likely never use it against you. Still, if she feels that you're botching up your marriage through inconsiderate behavior, or if she feels you could be earning more money than you do, she'll tell you about it. But, then, any wife would, really.

She'll never try to usurp your position as breadwinner of the family. She'll admire you for your ambition and drive. No one had better dare say one bad word about you in her presence. It's liable to cause her to break into tears. Pisces women are usually very sensitive beings and their reactions to adverse situations is sometimes nothing more than a plain, good, old-fashioned cry. They can weep buckets when inclined.

She'll have an extra-special dinner waiting for you to celebrate your landing a new and important account. Don't bother to go into the details, though, at the dinner table; she doesn't have much of a head for business matters, usually, and is only too happy to leave all that to you.

She can do wonders with a home. She's very fond of soft and beautiful things. There will always be a vase of fresh flowers on the hall table. She'll see to it that you always have plenty of socks and handkerchiefs in the top drawer of your dresser. You'll never have to shout downstairs, "Don't I have any clean shirts left?" She'll always see to it that you have. Treat her with tenderness and the relationship will be an enjoyable one.

She'll most likely be fond of chocolates. A bunch of beautiful flowers will make her eyes light up. See to it that you never forget her birthday or your anniversary. These things are very important to her. If you ever let them slip your mind, you can be sure of sending her off to the bedroom for an hour-long crying fit. An Arien with patience and tenderness can keep a Pisces woman happy for a lifetime.

She's not without faults herself, however, and after the glow of love-at-first-sight has faded away, you may find yourself standing in a tubful of hot water. You may find her lacking in imagination and zest. Her sensitivity is liable to get on your nerves after a while. You may even feel that she only uses tears in order to get her own way.

Pisces make strong, sacrificing mothers.

TAURUS
April 21 — May 20

CHARACTER
ANALYSIS

Of all the signs of the Zodiac, Taureans are perhaps the most diligent and determined. They are hardworkers and stick with something once it's begun. They are generally thorough people and are careful to avoid making mistakes. Patient, the Taurean knows how to bide his time. If something doesn't work out as scheduled, he will wait until the appropriate moment comes along, then forge ahead.

The person born under this sign is far from lazy. He will work hard to achieve whatever it is he desires. He is so determined that others often think of him as being unreasonably stubborn. He'll stick to a point he believes is right—nothing can force him to give up his chosen path once his mind is made up.

The Taurean takes his time in whatever he does. He wants to make sure everything is done right. At times this may exasperate people who are rather quick about things. Still and all, a job done by a Taurean is generally a job well done. Careful, steady, and reliable, the Taurus person is just the opposite of high-strung. This person can generally take a lot upon himself. Sometimes his burdens or worries are of such proportions that others would find them impossible to carry, but somehow the Taurean manages in his silent way.

The Taurean may be even-tempered, but he puts up with nonsense from no one. Others had better not take advantage of his balanced disposition. If they do, they are apt to rue the day.

The Taurus man or woman plans well before taking any one line of action. He believes in being well-prepared before embarking on any one project. Others may see him as a sort of slow-poke, but he is not being slow—just sure. He is not the sort of person who would act on a whim or fancy. He wants to be certain of the ground he is standing on.

37

Material things make him feel comfortable and successful. Some have a definite love of luxury and the like. This may be the result of a slight feeling of inferiority. Material goods make him feel that he is doing well and that he is just as good as the next person.

The Taurean is someone who can be trusted at all times. Once he has declared himself a friend, he remains so. He is loyal and considerate of others. In his circle of friends he is quite apt to be one of the successful people. The Taurean admires success; he looks up to people who have made something of themselves.

On the whole, the Taurean is a down-to-earth person. He is not pretentious or lofty, but direct and earnest. Things that are a bit abstract or far-fetched may not win his immediate approval. He believes in being practical. When he makes a decision, it is generally one with a lot of thought behind it.

Health

People born under this second sign of the zodiac generally are quite fit physically. They are often gifted with healthy constitutions and can endure more than others in some circumstances. The Taurean is often quite vigorous and strong. At times his strength may astonish others. He can put up with more pressure than most. Pain or the threat of it generally does not frighten him.

He can be rather proud of his good health. Even when he is ill, he would rather not give in to it or admit it. But when a disability becomes such that it cannot be ignored, the Taurean becomes rather sad and depressed. For him it is a kind of insult to be ill. When he is laid up with an illness, it generally takes quite a while for him to recover. Although his constitution is strong, when struck down by a disease, his powers for recuperation are not very great. Getting better is a very slow and gradual process for the average Taurus person.

Males born under this sign are often broad and stocky. They may be wide-shouldered and quite powerfully built. They are seldom short on muscle. As they age, they sometimes become a bit fat.

Females born under the sign of Taurus are often quite attractive and charming. They are fond of pretty things and like to see to it that they are looking well. Although they are often beautiful when young, as they grow older some of them tend to put on a little extra weight. They often have unusually attractive eyes and their complexions are generally quite clear and healthy-looking.

The weakest part of a Taurean's body is his throat. If ever he is sick, this part of his body is often affected. Sore throats and the like are often common Taurean complaints.

Occupation

The Taurus man or woman can do a good job—no matter what the work is. They have the ability to be thorough and accurate. They never shirk their duties. They may be looked upon as being rather slow—especially when they begin a task; but after they are thoroughly familiar with what they are doing, they work at an even and reasonable pace. They are methodical and that counts a good deal. They are quite good at working with detail. They seldom overlook anything.

Not all Taureans are slow. Some of them are rather quick and brilliant. In many cases, it depends on the circumstances they have to deal with. In any event, they never forget anything once they have learned it. They can be quite shrewd in business matters and are often highly valued in their place of business.

The average Taurean has plenty of get-up-and-go. He is never lazy or neglectful in his work. He enjoys working and does what he can to bring about favorable results.

In business, he will generally shy away from anything that involves what seems to be an unnecessary risk. He likes the path he trods to be a sure one; one that has been well laid out. When he has to make his own way, he sees to it that he is certain of every step of the route. This may often exasperate his co-workers or colleagues. His plodding ways generally pay off in the end, however. In spite of this, and because of his distrust of change, he often misses out on a good business deal. His work may become rather humdrum and dull due to his dislike of change in work routine or schedule.

The Taurus man or woman does well in a position of authority. He is a good manager and knows how to keep everything in order. Discipline is no problem to him. He knows what scheme to follow and sticks to it. Because his own powers of self-control are so well developed, he has no problem in managing others. The Taurean is not frightened by opposition. He knows how to forge ahead with his plans and will not stop until everything comes out the way he planned.

The Taurean is a stickler for detail. Every little point has to be thoroughly covered before he is satisfied. Because he is a patient person, he knows how to bide his time; he is the kind of person who will wait for the right opportunity to come along, if need be. This sort of person excels in a position where he can take his time in doing things. Any job that requires thoroughness and painstaking effort is one in which a Taurean is likely to do well. They make good managers and can handle certain technical and industrial jobs quite well. Some of them are gifted with the ability to draw or design. The Taurean sometimes does well in the world of architecture. Many of them are quite artistic and it depends on the proper circumstances to bring this out. In most cases, however, the Taurean is content with doing work that is sure and calculated. His creative ability may not have the proper chance to surface, and it is only through cultivation that he is able to make a broad use of it.

Although many people born under this sign work in the city, they prefer the peace and quiet of remote places to the hustle and bustle of the busy metropolis. Many of them do well in the area of agriculture. They have a way with growing things. A Taurus man or woman could easily become a successful dairyman or poultry farmer. They find it easy to relate to things rural or rustic. Many of them are gifted with green thumbs.

When working with others, he can be relied upon. His partner if possible should be similar in nature. The Taurus person may become annoyed if he works with someone who is always changing his mind or schedule. He doesn't care much for surprises or sudden changes. New ideas may not appeal to him at first; he has to have time to get used to them. Generally speaking, he likes to think of something new as being a creation of his own and by taking his time in approaching it, he tends to see it in that light. He is the sort of person who should be gently coaxed, when working with others. He will give his consent to new ideas if his colleagues are subtle enough in their presentation.

Although the Taurus man or woman may not hold an important position in the place where he works, this does not disturb him. He doesn't mind working under others—especially if they are good and able leaders or managers. The Taurean makes a good and loyal worker. He can always be depended on to complete his tasks.

The Taurus man or woman understands the value of money and appreciates the things it can do. He may not be a millionaire but he does know how to earn and save well enough so that he can acquire those material items he feels are important. Some people born under this sign can easily acquire a greedy streak if they don't watch out. So obsessed with material gain are some Taureans that they do not take time to relax and enjoy other things that life has to offer. Money-oriented, the ambitious Taurean sometimes turns into someone who is all work and no play. It is not surprising, then, that a great many bankers and financiers are born under this sign of the Zodiac.

The Taurus person is generally straight-forward and well-meaning. If someone is in need, he will not hesitate to assist them financially. Taureans as children are sometimes rather stingy, but as they grow up and have enough money, they become reasonably free in their use of it. Still and all, the average Taurean will never invest all the money he has in anything—he always likes to keep a good portion of it aside for that inevitable rainy day. Although he may not be interested in taking many risks, the person born under this sign is often lucky. When he does take a chance and gambles, he quite often turns out the winner.

When the person born under the sign of Taurus puts his best foot forward, he can achieve almost anything—even though it may take a little longer than it does with most. He has many hidden strengths and positive characteristics that help him to get ahead.

Home and Family

The Taurus person is a lover of homelife. He likes to be surrounded by familiar and comfortable things. He is the kind of person who calls his home his castle. Generally speaking, the home of a Taurus person radiates comfort and hospitality. The Taurus woman generally knows how to decorate and arrange a house so that visitors feel immediately at home upon entering. The Taurus man is more often than not a good breadwinner. He sees to it that the members of his immediate family have everything they need.

Taurean homelife is generally happy and orderly. He is as thorough and correct in his home life as he is in his work.

The Taurus person usually likes the peace, quiet, and beauty of the country. If possible, he will see to it that he lives there—for part of the year if not for the whole year. The Taurus housewife has her work down to an efficient routine. She is interested in keeping everything neat and orderly. She makes a very good hostess and knows how to make people feel at ease.

Being well-liked is important to someone born under this sign. He likes to be surrounded by good friends. He admires important people and likes to include them in his social activities if possible. When entertaining, the Taurus woman usually outdoes herself in preparing all sorts of delicious items. She is well skilled in the culinary arts. If ever she is poorly entertained or fed by others, she feels rather badly about it.

The Taurus man or woman usually has a tastefully furnished home. But what is more important to the Taurean than beauty is comfort. His house must be a place where he can feel at home.

Taureans can be rather strict with their children; they stand for no nonsense. They are interested in seeing that their children are brought up correctly. It is important for them that their offspring reflect the good home they come from. Compliments from others about the behavior of their children make the Taurus parents quite happy and proud. As the children grow older, however, and reach the teen-age stage, some difficulties may occur in the beginning, for the Taurus mother or father may resent the sudden change in the relationship as the child tries to assert his own individuality.

Social Relationships

The Taurus person generally does what he can to be popular among his friends. He is loyal and caring with people who are close to him. Because he is quite sincere and forthright, people generally seek him out as a friend. He makes a good talker as well as a listener. People in difficulties often turn to him for advice.

The Taurus person is genuinely interested in success and there is nothing he admires more than someone who has achieved his goal. In making friends, it seems as though a person born under this sign gravitates toward people who have made a success of themselves or people on their way up. Influential people are admired by the Taurean in general. Being surrounded by people who have met with some success in life makes the person born under this sign feel somewhat successful too.

The Taurus person is one who generally likes to keep his family matters to himself. He resents the meddling of friends—even close friends.

He is a person who sticks to his principles and as a result he may make an enemy or two as he goes along.

LOVE AND MARRIAGE

In love matters, the people born under this sign may go through a series of flings—many of them light-hearted—before settling down with the "right" person. By nature, the Taurean is serious. In love matters, his feelings are liable to run quite deep; however he will take steps to guard himself against disappointment if he feels the affair won't be lasting. The Taurean can be rather romantic. As with everything, once he has made up his mind about someone, nothing will stand in his way; he'll win the object of his affection if it's the last thing he does. Other suitors don't frighten him in the least.

Younger Taureans have nothing against light romances, but as they grow older they look for stability and deep affection in a love affair. Faithful in love as they are in most things, they look for persons who are apt to feel the way they do.

The Taurean in love does not generally attempt a coy approach. More likely than not he'll be direct in expressing his feelings. Once he has won the person he loves, the average Taurean is quite often possessive as well as protective.

Persons born under this sign generally do well in a marriage relationship. Matters at home go well so long as he is treated fairly by his mate. If conditions at home are not to his liking he can be rather biting and mean.

There is no halfway in marriage as far as the person born under the sign of Taurus is concerned; it's a matter of two people giving themselves completely. As husbands and wives, they make ideal mates in many respects. They are usually quite considerate and generous. They like looking after the other members of their families. They are very family-oriented types and nothing pleases them more than to be able to spend time at home with their loved ones.

Romance and the Taurus Woman

The Taurus woman has a charm and beauty that are hard to define. There is generally something elusive about her that attracts the opposite sex—something mysterious. Needless to say, she is much sought after. Men find her a delight to be with. She is generally an easy-going person—relaxed and good-natured. The opposite sex find her a joy to be with because they can be themselves. They don't have to try to impress her by being something they are not.

Although she may have a series of romances before actually settling down, everytime she falls in love it is the real thing. She is not superficial or flighty in romance. When she gives her heart she hopes it will be forever. When she does finally find the right person, she has no trouble in being true to him for the rest of her life.

In spite of her romantic nature, the female Taurean is quite practical, too, when it comes to love. She wants a man who can take care of her. Someone on whom she can depend. Someone who can provide her with the comforts she feels she needs. Some Taureans make it a point to look for men who are well-to-do or who have already achieved success. To them, the practical side of marriage is just as important as the romantic. However, not all Taurus women are like this. Some are attracted to sincere, hardworking men who are good company and faithful in the relationship. A Taurus wife sticks by the man of her choice. She will do everything in her power to give her man the spiritual support he needs in order to advance in his career.

The Taurus woman likes pretty, gentle things. They are quite domestic and enjoy making their home a comfortable and attractive one. They are often quite artistic and their taste in furnishings is often flawless. They know how to make a house comfortable and inviting. The Taurus woman is quite interested in material things. They make her feel secure and loved. Her house is apt to be filled with various objects that have an important meaning for her alone.

Generally speaking, she is even-tempered and does what she can to get along with her mate or loved one, but once she is rubbed the wrong way she can become very angry and outspoken. The considerate mate or lover, however, has no problem with his Taurus woman. When treated well, she maintains her pleasant disposition, and is a delight to be with. She is the kind of woman who is kind and warm when she is with the man of her choice. A man who is strong, protective, and financially sound is the sort of man who can help bring out the best in a woman born under this sign. She enjoys being flattered and being paid small attentions. It is not that she is excessively demanding, but just that she likes to have evidence from time to time that she is well loved.

The Taurus woman is very dependable and faithful. The man who wins her is indeed lucky. She is quite domestic and enjoys making things comfortable for the man she loves. She seldom complains. She is quite flexible and can enjoy the good times or suffer the bad times with equal grace. Although she does enjoy luxury, if difficult times come about, she will not bicker but stick beside the man she loves. For her marriage is serious business. It is very unlikely that a woman born under this sign would ever seek a divorce unless it was absolutely necessary.

A good homemaker, the Taurus woman knows how to keep the love of her man alive once she has won him. To her love is a way of life. She will live entirely for the purpose of making her man happy and contented. Men married to a woman of this sort seldom ever have reason to be dissatisfied. Their affections never stray. Taurus women are determined people. When they put their minds to making a marriage or love relationship work it seldom fails. They'll work as hard at love and romance as they will at anything else they want.

As a mother, the Taurus woman does what she can to see that her children are brought up correctly. She likes her children to be polite and obedient. She can be rather strict when she puts her mind to it. It is important to her that her offspring learn the right things in life—even if they don't seem to want to. She is not at all permissive as a parent. Her children must respect her and do as she says. She won't stand for insolence or disobedience. She is well-meaning in her treatment of her offspring. Although the children may resent her strictness somewhat as they are growing up, in later life they see that she was justified in the way she handled them.

Romance and the Taurus Man

The Taurus man is as determined in love as he is in everything else. Once he sets his mind on winning a woman, he keeps at it until he has achieved his goal.

Women find him quite attractive. The Taurus man has a protective way about him. He knows how to make a woman feel wanted and well taken care of. Taurus men are often fatherly and girls looking for protection and unwavering affection are often attracted to them. Quite often because of their he-man physiques, and sure ways, they have no trouble in the department of romance. The opposite sex find their particular brand of charm difficult to resist.

He can be a very romantic person. The number of romances he is likely to have before actually settling down may be many. But he is faithful. He is true to the person he loves for as long as that relationship lasts. When he finds a girl who really is suited to him, he devotes the rest of his life to making her happy.

Married life agrees with the man born under the Taurus sign. They make good, dependable husbands and excellent, concerned fathers. Like any man, the Taurus man is of course attracted to a woman who is good-looking and charming. But the qualities that most appeal to this sort of man often lie deeper than the skin. He is not interested in glamor alone. The girl of his choice must be a good home-maker, resourceful, and loving. Someone kind and considerate is apt to touch his heart-strings more than a pretty one-dimensional face. He is looking for a woman to settle down with for a lifetime.

Marriage is important to him because it means stability and security. These things are important to a man born under the sign of Taurus. He is serious about marriage. He will do his best to provide for his family in a way he feels is correct and responsible. He is not one to shirk his family responsibilities. He likes to know that the woman he has married will stand beside him in all that he does.

The Taurus man believes that only he should be boss of the family. He may listen and even accept the advice of his spouse, but he is the one who runs things. He likes to feel that he is the king in his castle.

He likes his home to be comfortable and inviting. He may be a big man, but still, in spite of this, the Taurean has a liking for soft things; he likes to be babied a little by the woman he loves. He may be a strict parent but he feels it is for the children's own good.

Woman—Man

TAURUS WOMAN
ARIES MAN

Although it is possible that you could be attracted to a man born under the sign of the Ram, it is not certain as to how far the relationship would go. An Arien who has made his mark in the world and is somewhat steadfast in his outlook and attitudes could be quite a catch for you. On the other hand, men under this sign are swiftfooted and quick-minded; their industrious manner may often fail to impress you, particularly when you become aware that their get-up-and-go sometimes leads to nowhere. When it comes to a fine romance, you want a nice broad shoulder to lean on; you are liable to find a relationship with someone who doesn't like to stay put for too long a time somewhat upsetting. Then, too, the Aries man is likely to misunderstand your interest in a slow-but-sure approach to most matters. He's liable to find you a stick-in-the-mud. What's more, he's liable to tell you so if you make him aware of it too often. Ariens tend to speak their minds, sometimes at the drop of a hat.

You may find a man born under this sign too demanding. He may give you the feeling that he wants you to be at all places at the same time. Even though he realizes that this is impossible, he may grumble at you for not at least having tried. You have a barrelful of patience at your disposal and he may try every last bit of it. Whereas you're a thorough person, he is liable to overshoot something that is very essential to a project or a relationship due to his eagerness to quickly achieve his end.

Being married to an Arien does not mean that you'll necessarily have a secure and safe life as far as finances are concerned. Ariens are not all rash with cash but they lack the sound head that you have for putting something away for that inevitable rainy day. He'll do his best, however, to see that you're well provided for—even though his efforts may leave something to be desired as far as you're concerned.

He'll love the children. Ariens make wonderful fathers. Kids take to them like ducks to water, probably because of their quick minds and zestful behavior. Sometimes Aries fathers are given to spoiling their children and here is where you'll most likely have to step in. You'll have to be careful, however, in being strict with them unless you want to drive most of their affection over to their father. When they reach the adolescent stage and become increasingly difficult to manage, it would perhaps be better for you to take a back

seat and rely on your Aries-husband's sympathy and his understanding of this stage of life.

Although there is liable to be a family squabble occasionally,
you, with your steady nature and love of permanence, will learn to
take it in your stride and make your marriage a success.

TAURUS WOMAN
TAURUS MAN

Although a man born under the same sign as you may seem like
a "natural," better look twice before you leap. It can also be that he
resembles you too closely to be compatible. You can be pretty set in
your ways when you want to and when you encounter someone with
just as much willpower or stubbornness, then a royal fireworks display can be the result. When two Taureans lock horns it can be a
very exhausting and totally frustrating get-together. However, if the
man of your dreams is one born under your sign and you're sure
that no other will do, then proceed with extreme caution. Even
though you know yourself well—or think you do—it does not necessarily mean that you will have an easy time understanding him.
Since you both are practical, however, you should try a rational
approach to your relationship: put all the cards on the table, discuss
the matter, and decide whether to cooperate, compromise, or call it
a day.

If you both have your sights set on the same goals, a life together
could be just what the doctor ordered. You both are affectionate
and have a deep need for affection. Being loved, understood, and
appreciated are most important for your mutual well-being.

Essentially, you are both looking for peace, security, and harmony in your lives. Working towards these goals together may be a
good way of eventually attaining them, especially if you are honest
and tolerant of each other.

If you should marry a Taurus man, you can be sure that the wolf
will stay far away from the door. They are notoriously good providers and do everything to make their families comfortable and happy. He'll appreciate the way you have of making a home warm and
inviting. Slippers and pipe, and the evening papers are essential
ingredients in making your Taurus husband happy at the end of
the day when he comes home from work. Although he may be a
big lug of a guy, he'll be pretty fond of gentle treatment and soft
things. If you puff up his pillow and tuck him in at night, he won't
complain. He'll eat it up and ask for more.

In friendships, you'll both most likely be on even footing. You
both tend to seek out friends who are successful or prominent. You

admire people who work hard and achieve what they set out for. It helps to reassure your way of looking at things.

Taurus parents love their children very much but never sacrifice a show of affection for the sake of perhaps spoiling them. Since you both are excellent disciplinarians where bringing up children is concerned, you should try to balance your tendency to be strict with a healthy amount of tenderness and affection.

TAURUS WOMAN
GEMINI MAN

Gemini men, in spite of their charm and dash, may tend to make your skin crawl. They seem to lack that sort of common sense you set so much store in. Their tendencies to start a half-dozen projects, then toss them up in the air out of boredom, may do nothing more than exasperate you. You may be inclined to interpret their jumping around from here to there as childish if not downright psychotic. A man born under this sign will never stay put and if you should take it into your head to try and make him sit still, he's liable to resent it strongly.

On the other hand, he's likely to think you're an old slow poke and far too interested in security and material things. He's attracted to things that sparkle and bubble—not necessarily for a long time. You are likely to seem quite dull and uninteresting—what with your practical head and feet firm on the ground—to this sort of gadabout. If you're looking for a life of security and steadiness—And what Taurean isn't?—then Mr. Right he ain't.

Chances are you'll be taken in by his charming ways and facile wit. Few women can resist Geminian charm. But after you've seen through his live-for-today, gossamer facade, you'll most likely be very happy to turn your attention to someone more stable, even if he is not as interesting. You want a man who's there when you need him, someone on whom you can fully rely. Keeping track of Gemini's movements will make your head spin. Still, being a Taurean, you're a patient woman who can put up with almost anything if you think it will be worth the effort.

A successful and serious-minded Gemini could make you a very happy woman, perhaps, if you gave him half the chance. Although he may give you the impression that he has a hole in his head, the Gemini man generally has a good head on his shoulders and can make efficient use of it when he wants. Some of them, who have learned the art of being steadfast have risen to great heights in their professions. President Kennedy was a Gemini as was Thomas Mann and William Butler Yeats.

Once you convince yourself that not all people born under the sign of the Twins are witless grasshoppers, you won't mind dating a few to support your newborn conviction. If you do find yourself walking down the aisle with one, accept the fact that married life with him will mean taking the bitter with the sweet.

Life with a Gemini man can be more fun than a barrel of clowns. You'll never experience a dull moment. You'd better see to it, though, that you get his paycheck every payday. If you leave the budgeting and bookkeeping to him you'll wind up behind the eight ball.

He's apt to let children walk all over him so you'd better take charge of them most of the time.

TAURUS WOMAN
CANCER MAN

The man born under the sign of Cancer may very well be the man after your own heart. Generally, Cancerians are steady people. They share Taureans' interest in security and practicality. Despite their sometimes seemingly grouchy exterior, men born under the sign of the Crab are rather sensitive and kind individuals. They are almost always hard workers and are very interested in making successes of themselves in business as well as socially. You'll find that his conservative outlook on many things often agrees with yours. He'll be a man on whom you can depend come rain or come shine. He'll never shirk his responsibilities as a provider and will always see to it that his wife and family never want.

Your patience will come in handy, if you decide it's a Cancerian you want for a mate. He isn't the type that rushes headlong into romance. He wants to be sure about love as you do. If after the first couple of months of dating, he suggests that you take a walk with him down lovers' lane, don't jump to the conclusion that he's about to make his "great play." Chances are he'll only hold your hand and seriously observe the stars. Don't let his coolness fool you, though. Underneath his starched reserve is a very warm heart. He's just not interested in showing off as far as affection is concerned. Don't think his interest is wandering if he does not kiss you good night at the bus stop; that just isn't his style. For him, affection should only be displayed for two sets of eyes—yours and his. If you really want to see him warm up to you, you'd better send your roommate off to the municipal museum, then bolt the doors and windows—to insure him that you won't be disturbed or embarrassed. He will never step out of line—he's too much of a gentleman for that, but it is likely that in such a sealed off atmosphere, he'll pull out an engagement ring (that used to belong to his grandmother) and slip it on your trembling finger.

Speaking of relatives, you'll have to get used to the fact that Cancerians are overly fond of their mothers. When he says his mother's the most wonderful woman in the world, you'd better agree with him—that is, if you want to become his wife. It's a very touchy area for him. Say one wrong word about his mother or let him suspect that your interest in her is not real, and you'd better go looking for husband material elsewhere.

He'll always be a faithful husband; Cancerians never pussyfoot around after they've taken that vow. They don't take their marriage responsibilities lightly. They see to it that everything in their homes runs smoothly. Bills will always be paid promptly. He's liable to take out all kinds of insurance policies on his family and property. He'll see to it that when retirement time rolls around, you'll both be very well off.

Men under this sign make patient and understanding fathers.

TAURUS WOMAN
LEO MAN

To know a man born under the sign of the Lion is not necessarily to love him—even though the temptation may be great. When he fixes most girls with his leonine double-whammy, it causes their hearts to pitter-pat and their minds to cloud over. But with you, the sensible Taurean, it takes more than a regal strut and a roar to win you over. There's no denying that Leo has a way with women—even practical Taurus women. Once he's swept you off your feet it may be hard to scramble upright again, still you're no pushover for romantic charm if you feel there may be no security behind it. He'll wine you and dine you in the fanciest places, croon to you under the moon, and shower you with diamonds if he can—still it would be wise to find out just how long the shower's going to last before consenting to be his wife. Lions in love are hard to ignore, let alone brush off. Your "no" will have a way of nudging him on until he feels he has you completely under his spell. Once mesmerized by this romantic powerhouse, you will most likely find yourself doing things you never dreamed of. Leos can be like vain pussycats when involved in romance; they like to be cuddled and curried, tickled under the chin and told how wonderful they are. This may not be your cup of tea, exactly; still when you're romancing with a man born under the sign of Leo, you'll find yourself doing all kinds of things to make him purr. Although he may be sweet and gentle when trying to win you, he'll let out a blood-curdling roar if he feels he's not getting the tender love and care he feels is his due. If you keep him well supplied with affection, you can be sure his eyes will never stray and his heart will never wander.

Leo men often turn out to be leaders. They're born to lord it over others in one way or another, it seems. If he is top banana in his firm, he'll most likely do everything he can to stay on top. And if he's not number one yet, then he's working on it, and will see to it that he's sitting on the throne before long.

You'll have more security than you can use if he's in a position to support you in the manner to which he feels you should be accustomed. He's apt to be too lavish, though, and although creditors may never darken your door, you'll most likely take it upon yourself to handle as much of the household bookkeeping as you can to put your mind at ease.

He's a natural-born friend-maker and entertainer. At a party, he may do everything short of dancing the fandango on a glass table top to attract attention. Let him. If you allow him his occasional ego trips without quibbling, your married life will be one of warmth, wealth, and contentment.

Although they're not big-family raisers, when Junior does come along he'll be brought up like one of the landed gentry if Papa Leo has anything to say about it.

TAURUS WOMAN
VIRGO MAN

Although the Virgo man may be a bit of a fuss-budget at times, his seriousness and dedication to common sense may help you to overlook his tendency to sometimes be overcritical about minor things.

Virgo men are often quiet, respectable types who set great store in conservative behavior and level-headedness. He'll admire you for your practicality and tenacity, perhaps even more than for your good looks. He's seldom bowled over by a glamor-puss. When he gets his courage up, he turns to a serious and reliable girl for romance. He'll be far from a Valentino while dating. In fact, you may wind up making all the passes. Once he does get his motor running, however, he can be a warm and wonderful fellow—to the right girl.

He's gradual about love. Chances are your romance with him will most likely start out looking like an ordinary friendship. Once he's sure you're no fly-by-night flirt and have no plans of taking him for a ride, he'll open up and rain sunshine all over your heart.

Virgo men tend to marry late in life. He believes in holding out until he's met that right girl. He may not have many names in his little black book; in fact, he may not even have a little black book. He's not interested in playing the field; leave that to men of the more flamboyant signs. The Virgo man is so particular that he may remain romantically inactive for a long period. His girl has to be perfect or it's no go. If you find yourself feeling weak-kneed for a Virgo, do your best to convince him that perfect is not so important when it comes to love. Help him to realize that he's missing out on a great deal by not considering the near-perfect or whatever you consider yourself to be. With your sure-fire perserverance, you'll most likely be able to make him listen to reason and he'll wind up reciprocating your romantic interests.

The Virgo man is no block of ice. He'll respond to what he feels to be the right feminine flame. Once your love-life with a Virgo starts to bubble, don't give it a chance to fall flat. You may never have a second chance at winning his heart.

If you should ever have a falling out with him, forget about patching up. He'd prefer to let the pieces lie scattered. Once married, though, he'll stay that way—even if it hurts. He's too conscientious to try to back out of a legal deal of any sort.

A Virgo man is as neat as a pin. He's thumbs down on sloppy housekeeping. An ashtray with just one stubbed-out cigarette is apt to make him see red. Keep everything bright, neat, and shiny—and that goes for the children, too, at least by the time he gets home from work. Chocolate-coated kisses from Daddy's little girl go over like a lead balloon with him.

TAURUS WOMAN
LIBRA MAN

Taureans are apt to find men born under the sign of Libra too wrapped up in a dream world ever to come down to earth. Although he may be very careful about weighing both sides of an argument, that does not mean he will ever make a decision about anything. Decisions large and small are capable of giving a Libran the willies. Don't ask him why. He probably doesn't know, himself. As a lover, you—who are interested in permanence and constancy in a relationship—may find him a puzzlement. One moment he comes hard and strong with "I love you", the next moment you find that he's left you like yesterday's mashed potatoes. It does no good to wonder "What did I do now?" You most likely haven't done anything. It's just one of Libra's ways.

On the other hand, you'll appreciate his admiration of harmony and beauty. If you're all decked out in your fanciest gown or have a tastefully arranged bouquet on the dining room table, you'll get a ready compliment—one that's really deserved. Librans don't pass out compliments to all and sundry. Generally, he's tactful enough to remain silent if he finds something distasteful or disagreeable.

He may not be as ambitious as you would like your lover or husband to be. Where you do have drive and a great interest in getting ahead, the Libran is often content to just drift along. It is not that he is lazy or shiftless, it's just that he places greater value on aesthetic things than he does in the material. If he's in love with you, however, he'll do anything in his power to make you happy.

You may have to give him a good nudge now and again to get him to see the light, but on the whole he'll be happy wrapped up in his artistic dreams when you're not around to remind him that the rent is almost due.

If you love your Libran don't be too harsh or impatient with him. Try to understand him. Don't let him see the stubborn side of your nature too often, or you'll scare him away. Librans are peace-loving people and hate any kind of confrontation that may lead to an argument. Some of them will do almost anything to keep the peace—even tell little white lies, if necessary.

Although you possess gobs of patience, you may find yourself losing a little of it when trying to come to grips with your Libran. He may think you're too materialistic or mercenary, but he'll have the good grace not to tell you, for fear you'll perhaps chew his head off.

If you find yourself deeply involved with a Libran, you'd better see to it that you help him manage his money. It's for his own good. Money will never interest him as much as it should and he does have a tendency to be too generous when he shouldn't be.

Although he may make a gentle and understanding father, he'll see to it that he never spoils his children.

TAURUS WOMAN
SCORPIO MAN

Many people have a hard time understanding the Scorpio man. Few, however, are able to resist his fiery charm. When angered, he can act like a nestful of wasps, and his sting is capable of leaving an almost permanent mark. If you find yourself interested in a man born under this sign, you'd better learn how to keep on his good side.

The Scorpio man is capable of being very blunt, and he can act like a brute or a cad. His touchiness may get on your nerves after a while and if it does, you'd better tiptoe away from the scene rather than chance an explosive confrontation. He's capable of giving you a talking to that would make you pack your bags and go back to mother . . . for good.

It's quite likely that he will find your slow, deliberate manner a little irritating. He's liable to misinterpret your patience for indifference. On the other hand, you're the kind of woman who can adapt to almost any sort of situation or circumstance if you put your mind and heart to it. Scorpio men are quite perceptive and intelligent. In some respects, they know how to use their brains more effectively and quicker than most. They believe in winning in everything; in business, they usually achieve the position they desire through drive and intellect.

Your interest in your home is not likely to be shared by him. No matter how comfortable you've managed to make the house, it will have very little influence on him as far as making him aware of his family responsibilities. He doesn't like to be tied down, generally, and would rather be out on the battlefield of life, belting away at what he feels is a just and worthy cause, then puttering around in the garden or mowing the front lawn.

He is passionate in his business affairs and political interests. He is just as passionate—if not more so—in romance. Most women are easily attracted to him—and the Taurus woman is no exception, that is, at least before she knows what she might be getting into. Those who allow their hearts to be stolen by a Scorpio man, shortly find that they're dealing with a cauldron of seething excitement. He's passion with a capital P, make no bones about that.

Scorpios are straight to the point. They can be as sharp as a razor blade and just as cutting. If there's not enough powder on your nose or you've just goofed with a sure-fire recipe for beef Stroganoff, he'll let you know about it in short order. He might say that your *big* nose is shiny and that he wouldn't serve the Stroganoff to his worst enemy—not even your mother.

In spite of everything, Scorpios get along well with children and quite often father large families.

TAURUS WOMAN
SAGITTARIUS MAN

The Taurus woman who has her cap set for a man born under the sign of Sagittarius may have to apply large amounts of strategy before being able to make him pop that question. When visions of the altar enter the romance, Sagittarians are apt to get cold feet. Although you may become attracted to a man born under this sign, because of his positive, winning manner, you may find the relationship loses some of its luster when it assumes a serious hue. Sagittarians are full of bounce—perhaps too much bounce to suit you. They are often hard to pin down and dislike staying put. If ever there's a chance to be on the move, he'll latch on to it post haste. They're quick people, both in mind and spirit. And sometimes because of their zip, they make mistakes. If you have good advice to offer, he'll tell you to keep it. Sagittarians like to rely on their own wit whenever possible. His up-and-at-'em manner about most things is likely to drive you up the wall occasionally. Your cautious, deliberate manner is likely to make him cluck his tongue impatiently. "Get the lead out of your shoes," is something he's liable to say when you're accompanying him on a stroll or jogging through the park on a Sunday morning. He can't abide a slow-poke. At times, you'll find him too breezy and kiddish. However, don't mistake his youthful demeanor for premature senility. Sagittarians are equipped with first-class brain power and know well how to put it to use. They're often full of good ideas and drive. Generally they're very broad-minded people and are very much concerned with fair play and equality.

In the romance department, he's quite capable of loving you whole-heartedly while treating you like a good pal. His hail-fellow-well-met manner in the arena of love is likely to scare a dainty sort of a damsel off. However, a woman who knows that his heart is in the right place, won't mind it too much if once in a while, he slaps her (lightly) on the back instead of giving her a gentle embrace.

He's not much of a homebody. He's got ants in his pants and enjoys being on the move. Hum-drum routine, especially at home, bores him to distraction. At the drop of a hat he may ask you to whip off your apron and dine out for a change instead. He's fond of coming up with instant surprises. He'll love to keep you guessing. His friendly, candid nature gains him many friends.

When it comes to children, you may find that you've been left holding the bag. Sagittarians feel helpless around little shavers. When children become older, he will develop a genuine interest in them.

TAURUS WOMAN
CAPRICORN MAN

A Taurus woman is often capable of bringing out the best in a man born under the sign of Capricorn. While other women are puzzled by his silent and slow ways, the Taurean, with her patience and understanding, can lend him the confidence he perhaps needs in order to crawl out of his shell.

Quite often, the Capricorn man is not the romantic kind of lover that attracts most women. Still, behind his reserve and calm, he's a pretty warm guy. He is capable of giving his heart completely once he has found the right girl. The Taurus woman who is deliberate by nature and who believes in taking time to be sure about everything she undertakes, is likely to find her kind of man in a Capricorn. He is slow and deliberate about almost everything—even romance. He doesn't believe in flirting and would never let his heart be led on a merry chase. If you win his trust, he'll give you his heart on a platter. Quite often, it is the woman who has to take the lead when romance is in the air. As long as he knows you're making the advances in earnest he won't mind. In fact, he'll probably be grateful.

Don't think that he's all cold fish; he isn't. Although some Capricorns have no difficulty in expressing passion, when it comes to displaying affection, they're all at sea. But with an understanding and patient girl he should have no trouble in learning to express himself in this area, especially if you let him know how important affection is to you, and for the good of your relationship.

The Capricorn man is very interested in getting ahead. He's quite ambitious and usually knows how to apply himself well to whatever task he undertakes. He's far from a spendthrift and tends to manage his money with extreme care. But a Taurus woman with a knack for putting away money for that rainy day should have no trouble in understanding this.

The Capricorn man thinks in terms of future security. He wants to make sure that he and his wife have something to fall back on when they reach retirement age.

He'll want you to handle the household efficiently, but that's no problem for most Taureans. If he should check up on you from time to time about the price of this and the cost of that, don't let it irritate you. Once he is sure you can handle this area to his liking, he'll leave it all up to you.

Although he may be a hard man to catch when it comes to marriage, once he's made that serious step, he's quite likely to become possessive. Capricorns need to know that they have the support of their women in whatever they do, every step of the way. Your Capricorn man, because he's waited so long for that right girl, may be considerably older than you.

Capricorn fathers never neglect their children and seem to know what is good for them.

TAURUS WOMAN
AQUARIUS MAN

The Aquarius man in your life is perhaps the most broadminded you have ever met; still, you're liable to think he is the most impractical. He's more of a dreamer than a doer. If you don't mind putting up with a man whose heart and mind are as wide as the Missouri but his head is almost always up in the clouds, then start dating that Aquarius man who somehow has captured your fancy. Maybe you, with your Taurean good sense, can bring him back down to earth before he gets too starry-eyed.

He's no dumbbell; make no mistake about that. He can be busy making some very complicated and idealistic plans when he's got that out-to-lunch look in his eyes. But more than likely, he'll never execute them. After he's shared one or two of his progressive ideas with you, you're liable to ask yourself "Who is this nut?" But don't go jumping to any wrong conclusions. There's a saying that as far as thinking is concerned, Aquarians are a half-century ahead of everybody else. If you do decide to say yes to his will-you-marry-me, you'll find out how right some of his zany whims are on your golden anniversary. Maybe the waiting will be worth it. Could be that you have an Einstein on your hands—and heart.

Life with an Aquarian won't be one of total despair for you if you learn to balance his airiness with your down-to-brass-tacks practicality. He won't gripe if you do. Being the open-minded man he is, the Aquarian will entertain all your ideas and opinions. He may not agree with them, but he'll give them a trial airing out, anyway.

Don't go tearing your hair out when you find that it's almost impossible to hold a normal conversation with your Aquarius friend. He's capable of answering your how-do-you-do with a rundown of the cost of Arizona sugar beets. Always keep in mind that he means well. His broadmindedness doesn't end with your freedom and individuality come into the picture.

He'll be kind and generous as a husband and will never lower himself by quibbling over petty things. You take care of the budgeting and bookkeeping; that goes without saying. He'll be thankful that you do such a good job of keeping track of all the pennies and nickels that would otherwise burn a hole in his pocket.

In your relationship with a man born under Aquarius you'll have plenty of opportunities to put your legendary patience to good use. At times, you may feel like tossing in the towel and calling it quits, but try counting up to ten before deciding that it's the last straw.

He'll be a good family man. He's very understanding with children and will overlook a naughty deed now and then or at least try to see it in its proper perspective.

TAURUS WOMAN
PISCES MAN

The Pisces man could be the man you've looked for high and low and thought never existed. He's terribly sensitive and terribly romantic. Still, he has a very strong individual character and is well aware that the moon is not made of green cheese. He'll be very considerate of your every wish and will do his best to see to it that your relationship is a happy one.

The Pisces man is great for showering the object of his affection with all kinds of little gifts and tokens of his love.

He's just the right mixture of dreamer and realist; he's capable of pleasing most women's hearts. When it comes to earning bread and butter, the strong Pisces will do all right in the world. Quite often they are capable of rising to very high positions. Some do extremely well as writers or psychiatrists. He'll be as patient and understanding with you as you will undoubtedly be with him. One thing a Pisces man dislikes is pettiness; anyone who delights in running another into the ground is almost immediately crossed off his list of possible mates. If you have any small grievances with your girlfriends, don't tell him about them. He couldn't care less and will think less of you if you do.

If you fall in love with a weak Pisces man, don't give up your job at the office before you get married. Better hang onto it until a good time after the honeymoon; you may still need it. A funny thing about the man born under this sign is that he can be content almost anywhere. This is perhaps because he is quite inner-directed and places little value on material things. In a shack or in a palace, the Pisces man is capable of making the best of all possible adjustments. He won't kick up a fuss if the roof leaks and if the fence is in sad need of repair, he's liable to shrug his shoulders and say "*mañana.*" He's got more important things on his mind, he'll tell you. At this point, you're quite capable of telling him to go to blazes. Still and all, the Pisces man is not shiftless or aimless, but it is important to understand that material gain is never an urgent goal for him.

Pisces men have a way with the sick and troubled. It's often his nature to offer his shoulder to anyone in the mood for a good cry. He can listen to one hard luck story after another without seeming to tire. He quite often knows what's bothering a person before the person knows it himself.

As a lover, he'll be quite attentive. You'll never have cause to doubt his intentions or sincerity. Everything will be above-board in his romantic dealings with you.

Children are often delighted with the Pisces man because they can often have their own way with him.

Man—Woman

TAURUS MAN
ARIES WOMAN

The Aries woman may be a little too bossy and busy for you. Generally speaking, Ariens are ambitious creatures and they can become a little impatient with people who are more thorough and deliberate than they are—especially when they feel it's taking too much time. Unlike you, the Aries woman is a fast worker—in fact, sometimes she's so fast, she forgets to look where she's going. When she stumbles or falls, it's a nice thing if you're there to grab her. She'll be grateful. Don't ever tell her "I told you so" when she errs. Ariens are proud women and don't like people to stick their tongues out at them. Such things can turn them into blocks of ice. And don't think that an Aries woman will always get tripped up in her plans because she lacks patience. Quite often they are capable of taking aim and hitting the bull's-eye. You'll be flabbergasted at times by their accuracy as well as by their ambition. On the other hand, because of your interest in being sure and safe, you're apt to spot many a mistake or flaw in your Aries friend's plans before she does.

In some respects, the Aries-Taurus relationship is like that of the tortoise and the hare. Although it may seem like plain plodding along to Miss Aries, you're quite capable of attaining exactly what she has her sights set on; it may take a bit longer but you generally do not make any mistakes along the way.

Taurus men are renowned lovers. With some of them, it's almost a way of life. When you are serious about a girl, you want her to be as earnest and as giving as you are in the relationship. Girls who have their hearts packed in ice-cubes are not likely to interest you very much, even though there is enough flame in you to melt an iceberg. An Aries woman can be giving when she feels her partner is deserving. She needs a man she can look up to and be proud of. If the shoe fits, slip into it. If not, better put your sneakers back on and quietly tiptoe out of her sight. She can cause you plenty of heartache if you've made up your mind about her but she hasn't made up hers about you. Aries women are very demanding, or at least they can be if they feel it's worth their while. They're high-strung at times and can be difficult if they feel their independence is being hampered.

If you manage to get to first base with the Aries girl of your dreams, keep a pair of kid gloves in your back pocket. You'll need them for handling her. Not that she's all that touchy; it's just that your relationship will have a better chance of progressing if you handle her with tender loving care. Let her know that you like her for her brains as well as for her good looks. Don't even begin to look like you're just about to admire the legs of that girl sitting opposite you in the bus. When your Aries date sees green, you'd better forget about a rosy future together.

TAURUS MAN
TAURUS WOMAN

Although two Taureans may be able to understand each other and even love each other, it does not necessarily hold true that theirs will be a stable and pleasant relationship. The Taurus woman you are dating may be too much like you in character to ever be compatible. You can be pretty set in your ways. When you encounter someone with just as much willpower or stubbornness, the results can be anything but pleasant. Whenever two Taureans lock horns it can be a very exhausting and unsatisfactory get-together. However, if the girl you have a hankering for was born under the sign of the Bull and you are convinced that no other will do, then proceed—but with caution. Even though you know yourself well—or, at least, think you do—it does not necessarily mean that you will have an easy time understanding Miss Taurus. However, since both of you are basically practical people, you should try a rational approach to your relationship: put your cards on the table, talk it over, then decide whether you should or could cooperate, compromise, or call it a day. If you both have your sights set on the same goal, life together could be just what the doctor ordered.

Both of you are very affectionate people and have a deep need for affection. Being loved, understood, and appreciated are very important for your well-being. You need a woman who is not stingy with her love because you're very generous with yours. In the Taurus woman you'll find someone who is attuned to your way of feeling when it comes to romance. Taureans, although practical and somewhat deliberate in almost everything they do, are, relatively speaking, very passionate people. They are capable of being very warm and loving when they feel that the relationship is an honest one and that their feelings will be reciprocated. In the area of home-life, two Taureans should be able to hit it off very well. Taurus wives are very good at keeping the household ship-shape. They know how to market wisely, how to budget, and how to save. If you and your

Taurus wife decide on a particular amount of money for housekeeping purposes each month, you can bet your bottom dollar that she'll stick to it right up to the last penny.

You're an extremely ambitious person—all Taureans are—and your chances for a successful relationship with a Taurus woman will perhaps be better if she is a woman of some standing. It's not that you're a social climber or that you are cold and calculating when it comes to love, but you are well aware that it is just as easy to fall in love with a rich or socially prominent woman as it is with a poor one.

Both of you should be careful in bringing up your children. Taureans have a tendency to be rather strict. When your children grow up and become independent, they could turn against you as a result.

TAURUS MAN
GEMINI WOMAN

The Gemini woman may be too much of a flirt ever to take your honest heart too seriously. Then again, it depends on what kind of a mood she's in. Gemini women can change from hot to cold quicker than a cat can wink its eye. Chances are her fluctuations will tire you after a time, and you'll pick up your heart—if it's not already broken into small pieces—and go elsewhere. Women born under the sign of the Twins have the talent of being able to change their moods and attitudes as frequently as they change their party dresses. Quite often they're good-time girls who like nothing better than to whoop it up and burn the candle to the wick. You'll always see them at parties, surrounded by men of all types, laughing gaily or kicking up their heels at every opportunity. Wallflowers they're not. The next day you may bump into the same girl at the neighborhood library and you'll hardly be able to recognize her for her "sensible" clothes and thick glasses. She'll probably have five or six books under her arms—on five or six different subjects. In fact, she may even work there. Don't greet her in too loud a voice; she's liable to put her finger to her lips and say "Shhh!" If you think you've met the twin sister of Dr. Jekyll and Mr. Hyde, you're most likely right.

You'll probably find her a dazzling and fascinating creature—for a time, at any rate—just as the majority of men do. But when it comes to being serious you may find that that sparkling Geminian leaves quite a bit to be desired. It's not that she has anything against being serious, it's just that she might find it difficult trying to be serious with you. At one moment she'll be capable of praising you for your steadfast and patient ways, the next moment she'll tell you in a cutting way that you're an impossible stick-in-the-mud.

Don't even try to fathom the depths of her mercurial soul—it's full of false bottoms. She'll resent close investigation, anyway, and will make you rue the day you ever took it into your head to try to learn more about her than she feels is necessary. Better keep the relationship fancy-free and full of fun until she gives you the go-ahead sign. Take as much of her as she's willing to give and don't ask for more. If she does take a serious interest in you and makes up her fickle mind about herself and you, then she'll come across with the goods.

There will come a time when the Gemini girl will realize that she can't spend her entire life at the ball and that the security and warmth you offer is just what she needs in order to be a happy, fulfilled woman.

Don't try to cramp her individuality; she'll never try to cramp yours.

Gemini women aren't really cut out to be good housewives, but she'll do her best if she feels it's very important to you. You may have to ask her five times to sew that button on your shirt and she's quite capable of letting the roast burn in the oven while she's wrapped up in the Sunday crossword puzzle.

TAURUS MAN
CANCER WOMAN

The girl born under Cancer needs to be protected from the cold, cruel world. She'll love you for your masculine yet gentle manner; you make her feel safe and secure. You don't have to pull any he-man or heroic stunts to win her heart; that's not what interests her. She's more likely to be impressed by your sure, steady ways—the way you have of putting your arm around her and making her feel that she's the only girl in the world. When she's feeling glum and tears begin to well up in her eyes, you have that knack of saying just the right thing—you know how to calm her fears, no matter how silly some of them may seem.

The girl born under this sign is inclined to have her ups and downs. You have the talent for smoothing out the ruffles in her sea of life. She'll most likely worship the ground you walk on or put you on a terribly high pedestal. Don't disappoint her if you can help it. She'll never disappoint you. This is the kind of woman who will take great pleasure in devoting the rest of her natural life to you. She'll darn your socks, mend your overalls, scrub floors, wash windows, shop, cook, and do just about anything short of murder in order to please you and to let you know that she loves you. Sounds like that legendary good old-fashioned girl, doesn't it? Contrary to popular belief, there are still a good number of them around—and many of them are Cancerians.

Of all the signs in the Zodiac, the women under the Cancer sign are the most maternal. In caring for and bringing up children, they know just how to combine the right amount of tenderness with the proper dash of discipline. A child couldn't ask for a better mother. Cancer women are sympathetic, affectionate, and patient with children.

While we're on the subject of motherhood, there's one thing you should be warned about: never be unkind to your mother-in-law. It will be the only golden rule your Cancerian wife will probably expect you to live up to. No mother-in-law jokes in the presence of your Mrs., please. With her, they'll go over like a lead balloon. Mother is something pretty special for her. She may be the crankiest, noisiest old bat this side of the Great Divide, still if she's your wife's mother, you'd better treat her like she's one of the landed gentry. Sometimes this may be difficult to swallow. But if you want to keep your home together and your wife happy, you'd better learn to grin and bear it.

Your Cancer wife will prove to be a whiz in the kitchen. She'll know just when you're in the mood for your favorite dish or snack, and she can whip it up in a jiffy.

Treat your Cancer wife fairly, and she'll treat you like a king.

TAURUS MAN
LEO WOMAN

The Leo woman can make most men roar like lions. If any woman in the Zodiac has that indefinable something that can make men lose their heads and find their hearts, it's the Leo woman. She's got more than her share of charm and glamor and she knows how to put them to good use, especially when she's in the company of the opposite sex. Jealous men either lose their sanity or at least their cool when trying to woo a woman born under the sign of the Lion. She likes to kick up her heels quite often and doesn't care who knows it. She often makes heads turn and tongues wag. You don't necessarily have to believe any of what you hear—it's most likely just jealous gossip or wishful thinking. Needless to say, other women in her vicinity turn green with envy and will try anything short of shoving her into the nearest lake in order to put her out of commission.

Although this vamp makes the blood rush to your head and you momentarily forget all of the things that you thought were important and necessary in your life, when you come back down to earth and are out of her bewitching presence, you'll probably come to the conclusion that although this vivacious creature can make you feel pretty wonderful, she just isn't the kind of girl you'd planned to bring home to mother. Not that your mother would necessarily disapprove of your choice—*you might,* after the shoes and rice are a thing of the past. Although she'll certainly do her best to be a good wife for you, she most likely will not live up to (or even try to) your idea of what your wife should be like.

If you're planning on not going as far as the altar with that Leo woman who has you flipping your lid, you'd better be financially equipped for some very expensive dating. Be prepared to shower her with expensive gifts, take her dining and dancing in the smartest nightspots in town. Promise her the moon, if you're in a position to go that far. Luxury and glamor are two things that are bound to lower a Leo's resistance. She's got expensive tastes and you'd better cater to them if you expect to get to first base with this gal.

If you've got an important business deal to clinch and you have doubts as to whether it will go over well or not, bring your Leo girlfriend along to that business luncheon and it will be a cinch that you'll have that contract—lock, stock, and barrel—in your pocket before the meeting is over. She won't have to say or do anything— just be there at your side. The grouchiest oil magnate can be transformed into a gushing, obedient schoolboy if there's a charm-studded Leo woman in the room.

TAURUS MAN
VIRGO WOMAN

The Virgo woman is pretty particular about choosing her men friends. She's not interested in just going out with anybody; she has her own idea of what a boyfriend or prospective husband should be —and it's quite possible that that image has something of you in it. Generally speaking, she's a quiet girl; she doesn't believe that nonsense has any place in a love affair. She's serious and will expect you to be. She's looking for a man who has both of his feet on the ground—someone who can take care of himself as well as take care of her. She knows the value of money and how to get the most out of a dollar. She's far from being a spendthrift. Throwing money around turns her stomach, even if it isn't her money that's being tossed to the winds.

She'll most likely be very shy about romancing. Even the simple act of holding hands may make her blush—on the first couple of dates. You'll have to make all the advances, which is how you feel it should be. You'll have to be careful not to make any wrong moves.

She's capable of showing anyone who oversteps the boundaries of common decency the door. It may even take quite a long time before she'll accept that goodnight kiss at the front gate. Don't give up. You're exactly the kind of man who can bring out the woman in her. There is warmth and tenderness underneath Virgo's seemingly frigid facade. It will take a patient and understanding man to bring it out into the open. She may have an idea that sex is something very naughty, if not downright unnecessary. The right man could make her put this old-fashioned idea in the trunk up in the attic along with her great grandmother's woolen nightie.

You'll find her a very sensitive girl, perhaps more sensitive than is good for her. You can help her overcome this by treating her with gentleness and affection.

When a Virgo has accepted you as a lover or mate, she won't stint on giving her love in return. With her, it's all or nothing at all. You'll be surprised at the transformation your earnest attention can bring about in this quiet kind of woman. When in love, Virgos only listen to their hearts, not to what the neighbors say.

Virgo women are honest in love once they've come to grips with it. They don't appreciate hypocrisy, particularly in this area of life. They believe in being honest to their hearts, so much so that once they've learned the ropes of romance and they find that their hearts have stumbled on another fancy, they're liable to be true to a new heart-throb and leave you standing in the rain. But if you're earnest about your interest in her, she'll know and reciprocate your affection. Do her wrong once, however, and you can be sure she'll snip the soiled ribbon of your relationship.

TAURUS MAN
LIBRA WOMAN

It's written that it is a woman's prerogative to change her mind. The writer must have had a woman born under the sign of Libra in his thoughts. Her changeability, in spite of its undeniable charm (sometimes) could actually drive even a man of your patience up the wall. She's capable of smothering you with love and kisses one day and the next day she's apt to avoid you like the plague. If you think you're a man of steel nerves then perhaps you can tolerate her sometime-ness without suffering too much. However, if you own up to the fact that you're only a mere mortal of flesh and blood, then you'd better try to fasten your attention on a girl who's somewhat more constant. But don't get the wrong idea: a love affair with a Libran is not all bad. In fact, it has an awful lot of positives. Libra women are soft, very feminine, and warm. She doesn't have to vamp all over the place in order to gain a man's attention. Her delicate presence is enough to warm the cockles of any man's heart. One smile and you're like a piece of putty in the palm of her hand.

She can be fluffy and affectionate, things you like in a girl. On the other hand, her indecision about what dress to wear, what to cook for dinner, or whether or not to redo the rumpus room could make you tear your hair out. What will perhaps be more exasperating is her flat denial that she can't make a simple decision when you accuse her of this. The trouble is that she wants to be fair to just about everything and thinks that the only way to do this is to weigh both sides of the situation before coming to a decision. A Libran can go on weighing things for days, months, or years if allowed the time.

The Libra woman likes to be surrounded with beautiful things. Money is no object when beauty is concerned. There'll always be plenty of flowers around her apartment. She'd rather die than do without daisies and such. She'll know how to arrange them tastefully, too. Women under this sign are fond of beautiful clothes and furnishings. They'll run up bills without batting an eye (if given the chance) in order to surround themselves with luxury.

Once she's cottoned to you, the Libra woman will do everything in her power to make you happy. She'll wait on you hand and foot when you're sick, bring you breakfast in bed Sundays, and even read you the funny papers if you're too sleepy to open your eyes. She'll be very thoughtful about anything that concerns you. If anyone dares suggest you're not the grandest man in the world, your Libra wife will give him or her a good talking to.

They work wonders in bringing up children. Gentle persuasion and affection is all she uses when dealing with them. Children love and respect her.

TAURUS MAN
SCORPIO WOMAN

When the Scorpio woman gets upset, be prepared to run for cover. There is nothing else to do. When her temper flies, so does everything else that's not bolted down. On the other hand, when she chooses to be sweet, you're apt to conclude that butter wouldn't have a chance of melting in her mouth. It would, of course. She can be as hot as a *tamale* or as cool as a cucumber, but whatever mood she happens to be in, it's for real. She doesn't believe in poses or hypocrisy. The Scorpio woman is often seductive and sultry—her *femme fatale* charm can pierce through the hardest of hearts like a laser ray. She doesn't have to look like Mata Hari (many resemble the tomboy next door), but once you've looked into those tantalizing eyes, you're a goner.

The Scorpio woman can be a whirlwind of passion—perhaps too much passion to suit even a hot-blooded Taurean. Life with a girl born under this sign will not be all smiles and smooth sailing. When prompted, she can unleash a gale of venom. If you think you can handle a woman who can purr like a pussycat when handled correctly but spit bullets once her fur is ruffled, then try your luck. Your stable and steady nature will most likely have a calming effect on her. But never cross her, even on the smallest thing. If you do, you'd better tell Fido to make room for you in the doghouse; you'll be his guest for the next couple of days.

Generally, the Scorpio woman will keep family battles within the walls of your home. When company visits, she's apt to give the impression that married life is one great big joy-ride. It's just her way of expressing loyalty to you, at least in front of others. She may fight you tooth and nail in the confines of your living room, but at the ball or during an evening out, she'll hang on your arm and have stars in her eyes. She doesn't consider this hypocrisy, she just believes that family quarrels are a private matter and should be kept so. She's pretty good at keeping secrets. She may even keep a few from you if she feels like it.

By nature, you're a calm and peace-loving man. You value dependability rather highly. A Scorpio may be too much of a pepper-pot for your love diet; you're liable to wind up a victim of chronic heartburn. She's rather an excitable and touchy woman. You're looking for someone whose emotions are more steady and reliable to settle down with. You may find a relationship with a Scorpio too draining.

Never give the Scorpio girl reason to think you've betrayed her. She's an eye-for-an-eye woman. She's not keen on forgiveness when she feels she's been done wrong.

If you've got your sights set on a shapely Scorpio siren, you'd better be prepared to take the bitter with the sweet.

TAURUS MAN
SAGITTARIUS WOMAN

The Sagittarius woman is hard to keep track of. First she's here then she's there. She's a woman with a severe case of itchy feet. She'll most likely win you over with her hale-fellow-well-met manner and breezy charm. She's constantly good-natured and almost never cross. She's the kind of girl you're likely to strike up a palsy-walsy relationship with, but you might not be interested in letting it go any further. She probably won't sulk if you leave it on a friendly basis, either. Treat her like a kid-sister and she'll love you all the more for it.

She'll probably be attracted to you because of your restful, self-assured manner. She'll need a friend like you to rely on and will most likely turn to you frequently for advice.

There's nothing malicious about a girl born under this sign. She'll be full of bounce and good cheer. Her sunshiny disposition can be relied upon even on the rainiest of days. No matter what she'll ever say or do, you'll know that she means well. Sagittarians are quite often short on tact and say literally anything that comes into their pretty little heads, no matter what the occasion. Sometimes the words that tumble out of their mouths seem downright cutting and cruel. She never meant it that way, however. She is quite capable of losing her friends and perhaps even yours, through a careless slip of the lip. On the other hand, you're liable to appreciate her honesty and good intentions.

She's not a girl that you'd most likely be interested in marrying, but she'll certainly be a lot of fun to pal around with. Quite often, Sagittarius women are the outdoor type. They're crazy about hiking, fishing, white-water canoeing, and even mountain-climbing. She's a busy little lady and no one could ever accuse her of being a slouch. She's great company most of the time and can be more fun than a three-ring circus when treated fairly. You'll like her for her candid and direct manner. On the whole, Sagittarians are very kind and sympathetic women.

If you do wind up marrying this girl-next-door type, you'll perhaps never regret it. Still there are certain areas of your home life that you'll have to put yourself in charge of, just to keep matters on an even keel. One area is savings. Sagittarians often do not have heads for money and as a result can let it run through their fingers like sand before they realize what has happened to it. Another area is children. She loves kids so much, she's apt to spoil them silly. If you don't step in, she'll give them all of the freedom they think they need.

TAURUS MAN
CAPRICORN WOMAN

You'll probably not have any difficulty in understanding the woman born under the sign of Capricorn. In some ways, she's just like you. She is faithful, dependable, and systematic in just about everything that she undertakes. She is quite concerned with security and sees to it that every penny she spends is spent wisely. She is very economical in using her time, too. She doesn't believe in whittling away her energy in a scheme that is bound not to pay off.

Ambitious themselves in a way, they're quite often attracted to ambitious men—men who are interested in getting somewhere in life. If a man of this sort wins her heart, she'll stick by him and do all she can to see to it that he gets to the top. The Capricorn woman is almost always diplomatic and makes an excellent hostess. She can be very influential when business acquaintances come to dinner.

She's not the most romantic woman of the Zodiac, but she's far from being frigid when she meets the right man. She believes in true love and doesn't appreciate getting involved in flings. To her, they're just a waste of time. She's looking for a man who means "business"—in life as well as in love. Although she can be very affectionate with her boyfriend or mate, she tends to let her head govern her heart. That is not to say that she is a cool, calculating cucumber. On the contrary, she just feels she can be more honest about love if she consults her brains first. She'll want to size up the situation first before throwing her heart in the ring. She wants to make sure that it won't get stepped on.

A Capricorn woman is likely to be very concerned, if not downright proud, about her family tree. Relatives are pretty important to her, particularly if they've been able to make their mark in life. Never say a cross word about her family members, either. That can really go against her grain and she won't talk to you for days on end.

She's generally thorough in whatever she undertakes: cooking, cleaning, entertaining. Capricorn women are well-mannered and gracious, no matter what their background. They seem to have it in their natures to always behave properly.

If you should marry a woman born under this sign you need never worry about her going on a wild shopping spree. They understand the value of money better than most women. If you turn over your paycheck to her at the end of the week, you can be sure that a good hunk of it will go into the bank and that all the bills will be paid on time.

With children, the Capricorn mother is both loving and correct. She'll see to it that they're polite and respectful to others.

TAURUS MAN
AQUARIUS WOMAN

The woman born under the sign of the Water Bearer can be pretty odd and eccentric at times. Some say that this is the source of her mysterious charm. You're liable to think that she's just a plain nut, and you may be fifty percent right. Aquarius women have their heads full of dreams, and stars in their eyes. By nature, they are often unconventional and have their own ideas about how the world should be run. Sometimes their ideas may seem pretty weird, but more likely than not, they are just a little too progressive for their time. There's a saying that runs "the way Aquarius thinks, so will the world in fifty years."

If you find yourself falling in love with a woman born under this sign, you'd better fasten your safety belt. It may take some time before you really know what she's like and even then you may have nothing more to go on but a string of vague hunches. She can be like a rainbow, full of dazzling colors. She's like no other girl you've ever known. There's something about her that is definitely charming, yet elusive; you'll never be able to put your finger on it. She seems to radiate adventure and magic without even half trying. She'll most likely be the most tolerant and open-minded woman you've ever encountered.

If you find that she's too much mystery and charm for you to handle—and being a Taurean, chances are you might—just talk it out with her and say that you think it would be better if you called it quits. She'll most likely give you a peck on the cheek and say she thinks you're one hundred percent right but still there's no reason why you can't remain friends. Aquarian women are like that. And perhaps you'll both find it easier to get along in a friendship than in a romance.

It is not difficult for her to remain buddy-buddy with someone she has just broken off with. For many Aquarians, the line between friendship and romance is a pretty fuzzy one.

She's not a jealous person and, while you're romancing her, she'll expect you not to be, either. You'll find her a pretty free spirit most of the time. Just when you think you know her inside-out, you'll discover that you don't really know her at all. She's a very sympathetic and warm person. She can be helpful to people in need of assistance and advice.

She's a chameleon and can fit in anywhere. She'll seldom be suspicious even when she has every right to be. If the man she loves slips and allows himself a little fling, chances are she'll just turn her head the other way and pretend not to notice that the gleam in his eye is not meant for her.

She makes a fine mother, of course. Her positive and big-hearted qualities are easily transmitted to her offspring.

TAURUS MAN
PISCES WOMAN

The Pisces woman places great value on love and romance. She's gentle, kind and romantic. Perhaps she's that girl you've been dreaming about all these years. Like you, she has very high ideals; she will only give her heart to a man who she feels can live up to her expectations.

She'll never try to wear the pants in the family. She's a staunch believer in the man being the head of the house. Quite often, Pisces women are soft and cuddly. They have a feminine, domestic charm that can win the heart of just about any man.

Generally, there's a lot more to her than just a pretty exterior and womanly ways. There's a brain ticking behind that gentle face. You may not become aware of it—that is, until you've married her. It's no cause for alarm, however. She'll most likely never use it against you. But if she feels you're botching up your married life through careless behavior or if she feels you could be earning more money than you do, she'll tell you about it. But any wife would, really. She'll never try to usurp your position as head and breadwinner of the family. She'll admire you for your ambition and drive. If anyone says anything against you in her presence, she'll probably break out into tears. Pisces women are usually very sensitive and their reaction to frustration and anger is often just a plain good old-fashioned cry. They can weep buckets when inclined.

She'll have an extra-special dinner waiting for you when you call up and tell her that you've just landed a new and important account. Don't bother to go into the details, though, at the dinner table; she doesn't have much of a head for business matters, usually, and is only too happy to leave that up to you.

She is a wizard in decorating a home. She's fond of soft and beautiful things. There will always be a vase of fresh flowers on the dining-room table. She'll see to it that you always have plenty of socks and underwear in the top drawer of your dresser.

Treat her with tenderness and your relationship will be an enjoyable one. Pisces women are generally fond of sweets, so keep her in chocolates (and flowers, of course) and you'll have a very happy wife. Never forget birthdays, anniversaries, and the like. These are important occasions for her. If you ever let such a thing slip your mind, you can be sure of sending her off to the bedroom for an hour-long cry.

Your Taurus talent for patience and gentleness can pay off in your relationship with a Pisces woman. Chances are she'll never make you sorry that you placed that band of gold on her finger.

There is usually a strong bond between a Pisces mother and her children. She'll try to give them things she never had as a child and is apt to spoil them as a result.

GEMINI
May 21—June 20

CHARACTER
ANALYSIS

Persons born under this third sign of the Zodiac are generally known for their versatility, their duality. Quite often they are able to manage several things at the same time. Some of them have two or more sides to their personalities. At one moment they can be happy and fun-loving, the next they can be sullen and quite morose. For the outsider, this sudden change may be difficult to understand or appreciate.

The Gemini man or woman is interested in all sorts of things and in different ways. Many of the subjects that attract them seem contrary and dissimilar. To the Gemini person, they're not.

The person born under the sign of the Twins has a mercurial nature. He can fly into a rage one moment, then be absolutely loveable the next. Chances are he won't even remember what all the fuss was about after a few moments have passed.

The Gemini man or woman is rather spiritual in nature. Intellectual challenges whet his appetite. He's a sensitive person. His mind is active, alert. He could even be described as idea-hungry, always on the lookout for new concepts, new ways of doing things. He is always moving along with the times. On the whole, the person born under this sign is very energetic. However, he is apt to bite off more than he can chew at times. He may begin a dozen different projects at once—and never finish any. It's often the doing—starting something—that he finds interesting. As soon as something becomes too familiar or humdrum he is likely to drop it like a hot coal and begin something else. The cultivated Geminian, however, does not have this problem. He has learned by experience that constancy pays off. He knows how to limit his interests—no matter how great the temptation may be to take on more—and how to finish the work that he has begun. It's a hard lesson for the natural Geminian to learn, but it can be done.

In school, persons born under this sign are generally quite popular and often at the top of their class. They learn quickly, and when they apply themselves, they can make good use of their powers of concentration. Many do well in languages. They are clever conversationalists; they can keep an audience entranced for hours. Still and all, the depth of their knowledge may be rather slight. They know how to phrase things well, and this gives the impression of deep learning. They read things too quickly at times and often miss important points. Sometimes they will insist that something is right when in fact it isn't.

Generally speaking, the Gemini person has a good sense of humor. He knows how to appreciate a good joke and this is apt to make him quite popular with others. He seldom fails to see the humorous side of life. In fact, he may irritate others by not acknowledging the serious side of a particular situation when it is necessary.

All in all, the person born under this sign of the Twins is openminded. He is tolerant of others no matter what their views are. He can get along well with various sorts of people. He's a great mixer. He never has much trouble understanding another's viewpoint.

It is held that the Gemini person is one who prefers to work with concrete things; high-blown ideas do not interest him. To him, facts are more important than fantasy. He's practical—or at least attempts to be. He can be quite goal-directed; there is always a reason for what he does. An ambitious person, on the whole, he is never short on projects; there is always something that he has to get done. He could be described as restless; he doesn't like sitting still for long periods of time. He's got to be on the go.

Health

The Geminian usually is an active person. He generally has plenty of energy stored up. Still, he has to be careful at times because he is liable to strain himself emotionally. He gets too wound up and finds it a bit difficult to relax. Troubles, small and large, can turn him into a nervous person, if he doesn't look out for himself. Weak points of his body are his lungs, arms, and nervous system. During the winter months, some people born under this sign have one cold after another. Sore throats are sometimes a common Geminian complaint.

On the whole, however, the Gemini has a pretty good constitution. He's healthy, but he has to learn how to take care of his health. People often think of the Gemini person as being weak and sickly, but this isn't so. His physique is often thin and wiry. He may not look like he can endure too much pressure, but his powers for endurance are often amazing. He is not delicate, by any stretch of the imagination.

Although the person born under this sign may be bothered by one minor ailment or another, Geminis seldom contract serious illnesses—if they take proper care of themselves. The wise Geminian acknowledges his limits and never tries to exceed them. He will never take on more work than he can comfortably handle. It is important that the Gemini man or woman learns how to relax. Sleep is also an important ingredient for good health. Some people born under this sign feel they have to be constantly on the go; it is as if they were on a treadmill. Of course, they can only keep it up for a short while, then they have to pay the consequences.

The Gemini man or woman is often gifted with handsome looks. Others find them winsome and attractive. Their faces are very lively and expressive; their smiles charming. Most of them tend to be on the slim side. They may seem rather restless or fidgety.

Occupation

Geminians are ambitious; they have plenty of drive. They like to keep busy. Most of them do well in jobs that give them a chance to make full use of their intellects. They like to use their minds more than their hands. They are good talkers, generally, and do well in positions where they have to deal directly with the public. They are clever with words and are persuasive in their arguments. Also, they know how to make people feel at ease by making use of their sense of humor. A good well-placed joke can work wonders when dealing with the public.

They quite often know how to turn a disadvantage to advantage. They know how to bargain. They are seldom made fools of when it comes to trading. Some of them make excellent salesmen and it is little wonder. Because they can juggle words so well and they have a deep interest in facts, they often turn into quite capable journalists. Some of them make good theater or film critics. Writing is one of their chief talents. They generally do well in the arts.

Anything to do with negotiating or bargaining is something in which the Geminian is apt to excel. They know how to phrase things; to put them in a favorable light.

One is apt to find Geminians in such professions as dentistry, medicine, law, engineering. They seem to fit in almost anywhere. Some of them have a head for mathematics and make good accountants.

When working with others, they will do what is necessary to make the project successful. However, they do like to be able to go their own way. They do not like someone looking over their shoulder constantly, advising them how something should be done. They like to move around quite a bit; nothing pleases them more than a job where they are free to come and go as they please. They generally find it difficult to sit down at a desk for long stretches at a time. Geminians often like movement for its own sake. They are not particularly interested in destinations. It's getting there that absorbs their interest.

They are generally not contented with being busy with just one thing. They are apt to try to hold down two jobs at the same time just to be active. Their hobbies are usually varied; some of them they manage to develop into side-occupations. They abhor dull routine and are often creative in their approach to a familiar scheme. They will do what they can to make their work interesting. If they are placed in the wrong position—that is, a position that does not coincide with their interests—they are apt to be rather grumpy and difficult to get along with.

Geminians aren't money-hungry, generally speaking, but somehow or other they always manage to find jobs that are well-paying. They are not the kind of people who would be willing to work for nothing. They value their own skills and generally know how much they are worth.

They like to be attached to modern, progressive concerns. They dislike job situations that are old-fashioned and tiresome.

Money interests the Gemini man or woman because it represents security. The uncultivated Geminian however, spends his earnings rather carelessly. He doesn't run out of money, but he mismanages what he has. When he has learned how to economize, he does quite well. He's always looking for a way to better his financial situation. Some Gemini people are job-hoppers; they are never satisfied with the position they have and they go from one job to another looking for their "proper niche," they think. It is the Geminian who knows how to make the best out of a job-situation he already has who wins the day. Job-changing becomes a sort of chronic disease; it never seems to stop and in the end, the job-hopper has nothing to show for all his changing.

People born under this sign usually know how to win the sympathy of influential people. They are often helped, advised, and

CHARACTER ANALYSIS / 77

encouraged by people who hold important positions. People find it easy to believe in them.

The Gemini man or woman is often quite generous with what he has; he does not mind sharing. He can be rather expansive and doesn't mind paying for others if he can afford it. Once in a while, he may do something unwise with his finances, but, all in all, he manages to keep his head above water as far as money matters are concerned.

Home and Family

The Gemini is quite adaptable. He is willing to do without if it is necessary, but if he can have his own way, he likes to be surrounded by comfortable and harmonious things. Home is important to him. He likes a house that radiates beauty and calm.

He likes to invite people to his home; he likes entertaining. It is important to the Geminian that people feel at home while visiting him. Because he is such a ready host, his house is often full of people—of all description. Although he may be at a loss how he should handle some household matters, he always seems to manage in one way or another. His home is likely to be modern —equipped with all of the latest conveniences and appliances. He is often amused by gadgets.

Although his home may be important to him, he likes to be able to feel that he can pick up and go off somewhere whenever the mood strikes him. He doesn't like the feeling of being tied down. Home is where he hangs his hat, he likes to think. A Geminian is apt to change his address more than once in his lifetime. This may or may not upset his family ties to a certain extent. Still, if they understand him, they will give in to his plans. No one is more difficult to live with than a dissatisfied Geminian. Still, more than likely the Geminian has his family conditioned to his moods and there is enough understanding to make life together possible. The cultivated Geminian learns to stay put, however, and make the most of the home he has.

The Gemini man or woman is a great fixer. He likes to make minor repairs, changing appliances, paintings, wallpapering, and the like. He will do many things to make improvements on his home. Sometimes he will go ahead and make changes without consulting those he lives with and, of course, this is apt to cause unpleasantness.

Outsiders may not think of Gemini as the ideal parent or family man. In fact, they may be open in their criticism. The Geminian might resent this quite strongly because he feels that it just isn't true. Children, however, are apt to get on the Gemini man or woman's nerves now and again. They like their offspring to be as expressive and creative as they are; however, they do enjoy moments of peace and quiet. Generally speaking, they know how to get along well with their children. This may be because they do have a youthful streak themselves. They understand the ups and downs of childhood; the trials and tribulations of growing up—also the joys. They may scold once in a while, but children who know them will never pay too much attention to them. The Gemini parent is generally a pushover for the wilful child.

Gemini children are sometimes difficult to manage. They usually don't like to be hampered by parental guidance. They like to be allowed to do as they please when they please. They often show signs of artistic ability at a very early age. The perceptive parent knows how to encourage them and to help them develop the characteristics that will help them later on in life.

Social Relationships

The person born under the sign of the Twins is usually easy to get along with. He likes people and knows how to make them like him. He seldom has serious enemies; he's too friendly for that. Because of his light-hearted and jovial ways many people are drawn to him. He is generally sincere in his friendships and expects that sincerity to be reciprocated. A sensitive person, he never forgets or forgives an offense.

Gemini people like to be in a crowd—a friendly crowd. They seldom like to be alone for long stretches at a time. They like their friends to be as active and as enthusiastic as they are. Social involvement is important to them. They are apt to throw a party at the drop of a hat. The Gemini man or woman enjoys making others feel good. They make excellent hosts and try to anticipate their guests' needs. A Geminian could never be called unhospitable.

Their friends are apt be very different from each other. The Geminian gets along well with all sorts of people. Their social needs are apt to seem contradictory to someone who does not understand the Geminian nature. The cultivated person born under this sign knows how to keep apart those friends who are not likely to get along. He'll avoid social conflict among his friends at all costs.

Meeting new people is important to the man or woman born under the third sign of the Zodiac. He thrives on social activities. He likes exchanging views and ideas.

The Geminian does not demand that his friends be his intellectual equal. He can be quite content discussing trivial matters as well as profound ones. He likes people he can relax with.

Friends may like the Gemini person, but find him hard to understand really. They can seem to be so many different things at the same time. They are difficult to pin down.

People are always inviting Geminians to parties; any social affair would seem incomplete without someone born under the sign of Gemini. Their charm and liveliness is contagious. People enjoy being around them. They can be rather loose-tongued at social gatherings, however, and sometimes divulge information about themselves or others that they shouldn't. They can be rather severe, too, in their criticisms. Whenever others find them unpleasant it is usually due to this. A Gemini's sharp tongue has cut many a social tie.

LOVE AND MARRIAGE

The person born under the sign of Gemini longs for affection and understanding. He doesn't always find it, though. Although, he's honest in his search, the Geminian is apt to be too critical. Once he's won someone, he finds fault with them. The cultivated Geminian learns to take the bitter with the sweet; he realizes that no one is perfect, and he accepts the love of his life for what she is.

It is quite possible for the Gemini to have many love relationships before he ever thinks of settling down with one person. He may not really be an intense lover. He loves being affectionate, however. Flattery can turn his head.

The person born under this sign does not like to feel that he is tied down. He likes someone who will give him the freedom he feels he needs. He doesn't like to feel imprisoned by love. He is often attracted to someone who is as independent in spirit as he is. He likes a witty and intelligent companion; someone who can discuss things rationally.

It is sometimes difficult for the natural Gemini to give himself to any one person. He does not like being limited in his affections. He is liable to flirt quite a bit just for the pleasure of flirting. He enjoys attention and will go to great lengths to get it, at times. He likes variety in romance. The same love diet is apt to bore him after a short time.

In spite of his changeability, the intelligent Gemini can settle down to one partner, once he puts his mind to it. The person who wins a Geminian is usually quite gifted and clever; someone who is very adaptable and knows how to change with his moods. The Gemini person is generally not difficult to get along with. He is pleasant and gentle, for the most part. He likes people who are responsive to his moods. If he really loves someone he sees to it that his demands are not too unreasonable. He's willing to make compromises.

Even after he's married, the average Geminian is given to flirting, but it's nothing for his mate to be concerned about: he'll keep it at a harmless level. He will not risk a love relationship that contains those benefits he appreciates.

Marriage for the Geminian is a relationship that should be lively and exciting. He's not the kind of person who enjoys a humdrum homelife. He likes a family that is as active as he is.

Romance and the Gemini Woman

The Gemini woman has no trouble attracting members of the opposite sex. They find her dazzling and glamorous. Her disposition is almost always gay and fun-loving. She knows how to make her suitors feel appreciated and wanted. However, she is a bit restless and can change from one mood to the other quite easily. This often mystifies and disappoints people who have an interest in her. Sometimes she seems easy to please, and other times not. People who don't understand her are apt to call her difficult and egocentric.

The Gemini woman likes variety in her love relationships. She may go through many romances before she thinks of marrying and settling down. Generally speaking, she admires a man who can accept her as an equal, intellectually and emotionally. She is not too fond of domestic duties. After marriage, she wants to be able to pursue her various interests just as she did when she was single.

An intellectual sort of man is apt to appeal to her when she is interested in a serious love relationship. A man who can win her mind, can win her heart. This sort of woman seldom marries someone she considers her inferior intellectually. She wants someone she can look up to—or, if not that, at least eye to eye.

The single Gemini woman can be quite flirtatious. She may even toy with the affections of someone she is not seriously interested in. When she feels a romance has come to an end, she'll say so bluntly and move on. She likes her love relationships to be an adventure—full of amusement and excitement. Men looking for a housekeeper instead of a partner are wasting their time when courting a Gemini woman. She'll never tie herself to the kitchen for the love of a man. She is interested in too many other things.

The considerate Gemini woman, however, will cut down on her interests and confine most of her activities to the home if she feels the love of her man is worth the sacrifice.

The Gemini woman has good taste in decorating a home. She knows how to arrange rooms and how to use color tastefully. She can become a good homemaker once she puts her mind to it. She likes things tidy and neat but is not too fond of domestic chores. If possible, she will see to it that she has some help in carrying out household duties.

Romance and the Gemini Man

The man born under the sign of Gemini is interested in change and adventure in his romantic activities. The woman who desires to keep up with him has to be quick on her feet. His restlessness is apt to puzzle even those who love him. He is quick-witted and fond of change. Someone who is likely to drag him into a life of humdrum domesticity is not apt to win him.

In spite of the fact that he may go from romance to romance quite easily, the Gemini man is really in search of a true and lasting love relationship. He is popular with women. They like him because of his charm and intelligence. If he cares for a woman, he can make her feel like the most important person in his life. He is capable of steadfastness in his affections, but there is no guarantee how long this will last.

A girl interested in home and a family—and nothing else—is not one who will appeal to him. He wants someone who is a good companion; someone who can share his interests as well as his moods. He wants someone he can talk with as an equal—someone whose interests go beyond those of managing household matters.

In love, he can be either passionate or mild; it depends on his partner and the circumstances. Some Geminians are easily distracted in romance and their interests travel from one woman to the other with appalling ease.

When he does meet that unusual girl he is looking for, the Geminian proves himself to be a loving and responsible mate. He does his best to protect the interests of his family and is willing to make the sacrifices necessary to keep his home life in order. He may flirt occasionally after marriage but it seldom goes beyond that. The woman who marries him must allow him his little romantic fantasies. He's liable to become unreasonable if he is reproached for flirting harmlessly.

He will be faithful to the woman who allows him his freedom—the woman who is not suspicious and trusts him.

Life with a Gemini man can be a happy one indeed, but the woman who plans to go through life at his side has to be as adaptable and active as he is.

Woman—Man

GEMINI WOMAN
ARIES MAN

The man born under the sign of Aries is often attracted to the Gemini woman. In you he can find that mixture of intellect and charm that is so often difficult to find in a woman. Like you, he often resembles that intellectual mountain goat that leaps from crag to crag. He has an insatiable thirst for knowledge of all kinds. Unlike you, however, the Aries man usually sees to it that he finishes whatever it is he had begun. He can do with a woman like you—someone attractive, quick-witted, and intelligent. He'll admire you for your independence. He's not interested in a clinging vine kind of a wife, but someone who is there when he needs her; someone who listens and understands what he says; someone who can give advice if he should ever happen to ask for it, which is not likely to be often. The Aries man wants a woman who is a good companion and a good sport. He is looking for a woman who will look good on his arm without hanging on it too heavily. He is looking for a woman who has both feet on the ground and yet is mysterious and enticing, a kind of domestic Helen of Troy whose face or fine dinner can launch a thousand business deals, if need be. That woman he is in search of sounds a little like you, doesn't it. If the shoe fits, put it on. You won't be sorry.

The Aries man makes a good husband. He is faithful and attentive. He is an affectionate man. He'll make you feel needed and loved. Love is a serious matter for the Aries man. He does not believe in flirting or playing the field—especially after he's found the woman of his dreams. He'll expect you to be as constant in your affection as he is in his. Try to curb your bent for harmless flirting if you have your heart set on an Arien. He'll expect you to be a hundred percent his; he won't put up with any nonsense while romancing you.

The Aries man may be pretty progressive and modern about

many things, but when it comes to pants wearing, he's downright conventional: it's strictly male attire. The best position you can take in the relationship is a supporting one. He's the boss and that's that. Once you have learned to accept that, you'll find the going easy.

The Aries man, with his endless energy and drive, likes to relax in comfort at the end of the day. The Gemini woman who is a good homemaker can be sure of his undying affection. He's a lover of slippers and pipe, and a comfortable armchair. If you see to it that everything in the house is where he expects to find it, you'll have no difficulty keeping the relationship on an even keel.

The Arien is generally a good provider. He'll see to it that you never want. Although he is interested in security, he's a man who is not afraid to take risks. Quite often, his gambling pays off.

Life and love with an Aries man may be just the medicine you need.

GEMINI WOMAN
TAURUS MAN

If you've got your heart set on a man born under the sign of Taurus, you'll have to learn the art of being patient. Taureans take their time about everything—even love.

The steady and deliberate Taurean is a little slow on the draw; it may take him quite a while before he gets around to popping that question. For the Gemini woman who is pretty adept at twiddling her thumbs, the waiting and anticipating almost always pays off in the end. Taurus men want to make sure that every step they take is a good one, particularly if they feel that the path they're on could lead to the altar.

If you are in the mood for a whirlwind romance, you had better cast your net in shallower waters. Moreover, most Taureans prefer to do the angling themselves. They are not keen on women taking the lead—once she does, he's liable to drop her immediately. Once the Gemini woman lets herself get caught on his terms, she'll find that her Taurean has fallen for her—hook, line, and sinker.

The Taurus man is fond of a comfortable homelife. It is very important to him. If you keep those home fires burning you will have no trouble keeping that flame in your Taurean's heart aglow. You have a talent for homemaking. You are an old hand at harmony and color use. Your taste in furnishings is excellent. Perhaps, with your moodiness, sense of adventure, and love of change, you could turn out to be a challenging mate for the strong, steady, and protective Bull. It could be that he is the answer to your prayer. Perhaps he could be the anchor for your dreams and plans; he could help you acquire a more balanced outlook and approach to your life. Not one for wild schemes, himself, the Taurean can constructively help you to curb your impulsiveness. He's the man who is always there when you need him.

When you tie the knot with a man born under Taurus, you can put away fears about creditors pounding on the front door. Taureans are practical about everything including bill-paying. When he carries you over that threshold, you can be certain that the entire house is paid for.

As a housewife, the Gemini woman married to a Taurus man need not worry about having to put aside her many interests for the sake of back-breaking house chores. He'll see to it that you have all the latest time-saving appliances and comforts.

You also can forget about acquiring premature gray hairs due to unruly, ruckus-raising children under your feet. Papa Taurus is a master at keeping offspring in line. He's crazy about kids but he also knows what's good for them.

The Taurus man is steady—the kind of man the Gemini woman often needs.

GEMINI WOMAN
GEMINI MAN

The Gemini man and the Gemini woman are a couple that understand each other. They are so much alike, how could they but help it. Both are intelligent, witty, outgoing, and tend to be rather versatile. The Gemini man could easily turn out to be your better half. One thing that causes a Twin's mind and affection to wander is a bore, and it's highly unlikely that an active Gemini woman would ever allow herself to be accused of that. The Gemini man that has caught your heart will admire you for your ideas and intellect—perhaps even more than for your good cooking and flawless talent for homemaking. The Gemini woman needn't feel that once she's made her marriage vows that she'll have to put her interests and ambition in storage. The Gemini man will admire you for your zeal and liveliness. He's the kind of guy who won't pout and scowl if you let him shift for himself in the kitchen once in a while. In fact, he'll enjoy the challenge of wrestling with pots and pans himself for a change. Chances are, too, that he might turn out to be a better cook than you—that is, if he isn't already.

The man born under the sign of the Twins is a very active person. There aren't many women who have enough pep to keep up with him. But this doesn't set a problem for the spry Gemini woman. You are both dreamers, planners, and idealists. The strong Gemini woman can easily fill the role of rudder for her Gemini man's ship-without-a-sail. If you happen to be a cultivated Gemini, he won't mind it too much. The intelligent Twin is often aware of his shortcomings and he doesn't resent it if someone with better bearings gives him a shove in the right direction when it's needed. The average Gemini does not have serious ego-hangups and will even accept a well-deserved chewing out from his mate quite gracefully.

When you and your Gemini man team up, you'll probably always have a houseful of people to entertain . . . interesting people, too. Geminis find it hard to tolerate sluggish minds and dispositions.

Gemini men are always attractive to the opposite sex. You'll perhaps have to allow him an occasional harmless flirt—it will seldom amount to more than that if you're his proper mate. It will help keep his spirits up. A Twin out-of-sorts (as you well know), is capable of brewing up a whirlwind of trouble. Better to let him hanky-pank—within eyeshot, of course—than to lose your cool.

As far as children go, you are both pushovers. One of you will have to learn to fill the role of house disciplinarian, otherwise chaos will reign.

GEMINI WOMAN
CANCER MAN

Chances are you won't hit it off too well with the man born under Cancer, but then Cupid has been known to do some pretty unlikely things. The Cancerian is a very sensitive man—thin-skinned and occasionally moody. You've got to keep on your toes, and not step on his if you're determined to make a go of the relationship.

The Cancer man may be lacking in many of the qualities you seek in a man, but when it comes to being faithful and being a good provider, he's hard to beat.

It is the perceptive Gemini woman who will not mistake the Crab's quietness for sullenness or his thriftiness for pennypinching. In some respects he can be like the wise old owl out on a limb; he may look like he's dozing but actually he hasn't missed a thing. Cancerians often possess a well of knowledge about human behavior; they can come across with some pretty helpful advice to those in trouble or in need. He can certainly help to keep you from making unwise investments in time and—especially—money. He may not say much, but he's always got his wits about him.

The Crab may not be the match or catch for many a Gemini woman; in fact, he is likely to seem downright dull to the on-the-move Gemini girl. True to his sign, he can be fairly cranky and crabby when handled the wrong way. He is perhaps more sensitive than he should be.

Gemini people are usually as smart as a whip. If you're clever you will never, in any way, convey the idea that you consider your Cancerian a little short on brain power. Browbeating is a sure-fire way of sending the Crab angrily scurrying back to his shell—and it's quite possible that all of that lost ground may never be recovered.

The Crab is most comfortable at home. Once settled in for the night or for the weekend, wild horses couldn't drag him any further than the gatepost—that is, unless those wild horses were dispatched by his mother. The Crab is sometimes a Mama's boy. If his mate does not put her foot down, he will see to it that his mother comes first whenever possible. No self-respecting Geminian would ever allow herself to play second fiddle—even if it is to her old gray-haired mother-in-law. If she's a tactful Geminian, she may find that slipping into number-one position can be as easy as pie (that legendary apple one his mother used to make).

If you take enough time to pamper your Cancer man with good cooking and comfort, you'll find that "Mother" turns up less and less—at the front door as well as in daily conversations.

Cancerians make protective, proud, and patient fathers.

GEMINI WOMAN
LEO MAN

For the Gemini woman who enjoys being swept off her feet in a romantic whirlwind fashion, Leo is the sign of love. When the Lion puts his mind to romancing, he doesn't stint. It's all wining, dining, and dancing till the wee hours of the morning.

Leo is all heart and knows how to make his woman feel like a woman. The Gemini girl in constant search of a man she can look up to need go no farther; Leo is ten-feet tall—in spirit if not in stature. He's a man not only in full control of his faculties but he also manages to have full control of just about any situation he finds himself in. He's a winner.

The Leo man may not look like Tarzan, but he knows how to roar and beat his chest if he has to. The Gemini woman who has had her fill of weak-kneed men, finds in a Leo someone she can at last lean upon. He can support you not only physically, but also where your plans and projects are concerned. He's good at giving advice that pays off. Leos are direct people. They don't believe in wasting time or effort. They almost never make unwise investments—something that a Gemini often does.

Many Leos rise to the top of their profession and through their example, prove to be a great inspiration to others.

Although he's a ladies' man, Leo is very particular about his ladies. His standards are high when it comes to love interests. The idealistic and cultivated Geminian should have no trouble keeping her balance on the pedestal the Lion sets her on. Leo believes that romance should be played on a fair give-and-take basis. He won't stand for any monkey business in a love relationship. It's all or nothing.

You'll find him a frank, straight-from-the-shoulder person; he generally says what is on his mind.

The Gemini woman who does decide upon a Leo for a mate, must be prepared to stand squarely behind her man. He expects it—and usually deserves it. He's the head of the house and can handle that position without a hitch. He knows how to go about breadwinning and, if he has his way (and most Leos do have their own way), he'll see to it that you'll have all the luxuries you crave and the comforts you need.

It's unlikely that the romance in your marriage will ever die out. Lions need love like flowers need sunshine. They're ever amorous and generally expect similar attention and affection from their mate. Lions are fond of going out on the town; they love to give parties. You should encounter no difficulties in sharing his interest in this direction.

Leos make strict fathers, generally. You'll have to smooth over your children's roughed-up feelings.

GEMINI WOMAN
VIRGO MAN

The Virgo man is all business—or he may seem so to you. He is usually very cool, calm, and collected. He's perhaps too much of a fuss-budget to wake up deep romantic interests in a Geminian. Torrid romancing to him is just so much sentimental mush. He can do without it and can make that quite evident in short order. He's keen on chastity and, if necessary, he can lead a sedentary, sexless life without caring too much about the fun others think he is missing. In short, you are liable to find him a first-class dud. His lack of imagination and dislike for flights of fancy can grate on a Gemini woman's nerves no end. He is always correct and likes to be handled correctly. Almost everything about him is orderly. "There's a place for everything . . ." is likely to be an adage he'll fall back on quite regularly.

He does have an honest-to-goodness heart, believe it or not. The Geminian who finds herself strangely attracted to his cool, feet-flat-on-the-ground ways, will discover that his is a constant heart, not one that goes in for flings or sordid affairs. Virgos take an awfully long time to warm up to someone. A practical man, even in matters of the heart, he wants to know just what kind of a person you are before he takes a chance on love.

The impulsive Gemini girl had better not make the mistake of kissing her Virgo friend on the street—even if it's only a peck on the cheek. He's not at all demonstrative and hates public displays of affection. Love, according to him, should be kept within the confines of one's home—with the curtains drawn. Once he believes that you are on the level with him as far as your love is concerned, you'll see how fast he loses his cool. Virgos are considerate, gentle lovers. He'll spend a long time, though, getting to know you. He'll like you before he loves you.

A Gemini-Virgo romance can be a sometime—or, rather a one-time—thing. If the bottom ever falls out, don't bother to pick up the pieces. Nine times out of ten, he won't care about patching up. He's a once-burnt-twice-shy guy. When he crosses your telephone number out of his address book, he's crossing you out of his life—for good.

Neat as a pin, he's thumbs-down on what he considers "sloppy" housekeeping. An ashtry with just one stubbed-out cigarette in it can be annoying to him, even if it's just two seconds old. Glassware should always sparkle and shine.

If you wind up marrying a Virgo man, keep your kids spic-and-span, at least by the time he gets home from work. Train the children to be kind, respectful and courteous. He'll expect it.

GEMINI WOMAN
LIBRA MAN

If there's a Libran in your life, you are most likely a very happy woman. Men born under this sign have a way with impulsive, intelligent women. You'll always feel at ease in his company; you can always be yourself when you're with him.

Like you, he's given to occasional fits of impulsiveness. His moods are apt to change quite rapidly. One moment he comes on hard and strong with "I love you", and next moment you find that he's left you like yesterday's mashed potatoes. He'll come back to you, though; don't worry. Librans are like that. Deep down inside he really knows what he wants even though he may not appear to.

You'll appreciate his admiration of beauty and harmony. If you're dressed to the teeth and never looked better in your life, you'll get a ready compliment—and one that's really deserved. Librans don't indulge in idle flattery. If they don't like something, they are tactful enough to remain silent.

Librans will go to great lengths to preserve peace and harmony—even tell a fat lie if necessary. They don't like showdowns or disagreeable confrontations. The frank Gemini woman is all for getting whatever is bothering her off her chest and out into the open, even if it comes out all wrong. To the Libran, making a clean breast of everything sometimes seems like sheer folly.

You may lose your patience while waiting for your Libra friend to make up his mind. It takes him ages to make a decision. He weighs both sides carefully before committing himself to anything. You seldom dillydally—at least about small things—and so it's likely that you will find it difficult to see eye to eye with a hesitating Libra when it comes to decision-making methods.

All in all, though, he is a kind, gentle, and fair person. He is interested in the "real" truth; he'll try to balance everything out until he has all the correct answers. It is not difficult for him to see both sides of the story.

He's a peace-loving man. The sight of blood is apt to turn his stomach.

Librans don't dance on table-tops like Leos are liable to do. They're not showoffs. Generally, they are well-balanced people. love entanglement they have. If he should find that the girl he's datlove entaglement they have. If he should find that the girl he's dating is not really suited to him, he will end the relationship in such a tactful manner that no hard feelings will come about.

He never lets money burn holes in his pockets. You don't have to worry about him throwing his money all over the place, though; most likely he'll spend it all on you—and lavishly.

The Libra father is firm, gentle, and patient.

GEMINI WOMAN
SCORPIO MAN

Many find the Scorpio's sting a fate worse than death. The Gemini woman quite often is no exception. When his anger breaks loose, you had better clear out of the vicinity.

The average Scorpio man may strike the Gemini woman as being a brute. He'll stick pins into the balloons of your plans and dreams if they don't line up with what he thinks is right. If you do anything to irritate him—just anything—you'll wish you hadn't. He'll give you a sounding out that would make you pack your bags and go back to Mother—if you were that kind of a girl.

The Scorpio man hates being tied down to homelife—and so do you to a certain extent. Instead of wrestling with pots and pans, you'd rather be out and about, devoting plenty of time to your many interests. The Scorpio man would rather be out on the battlefield of life, belting away at whatever he feels is a just and worthy cause, instead of staying home nestled in a comfortable armchair with the evening paper. If you're one of those Gemini girls that has a strong homemaking streak, don't keep those homefires burning too brightly too long; you may just run out of firewood.

As passionate as he is in business affairs and politics, the Scorpio man has plenty of pep and ginger stored away for love-making. Most women are easily attracted to him—and the Gemini woman is no exception—that is, at least before she is really aware of what she might be getting into. Those who allow a man born under this sign to sweep them off their feet, shortly find that they're dealing with a pepperpot of seething excitement. The Scorpio man is passionate with a capital P, you can be sure of that. But he's capable of dishing out as much pain as pleasure. Damsels with fluttering hearts who, when in the embrace of a Scorpio, think "This is it," had better be in a position moments later to admit that perhaps it isn't. Scorpios are blunt. An insult is likely to whiz out of his mouth much quicker than a compliment.

If you're the kind of Gemini who can keep a stiff upper lip, take it on the chin, turn a deaf ear, and all of that, because you feel you are still under his love-spell in spite of everything: lots of luck.

If you have decided to take the bitter with the sweet, prepare yourself for a lot of ups and downs. Chances are you won't have as much time for your own affairs and interests as you'd like. The Scorpio's love of power may cause you to be at his constant beck-and-call.

Scorpios like fathering large families but they seldom give them the attention they need.

GEMINI WOMAN
SAGITTARIUS MAN

The Gemini woman who has set her cap for a man born under the sign of Sagittarius may have to apply an awful amount of strategy before she can get him to say "Will you marry me?" Although some Sagittarians may be marriage-shy, they're not ones to skitter away from romance. A Gemini woman may find a relationship with a Sagittarian—whether a fling or "the real thing"—a very enjoyable experience.

As a rule, Sagittarians are bright, happy, and healthy people. They have a strong sense of fair play. Often they're a source of inspirations to others. They're full of ideas and drive.

You'll be taken by the Sagittarian's infectious grin and his light-hearted friendly nature. If you do wind up being the woman in his life, you'll find that he's apt to treat you more like a buddy than the love of his life. It's just his way. Sagittarians are often chummy instead of romantic.

You'll admire his broadmindedness in most matters—including that of the heart. If, while dating you, he claims that he still wants to play the field, he'll expect you to enjoy the same liberty. Once he's promised to love, honor, and obey, however, he does just that. Marriage for him, once he's taken that big step, is very serious business. The Gemini woman with her keen imagination and love of freedom will not be disappointed if she does tie up with a Sagittarian. The Sagittarius man is quick-witted—but not as quick-witted as you sometimes. Generally, men of this sign have a genuine interest in equality. They hate prejudice and injustice.

If he insists on a night out with the boys once a week, he won't scowl if you decide to let him shift for himself in the kitchen once a week while you go out with the girls.

He's not much of a homebody. Quite often he's occupied with far away places either in his dreams or in reality. He enjoys—just as you do—being on the go or on the move. He's got ants in his pants and refuses to sit still for long stretches at a time. Humdrum routine—especially at home—bores him. At the drop of a hat, he may ask you to whip off your apron and dine out instead. He'll take great pride in showing you off to his friends. He'll always be a considerate mate; he will never embarrass or disappoint you intentionally.

His friendly, sunshiny nature is capable of attracting many people. Like you, he's very tolerant when it comes to friends, and you'll most likely spend a great deal of time entertaining people.

Sagittarians are all thumbs when it comes to little shavers. He'll develop an interest in them, though, when they get older.

GEMINI COMAN
CAPRICORN MAN

The with-it Gemini girl is likely to find the average Capricorn man a bit of a drag. The man born under the sign of the Goat is often a closed person and difficult to get to know. Even if you do get to know him, you may not find him very interesting.

In romance, Capricorn men are a little on the rusty side. You'll probably have to make all the passes.

You may find his plodding manner irritating, and his conservative, traditional ways downright maddening. He's not one to take chances on anything. "If it was good enough for my father, it's good enough for me" may be his motto. He follows a way that is tried and true.

Whenever adventure rears its tantalizing head, the Goat will turn his head the other way; he's just not interested.

He may be just as ambitious as you are—perhaps even more so, but his ways of accomplishing his aims are more subterranean or, at least, seem so. He operates from the background a good deal of the time. At a gathering you may never even notice him, but he's there, taking in everything and sizing up everyone, planning his next careful move.

Although Capricorns may be intellectual, it is generally not the kind of intelligence a Geminian appreciates. He may not be as bright or as quick as you are; it may take ages for him to understand a simple joke.

The Gemini woman who does take up with a man born under this sign, must be pretty good in the "Cheering Up" department, as the man in her love-life may act as though he's constantly being followed by a cloud of gloom.

The Capricorn is happiest in the comfort and privacy of his own home. The security possible within four walls can make him a happy man. He'll spend as much time as he can at home. If he is loaded down with extra work, he'll bring it home instead of staying at the office.

You'll most likely find yourself frequently confronted by his relatives. Family is very important to the Capricorn—*his* family, that is. They had better take a pretty important place in your life, too, if you want to keep your home a happy one.

Although his caution in most matters may all but drive you up the wall, you'll find his concerned way with money justified most of the time. He is no squanderer. Everything is planned right down to the last red penny. He'll see to it that you never want.

He can be quite a scold when it comes to disciplining children. You'll have to step in and smooth things over when he goes too far.

GEMINI WOMAN
AQUARIUS MAN

You've never known love unless you've know a man born under the sign of Aquarius. The Gemini woman is likely to find Aquarians dazzling.

As a rule, Aquarians are extremely friendly and open. Of all the signs, they are perhaps the most tolerant. In the thinking department, they are often miles ahead of others.

The Gemini woman will most likely not only find her Aquarius man intriguing and interesting, but she'll find the relationship she has with him a challenging one, as well. Your high respect for intelligence and imagination may be reason enough for you to settle your heart on a Water Bearer. You'll find that you can learn a lot from him.

Aquarians love everybody—even their worst enemies, sometimes. Through your relationship with an Aquarian, you'll find yourself running into all sorts of people, ranging from near-genius to downright insane—and they're all friends of his.

In the holding-hands phase of your romance, you may find that your Water Bearing friend has cold feet. Aquarians take quite a bit of warming up before they're ready to come across with that first goodnight kiss. More than likely, he'll just want to be your pal in the beginning. For him, that's an important first step in any relationship—love, included. The "poetry and flowers" stage—if it ever comes—will come much later. The Aquarian is all heart; still when it comes to tying himself down to one person and for keeps, he is liable to hesitate. He may even try to get out of it if you breath down his neck too hard.

The Aquarius man is no Valentino and wouldn't want to be. The Gemini woman is likely to be more impressed by his broadmindedness and high moral standards than by his feeble attempts at romance.

You won't find it difficult to look up to a man born under the sign of the Water Bearer, but you may find the challenge of trying to keep up with him dizzying. He can pierce through the most complicated problem as if it were a matter of 2 + 2. You may find him a little too lofty and high-minded—but don't judge him too harshly if that's the case: he's way ahead of his time—your time, too, most likely.

If you marry this man, he'll stay true to you. He'll certainly admire you for your intelligence and wit. Don't think that, once you're married, he'll keep you chained to the kitchen sink. He'll encourage you to go ahead in your pursuit of knowledge. You'll most likely have a minor tiff with him every now and again but never anything serious.

Kids love him and vice-versa. He'll be as tolerant with them as he is with adults.

GEMINI WOMAN
PISCES MAN

The man born under Pisces is quite a dreamer. Sometimes he's so wrapped up in his dreams that he's difficult to reach. To the average Gemini woman, he may seem a little sluggish.

He's easy-going most of the time. He seems to take things in his stride. He'll entertain all kinds of views and opinions from just about anyone, nodding or smiling vaguely, giving the impression that he's with them one hundred percent while that may not be the case at all. His attitude may be "why bother" when he is confronted with someone wrong who thinks he's right. The Pisces man will seldom speak his mind if he thinks he'll be rigidly opposed.

The Pisces man is oversensitive at times—he's afraid of getting his feelings hurt. He'll sometimes imagine a personal injury when none's been made. Chances are you'll find this maddening; at times you may feel like giving him a swift kick where it hurts the most. It wouldn't do any good, though. It would just add fuel to the fire of his persecution complex.

One thing you'll admire about this man is his concern for people who are sickly or troubled. He'll make his shoulder available to anyone in the mood for a good cry. He can listen to one hard-luck story after another without seeming to tire. When his advice is asked, he is capable of coming across with some words of wisdom. He often knows what is bugging someone before that person is aware of it himself. It's almost intuitive with Pisceans, it seems. Still, at the end of the day, this man will want some peace and quiet. If you've got a problem on your mind when he comes home, don't unload it in his lap. If you do, you are liable to find him short-tempered. He's a good listener, but he can only take so much.

Pisces are not aimless although they may seem so at times. The positive sort of Pisces man is quite often successful in his profession and is likely to wind up rich and influential. Material gain, however, is not a direct goal for a man born under this sign.

The weaker Pisces are usually content to stay put on the level where they find themselves. They won't complain too much if the roof leaks and the fence is in need of repair. He'll just shrug and say, "C'est la vie."

Because of their seemingly laissez-faire manner, people under this sign—needless to say—are immensely popular with children. For tots they play the double role of confidant and playmate. It will never enter his mind to discipline a child, no matter how spoiled or incorrigible that child becomes.

Man—Woman

GEMINI MAN
ARIES WOMAN

The Aries woman is quite a charmer. When she tugs at your heart, you'll know it. She's a woman in search of a knight in shining armour. She is a very particular person with very high ideals. She won't accept anyone other than the man of her dreams.

The Aries woman never plays around with passion; she means business when it comes to love.

Don't get the idea that she's a dewy-eyed Miss. She isn't. In fact, she can be pretty practical and to-the-point when she wants. She's a girl with plenty of drive and ambition. With an Aries woman behind you, you are liable to go far in life. She knows how to help her man get ahead. She's full of wise advice; you only have to ask. In some cases, Aries women have a keen business sense; many of them become successful career women. There is nothing backward or retiring about her. She is equipped with a good brain and she knows how to use it.

An Aries-Gemini union could be something strong, secure, and romantic. If both of you have your sights fixed in the same direction, there is almost nothing that you could not accomplish.

The Gemini man will have to give up flirting if he decides to settle for an Aries girlfriend or wife. The Aries woman is proud, and capable of being quite jealous. While you're with her, never cast your eye in another woman's direction. It could spell disaster for your relationship. The Aries woman won't put up with romantic nonsense even if it's done only in fun.

If the Aries woman backs you up in your business affairs, you can be sure of succeeding. However, if she is only interested in advancing her own career and puts her own interests before yours, she can be sure of rocking the boat. It will put a strain on the relationship. The over-ambitious Aries woman can be a pain in the neck and make you forget that you were in love with her once.

The cultivated Aries woman makes a wonderful wife and mother. She has a natural talent for homemaking. With a pot of paint and some wallpaper she can transform the dreariest domicile into an abode of beauty and snug comfort. The perfect hostess—even when friends just happen by—she knows how to make guests feel at home.

You'll admire your Arien, too, because she knows how to stand on her own two feet. Hers is an independent nature. She won't break down and cry when things go wrong, but she'll pick herself up and try to patch up matters.

Like you she's pretty social-minded. In the wit department, she can run you a close second. She'll love you as long as she can look up to you.

She makes a fine, affectionate mother.

GEMINI MAN
TAURUS WOMAN

The woman born under the sign of Taurus may lack a little of the sparkle and bubble you like in a woman. The Taurus woman is generally down-to-earth and never flighty. It's important to her that she keep both feet flat on the ground. She may fail to appreciate your willingness to run here and there—especially if she's under the impression that there's no profit in it.

On the other hand, if you hit it off with a Taurus woman, you won't be disappointed at all in the romance area. The Taurus woman is all woman, and proud of it, too. She can be very devoted and loving once she decides that her relationship with you is no fly-by-night romance. Basically, she's a passionate person. In sex, she's direct and to-the-point. If she really loves you, she'll let you know that she's yours—and without reservations. Better not flirt with other women once you've committed yourself to her. She can be jealous and possessive.

She'll stick by you through thick and thin. It's almost certain that if the going ever gets rough, she won't go running home to Mother. She can adjust to hard times just as graciously as she can to good times.

Taureans are, on the whole, pretty even-tempered. They like to be treated with kindness. Pretty things and soft things make them purr like kittens.

With your quick wit and itchy feet, you may find yourself miles ahead of your Taurus woman. At times you are likely to find this distressing. But if you've developed a talent for patience, you won't mind waiting for her to catch up. Never try grabbing her hand and pulling her along at your normal speed—it is likely not to work. It could lead to flying pots and pans and a fireworks display that would put July Fourth to shame. The Taurus woman doesn't anger readily but when prodded often enough, she's capable of letting loose with a cyclone of ill-will. If you treat her correctly, you'll have no cause for complaint.

The Taurean loves doing things for her man. She's a whiz in the kitchen and can whip up feasts fit for a king if she thinks they'll be appreciated. She may not fully understand you, but she'll adore you and be faithful to you if she feels you're worthy of it.

The woman born under Taurus will make a wonderful mother for your children. She knows how to keep her children well-loved, cuddled and warm. She may not be too sympathetic toward them when they reach the teenage stage, however. Their changeability tends to irk her steadfast ways.

GEMINI MAN
GEMINI WOMAN

Although you and your Gemini woman may be as alike as peas in a pod, there will be certain barriers to overcome in order to make your relationship a smooth-running one. Before settling on anything definite, it would be wise for you both to get to know each other as you really are—without the sparkling veneer, the wit, the irresistible charm that Geminians are so well known for. You're both talkers and if you don't understand each other well enough you are liable to have serious arguments. Get to know each other well; learn what it is that makes you really tick. Two Gemini people without real knowledge of themselves and their relationship can easily wind up behind the eight ball. Two cultivated, positive Geminians can make a love relationship or marriage work where other fail.

You are likely to find a romance with a woman born under this sign a many-splendored thing. In her you can find the intellectual companionship you crave and so seldom find. A Gemini woman can appreciate your aims and desires because she travels pretty much the same road as you do, intellectually and emotionally. You'll admire her for her liveliness and mental agility. You'll be attracted by her warmth and grace.

While she's on your arm, you'll probably notice that many male eyes are drawn to her; she may even return a gaze or two, but don't let that worry you. Women born under this sign (the men, too, for that matter) have nothing against a harmless flirt or two; they enjoy this sort of attention and if she feels she's already spoken for, she'll never let it get out of hand.

Although she may not be very handy in the kitchen, you'll never go hungry for a filling and tasty meal. She's in as much a hurry as you are most of the time, and won't feel like she's cheating by breaking out the instant mashed potatoes. She may not feel totally at home at the kitchen range, but she can be clever; with a dash of this and a little bit of that, she can make an uninteresting TV dinner taste like something out of a Jim Beard cookbook. Then again, there are some Gemini girls who find complicated recipes a challenge to their intellect. Every meal they prepare turns out to be a tantalizing and mouth-watering surprise.

The Gemini woman loves people as much as you do—all kinds of people. Together you'll most likely throw some very interesting and successful parties. Geminians do well in organizing social affairs. Everyone invited is bound to have the time of his life.

People may not have the impression that your Gemini wife is the best of mothers—but the children themselves seldom have reason to complain. Gemini women get along with their kids so well because they have a child-like quality to their natures.

GEMINI MAN
CANCER WOMAN

If you fall in love with a Cancer woman, be prepared for anything. Cancerians are sometimes difficult to understand when it comes to love. In one hour, she can unravel a range of emotions that will leave you dizzy. She'll keep you guessing, that's for sure.

You may find her a little too uncertain and sensitive for your tastes. You'll most likely spend a good deal of time encouraging her—helping her to erase her foolish fears. Tell her she's a living doll a dozen times a day and you'll be well loved in return.

Be careful of the jokes you make when in her company—don't let them revolve around her, her personal interests, or her family. If you do, you'll most likely reduce her to tears. She can't stand being made fun of. It will take bushels of roses and tons of chocolates to get her to come back out of her shell.

In matters of money-managing, she may not easily come around to your way of thinking. Geminians rarely let money burn a hole in their pockets. Cancerians are just the opposite. You may get the notion that your Cancerian sweetheart of mate is a direct descendent of Scrooge. If she has her way, she'll hang onto that first dollar you earned. She's not only that way with money, but with everything from bakery string to jelly jars. She's a saver; she never throws anything away, no matter how trivial.

Once she returns your "I love you," you'll find that you have a very loving, self-sacrificing, and devoted friend on your hands. Her love for you will never alter. She'll put you high on a pedestal and will do everything—even if it's against your will—to keep you up there.

Cancer women love homelife. For them, marriage is an easy step. They're domestic with a capital D. She'll do her best to make your home comfortable and cozy. She feels more comfortable at home than anywhere else. She makes an excellent hostess.

Cancer women make the best mothers of all the signs of the

zodiac. She'll consider every minor complaint of her child a major catastrophe. She's not the kind of mother who will do anything to get the children off her hands. With her, kids come first. If you are lucky, you'll run a close second. You'll perhaps see her as too devoted to the children; you may have a hard time convicing her to untie her apron strongs. When Junior or Sis is ready for that first date, you may have to lock your Cancer wife up in the broom closet to keep her from going along.

GEMINI MAN
LEO WOMAN

If you can manage a girl who likes to kick up her heels every now and again, then Leo is for you. You'll have to learn to put away jealous fears when you take up with a woman born under this sign; she's the kind that makes heads turn and tongues wag. You don't necessarily have to believe any of what you hear—it's most likely just jealous gossip or wishful thinking.

The Leo girl has more than a fair share of grace and glamor. She knows it, and knows how to put it to good use. Needless to say, other women turn green with envy and will try anything, short of shoving her into the nearest lake, in order to put her out of the running.

If she's captured your heart and fancy, woo her full-force if your intention is to win her. Shower her with expensive gifts and promise her the moon—if you're in a position to go that far; then you'll find her resistance weakening. It's not that she's such a difficult cookie—she'll probably make a lot over you once she's decided you're the man for her; but she does enjoy a lot of attention. What's more, she feels she's entitled to it. Her mild arrogance, though, is becoming. The Leo woman knows how to transform the crime of excessive pride into a very charming misdemeanor. It sweeps most men right off their feet . . . rather, all men. Those who do not succumb to her leonine charm are few and far between.

If you've got an important business deal to clinch and you have doubts as to whether or not it will go over well, bring your Leo wife along to the business luncheon or cocktail party and it'll be a cinch that you'll have that contract in your pocket before the meeting is over. She won't have to say or do anything; just be there, at your side. The grouchiest oil magnate can be transformed into a gushing, obedient schoolboy if there's a Leo woman in the room.

If you're a rich Geminian, you may have to see to it that your Leo wife doesn't get too heavy-handed with the charge accounts and credit cards. When it comes to spending, Leos tend to overdo. They're even worse than Geminians. If you're a poor Gemini man, you'll have nothing to worry about because Miss Leo, with her love of luxury, will most likely never give you the time of day, let alone consent to be your wife.

As a mother, she can be both strict and easy-going. She can pal around with her children and still see to it that they know their places. She won't be so apt to spoil them as you will, still she'll be a loving and devoted parent.

GEMINI MAN
VIRGO WOMAN

The Virgo woman may be a little too difficult for you to understand at first. Her waters run deep. Even when you think you do know her, don't take any bets on it. She's capable of keeping things hidden in the deep recesses of her womanly soul—things she'll only release when she's sure that you're the man she's been looking for. It may take her some time to come around to this decision. Virgo women are finicky about almost everything; everything has to be letter-perfect before they're satisfied. Many of them have the idea that only Virgos can do things correctly.

Nothing offends a Virgo woman more than slovenly dress, sloppy character, or a careless display of affection. Make sure your tie is straight and that your shoes sport a bright shine before you go calling on this lady. Save your off-color jokes for the locker-room; she'll have none of that. Take her arm when crossing the street. Don't rush the romance. Trying to corner her in the back of a cab may be one way of striking out. Never criticize the way she looks—in fact, the best policy would be to agree with her as much as possible. Still, you're an impulsive, direct Gemini; all those do's and don'ts you'll have to observe if you want to get to first base with a Virgo may be just a little too much to ask of you. After a few dates, you may come to the conclusion that she just isn't worth all that trouble. However, the Virgo woman is mysterious enough, generally speaking, to keep her men running back for more. Chances are you'll be intrigued by her airs and graces.

Love-making means a lot to you. You may be disappointed at first in her cool Virgo ways. However, under her glacial facade, there lies a hot cauldron of seething excitement. If you're patient and artful in your romantic approach, you'll find that all that caution was well worth the trouble. When Virgos really love, they don't stint. It's all or nothing as far as they're concerned. Once they're convinced that they love you, they go all the way, right off the bat—tossing all cares to the wind.

One thing a Virgo woman can't stand in love is hypocrisy. They don't give a hoot about what the neighbors might say, if their hearts tell them "Go Ahead." They're very concerned with human truths. So much so that if their hearts stumble upon another fancy, they're liable to be true to that new heart-throb and leave you standing in the rain. She's that honest—to her heart, at any rate. But if you are honest about your interest in her, she'll know and she'll respect and reciprocate your interest. Do her wrong once, however, and you can be sure she'll put an end to the relationship for good.

She's both strict and tender with children. She can be a devoted and loving wife. It really depends on you.

GEMINI MAN
LIBRA WOMAN

You'll probably find that the girl born under the sign of Libra is worth more than her weight in gold. She's a woman after your own heart.

With her, you'll always come first—make no mistake about that. She'll always support you 100 percent, no matter what you do. When you ask her advice about almost anything, you'll most likely get a very balanced and realistic opinion. She is good at thinking things out and never lets her emotions run away with her when clear logic is called for.

As a homemaker she is hard to beat. She is very concerned with harmony and balance. You can be sure she'll make your house a joy to live in; she'll see to it that the house is tastefully furnished and decorated. A Libran cannot stand filth or disarry—it gives her goose-bumps. Anything that does not radiate harmony, in fact, runs against her orderly grain.

She is chock-full of charm and womanly ways. She can sweep just about any man off his feet with one winning smile. When it comes to using her brains, she can out-think almost anyone and, sometimes, with half the effort. She is diplomatic enough, though, never to let this become glaringly apparent. She may even turn the conversation around so that you think you were the one who did all the brain-work. She couldn't care less, really, just as long as you end up doing what is right.

The Libra woman will put you up on a pretty high pedestal. You are her man and her idol. She'll leave all the decision-making—large or small—up to you. She's not interested in running things and will only offer her assistance if she feels you really need it.

Some find her approach to reason masculine. However, in the

areas of love and affection the Libra woman is *all* woman. She'll literally shower you with love and kisses during your romance with her. She doesn't believe in holding out. You shouldn't, either, if you want to hang on to her.

She is the kind of girl who likes to snuggle up to you in front of the fire on chilly autumn nights. The kind of girl who will bring you breakfast in bed Sunday mornings. She'll be very thoughtful about anything that concerns you. If anyone dares suggest you're not the grandest guy in the world, your Libran woman is bound to defend you. When she makes those marriage vows she means every word she says.

The Libra woman will be everything you want her to be.

She makes a sensitive and loving mother. When the little ones come along, you don't have to worry about taking the backseat. You will always come first with her.

GEMINI MAN
SCORPIO WOMAN

The Scorpio woman can be a whirlwind of passion—perhaps too much passion to really suit you. When her temper flies, you'd better lock up the family heirlooms and take cover. When she chooses to be sweet, however, you're apt to think that butter wouldn't melt in her mouth. But, of course, it would

The Scorpio woman can be as hot as a tamale or as cool as a cucumber, but whatever mood she's in, she's in it for real. She does not believe in poses or putting on airs.

The Scorpio woman is often sultry and seductive—her *femme fatale* charm can pierce the hardest of hearts like a laser ray. She may not look like Mata Hari (quite often Scorpios resemble the tomboy next door) but once she's fixed you with her tantalizing eyes, you're a goner.

Life with the Scorpio woman will not be all smiles and smooth-sailing; when prompted, she can unleash a gale of venom. Generally, she'll have the good grace to keep family battles within the walls of your home. When company visits, she's apt to give the impression that married life with you is one great big joy-ride. It's just one of her ways of expressing her loyalty to you—at least in front of others. She may fight you tooth and nail in the confines of your livingroom, but at a ball or during an evening out, she'll hang on your arm and have stars in her eyes.

Scorpio woman are good at keeping secrets. She may even keep a few buried from you if she feels like it.

Never cross her up on even the smallest thing. When it comes to revenge, she's an eye-for-an-eye woman. She's not too keen on forgiveness—especially when she feels she's been wronged. You'd be well-advised not to give her any cause to be jealous, either . . . as difficult as that may sound to Geminian ears. When the Scorpio woman sees green, your life will be made far from rosy. Once she's put you in the dog-house, you can be sure that you're going to stay there an awfully long time.

You may find life with the Scorpio woman too draining. Although she may be full of the old paprika, it's quite likely that she's not the kind of girl you'd like to spend the rest of your natural life with. You'd prefer someone gentler and not so hot-tempered; someone who can take the highs with the lows and not bellyache; someone who is flexible and understanding. If you've got your sights set on a shapely Scorpion, forget about that sweet girl of your dreams. A woman born under Scorpio can be heavenly, but she can also be the very devil when she chooses.

As a mother, a Scorpio is protective and encouraging.

GEMINI MAN
SAGITTARIUS WOMAN

You'll most likely never come across a more good-natured girl than the one born under the sign of Sagittarius. Generally, they're full of bounce and good cheer. Their sunny dispositions seem almost permanent and can be relied upon even on the rainiest days.

Women born under this sign are almost never malicious. If ever they seem to be it is probably due to the fact that Sagittarians are often a little short on tact. They say literally anything that comes into their pretty little heads—no matter what the occasion. Sometimes the words that tumble out of their mouths seem downright cutting and cruel. Still, no matter what she says, she means well. The Sagittarius woman is quite capable of losing some of her friends—and perhaps even some of yours—through a careless slip of the lip.

On the other hand, you are liable to appreciate her honesty and good intentions. To you, qualities of this sort play an important part in life. With a little patience and practice, you can probably help cure your Sagittarian of her loose tongue; in most cases, she'll give in to your better judgement and try to follow your advice to the letter.

Chances are, she'll be the outdoors type of girlfriend. Long hikes, fishing trips, and white-water canoeing will most likely appeal to her. She's a busy person; no one could ever call her a slouch. She sets great store in mobility. Like you, she possesses a pair of itchy feet. She won't sit still for a minute if she doesn't have to.

She is great company most of the time and, generally, lots of fun. Even if your buddies drop by for poker and beer, she won't have any trouble fitting in.

On the whole, she is a very kind and sympathetic woman. If she feels she's made a mistake, she'll be the first to call your attention to it. She's not afraid to own up to her faults and shortcomings.

You might lose your patience once or twice with her. After she's seen how upset her shortsightedness or tendency to blabbermouth has made you, she'll do her best to straighten up.

The Sagittarian woman is not the kind who will pry into your business affairs. But she'll always be there, ready to offer advice if you need it. If you come home from a night out with the boys and you tell your Sagittarian wife that the red stains on your collar came from cranberry sauce and not lipstick, she'll believe you. She'll seldom be suspicious; your word will almost always be good enough for her.

She is a wonderful and loving friend to her children.

GEMINI MAN
CAPRICORN WOMAN

If you are not a successful business man or, at least, on your way to success, it's quite possible that a Capricorn woman will have no interest in entering your life. Generally speaking, she's a very security-minded female; she'll see to it that she invests her time only in sure things. Men who whittle away their time with one unsuccessful scheme or another, seldom attract a Capricorn. Men who are interested in getting somewhere in life and keep their noses close to the grindstone quite often have a Capricorn woman behind them, helping them to get ahead.

Although she is a kind of "climber", she is not what you could call cruel or hard-hearted. Beneath that cool, seemingly calculating, exterior, there's a warm and desirable woman. She just happens to think that it is just as easy to fall in love with a rich or ambitious man as it is with a poor or lazy one. She's practical.

The Capricorn woman may be keenly interested in rising to the top, but she'll never be aggressive about it. She'll seldom step on someone's feet or nudge competitors away with her elbows. She's quiet about her desires. She sits, waits, and watches. When an opening or opportunity.does appear, she'll latch on to it licketysplit. For an on-the-move Geminian, an ambitious Capricorn wife or girlfriend can be quite an asset. She can probably give you some very good advice about business matters. When you invite the boss and his wife for dinner, she'll charm them both right off the ground.

The Capricorn woman is thorough in whatever she does: cooking, cleaning, making a success out of life. Capricorns make excellent hostesses as well as guests. Generally, they are very well-mannered and gracious, no matter what their backgrounds are. They seem to have a built-in sense of what is right. Crude behavior or a careless *faux-pas* can offend them no end.

If you should marry a woman born under Capricorn you need never worry about her going on a wild shopping spree. Capricorns are very careful about every cent that comes into their hands. They understand the value of money better than most women and have no room in their lives for careless spending. If you turn over your paycheck to her at the end of the week, you can be sure that a good part of it will wind up in the bank.

Capricorn girls are generally very fond of family—their own, that is. With them, family ties run very deep. Don't make jokes about her relatives—close or distant. She won't stand for it. It would be good for you to check out her family before you decide to get down on bended knee. After your marriage, you'll undoubtedly be seeing lots of them.

With children, she is both loving and correct. Her children are polite and well brought up.

GEMINI MAN
AQUARIUS WOMAN

If you find that you've fallen head over heels for a woman born under the sign of the Water Bearer, you'd better fasten your safety belt. It may take you quite a while to actually discover what this girl is like—and even then, you may have nothing to go on but a string of vague hunches. The Aquarian is like a rainbow, full of bright and shining hues; she is like no other girl you've ever known. There is something elusive about her—something delightfully mysterious. You'll most likely never be able to put your finger on it. It's nothing calculated, either; Aquarians don't believe in phony charm.

There will never be a dull moment in your life with this Water Bearing woman; she seems to radiate adventure and magic. She'll most likely be the most open-minded and tolerant woman you've ever met. She has a strong dislike for injustice and prejudice. Narrow-mindedness runs against her grain.

She is very independent by nature and quite capable of shifting for herself if necessary. She may receive many proposals for marriage from all sorts of people without ever really taking them seriously. Marriage is a very big step for her; she wants to be sure she knows what she's getting into. If she thinks that it will seriously curb her independence, she's liable to shake her head and return the engagement ring—if indeed she's let the romance get that far.

The line between friendship and romance is a pretty fuzzy one for an Aquarian. It's not difficult for her to remain buddy-buddy with someone with whom she's just broken off. She's tolerant, remember? So, if you should ever see her on the arm of an ex-lover, don't jump to any hasty conclusions.

She's not a jealous person herself and doesn't expect you to be, either. You'll find her pretty much of a free spirit most of the time. Just when you think you know her inside-out, you'll discover that you don't really know her at all.

She's a very sympathetic and warm person; she can be helpful to people in need of assistance and advice.

The Aquarius woman is like a chameleon in some respects; she can fit in anywhere without looking like she doesn't belong.

She'll seldom be suspicious even if she has every right to be. If the man she loves slips and allows himself a little fling, chances are she'll just turn her head the other way and pretend not to notice that gleam in his eye is not meant for her. That's pretty understanding. Still, a man married to an Aquarian should never press his luck in hanky-panky. Her tolerance does have its limits.

She makes a fine, big-hearted mother; her good qualities rub off on her offspring.

GEMINI MAN
PISCES WOMAN

Many a man dreams of a Piscean kind of a girl. You're perhaps no exception. She's soft and cuddly—very domestic. She'll let you be the brains of the family; she's contented to just lean on your shoulder and let you be master of the household.

She can be very ladylike and proper. Your business associates and friends will be dazzled by her warmth and femininity. Although she's a charmer, there is a lot more to her than just a pretty exterior. There is a brain ticking away behind that soft, womanly facade. You may never become aware of it—that is, until you're married to her. It's no cause for alarm, however; she'll most likely never use it against you.

If she feels you're botching up your married life through careless behavior or if she feels you could be earning more money than you do, she'll tell you about it. But any wife would, really. She will never try to usurp your position as head and breadwinner of the family.

No one had better dare say one uncomplimentary word about you in her presence. It's liable to cause her to break into tears. Pisces women are usually very sensitive. Their reactions to adversity, frustration, or anger is just a plain, good, old-fashioned cry. They can weep buckets when inclined.

She'll have an extra-special dinner waiting for you when you phone to tell her that you've just landed a new and important account. Don't bother to go into details, though, at the dinner table; she doesn't have much of a head for business matters, usually, and is only too happy to leave that up to you.

She can do wonders with a house. She is very fond of soft and beautiful things. There will always be plenty of fresh-cut flowers around the house. She'll see that you always have plenty of socks and underwear in that top drawer of your dresser.

Treat her with tenderness and your relationship will be an enjoyable one. She's most likely fond of chocolates. A bunch of beautiful roses will never fail to make her eyes light up. See to it that you never forget her birthday or your anniversary. These things are very important to her. If you let them slip your mind, you'll send her into a crying-fit that could last for hours. If you are patient and kind, you can keep a Pisces woman happy for a lifetime. She, however, is not without her faults. Her "sensitivity" may get on your nerves after a while; you may find her lacking in imagination and zest. You may even feel that she only uses her tears as a method of getting her own way.

She makes a strong, self-sacrificing mother. She'll find it difficult to refuse children anything.

CANCER
June 21 — July 20

CHARACTER ANALYSIS

The Cancerian is generally speaking a rather sensitive person. He is quite often a generous person by nature, and he is willing to help almost anyone in need. He is emotional and often feels sorry for persons less fortunate than he. He could never refuse to answer someone's call for help. It is because of his sympathetic nature that others take advantage of him now and again.

In spite of his willingness to help others, the Cancer man or woman may seem difficult to approach by people not well acquainted with his character. On the whole, he seems rather subdued and reserved. Others may feel there is a wall between them and the Cancerian while this may not be the case at all. The person born under this sign is careful not to let others hurt him; he has learned through hard experience that protection of some sort is necessary in order to get along in life. The person who wins his confidence and is able to get beyond this barrier will find him a warm and loving person.

With his family and close friends, he is a very faithful and dependable person. In his quiet way, he can be affectionate and loving. He is generally not one given to demonstrative behavior. He can be fond of someone without telling them so a dozen times a day. With people he is close to, the Cancerian is bound to be more open about his own need for affection, and he enjoys being made over by his loved ones. He likes to feel wanted and protected.

When he has made up his mind about something, he sticks to it, and is generally a very constant person. He knows how to hold his ground. He never wavers. People who don't know him may think him weak and easily managed, because he is so quiet and modest, but this is far from true. He can take a lot of punishment

109

for an idea or a cause he believes in. For the Cancerian, right is right. In order to protect himself, the person born under this sign will sometimes put up a pose as someone bossy and domineering. Sometimes he is successful in fooling others with his brash front. People who have known him for a while, however, are seldom taken in.

Many people born under this sign are rather shy and seemingly lacking confidence. They know their own minds, though, even if they do not seem to. He responds to kindness and encouragement. He will be himself with people he trusts. A good person can bring out the best in this person. Disagreeable or unfeeling people can send him scurrying back into his shell. He is a person who does not appreciate sharp criticism. Some people born under this sign are worriers. They are very concerned about what others may think of them. This may bother them so much that they develop a deep feeling of inferiority. Sometimes this reaches the point where he is so unsure of himself in some matters that he allows himself to be influenced by someone who has a stronger personality. The Cancerian is sometimes afraid that people will talk behind his back if he doesn't comply to their wishes. However, this does not stop him from doing what he feels is right. The cultivated Cancerian learns to think for himself and has no fear of disapproval.

The Cancer man or woman is most himself at home. The person born under this sign is a real lover of domesticity. He likes a place where he can relax and feel properly sheltered. Cancerians like things to stay as they are; they are not fond of changes of any sort. They are not very adaptable people. When visiting others or going to unfamiliar places, they are not likely to feel very comfortable. They are not the most talkative people at a party. In the comfort of their own homes, however, they blossom and bloom.

The Cancer man or woman sticks by the rules, whatever the game. He is not a person who would ever think of going against an established grain. He is conventional and moderate in almost all things. In a way he likes the old-fashioned things; however, in spite of this, he is interested in new things and does what he can to keep up with the times. In a way, he has two sides to his character. He is seldom forgetful. He has a memory like an elephant and can pick out any detail from the past with no trouble at all. He often reflects on things that have happened. He prefers the past to the future, which sometimes fills him with a feeling of apprehension.

This fourth sign of the Zodiac is a motherly one. Even the Cancer man has something maternal about him. He is usually kind and considerate; ready to help and protect. Others are drawn to them because of these gentle qualities. People in trouble often turn to him for advice and sympathy. People find him easy to confide in.

The Cancer person in general is a very forgiving person. He almost never holds a grudge. Still, it would not be wise to anger him. Treat him fairly and he will treat you the same. He does not appreciate people who lose patience with him. The Cancerian is usually proud of his mind and does not like to be considered unintelligent. Even if others feel that he is somewhat slow in some areas, he would rather not have this opinion expressed in his presence. He's not a person to be played with; he can tell when someone is treating him like a fool.

Quite often people born under this sign are musically inclined. Some of them have a deep interest in religious matters. They are apt to be interested in mystical matters, as well. Although they are fascinated by these things, they may be somewhat afraid of being overwhelmed if they go into them too deeply. In spite of this feeling of apprehension, they try to satisfy their curiosity in these matters.

Health

For the person born under the sign of Cancer, the stomach is his weak point. Chances are that the Cancerian is very susceptible most of the time to infectious diseases. Sometimes his health is affected by nervousness. He can be quite a worrier; even little things eat at him from time to time and this is apt to lower his resistance to infectious illnesses. He is often upset by small matters.

The Cancerian as a child is sometimes rather sickly and weak. His physique during this period of growth can be described in most cases as fragile. Some develop into physically strong adults, others may have the remnants of childhood ailments with them for a good part of their adult lives. They are rather frightened of being sick. Illness is a word they would rather not mention. Pain is also a thing they fear.

They are given to quick-changing moods at times and this often has an effect on their overall health. Worry or depression can have a subliminal effect on their general health. Usually their illnesses are not as serious as they imagine them to be. They sometimes find it easy to feel sorry for themselves.

On the whole, the Cancer man or woman is a quiet person. He is not one to brag or push his weight around. However, let it not be thought that he lacks the force that others have. He can be quite purposeful and energetic when the situation calls for it. However, when it comes to tooting their own horn, they can be somewhat shy and reticent. They may lack the get-up-and-go that others have when it comes to pushing their personal interests ahead.

Some Cancerians are quite aware of the fact that they are not what one would call sturdy in physique or temperament, and often they go through life rather painfully trying to cover up the weak side of their nature.

The man or woman born under the sign of Cancer is not apt to be very vigorous or active. As a rule, they are not too fond of physical exercise, and they have a weakness for rich and heavy foods. As a result, in later life they could end up overweight. Some Cancerians have trouble with their kidneys and intestines. Others digest their food poorly. The wise Cancer man or woman, however, adheres to a strict and well-balanced diet with plenty of fresh fruit and vegetables. Moreover, they see to it that they properly exercise their bodies daily. The Cancer man or woman who learns to cut down on rich foods and worry, often lives to a ripe old age.

Occupation

The Cancer person generally has no trouble at all establishing himself in the business world. He has all those qualities that generally make one a success professionally. He is careful with his equipment as well as his money. He is patient and he knows how to persevere. Any job where he has a chance to use his mind instead of his body is usually a job in which he has no trouble succeeding. He can work well with people—especially persons situated in dire straits. Welfare work is the kind of occupation in which he usually excels. He can really be quite a driving person if his job calls for it. The Cancerian is surprisingly resourceful. In spite of his retiring disposition, he is capable of accomplishing some very difficult tasks.

The Cancerian can put on an aggressive front, and in some cases it can carry him far. Quite often he is able to develop leadership qualities and make good use of them. He generally knows how to direct his energy so that he never becomes immediately exhausted. He'll work away at a difficult chore gradually; seldomly approaching anything head on. By working at something obliquely he often finds advantages along the way that are not apparent to others. In spite of his cautious approach, the Cancerian is often taxed by work that is too demanding of his energy. He may put up a good front of being strong and courageous while actually he is at the end of his emotional rope. Risks sometimes frighten the person born under this sign. It is often this fear which exhausts him. The

CHARACTER ANALYSIS / 113

possible dangers in the world of business set him to worrying.

The Cancerian does not boast about what he is going to do; he just quietly goes ahead and does it. Quite often he accomplishes more than others in this quiet way.

The person born under this sign enjoys helping others. By nature, he is quite a sympathetic individual. He does not like to see others suffer or do without. He is willing to make sacrifices for someone he trusts and cares for. The Cancerian, as was mentioned before, has a maternal streak in him, which is perhaps why he works so well with children. People born under the fourth sign of the Zodiac often make excellent teachers. They understand young people well and do what they can to help them grow up properly.

Cancerians also are fairly intuitive. In business or financial matters, they often make an important strike by playing a strong hunch. In some cases they are able to rely almost entirely on their feelings rather than on reason.

Water attracts the Cancer person. Often they have connections with the sea through their professions. The Cancerian housewife may find herself working with various liquids quite successfully while at home. Trade and commerce often appeal to the person born under this sign.

The average Cancerian has many choices open to him as far as a career is concerned. There are many things that he can do well once he puts his mind to it. In the arts he is quite likely to do well. The Cancer man or woman has a way with beauty, harmony, and creativity. Basically, he is a very capable person in many things; it depends on which of his talents he wants to develop to a professional point. He has a rich imagination and sometimes can make use of it in the area of painting, music, or sculpture.

When working for someone else, the Cancerian can always be depended upon. He makes a loyal and conscientious employee.

It is important for the Cancerian that he select a job that is well suited to his talents and temperament. Although he may feel that earning money is important, the Cancerian eventually comes to the point where he realizes that it is even more important to enjoy the work he is doing. He should have a position which allows him to explore the recesses of his personality and to develop. When placed in the wrong job, the Cancer man or woman is apt to spend a good deal of time wishing he were somewhere else.

Cancerians know the value of money. They are not the sort of people who go throwing money about recklessly. The Cancer person is honest and expects others to be the same. He is quite modest in most things and deplores extravagance and unnecessary display. There are many rich Cancerians. They have a genius for making money and for investing or saving it. Security is important to the person born under this sign. He'll always see to it that he has something put away for that inevitable rainy day.. He is also a hard worker and is willing to put in long hours for the money it brings him. Financial success is usually the result of his own perseverance and industry. Through his own need for security, it is often easy for the Cancerian to sympathize with those of like dispositions. He is a helpful person. If he sees someone trying to do his best to get ahead—and still not succeeeding--he is quite apt to put aside his own interests temporarily to help the other man. Sometimes the Cancerian worries over money even when he has it. He can never be too secure. It would be better for him to learn how to relax and not to let his worries undermine his health. Financial matters often cause him considerable concern—even when it is not necessary.

Home and Family

People born under this sign are usually great home-lovers. They are very domestic by nature; home for them spells security. The Cancerian is a family person. He respects those who are related to him. He feels a great responsibility toward all the members of his family. There is usually a very strong tie between the Cancer person and his mother that lasts through his whole life. Something a Cancerian will not tolerate is for someone to speak ill of a member of his family. This for him is a painful and deep insult. He has a great respect for his family and family traditions. Quite often the person under this sign is well-acquainted with his family tree. If he happens to have a relative who has been quite successful in life, he is quite proud of the fact. Once he is home for the weekend, he generally stays there. He does not particularly care for moving about. He is a born stay-at-home, in most cases.

The Cancerian is sentimental about old things and habits. He is apt to have many things stored away from years ago. Something that was dear to his parents will probably be dear to him as well.

Some Cancerians do travel about from time to time. But no matter what their destination, they are always glad to be back where they feel they belong.

The home of a person born under this sign is usually quite comfortable and tastefully furnished. The Cancerian is a bit of a romantic and usually this is reflected in the way his house is arranged.

The Cancer child is always attached to his home and family. He may not care to go out and play with other children very much but enjoys it when his friends come to his house.

The maternal nature of the Cancer person comes out when he gives a party. He is a very attentive host and worries over a guest like a mother hen—anxious to see that they are comfortable and lack nothing. He does his best to make others happy and at home, and he is admired and loved for that. People who visit Cancerians are usually deeply impressed by their out-going ways. The Cancer hostess prepares unusual and delicious snacks for her visitors. She is very concerned about them and likes to see to it that they are well-fed while visiting her.

Homebodies that they are, Cancerians generally do what they can to make their home a comfortable and interesting place for themselves as well as for others. They feel very flattered when a visitor pays them a compliment on their home.

Children play a very important part in the lives of people born under this sign. They like to fuss over their offspring and give them the things they feel that they need. They generally like to have large families. They like to see to it that their children are well-provided for and that they have the chances in life that their parents never had. The best mother of the Zodiac is usually someone born under the sign of Cancer. They have a strong protective nature. They usually have a strong sense of duty, and when their children are in difficulty they do everything they can to set matters right. Children, needless to say, are fond of their Cancerian parent, and do what they can to make the parent-child relationship a harmonious one.

Social Relationships

The Cancer person may seem rather retiring and quiet and this gives people the impression that he is not too warm or sympathetic. However, the person born under this sign is very sensitive and loving. His ability to understand and sympathize with others is great. He likes to have close friends—people who love and understand him as well as he tries to love and understand them. He wants to be well-liked—to be noticed by people who he feels should like him. If he does not get the attention and affection he feels he is entitled to, he is apt to become a little sullen and difficult to deal with.

The Cancer man or woman has strong powers of intuition and he can generally sense when he has met a person who is likely to turn into a good friend. The Cancerian suffers greatly if ever he should lose a friend. To him friendships are sacred. Sometimes the Cancerian sets his friends on too high a pedestal; he is apt to feel quite crest-fallen when he discovers that they have feet of clay. He is often romantic in his approach to friendship and is likely to seek people out for sentimental reasons rather than for practical ones.

The Cancerian is a very sensitive person and sometimes this contributes to making a friendship unsatisfactory. He sometimes makes the wrong interpretation of a remark that is made by a friend or acquaintance. He imagines something injurious behind a very innocent remark. He sometimes feels that people who profess to be his friends laugh at him cruelly behind his back. He has to be constantly reassured of a friend's sincerity, especially in the beginning of a relationship. If he wants to have the wide circle of friends he desires, the Cancerian must learn to curb these persecution fantasies.

LOVE AND MARRIAGE

The Cancer man or woman has to have love in his life, otherwise his existence is a dull and humdrum affair. When he loves someone, the Cancerian will do everything in his power to make her happy. He is not afraid to make sacrifices in order to make an important relationship work. To his loved one he is likely to seem uncertain and moody. The Cancer person is usually very influenced by the impression he has of his lover. He may even be content to let his romance partner have her own way in the relationship. He may not make many demands but be willing to follow those of his loved one. At times he may feel that he is not really loved, and draw away somewhat from the relationship. Sometimes it takes a lot of coaxing before he can be won over to the fact that he is indeed loved for himself alone.

The Cancerian is often possessive about people as well as material objects. This often makes the relationship difficult to accept for his partner.

His standards are sometimes impossibly high and because of this he is rather difficult to please. The Cancer man or woman is interested in finding someone with whom he can spend the rest of his life. He or she is not interested in any fly-by-night romance.

Romance and the Cancer Woman

The Cancer woman is usually a very warm and loving person. Her feelings run deep. She is sincere in her approach to love. Still and all, she is rather sensitive when in love and her lover may find her difficult to understand at times. The Cancer woman is quite given to crying and when she has been wronged or imagines she has, she is capable of weeping buckets. It may be quite a while before she comes out of her shell again.

Marriage is a union quite suited to the Cancer woman's temperament. She longs for permanence in a relationship and is not fond of flings or meaningless romantic adventures. Her emotions are usually very deep. She desires a man who is protective and affectionate; someone who can help and guide her through life.

She may be too possessive with her husband and this may cause discord. The demands she is likely to make on her family may be overbearing at times. She often likes to be reassured that she is loved and appreciated.

She makes a devoted and loving wife and mother who will do everything to keep her family life harmonious and affectionate.

Romance and the Cancer Man

Quite often the Cancer man is the reserved type. He may be difficult for some women to understand. Generally speaking, he is a very loving person; but sometimes he has difficulty in letting this appear so. He is a bit afraid of being rejected or hurt, so he is liable to keep his true feelings hidden until he feels that the intended object of his affection is capable of taking him seriously.

Quite often he looks for a woman who has the same qualities as his mother. He is more easily attracted to a woman who has old-fashioned traits than to a modern woman. He likes a woman who is a good cook; someone who does not mind household chores and a quiet life.

When deeply in love, the Cancer man does everything in his power to hold the woman of his choice. He is very warm and affectionate and may be rather extravagant from time to time in entertaining the woman he loves.

Marriage is something in which the Cancer man is seriously interested. He wants to settle down with a warm and loving wife—someone who will mother him to some extent. He makes a good father. He is fond of large families. His love of his children may be too possessive.

Woman—Man

CANCER WOMAN
ARIES MAN

Although it's possible that you could find happiness with a man born under the sign of the Ram, it's uncertain as to how long that happiness would last.

An Arien who has made his mark in the world and is somewhat steadfast in his outlooks and attitudes could be quite a catch for you. On the other hand, men under this sign are often swift-footed and quick-minded; their industrious mannerisms may fail to impress you, especially if you feel that much of their get-up-and-go often leads nowhere.

When it comes to a fine romance, you want someone with a nice, broad shoulder to lean on. You are likely to find a relationship with someone who doesn't like to stay put for too long somewhat upsetting.

The Arien may have a little trouble in understanding you, too . . . at least, in the beginning of the relationship. He may find you a bit too shy and moody. Ariens tend to speak their minds; he's liable to criticize you at the drop of a hat.

You may find a man born under this sign too demanding. He may give you the impression that he expects you to be at his beck-and-call. You have a barrelful of patience at your disposal and he may try every last bit of it. He is apt not to be as thorough as you are in everything that he does. In order to achieve success or a goal quickly, he is liable to overlook small but important details—and regret it when it is far too late.

Being married to an Arien does not mean that you'll have a secure and safe life as far as finances are concerned. Not all Ariens are rash with cash, but they lack that sound head you have for putting away something for that inevitable rainy day. He'll do his best, however, to see that you're adequately provided for—even though his efforts may leave something to be desired as far as you're concerned.

With an Aires man for a mate, you'll find yourself constantly among people. Ariens generally have many friends—and you may not heartily approve of them all. People born under this sign are more interested in "Interesting" people than they are in influential ones. Although there is liable to be a family squabble from time to time, you are stable enough to take it all in your stride. Your love of permanence and a harmonious homelife will help you to take the bitter with the sweet.

Aries men love children. They make wonderful fathers. Kids take to them like ducks to water. Their quick minds and behavior appeal to the young.

CANCER WOMAN
TAURUS MAN

Some Taurus men are strong and silent. They do all they can to protect and provide for the women they love. The Taurus man will never let you down. He's steady, sturdy, and reliable. He's pretty honest and practical, too. He says what he means and means what he says. He never indulges in deceit and will always put his cards on the table.

The Taurean is a very affectionate man. Being loved, appreciated, and understood is very important for his well-being. Like you, he is also looking for peace, harmony, and security in his life. If you both work toward these goals together, you'll find that they are easily attained.

If you should marry a Taurus man, you can be sure that the wolf will never darken your door. They are notoriously good providers and do everything they can to make their families comfortable and happy.

He'll appreciate the way you have of making a home warm and inviting. Slippers and pipe, and the evening papers are essential ingredients in making your Taurus husband happy at the end of the workday. Although he may be a big lug of a guy, you'll find he's pretty fond of gentleness and soft things. If you puff up his pillow and tuck him in at night, he won't complain. He'll eat it up and ask for more.

You probably won't complain about his friends. The Taurean tends to seek out friends who are successful or prominent. You admire people, too, who work hard and achieve what they set out for. It helps to reassure your way of life and the way you look at things.

Like you, the Taurus man doesn't care too much for change. He's a stay-at-home of the first degree. Chances are that the house you move into after you're married will be the house you'll live in for the rest of your life.

You'll find that the man born under this sign is easy to get along with. It's unlikely that you'll have many quarrels or arguments.

Although he'll be gentle and tender with you, your Taurus man is far from being a sensitive type. He's a man's man. Chances are he loves sports like fishing and football. He can be earthy as well as down-to-earth.

Taureans love their children very much but do everything they can not to spoil them. They believe in children staying in their places. They make excellent disciplinarians. Your children will be polite and respectful. They may find their Taurus father a little gruff, but as they grow older they'll learn to understand him.

CANCER WOMAN
GEMINI MAN

Gemini men, in spite of their charm and dashing manner, may make your skin crawl. They may seem to lack the sort of common sense you set so much store in. Their tendency to start something, then—out of boredom—never finish it, may do nothing more than exasperate you.

You may be inclined to interpret a Geminian's jumping around from here to there as childish if not downright neurotic. A man born under this sign will seldom stay put and if you should take it upon yourself to try and make him sit still, he's liable to resent it strongly.

On the other hand, the Gemini man is liable to think you're an old slowpoke—someone far too interested in security and material things. He's attracted to things that sparkle and dazzle; you, with your practical way of looking at things, are likely to seem a little dull and uninteresting to this gadabout. If your're looking for a life of security and permanence—and what Cancerian isn't—then you'd better look elsewhere for your Mr. Right.

Chances are you'll be taken in by his charming ways and facile wit—few women can resist Gemini-magic—but after you've seen through his live-for-today, gossamer facade, you'll most likely be very happy to turn your attention to someone more stable—even if he is not as interesting. You want a man who is there when you need him. You need someone on whom you can fully rely. Keeping track of a Gemini's movements will make you dizzy. Still, you are a patient woman, most of the time, and you are able to put up with something contrary if you feel that in the end it will prove well worth the effort.

A successful and serious Gemini could make you a very happy woman, perhaps, if you gave him half a chance. Although you may think that he has holes in his head, the Gemini man generally has a good brain and can make good use of it when he wants. Some Geminians who have learned the importance of being consequent have risen to great heights, professionally. President Kennedy was a Gemini as was Thomas Mann and William Butler Yeats. Once you can convince yourself that not all people born under the sign of the Twins are witless grasshoppers, you'll find you've come a long way in trying to understand them.

Life with a Gemini man can be more fun than a barrel of clowns. You'll never have a chance to experience a dull moment. He lacks your sense when it comes to money, however. You should see to it that you handle the budgeting and bookkeeping.

In ways, he's like a child himself; perhaps that is why he can get along so well with the younger generation.

CANCER WOMAN
CANCER MAN

You'll find the man born under the same sign as you easy to get along with. You're both sensitive and sensible people; you'll see eye-to-eye on most things. He'll share your interest in security and practicality.

Cancer men are always hard workers. They are very interested in making successes of themselves in business and socially. Like you, he's a conservative person who has a great deal of respect for tradition. He's a man you can depend on come rain or come shine. He'll never shirk his responsibilities as provider and will always see to it that you never want.

The Cancer man is not the type that rushes headlong into romance. Neither are you, for that matter. Courtship between the two of you will be a sensible and thorough affair. It may take months before you even get to that holding-hands stage of romance. One thing you can be sure of: he'll always treat you like a lady. He'll have great respect and consideration for your feelings. Only when he is sure that you approve of him as someone to love, will he reveal the warmer side of his nature. His coolness, like yours, is just a front. Beneath it lies a very affectionate heart.

Although he may seem restless or moody at times, on the whole the Cancer man is a very considerate and kind person. His standards are extremely high. He is looking for a girl who can measure up to his ideals . . . a girl like you.

Marriage means a lot to the Cancer male. He's very interested in settling down with someone who has the same attitudes and outlooks as he has. He's a man who loves being at home. He'll be a faithful husband. Cancerians never pussyfoot around after they've made their marriage vows. They do not take their marriage responsibilities lightly. They see to it that everything in this relationship is just the way it should be. Between the two of you, your home will be well managed; bills will be paid on time, there will be adequate insurance on everything of value, and there will be money in the bank. When retirement time rolls around, you both should be very well off.

The Cancer man has a great respect for family. You'll most likely be seeing a lot of his mother during your marriage, just as he'll probably be seeing a lot of yours. He'll do his best to get along with your relatives; he'll treat them with the kindness and concern you think they deserve. He'll expect you to be just as considerate with his relatives.

The Cancerian makes a very good father. He's very patient and understanding, especially when the children are young and dependent.

CANCER WOMAN
LEO MAN

To know a man born under the sign of the Lion is not necessarily to love him—even though the temptation may be great. When he fixes most girls with his leonine double-whammy, it causes their hearts to pitter-pat and their minds to cloud over.

But with you, the sensible Cancerian, it takes more than a regal strut and a roar to win you over. There is no denying that Leo has a way with women—even practical Cancerians—and that once he's swept a girl off her feet, it may be hard for her to scramble upright again. Still, you are no pushover for romantic charm when you feel there may be no security behind it.

He'll wine you and dine you in the fanciest places. He'll croon to you under the moon and shower you with diamonds if he can get a hold of them. Still, it would be wise to find out just how long that shower is going to last before consenting to be his wife.

Lions in love are hard to ignore, let alone brush off. Once mesmerized by this romantic powerhouse, you will most likely find yourself doing things you never dreamed of. Leos can be like vain pussycats when involved romantically. They like to be cuddled and curried, tickled under the chin and told how wonderful they are. This may not be your cup of tea, exactly, still when you're romantically dealing with a man born under the sign of Leo, you'll find yourself doing all kinds of things to make him purr.

Although he may be big and magnanimous while trying to win you, he'll let out a blood-curdling roar if he thinks he's not getting the tender love and care he feels is his due. If you keep him well supplied with affection, you can be sure his eyes will never stray and his heart will never wander.

Leo men often tend to be authoritarian—they are born to lord it over others in one way or another, it seems. If he is the top banana of his firm, he'll most likely do everything he can to stay on top. If he's not number one, he's most likely working on it and will be sitting on the throne before long. You'll have more security than you can use if he is in a position to support you in the manner to which he feels you should be accustomed. He's apt to be too lavish, though—at least, by your standards.

You'll always have plenty of friends when you have a Leo for a mate. He's a natural born friend-maker and entertainer. He loves to kick up his heels at a party.

As fathers, Leos tend to spoil their children no end.

CANCER WOMAN
VIRGO MAN

The Virgo man is often a quiet, respectable type who sets great store in conservative behavior and level-headedness. He'll admire you for your practicality and tenacity—perhaps even more than for your good looks. The Virgo man is seldom bowled over by glamour pusses. When looking for someone to love, he always turns to a serious, reliable girl.

He'll be far from a Valentino while dating. In fact, you may wind up making all the passes. Once he gets his motor running, however, he can be a warm and wonderful fellow—to the right girl.

The Virgo man is gradual about love. Chances are your romance with him will start out looking like an ordinary friendship. Once he's sure that you are no fly-by-night flirt and have no plans of taking him for a ride, he'll open up and rain sunshine all over your heart.

The Virgo man takes his time about romance. It may be many years before he seriously considers settling down. Virgos are often middle-age when they make their first marriage vows. They hold out as long as they can for that girl who perfectly measures up to their ideals.

He may not have many names in his little black book; in fact, he may not even have a little black book. He's not interested in playing the field; leave that to the more flamboyant signs. The Virgo man is so particular that he may remain romantically inactive for a long period of time. The girl he chooses has to be perfect or it's no go.

With your sure-fire perseverance, you'll most likely be able to make him listen to reason, as far as romance is concerned; before long, you'll find him returning your love. He's no block of ice and will respond to what he considers to be the right feminine flame.

Once your love-life with Virgo starts to bubble, don't give it a chance to die down. The Virgo man will never give a woman a second chance at winning his heart. If there should ever be a falling-out between you: forget about picking up the pieces. By him, it's one strike and you're out.

Once married, he'll stay that way—even if it hurts. He's too conscientious to back out of a legal deal of any sort. He'll always be faithful and considerate. He's as neat as a pin and will expect you to be the same.

If you marry a Virgo man, keep your kids spic-and-span, at least by the time he gets home from work. He likes children to be clean and polite.

CANCER WOMAN
LIBRA MAN

Cancerians are apt to find men born under the sign of Libra too wrapped up in their own private dreams to be romantically interesting. He's a difficult man to bring back down to earth, at times. Although he may be very careful about weighing both sides of an argument, he may never really come to a reasonable decision about anything. Decisons, large and small, are capable of giving a Libran the willies. Don't ask him why. He probably doesn't know, himself.

You are looking for permanence and constancy in a love relationship; you may find him a puzzlement. One moment he comes on hard and strong with declarations of his love; the next moment you find he's left you like yesterday's mashed potatoes. It does no good to wonder "what went wrong." Chances are: nothing, really. It's just one of Libra's strange ways.

On the other hand, you'll probably admire his way with harmony and beauty. If you're all decked out in your fanciest gown, you'll receive a ready compliment and one that's really deserved. Librans don't pass out compliments to all and sundry. If something strikes him as distasteful, he'll remain silent. He's tactful.

He may not seem as ambitious as you would like your lover or husband to be. Where you have a great interest in getting ahead, the Libran is often content just to drift along. It is not that he is lazy or shiftless; material gain generally means little to him. He is more interested in aesthetic matters. If he is in love with you, however, he'll do everything in his power to make you happy.

You may have to give him a good nudge now and again to get him to recognize the light of reality. On the whole, he'll enjoy the company of his artistic dreams when you're not around. If you love your Libran, don't be too harsh or impatient with him. Try to understand him.

Librans are peace-loving people. They hate any kind of confrontation that might lead to an argument. Some of them will do almost anything to keep the peace—even tell a little lie.

If you find yourself involved with a man born under this sign, either temporarily or permanently, you'd better take over the task of managing his money. It's for his own good. Money will never interest a Libran as much as it should; he often has a tendency to be generous when he shouldn't be.

Don't let him see the materialistic side of your nature too often. It's liable to frighten him off.

He makes a gentle and understanding father. He's careful not to spoil children.

CANCER WOMAN
SCORPIO MAN

Some people have a hard time understanding the man born under the sign of Scorpio; few, however, are able to resist his fiery charm. When angered, he can act like an overturned wasps' nest; his sting can leave an almost permanent mark.. If you find yourself interested in a man born under this sign, you'd better learn how to keep on his good side.

The Scorpio man can be quite blunt when he chooses; at times, he'll seem like a brute to you. He's touchy—more so than you—and it is liable to get on your nerves after a while. When you feel like you can't take it anymore, you'd better tiptoe away from the scene rather than chance an explosive confrontation. He's capable of giving you a sounding-out that will make you pack your bags and go back to Mother—for good.

If he finds fault with you, he'll let you know. He's liable to misinterpret your patience and think it a sign of indifference. Still and all, you are the kind of woman who can adapt to almost any sort of relationship or circumstance if you put your heart and mind to it.

Scorpio men are all quite perceptive and intelligent. In some respects, they know how to use their brains more effectively than most. They believe in winning in whatever they do; second-place holds no interest for them. In business, they usually achieve the position they want through drive and use of intellect.

Your interest in home-life is not likely to be shared by him. No matter how comfortable you've managed to make the house, it will have very little influence on him with regards to making him aware of his family responsibilities. He does not like to be tied down, generally, and would rather be out on the battlefield of life, belting away for what he feels is a just and worthy cause. Don't try to keep the homefires burning too brightly while you wait for him to come home from work—you may just run out of firewood.

The Scorpio man is passionate in all things—including love. Most women are easily attracted to him—and the Cancer woman is no exception . . . that is, at least before she knows what she might be getting into. Those who allow themselves to be swept off their feet by a Scorpio man, shortly find that they're dealing with a carton of romantic fireworks. The Scorpio man is passionate with a capital P, make no mistake about that.

Scorpio men are straight to the point. They can be as sharp as a razor blade and just as cutting. Always manage to stay out of his line of fire; if you don't, it could cost you your love-life.

Scorpio men like large families. They love children but they do not always live up to the role of father.

CANCER WOMAN
SAGITTARIUS MAN

Sagittarius men are not easy to catch. They get cold feet whenever visions of the altar enter the romance. You'll most likely be attracted to the Sagittarian because of his sun-shiny nature. He's lots of laughs and easy to get along with, but as soon as the relationship begins to take on a serious hue, you may feel yourself a little let-down.

Sagittarians are full of bounce; perhaps too much bounce to suit you. They are often hard to pin down; they dislike staying put. If he ever has a chance to be on-the-move, he'll latch on to it without so much as a how-do-you-do. Sagittarians are quick people —both in mind and spirit. If ever they do make mistakes, it's because of their zip; they leap before they look.

If you offer him good advice, he's liable not to follow it. Sagittarians like to rely on their own wits and ways whenever possible.

His up-and-at-'em manner about most things is likely to drive you up the wall at times. And your cautious, deliberate manner is likely to make him cluck his tongue occasionally. "Get the lead out of your shoes," he's liable to tease when you're accompanying him on a stroll or jogging through the park with him on a Sunday morning. He can't abide a slowpoke.

At times you'll find him too much like a kid—too breezy. Don't mistake his youthful zest for premature senility. Sagittarians are equipped with first-class brain power and know how to use it well. They are often full of good ideas and drive. Generally, they are very broad-minded people and very much concerned with fair play and equality.

In the romance department, he's quite capable of loving you whole-heartedly while treating you like a good buddy. His hail-fellow-well-met manner in the arena of love is likely to scare off a dainty damsel. However, a woman who knows that his heart is in the right place, won't mind it too much if, once in a while, he slaps her (lightly) on the back instead of giving her a gentle embrace.

He's not very much of a homebody. He's got ants in his pants and enjoys being on-the-move. Humdrum routine—especially at home—bores him silly. At the drop of a hat, he may ask you to whip off your apron and dine out for a change. He's a past-master in the instant-surprise department. He'll love keeping you guessing. His friendly, candid nature will win him many friends. He'll expect his friends to be yours, and vice-versa.

Sagittarians make good fathers when the children become older; with little shavers, they feel all thumbs.

CANCER WOMAN
CAPRICORN MAN

The Capricorn man is quite often not the romantic kind of lover that attracts most women. Still, with his reserve and calm, he is capable of giving his heart completely once he has found the right girl. The Cancer woman who is thorough and deliberate can appreciate these same qualities in the average Capricorn man. He is slow and sure about most things—love included.

He doesn't believe in flirting and would never lead a heart on a merry chase just for the game of it. If you win his trust, he'll give you his heart on a platter. Quite often, it is the woman who has to take the lead when romance is in the air. As long as he knows you're making the advances in earnest, he won't mind—in fact, he'll probably be grateful. Don't get to thinking he's all cold fish; he isn't. While some Capricorns are indeed quite capable of expressing passion, others often have difficulty in trying to display affection. He should have no trouble in this area, however, once he has found a patient and understanding girl.

The Capricorn man is very interested in getting ahead. He's quite ambitious and usually knows how to apply himself well to whatever task he undertakes. He's far from being a spendthrift. Like you, he knows how to handle money with extreme care. You, with your knack for putting pennies away for that rainy day, should have no difficulty in understanding his way with money. The Capricorn man thinks in terms of future security. He saves to make sure that he and his wife have something to fall back on when they reach retirement age. There's nothing wrong with that; in fact, it's a plus quality.

The Capricorn man will want to handle household matters efficiently. Most Cancerians have no trouble in doing this. If he should check up on you from time to time, don't let it irritate you. Once you assure him that you can handle this area to his liking, he'll leave it all up to you.

Although he's a hard man to catch when it comes to marriage, once he's made that serious step, he's quite likely to become possessive. Capricorns need to know that they have the support of their women in whatever they do, every step of the way.

The Capricorn man likes to be liked. He may seem like a dull, reserved person but underneath it all, he's often got an adventurous nature that has never had the chance to express itself. He may be a real dare-devil in his heart of hearts. The right woman, the affectionate, adoring woman, can bring out that hidden zest in his nature.

Although he may not understand his children fully, he'll be a loving and dutiful father.

CANCER WOMAN
AQUARIUS MAN

You are liable to find the Aquarious man the most broadminded man you have ever met; on the other hand, you are also liable to find him the most impractical. Oftentimes, he's more of a dreamer than a doer. If you don't mind putting up with a man whose heart and mind are as wide as the Missouri but whose head is almost always up in the clouds, then start dating that Aquarian who has somehow captured your fancy. Maybe you, with your good sense, can bring him back down to earth when he gets too starry-eyed.

He's no dumb-bell; make no mistake about that. He can be busy making some very complicated and idealistic plans when he's got that out-to-lunch look in his eyes. But more than likely, he'll never execute them. After he's shared one or two of his progressive ideas with you, you are liable to ask yourself "Who is this nut?" But don't go jumping to conclusions. There's a saying that Aquarians are a half-century ahead of everybody else in the thinking department.

If you decide to say "yes" to his "will you marry me", you'll find out how right his zany whims are on or about your 50th anniversary. Maybe the waiting will be worth it. Could be that you have an Einstein on your hands—and heart.

Life with an Aquarian won't be one of total despair if you can learn to temper his airiness with your down-to-earth practicality. He won't gripe if you do. The Aquarius man always maintains an open mind; he'll entertain the ideas and opinions of everybody. He may not agree with all of them.

Don't go tearing your hair out when you find that it's almost impossible to hold a normal conversation with your Aquarius friend at times. He's capable of answering your how-are-you-feeling with a run-down on the price of Arizona sugar beets. Always try to keep in mind: he means well.

His broadmindedness doesn't stop when it comes to you and your personal freedom. You won't have to give up any of your hobbies or projects after you're married; in fact, he'll encourage you to continue your interests.

He'll be a kind and generous husband. He'll never quibble over petty things. Keep track of the money you both spend. He can't. Money burns a hole in his pocket.

You'll have plenty of chances to put your legendary patience to good use during your relationship with an Aquarian. At times, you may feel like tossing in the towel, but you'll never call it quits.

He's a good family man. He understands children as much as he loves them.

CANCER WOMAN
PISCES MAN

The Pisces man is perhaps the man you've been looking all over for, high and low; the man you almost thought didn't exist.

The Pisces man is very sensitive and very romantic. Still, he is a reasonable person. He may wish on the moon, yet he's got enough good sense to know that it isn't made of green cheese.

He'll be very considerate of your every wish and whim. He will do his best to be a very compatible mate. The Pisces man is great for showering the object of his affection with all kinds of little gifts and tokens of his affection. He's just the right mixture of dreamer and realist that pleases most women.

When it comes to earning bread and butter, the strong Pisces man will do all right in the world. Quite often they are capable of rising to very high positions. Some do very well as writers or psychiatrists. He'll be as patient and understanding with you as you are with him.

One thing a Pisces man dislikes is pettiness. Anyone who delights in running another into the ground is almost immediately crossed off his list of possible mates. If you have any small grievances with any of your girl friends, don't tell him about them. He couldn't care less about them and will be quite disappointed in you if you do.

If you fall in love with a weak Pisces man, don't give up your job at the office before you get married. Better still: hang onto it until a good while after the honeymoon; you may need it.

A funny thing about the man born under this sign is that he can be content almost anywhere. This is perhaps because he is quite inner-directed and places little value on some exterior things.

In a shack or a palace, the Pisces man is capable of making the best of all possible adjustments. He won't kick up a fuss if the roof leaks or if the fence is in sad need of repair. He's got more important things on his mind, he'll tell you. Still and all, the Pisces man is not lazy or aimless. It's important to understand that material gain is never a direct goal for him.

Pisces men have a way with the sick and troubled. He'll offer his shoulder to anyone in the mood for a good cry. He can listen to one hard luck story after another without seeming to tire. Quite often he knows what is bothering someone before that person, himself, realizes what it is. It's almost intuitive with Pisceans, it seems.

As a lover, he'll be attentive and faithful. Children are often delighted with Pisces men. As fathers, they are never strict, always permissive.

Man—Woman

CANCER MAN
ARIES WOMAN

The Aires woman may be a little too bossy and busy for you. Generally speaking, Ariens are ambitious creatures. They can become a little impatient with people who are more thorough and deliberate than they are—especially if they feel such people are taking too much time. The Aries woman is a fast worker. Sometimes she's so fast she forgets to look where she's going. When she stumbles or falls, it would be nice if you were there to grab her. Ariens are proud women. They don't like to be told "I told you so" when they err. Tongue-wagging can turn them into blocks of ice. Don't begin to think that the Aires woman frequently gets tripped up in her plans. Quite often they are capable of taking aim and hitting the bull's-eye. You'll be flabbergasted at times by their accuracy as well as by their ambition. On the other hand, because of your interest in being sure and safe, you're apt to spot a flaw in your Arien's plans before she does.

You are somewhat slower than the Arien in attaining what you have your sights set on. Still, you don't make any mistakes along the way; you're almost always well-prepared.

The Aries woman is rather sensitive at times. She likes to be handled with gentleness and respect. Let her know that you love her for her brains as well as for her good looks. Never give her cause to become jealous. When your Aires date sees green, you'd better forget about sharing a rosy future together. Handle her with tender love and care and she's yours.

The Aires woman can be giving if she feels her partner is deserving. She is no iceberg; she responds to the proper flame. She needs a man she can look up to and feel proud of. If the shoe fits, put it on. If not, better put your sneakers back on and quietly tiptoe out of her sight. She can cause you plenty of heart ache if you've made up your mind about her but she hasn't made up hers about you. Aires women are very demanding at times. Some of them are high-strung; they can be difficult if they feel their independence is being hampered.

The cultivated Aires woman makes a wonderful homemaker and hostess. You'll find she's very clever in decorating and color-use. Your house will be tastefully furnished; she'll see to it that it radiates harmony. Friends and acquaintances will love your Aries wife. She knows how to make everyone feel at home and welcome.

Although the Aries woman may not be keen on burdening responsibilities, she is fond of children and the joy they bring.

CANCER MAN
TAURUS WOMAN

A Taurus woman could perhaps understand you better than most women. She is a very considerate and loving kind of person. She is methodical and thorough in whatever she does. She knows how to take her time in doing things; she is anxious to avoid mistakes. Like you, she is a careful person. She never skips over things that may seem unimportant; she goes over everything with a fine-tooth comb.

Home is very important to the Taurus woman. She is an excellent homemaker. Although your home may not be a palace, it will become, under her care, a comfortable and happy abode. She'll love it when friends drop by for the evening. She is a good cook and enjoys feeding people well. No one will ever go away from your house with an empty stomach.

The Taurus woman is serious about love and affection. When she has taken a tumble for someone, she'll stay by him—for good, if possible. She will try to be practical in romance, to some extent. When she sets her cap for a man, she keeps after him until he's won her. Generally, the Taurus woman is a passionate lover, even though she may appear otherwise at first glance. She is on the look-out for someone who can return her affection fully. Taureans are sometimes given to fits of jealousy and possessiveness. They expect fair play in the area of marriage; when it doesn't come about, they can be bitingly sarcastic and mean.

The Taurus woman is generally an easy-going person. She's

fond of keeping peace. She won't argue unless she has to. She'll do her best to keep a love relationship on even keel.

Marriage is generally a one-time thing for Taureans. Once they've made the serious step, they seldom try to back out of it. Marriage is for keeps. They are fond of love and warmth. With the right man, they turn out to be ideal wives.

The Taurus woman will respect you for your steady ways; she'll have confidence in your common sense.

Taurus women seldom put up with nonsense from their children. They are not so much strict as concerned. They like their children to be well-behaved and dutiful. Nothing pleases a Taurus mother more than a compliment from a neighbor or teacher about her child's behavior. Although children may inwardly resent the iron hand of a Taurus woman, in later life they are often quite thankful that they were brought up in such an orderly and conscientious way.

CANCER MAN
GEMINI WOMAN

The Gemini woman may be too much of a flirt ever to take your heart too seriously. Then again, it depends on what kind of mood she's in. Gemini women can change from hot to cold quicker than a cat can wink its eye. Chances are her fluctuations will tire you after a time, and you'll pick up your heart—if it's not already broken into small pieces—and go elsewhere. Women born under the sign of the Twins have the talent of being able to change their moods and attitudes as frequently as they change their party dresses.

Sometimes, Gemini girls like to whoop it up. Some of them are good-time girls who love burning the candle to the wick. You'll always see them at parties and gatherings, surrounded by men of all types, laughing gaily or kicking up their heels at every opportunity. Wallflowers, they're not. The next day you may bump into the same girl at the neighborhood library and you'll hardly recognize her for her "sensible" attire. She'll probably have five or six books under her arm—on five or six different subjects. In fact, she may even work there. If you think you've met the twin sister of Dr. Jekyll and Mr. Hyde, you're most likely right.

You'll probably find her a dazzling and fascinating creature—for a time, at any rate. Most men do. But when it comes to being serious about love you may find that that sparkling Eve leaves quite a bit to be desired. It's not that she has anything against being serious, it's just that she might find it difficult trying to be serious with you.

At one moment, she'll be capable of praising you for your steadfast and patient ways; the next moment she'll tell you in a cutting way that you're an impossible stick in the mud.

Don't even begin to fathom the depths of her mercurial soul—it's full of false bottoms. She'll resent close investigation anyway, and will make you rue the day you ever took it into your head to try to learn more about her than she feels is necessary. Better keep the relationship fancy free and full of fun until she gives you the go-ahead sign. Take as much of her as she is willing to give; don't ask for more. If she does take a serious interest in you, then she'll come across with the goods.

There will come a time when the Gemini girl will realize that she can't spend her entire life at the ball and that the security and warmth you offer is just what she needs to be a happy, fulfilled woman.

She'll be easy-going with her children. She'll probably spoil them silly.

CANCER MAN
CANCER WOMAN

The girl born under Cancer needs to be protected from the cold cruel world. She'll love you for your gentle and kind manner; you are the kind of man who can make her feel safe and secure.

You won't have to pull any he-man or heroic stunts to win her heart; she's not interested in things like that. She's more likely to be impressed by your sure, steady ways—the way you have of putting your arm around her and making her feel that she's the only girl in the world. When she's feeling glum and tears begin to well up in her eyes, you'll know how to calm her fears, no matter how silly some of them may seem.

The girl born under this sign—like you—is inclined to have her ups and downs. Perhaps you can both learn to smooth out the roughed-up spots in each other's life. She'll most likely worship the ground you walk on or place you on a very high pedestal. Don't disappoint her if you can help it. She'll never disappoint you. The Cancer woman is the sort who will take great pleasure in devoting the rest of her natural life to you. She'll darn your socks, mend your overalls, scrub floors, wash windows, shop, cook, and do anything short of murder in order to please you and to let you know that she loves you. Sounds like that legendary good old-fashioned girl, doesn't it? Contrary to popular belief, there are still a good number of them around and the majority of them are Cancerians.

Treat your Cancer mate fairly and she'll treat you like a king.

There is one ohing you should be warned about: never be unkind to your mother-in-law. It will be the only golden rule your Cancerian wife will probably expect you to live up to. Mother is something pretty special for her. You should have no trouble in understanding this, for your mother has a special place in your heart, too. It's always that way with people born under this sign. They have great respect and love for family-ties. It might be a good idea for you both to get to know each other's relatives before tying the marriage knot, because after the wedding bells have rung, you'll be seeing a lot of them.

Of all the signs in the Zodiac, the woman born under Cancer is the most maternal. In caring for and bringing up children, she knows just how to combine tenderness and discipline. A child couldn't ask for a better mother. Cancer women are sympathetic, affectionate, and patient with children. Both of you will make excellent parents—especially when the children are young; when they grow older you'll most likely be reluctant to let them go out into the world.

CANCER MAN
LEO WOMAN

The Leo woman can make most men roar like lions. If any woman in the Zodiac has that indefinable something that can make men lose their heads and find their hearts, it's the Leo woman.

She's got more than a fair share of charm and glamour and she knows how to make the most of her assets, especially when she's in the company of the opposite sex. Jealous men either lose their cool or their sanity when trying to woo a woman born under the sign of the Lion. She likes to kick up her heels quite often and doesn't care who knows it. She often makes heads turn and toungues wag. You don't necessarily have to believe any of what you hear—it's most likely just jealous gossip or wishful thinking. Needless to say, other women in her vicinity turn green with envy and will try anything short of shoving her into the nearest lake in order to put her out of commission.

Although this vamp makes the blood rush to your head and makes you momentarily forget all the things you thought were important and necessary in your life, you may feel differently when you come back down to earth and the stars are out of your eyes. You may feel that although this vivacious creature can make you feel pretty wonderful, she just isn't the kind of girl you planned to bring home to Mother. Not that your mother might disapprove of your choice—but *you might* after the shoes and rice are a thing of the past. Although the Leo woman may do her best to be a good wife for you, chances are she'll fall short of your idea of what a good wife should be.

If you're planning on not going as far as the altar with that Leo woman who has you flipping your lid, you'd better be financially equipped for some very expensive dating. Be prepared to shower her with expensive gifts and to take her dining and dancing to the smartest spots in town. Promise her the moon if you're in a position to go that far. Luxury and glamour are two things that are bound to lower a Leo's resistance. She's got expensive tastes and you'd better cater to them if you expect to get to first base with this femme.

If you've got an important business deal to clinch and you have doubts as to whether you can swing it or not, bring your Leo girl along to the business luncheon. Chances are that with her on your arm, you'll be able to win any business battle with both hands tied. She won't have to say or do anything—just be there at your side. The grouchiest oil magnate can be transformed into a gushing, obedient schoolboy if there's a charming Leo woman in the room.

Leo mothers are blind to the faults of their children. They make very loving and affectionate mothers and tend to spoil their offspring.

CANCER MAN
VIRGO WOMAN

The Virgo woman is pretty particular about choosing her men friends. She's not interested in just going out with anybody; she has her own idea of what a boyfriend or prospective husband should be—and it's quite possible that that image has something of you in it. Generally speaking, she's a quiet girl. She doesn't believe that nonsense has any place in a love affair. She's serious about love and she'll expect you to be. She's looking for a man who has both feet on the ground—someone who can take care of himself as well as her. She knows the value of money and how to get the most out of a dollar. She's far from being a spendthrift. Throwing money around turns her stomach—even when it isn't her money.

She'll most likely be very shy about romancing. Even the simple act of holding hands may make her turn crimson—at least, on the first couple of dates. You'll have to make all the advances—which is as it should be—and you'll have to be careful not to make any wrong moves. She's capable of showing anyone who oversteps the boundaries of common decency the door. It may even take quite a long time before she'll accept that goodnight kiss at the front gate. Don't give up. You are perhaps the kind of man who can bring out the warm woman in her. There is love and tenderness underneath Virgo's seemingly frigid facade. It will take a patient and understanding man to bring it out into the open. She may have the idea that sex is something very naughty, if not unnecessary. The right man could make her put this old-fashioned idea in the trunk up in the attic along with her great grandmother's wollen nighties.

She is a very sensitive girl. You can help her overcome this by treating her with gentleness and affection.

When a Virgo has accepted you as a lover or mate, she won't stint in giving her love in return. With her, it's all or nothing at all. You'll be surprised at the transformation your earnest attention can bring about in this quiet kind of woman. When in love, Virgos only listen to their hearts, not to what the neighbors say.

Virgo women are honest about love once they've come to grips with it. They don't appreciate hyprocrisy—particularly in this area of life. They will always be true to their hearts—even if it means tossing you over for a new love. But if you convince her that you are earnest about your interest in her, she'll reciprocate your love and affection and never leave you. Do her wrong once, however, and you can be sure she'll call the whole thing off.

Virgo mothers are tender and loving. They know what's good for their children and take great pains in bringing them up correctly.

CANCER MAN
LIBRA WOMAN

The song goes: It's a woman's prerogative to change her mind. The lyricist must have had the Libra woman in his thoughts when he jotted this ditty out. Her changeability, in spite of its undeniable charm (sometimes), could actually drive even a man of your patience up the wall. She's capable of smothering you with love and kisses one day and on the next, avoid you like the plague. If you think you're a man of steel nerves then perhaps you can tolerate her sometimey-ness without suffering too much. However, if you own up to the fact that you're a mere mortal who can only take so much, then you'd better fasten your attention on a girl who's somewhat more constant.

But don't get the wrong idea—a love affair with a Libran is not all bad. In fact, it can have an awful lot of plusses to it. Libra women are soft, very feminine, and warm. She doesn't have to vamp all over the place in order to gain a man's attention. Her delicate presence is enough to warm the cockles of any man's heart. One smile and you're like a piece of putty in the palm of her hand.

She can be fluffy and affectionate—things you like in a girl. On the other hand, her indecision about which dress to wear, what to cook for dinner, or whether or not to redo the rumpusroom could make you tear your hair out. What will perhaps be more exasperating is her flat denial to the accusation that she cannot make even the simplest decision. The trouble is that she wants to be fair or just in all matters; she'll spend hours weighing both sides of an argument or situation. Don't make her rush into a decision; that would only irritate her.

The Libra woman likes to be surrounded by beautiful things. Money is no object when beauty is concerned. There will always be plenty of flowers in her apartment. She'd rather die than do without daisies and such. She'll know how to arrange them tastefully, too. Women under this sign are fond of beautiful clothes and furnishings. They will run up bills without batting an eye—if given the chance.

Once she's cottoned to you, the Libra woman will do everything in her power to make you happy. She'll wait on you hand and foot when you're sick, bring you breakfast in bed on Sundays, and even read you the funny papers if you're too sleepy to open your eyes. She'll be very thoughtful and devoted. If anyone dares suggest you're not the grandest man in the world, your Libra wife will give that person a good sounding-out.

Librans work wonders with children. Gentle persuasion and affection are all she uses in bringing them up. It works.

CANCER MAN
SCORPIO WOMAN

When the Scorpio woman chooses to be sweet, she's apt to give the impression that butter wouldn't melt in her mouth . . . but, of course, it would. When her temper flies, so will everything else that isn't bolted down. She can be as hot as a *tamale* or as cool as a cucumber when she wants. Whatever mood she's in, you can be sure it's for real. She doesn't believe in poses or hypocrisy.

The Scorpio woman is often seductive and sultry. Her femme fatale charm can pierce through the hardest of hearts like a laser ray. She doesn't have to look like Mata Hari (many of them resemble the tomboy next door) but once you've looked into those tantalizing eyes, you're a goner.

The Scorpio woman can be a whirlwind of passion. Life with a girl born under this sign will not be all smiles and smooth-sailing. If you think you can handle a woman who can purr like a pussycat when handled correctly but spit bullets once her fur is ruffled, then try your luck. Your stable and steady nature will most likely have a calming effect on her. You're the kind of man she can trust and rely on. But never cross her—even on the smallest thing; if you do, you'd better tell Fido to make room for you in the dog-house—you'll be his guest for the next couple of days.

Generally, the Scorpio woman will keep family battles within the walls of your home. When company visits, she's apt to give the impression that married life with you is one big joy-ride. It's just her way of expressing her loyalty to you—at least, in front of others. She believes that family matters are and should stay private. She certainly will see to it that others have a high opinion of you both. She'll be right behind you in whatever it is you want to do. Although she's an individualist, after she has married she'll put her own interests aside for those of the man she loves. With a woman like this behind you, you can't help but go far. She'll never try to take over your role as boss of the family. She'll give you all the support you need in order to fulfill that role. She won't complain if the going gets rough. She knows how to take the bitter with the sweet. She is a courageous woman. She's as anxious as you are to find that place in the sun for you both. She's as determined a person as you are.

Although she may love her children, she may not be very affectionate toward them. She'll make a devoted mother, though. She'll be anxious to see them develop their talents. She'll teach the children to be courageous and steadfast.

CANCER MAN
SAGITTARIUS WOMAN

The Sagittarius woman is hard to keep track of: first she's here, then she's there. She's a woman with a severe case of itchy feet. She's got to keep on the move.

People generally like her because of her hail-fellow-well-met manner and her breezy charm. She is constantly good-natured and almost never cross. She is the kind of girl you're likely to strike up a palsy-walsy relationship with; you might not be interested in letting it go any farther. She probably won't sulk if you leave it on a friendly basis, either. Treat her like a kid-sister and she'll eat it up like candy.

She'll probably be attracted to you because of your restful, self-assured manner. She'll need a friend like you to help her over the rough spots in her life; she'll most likely turn to you for advice frequently.

There is nothing malicious about a girl born under this sign. She is full of bounce and good cheer. Her sunshiny dispositon can be relied upon even on the rainiest of days. No matter what she says or does, you'll always know that she means well. Sagittarians are sometimes short on tact. Some of them say anything that comes into their pretty little heads, no matter what the occasion. Sometimes the words that tumble out of their mouths seem downright cutting and cruel; they mean well but often everything they say comes out wrong. She's quite capable of losing her friends—and perhaps even yours—through a careless slip of the lip. Always remember that she is full of good intentions. Stick with her if you like her and try to help her mend her ways.

She's not a girl that you'd most likely be interested in marrying, but she'll certainly be lots of fun to pal around with. Quite often, Sagittarius women are outdoor types. They're crazy about things like fishing, camping, and mountain climbing. They love the wide open spaces. They are fond of all kinds of animals. Make no mistake about it: this busy little lady is no slouch. She's full of pep and vigor.

She's great company most of the time; she's more fun than a three-ring circus when she's in the right company. You'll like her for her candid and direct manner. On the whole, Sagittarians are very kind and sympathetic women.

If you do wind up marrying this girl-next-door type, you'd better see to it that you take care of all financial matters. Sagittarians often let money run through their fingers like sand.

As a mother, she'll smother her children with love and give them all of the freedom they think they need.

CANCER MAN
CAPRICORN WOMAN

The Capricorn woman may not be the most romantic woman of the Zodiac, but she's far from frigid when she meets the right man. She believes in true love; she doesn't appreciate getting involved in flings. To her, they're just a waste of time. She's looking for a man who means "business"—in life as well as in love. Although she can be very affectionate with her boyfriend or mate, she tends to let her head govern her heart. That is not to say that she is a cool, calculating cucumber. On the contrary, she just feels she can be more honest about love if she consults her brains first. She wants to size-up the situation first before throwing her heart in the ring. She wants to make sure it won't get stepped on.

The Capricorn woman is faithful, dependable, and systematic in just about everything that she undertakes. She is quite concerned with security and sees to it that every penny she spends is spent wisely. She is very economical about using her time, too. She does not believe in whittling away her energy on a scheme that is bound not to pay off.

Ambitious themselves, they are quite often attracted to ambitious men—men who are interested in getting somewhere in life. If a man of this sort wins her heart, she'll stick by him and do all she can to help him get to the top.

The Capricorn woman is almost always diplomatic. She makes an excellent hostess. She can be very influential when your business acquaintances come to dinner.

The Capricorn woman is likely to be very concerned, if not downright proud, about her family tree. Relatives are pretty important to her, particularly if they're socially prominent. Never say a cross word about her family members. That can really go against her grain and she'll punish you by not talking for days.

She's generally thorough in whatever she does: cooking, housekeeping, entertaining. Capricorn women are well-mannered and gracious, no matter what their backgrounds. They seem to have it in their natures to always behave properly.

If you should marry a woman born under this sign, you need never worry about her going on a wild shopping spree. They understand the value of money better than most women. If you turn over your paycheck to her at the end of the week, you can be sure that a good hunk of it will go into the bank and that all the bills will be paid on time.

With children, the Capricorn mother is both loving and correct. She'll see to it that they're polite and respectful.

CANCER MAN
AQUARIUS WOMAN

The woman born under the sign of the Water Bearer can be pretty odd and eccentric at times. Some say that this is the source of her mysterious charm. You're liable to think she's just a plain screwball; you may be 50 percent right.

Aquarius women often have their heads full of dreams and stars in their eyes. By nature, they are often unconventional; they have their own ideas about how the world should be run. Sometimes their ideas may seem pretty weird—chances are they're just a little bit too progressive. There is a saying that runs "The way the Aquarian thinks, so will the world in fifty years."

If you find yourself falling in love with a woman born under this sign, you'd better fasten your safety belt. It may take some time before you know what she's like and even then, you may have nothing to go on but a string of vague hunches.

She can be like a rainbow: full of dazzling colors. She's like no other girl you've ever known. There is something about her that is definitely charming—yet elusive, you'll never be able to put your finger on it. She seems to radiate adventure and optimism without even trying. She'll most likely be the most tolerant and open-minded woman you've ever encountered.

If you find that she's too much mystery and charm for you to handle—and being a Cancerian, chances are you might—just talk it out with her and say that you think it would be better if you called it quits. She'll most likely give you a peck on the cheek and say "Okay, but let's still be friends." Aquarius women are like that. Perhaps you'll both find it easier to get along in a friendship than in a romance.

It is not difficult for her to remain buddy-buddy with an ex-lover. For many Aquarians, the line between friendship and romance is a pretty fuzzy one.

She's not a jealous person and while you're romancing her, she won't expect you to be, either. You'll find her a pretty free spirit most of the time. Just when you think you know her inside-out, you'll discover that you don't really know her at all. She's a very sympathetic and warm person; she is often helpful to those in need of assistance and advice.

She'll seldom be suspicious even when she has every right to be. If the man she loves makes a little slip, she's liable to forget it.

She makes a fine mother. Her positive and big-hearted qualities are easily transmitted to her offspring.

CANCER MAN
PISCES WOMAN

The Pisces woman places great value on love and romance. She's gentle, kind, and romantic. Perhaps she's that girl you've been dreaming about all these years. Like you, she has very high ideals, she will only give her heart to a man who she feels can live up to her expectations.

She'll never try to wear the pants in the family. She's a staunch believer in the man being the head of the house. Quite often, Pisces women are soft and cuddly. They have a feminine, domestic charm that can win the heart of just about any man.

Generally, there's a lot more to her than just her pretty face and womanly ways. There's a brain ticking behind that gentle facade. You may not become aware of it—that is, until you've married her. It's no cause for alarm, however; she'll most likely never use it against you. But if she feels you're botching up your married life through careless behavior or if she feels you could be earning more money than you do, she'll tell you about it. But any wife would, really. She will never try to usurp your position as head and bread winner of the family. She'll admire you for your ambition and drive. If anyone says anything against you in her presence, she'll probably break out into tears. Pisces women are usually very sensitive. Their reaction to adversity or frustration is often just a plain good old fashioned cry. They can weep buckets when inclined.

She'll have an extra-special dinner waiting for you when you call up and tell her that you've just landed a new and important contract. Don't bother to go into the details at the dinner table, though; she probably doesn't have much of a head for business matters. She's only too glad to leave those matters up to you.

She's a wizard in decorating a house. She's fond of soft and beautiful things. She's a good housekeeper. She'll always see to it that you have plenty of socks and underwear in the top drawer of your dresser.

Treat her with tenderness and your relationship will be an enjoyable one. Pisces women are generally fond of sweets and flowers. Never forget birthdays, anniversaries, and the like. She won't.

Your talent for patience and gentleness can pay off in your relationship with a Pisces woman. Chances are she'll never make you sorry you placed that band of gold on her finger.

There's a strong bond between a Pisces mother and her children. She'll try to give them all the things she never had as a child. Chances are she'll spoil them a little.

LEO
July 21 — August 21

CHARACTER ANALYSIS

The person born under the sign of Leo usually knows how to handle a position of authority well. Others have a deep respect for the decisions he makes. The Leo man or woman generally has something aristocratic about him that commands respect. The person born under this fifth sign of the Zodiac generally knows·how to stand on his own two feet. He is independent in many things that he does. He knows how to direct his energies so that he will be able to achieve his ends. He seldom wastes time; he is to the point. In love matters, the Leo is quite passionate. He doesn't stint when it comes to romance and is capable of deep emotions. The Leo is a stable person; he has the ability to see things through to the end without wavering on his standpoint.

Leo people are quite generous in all that they do. They give themselves fully to every situation. To others they often appear quite lordly; they are often at the helm of organizations, running things.

The Leo person does not believe in being petty or small. Quite often he goes out of his way to make others happy. He would never stoop to doing anything which he felt was beneath his dignity. He has a deep feeling of self-respect. He would never treat others badly. He is kind-hearted, sometimes to a fault.

Leo people generally learn to shoulder certain responsibilities at an early age. They have an understanding of life that others sometimes never attain. They do not shy away from conflict or troubles. They believe in dealing with opposition directly. They are quite active in their approach to problems. Life, to them, should be attacked with zest and vigor.

When the Leo man or woman knows what he wants in life, he

goes out after it. He is not a person who gives up easily. He perseveres until he wins. He is not interested in occupying a position where he has to be told what to do. He is too independent for that sort of thing. He wants to be the person who runs things and he seems almost naturally suited for an authoritative position. His bearing is that of someone who expects others to listen to him when he speaks. He is a forceful person; he knows how to command respect. He is seldom unsure of himself, but when he is, he sees to it that others do not notice. He is quite clever at organizing things. He is a person who likes order. He knows how to channel his creative talents in such a way that the results of whatever he does are always constructive and original. Leadership positions bring out the best in a person born under this sign.

The Leo person is generally quite tolerant and open-minded. He believes in live-and-let-live so long as the other person does not infringe on what he believes to be his natural rights. In most things, he is fair. He believes in being frank and open. On the whole, the Leo person is active and high-strung. If something irritates him or runs against his grain, he will let it be known. He can be short-tempered if the occasion calls for it.

He is a person who believes in sticking to his principles. He is not interested in making compromises—especially if he feels that his standpoint is the correct one. He can become angry if opposed. But, all in all, his bad temper does not last for a long time. He is the kind of person who does not hold grudges.

The Leo person often has a flair for acting. Some of the best actors in the world have been people born under this sign. Their dramatic talents are often considerable; even as children Leo people have a strong understanding of drama. There is also something poetic about them. They can be quite romantic at times. They have a deep love and appreciation of beauty. They are fond of display and have a love of luxury that often startles modest people.

On the whole, he is a rather proud person. His head is easily turned by a compliment. The cultivated Leo, however, knows how to take flattery in his stride. Others may try to get around him by flattering him—they generally succeed with the weaker Leos, for they are quite caught up with themselves and feel that no compliment is too great. This should not be interpreted as pure vanity. The Leo person has a clear understanding of his own superiority and worth.

In spite of the fact that he is generous in most things, the person born under this sign may not appreciate others making demands of him. He may not mind offering favors, but he does not like them to be asked of him.

The person born under this sign feels that it is important to be your own boss. He does not like others to tell him what to do. He is quite capable, he feels, of handling his own affairs—and quite well. If he has to work with others, he may become rather impatient, especially if they are somewhat slow or unsure. He does not like to be kept waiting. Team work for him is sometimes a very frustrating experience. He likes to be on his own.

Health

The Leo person is generally well built. He is a sturdy person, capable of taking a lot of stress and strain if necessary. Still, he may take on more than he can manage from time to time, and this is likely to exhaust him physically. He enjoys challenge, however, and finds it difficult to turn down a proposition which gives him a chance to demonstrate his worth—even if it is beyond his real capabilities. Although he is basically an active person, he does have his limits. If he refuses to recognize them, he may become the victim of a nervous disorder. Some people born under this sign are fond of keeping late hours—in pursuit of pleasure or fame. They can keep this up for some time, but in the end it does have a telling effect on their health. People born under this sign often wear themselves out by going from one extreme to the other.

The weak parts of the Leo are his spine and heart. He should see to it that he does nothing that might affect these areas of his body. In many instances, the Leo has to restrain himself in order to protect his health. Heart disease or rheumatic fever sometimes strike people born under this sign. In spite of this, the Leo generally has a strong resistance to disease. His constitution is good; whenever he does fall ill, he generally recovers rather quickly. The Leo man or woman cannot stand being sick. He has to be up and around; lying in bed is quite bothersome for him.

On the whole, the Leo is a brave person. However, he may have to learn the art of being physically courageous. This is generally not one of his natural attributes. If ideas or principles are at stake he is not afraid to stand up and let others know his opinion; but where physical dangers are involved he may be somewhat fearful.

The Leo man or woman has a deep love of life. He can be quite pleasure-oriented. He likes the good things that life has to offer. Sometimes he is over-enthusiastic in his approach to things, and as a result accidents occur. Under certain conditions he may take chances that others wouldn't. It is important that the person born under this sign learn how to curb impulsiveness, as often it works against him.

The Leo woman is often charming and beautiful. She seldom has any trouble in finding a mate. Men are drawn to her almost automatically because of her grace and poise. They are known for their attractive eyes and regal bearing. Their features are often fine and delicate. There is seldom anything gross about a woman born under the sign of Leo, even when they tend to be heavy-set or large. There is always something fine that is easy to recognize in their build and carriage.

Even when they become older, Leo people remain energetic. Their zest for life never dies. They can prolong their lives, by avoiding excesses in drinking or in general life-style.

Occupation

The Leo seems to gravitate to jobs where he will have a chance to exercise his ability to manage. He is best suited to positions of authority; people respect the decisions he makes. He seems to be a natural-born leader. He knows how to take command of any situation in which he finds himself. The decisions he makes are usually just. He is direct in the way he handles his business affairs. When dealing with others he is open. He says what he means—even if he runs the danger of being blunt or offensive. He is the kind of person who believes that honesty is the best policy. Lies don't go down well with him. The truth—even if it is painful—is better than a kind lie.

In spite of the fact that the Leo person is sometimes critical to a fault, the people who work under him generally respect him and try to understand him. They seldom have reason to question his authority.

In work situations, the Leo always tries to do his best. His interest in being the top person has considerable motivational force. He is not interested in second place; only the top position is good enough for him. He will strive until he gets the position he feels is his due. The Leo person generally has a good understanding of the way things work and how to improve work situations so that better results can be obtained. He knows how to handle people—how they think and how they behave. His understanding of human nature is considerable. He is not the kind of person to rest on his laurels. He is always in search of ways to better an existing situation. He knows how to move along with the times and always tries to keep abreast of new developments in his field.

He is a proud person. In every struggle—be it physical or intellecutal—he fights to win. Failure is something he finds difficult to accept. He seldom considers the possibility; success is the only thing he keeps in mind as he works. He coordinates all of his energies and efforts so that success is almost guaranteed. Dull, routine work he is glad to leave to others. His interest lies in the decision-making area of business. He wants to discuss important issues and have a hand in making policies.

He leads things well; there can be no question of that. He is deeply interested in others, and he would never abuse his position as supervisor or manager, but use it to help those working under him.

On the whole, he is a responsible person. He handles his duties capably. He does not, however, enjoy being told what to do. When others try to lord it over him, he is likely to resent it—sometimes quite violently. He feels that no one is in a position to lead him. He often finds fault with the way others try to run things; sometimes he is quite just in his criticism.

The person born under this sign usually does well in a position where he has to deal with the public. He knows how to be persuasive in his argument. Others seldom have reason to doubt his word, for he is usually sure of what he has to say. A Leo person is likely to do well in any kind of business where he is given an opportunity to make use of his managerial skills. Politics is another area where the man or woman born under this sign is apt to do quite well.

As was mentioned before, many Leos seem to be natural-born actors. They have convincing ease when on the stage; they know how to immerse themselves completely in a dramatic role. They do well in almost any kind of creative work. They have the soul of an artist or poet. In whatever he does, theater work, politics, advertising, or industrial management, the Leo will do what he can to occupy the top position. If he does not have it in the beginning, you can be sure he is working toward it.

The Leo person is far from being stingy. He loves entertaining his friends and relatives in a royal manner. Generous, sometimes to a fault, he is far from being careless with his money. He has a deep-hidden fear of being poor. He'll do what he can to protect his interests. The Leo man or woman is generally fortunate enough to occupy a position that pays well. If he earns a lot, he is apt to spend a lot. He does not like to have to count pennies. Luxurious surroundings give him the feeling of success. Money is seldom a problem to the wise Leo man or woman. Some of them wind up considerably well-off early in life. They usually don't mind taking chances with their finances; quite often they are lucky in speculation or gambling.

If he feels that someone is in serious financial trouble he does not mind helping him out. He is generous and good-hearted when it comes to lending money; but he doesn't like to be taken advantage of. If someone makes unnecessary demands of him financially, he is apt to become disagreeable.

He likes giving people he cares for presents. The gifts he gives are usually expensive and in good taste. He likes to please others—to make them grateful for the gifts he has given them. He likes others to think well of him and that is perhaps why he is rather keen on giving presents. He likes to be the one others turn to when in trouble or lean on for support.

A show of wealth makes the Leo feel important. The cultivated Leo sees to it that his extravagance never becomes unreasonable or unbearable.

Home and Family

The Leo man or woman needs a place where he can relax in peace and quiet. His home is his castle. He likes to live in a place that radiates comfort and harmony. Home life is important to the Leo person. He likes to feel that his family needs him—financially as well as emotionally. He likes to be the one who runs things at home. He expects his standards to be upheld by the other members of his family. He is generally a good provider.

The Leo person makes an excellent host. He knows how to make his guests feel at home. He likes to entertain his close friends quite often. The Leo woman does everything she can to make her guests feel they are liked and cared for. She is usually a very attentive hostess.

When the Leo person spends money it is usually to show that he is capable of spending it. For him it is a display of power or success. It lets others know what he is worth. He sees to it that his home has all of the latest appliances and luxuries. He enjoys impressing others by his clothes and furnishings, even though this may encourage them to envy him.

The woman born under this sign usually enjoys dressing well. Her wardrobe is apt to be large. If she is able, she may not wear the same thing more than once or twice. She is very conscious of being in style. If her husband is not a big earner, she may be quite a burden, for her extravagance is sometimes boundless. If she is married to a man who is not in a top earning position, she will do what she can to help him achieve it.

The Leo person is fond of children. Leos enjoy taking care of them and seeing them grow up. Sometimes, however, they are too forceful as parents and don't give their children a chance to develop their own potential. They like to be proud of their offspring and appreciate it when others pay them compliments about their children's behavior. Some Leo parents love their children so much that they are blind to their faults. They become angry if others should accuse them of spoiling their children. They are anxious to see their children succeed and sometimes expect too much of them too soon. When the children reach adulthood and assert their own will, the Leo parent is apt to feel that his children are not appreciative for all that he has done for them. He may resent their show of independence.

Social Relationships

Leo people have no trouble making friends. People seem to gravitate to them. It is unusual for someone born under this sign not to be popular. They are warm, friendly, and considerate. People like them because of their sure, authoritative ways. Leo people know how to keep the friends they make. They are outgoing, open, and helpful. They never refuse someone in real need.

They usually have what is popularly known as "personality". They are never dull or retiring people. They are always out front where they can easily be seen. They like having a rich and active social life. Sometimes they make considerable gains in their business affairs, through social activities. For them, business and pleasure can mix. They are never short of important contacts.

Those who love Leos accept their leadership without having any qualms. They trust their good judgement; their ability to regulate things. They like mixing with people, but still, they may feel it necessary to keep some distance.

LOVE AND MARRIAGE

Love is an important area of the Leo's life. Leos are very emotional and apt to get carried away in love. They take all kinds of risks in order to win someone they are fond of. When amorous, Leos may lose all sense of what is wrong and what is right.

Leos are sentimental and easily moved. Every love affair is serious to them. They may flirt from time to time, but when earnest in love they do what they can to make it permanent. A Leo is very affectionate by nature and he displays this in private. He or she is not fond of being demonstrative in public places. Somehow Leo feels this is undignified. Love and affection should be kept between two people in private. When in love, Leos are faithful. They do not believe in cheating; constancy is important to them. Generally speaking, Leo people are attractive and are never at a loss for company. The opposite sex falls under the charm of a Leo person quite easily. When looking for a permanent mate, the wise and cultivated Leo chooses someone who is not jealous or possessive—someone who won't suspect him of infidelity if he finds someone else attractive and is quite frank about it.

Romance and the Leo Woman

The Leo woman is passionate by nature. She is very warm and giving when in love. Men find her a very desirable creature and are apt to lose their heads over her when in love. She has an undeniable charm for the opposite sex. Other women are not apt to care for her when men are in the vicinity, for she has no trouble in outshining them all. She is serious when it comes to love. She may have many love affairs before she settles down, but all of them will be serious; she almost never flirts. She doesn't like a jealous or possessive man; she wants the person she loves to trust her implicitly. She doesn't like her love to be doubted.

She likes to be active socially. She enjoys being catered to by the man who loves her. She is fond of parties and entertainment. The man who courts her may have to spend quite a bit of money in order to please her. Sometimes, she is rather dreamy when in love and chooses the wrong man for a partner.

She is the kind of woman who stands behind her man in all that she does. She does what she can to help him ascend the ladder of success. She is an intelligent conversationalist and can often entertain her husband's business associates in such a way that her husband can make important gains. She is a charming hostess.

The Leo mother is affectionate and understanding. She will do all she can to see to it that her children are brought up properly.

Romance and the Leo Man

The Leo man is considered a real Casanova by many. He is passionate when in love and will stop at nothing to please the object of his affection. Women love his fiery, sure nature. They feel safe and secure when they are with him. He is a difficult person for many a woman to resist. When romancing someone, the Leo does what he can to keep the affair exciting and happy. He lavishes gifts on the person he loves. Dining and dancing at the best places in town are something the Leo person is likely to be fond of when dating.

If the Leo person loves someone he is likely to be blind to her faults. He may be more in love with his idea of a person than with the person herself. So caught up is he in his passion that he is likely to forget all practical matters. Sometimes the Leo marries unluckily because of this. He idolizes his love to such an extent that he feels she is incapable of human faults and weaknesses.

The Leo man is a passionate lover. He woos the woman of his choice until he wins her. It is important for him to love, and to have that love returned. Women are easily attracted to him because of his charming ways. He knows how to make a woman feel important and wanted.

He is serious about love. He doesn't believe in meaningless flings. He is very concerned with appearance and is easily attracted to a goodlooking woman. He is apt to build a certain fantasy world around the woman he loves and set her on a high pedestal. He will do everything he can to make her happy. He is an attentive lover and is fond of presenting his loved one with presents. He does not like possessive or jealous women. He wants his sweetheart or wife to give him the freedom he feels he is entitled to. Although he may be attracted to other women after marriage, it is unlikely that he will ever be unfaithful.

As a parent and husband he is an excellent provider. He likes to be admired by his family. He may become rather irritable if he feels his family is not as loving and as affectionate as he is. He wants his family to be one he can be proud of.

Woman—Man

LEO WOMAN
ARIES MAN

The man born under the sign of Aries is often attracted to the Leo woman. In you he can find that mixture of intellect and charm that is often difficult to find in a woman.

In some ways, the Aries man resembles an intellectual mountain goat leaping from crag to crag. He has an insatiable thirst for knowledge. He is ambitious and is apt to have his finger in many pies. He can do with a woman like you—someone attractive, quick-witted, and smart.

He is not interested in a clinging vine kind of wife, but someone who is there when he needs her; someone who listens and understands what he says; someone who can give advice if he should ever have to ask for it—which is not likely to be often. The Aries man wants a woman who is a good companion and a good sport. He is looking for a woman who will look good on his arm without hanging on it too heavily. He is looking for a woman who has both feet on the ground and yet is mysterious and enticing—a kind of domestic Helen of Troy whose face or fine dinner can launch a thousand business deals if need be. That woman he is in search of sounds a little like you, doesn't it. If the shoe fits, wear it. It will make you feel like Cinderella.

The Aries man makes a good husband. He is faithful and attentive. He is an affectionate kind of man. He'll make you feel needed and loved. Love is a serious matter for the Aries man. He does not believe in flirting or playing the field—especially after he's found the woman of his dreams. He'll expect you to be as constant in your affection as he is in his. He'll expect you to be one hundred percent his; he won't put up with any nonsense while romancing you.

The Aries man may be pretty progressive and modern about

many things; however, when it comes to wearing the pants he's downright conventional; it's strictly male attire. The best position you can take in the relationship is a supporting one. He's the boss and that's that. Once you have learned to accept that, you'll find the going easy.

The Aries man, with his endless energy and drive, likes to relax in the comfort of his home at the end of the day. The good home-maker can be sure of holding his love. He's keen on slippers and pipe, and a comfortable armchair. If you see to it that everything in the house is where he expects to find it, you'll have no difficulty keeping the relationship on an even keel.

Life and love with an Aries man may be just the medicine you need. He'll be a good provider. He'll spoil you if he's financially able.

He's young at heart and can get along easily with children.

LEO WOMAN
TAURUS MAN

If you've got your heart set on a man born under the sign of Tau-rus, you'll have to learn the art of being patient. Taureans take their time about everything—even love.

The steady and deliberate Taurus man is a little slow on the draw; it may take him quite a while before he gets around to pop-ping that question. For the Leo woman who doesn't mind twid-dling her thumbs, the waiting and anticipating almost always pays off in the end. Taurus men want to make sure that every step they take is a good one—particularly, if they feel that the path they're on could lead to the altar.

If you are in the mood for a whirlwind romance, you had bet-ter cast your net in shallower waters. Moreover, most Taureans prefer to do the angling themselves. They are not keen on women taking the lead; once she does, he's liable to drop her like a dead fish. If you let yourself get caught on his terms, you'll find that he's fallen for you—hook, line, and sinker.

The Taurus man is fond of a comfortable homelife. It is very important to him. If you keep those home fires burning you will have no trouble keeping that flame in your Taurean's heart aglow. You have a talent for homemaking; use it. Your taste in furnish-ings is excellent. You know how to make a house come alive with inviting colors and decorations.

Taurus, the strong, steady, and protective Bull could be the answer to your prayers. Perhaps he could be the anchor for your dreams and plans. He could help you acquire a more balanced out-look and approach to your life. If you're given to impulsiveness, he could help you to curb it. He's the man who is always there when you need him.

When you tie the knot with a man born under Taurus, you can put away fears about creditors pounding on the front door. Taureans are practical about everything including bill-paying. When he carries you over that threshold, you can be certain that the entire house is paid for, not only the doorsill.

As a housewife, you won't have to worry about putting aside your many interests for the sake of back-breaking house chores. Your Taurus husband will see to it that you have all the latest time-saving appliances and comforts.

You can forget about acquiring premature gray hairs due to unruly, ruckus-raising children under your feet. Papa Taurus is a master at keeping offspring in line. He's crazy about kids but he also knows what's good for them.

LEO WOMAN
GEMINI MAN

The Gemini man is quite a catch. Many a woman has set her cap for him and failed to bag him. Generally, Gemini men are intelligent, witty, and outgoing. Many of them tend to be rather versatile. The Gemini man could easily wind up being your better half.

One thing that causes a Twin's mind and affection to wander is a bore, and it is unlikely that an active Leo woman would ever allow herself to be accused of that. The Gemini man that has caught your heart will admire you for your ideas and intellect—perhaps even more than for your home-making talents and good looks.

The Leo woman needn't feel that once she's made her marriage vows that she'll have to store her interests and ambition in the attic somewhere. The Gemini man will admire you for your zeal and liveliness. He's the kind of guy who won't scowl if you let him shift for himself in the kitchen once in a while. In fact, he'll enjoy the challenge of wrestling with pots and pans himself for a change. Chances are, too, that he might turn out to be a better cook than you—that is, if he isn't already.

The man born under the sign of the Twins is a very active person. There aren't many women who have enough pep to keep up with him. But pep is no problem for the spry Leo woman. You are both dreamers, planners, and idealists. The strong Leo woman can easily fill the role of rudder for her Geminian's ship-without-a-sail. If you are a cultivated, purposeful Leo, he won't mind it at all. The intelligent Twin is often aware of his shortcomings and doesn't resent it if someone with better bearings gives him a shove in the right direction—when it's needed. The average Gemini does not have serious ego-hangups and will even accept a well-deserved chewing out from his mate quite gracefully.

When you and your Gemini man team up, you'll probably always have a houseful of people to entertain—interesting people, too; Geminians find it hard to tolerate sluggish minds and dispositions.

People born under Gemini generally have two sides to their natures, as different as night and day. It's very easy for them to be happy-go-lucky one minute, then down in the dumps the next. They hate to be bored and will generally do anything to make their lives interesting, vivid, and action-packed.

Gemini men are always attractive to the opposite sex. You'll perhaps have to allow him an occasional harmless flirt—it will seldom amount to more than that if you're his proper mate.

The Gemini father is a pushover for children. He loves them so much, he generally lets them do what they want.

LEO WOMAN
CANCER MAN

Chances are you won't hit it off too well with the man born under Cancer if love is your object, but then Cupid has been known to do some pretty unlikely things. The Cancerian is a very sensitive man—thin-skinned and occasionally moody. You've got to keep on your toes—and not step on his—if you're determined to make a go of the relationship.

The Cancer man may be lacking in many of the qualities you seek in a man, but when it comes to being faithful and being a good provider, he's hard to beat.

It is the perceptive Leo woman who will not mistake the Crab's quietness for sullenness or his thriftiness for pennypinching. In some respects, he is like that wise old owl out on a limb; he may look like he's dozing but actually he hasn't missed a thing. Cancerians often possess a well of knowledge about human behavior; they can come across with some pretty helpful advice to those in trouble. He can certainly guide you in making investments both in time and in money. He may not say much, but he's always got his wits about him.

The Crab may not be the match or the catch for many a Leo woman; in fact, he is likely to seem downright dull to the on-the-move Leo girl. True to his sign, he can be fairly cranky and crabby when handled the wrong way. He is perhaps more sensitive than he should be.

Leo people are usually as smart as a whip. If you're clever, you will never in any way convey the idea that you consider your Cancerian a little short on brain power. Browbeating is a sure-fire way of sending the Crab angrily scurrying back to his shell—and it's quite possible that all of that lost ground will never be recovered.

The Crab is most himself at home. Once settled down for the night or the weekend, wild horses couldn't drag him any farther than the gatepost—that is, unless those wild horses were dispatched by his mother. The Crab is sometimes a Momma's boy. If his mate doesn't put her foot down, he will see to it that his mother always comes first. No self-respecting Leo would ever allow herself to play second fiddle—even if it's to her old gray-haired mother-in-law. If she's tactful, she'll discover that slipping into number one position is as easy as pie (that legendary one his mother used to bake).

If you pamper your Cancer man, you'll find that "mother" turns up increasingly less—at the front door as well as in conversations.

Cancerians make protective, proud, and patient fathers.

LEO WOMAN
LEO MAN

You probably won't have any trouble understanding the Leo man as you were born under the same sign. Still, some conflict is possible due to the fact that you both are very much alike. Be tactful and tolerant in a Leo-Leo relationship.

For many women, Leo is the sign of love. When the Lion puts his mind to romance, he doesn't stint. If he has it his way, it will be all wining, dining, and dancing till the wee hours of the morning.

The Leo man is all heart and knows how to make his woman feel like a woman. More often than not, he is a man a woman can look up to. He's a man who manages to have full control of just about any situation he finds himself in. He's a winner.

The Leo man may not look like Tarzan, but he knows how to roar and beat his chest if he has to. He's the kind of man you can lean upon. He'll also give you support in your plans and projects. He's often capable of giving advice that pays off. Leo men are direct. They don't pussyfoot around.

Leo men often rise to the top of their profession and through their examples, prove to be great sources of inspiration to others.

Although he's a ladies' man, the Leo man is very particular about his ladies. His standards are high when it comes to love interests. He believes that romance should be played on a fair give-and-take basis. He won't put up with any monkey-shines in a love relationship. It's all or nothing.

You'll find him a frank, off-the-shoulder person; he generally says what is on his mind.

If you decide that a Leo man is the one for you, be prepared to stand behind him full-force. He expects it—and usually deserves it. He's the head of the house and can handle that position without a hitch. He knows how to go about breadwinning and, if he has his way (and most Leos do have their own way), he'll see to it that you'll have all the luxuries you crave and the comforts you need.

It's unlikely that the romance in your marriage will ever die out. Lions need love like flowers need sunshine. They're ever-amorous and generally expect like attention and affection from their mate. Lions are fond of going out on the town; they love to give parties as well as go to them. You should encounter no difficulties in sharing his interests in this direction.

Leos make strict fathers, generally. You'll have to do your best to smooth down your children's roughed-up feelings.

LEO WOMAN
VIRGO MAN

The Virgo man is all business—or he may seem so to you. He is usually very cool, calm, and collected. He's perhaps too much of a fuss-budget to wake up deep romantic interests in a Leo woman. Torrid romancing to him is just so much sentimental mush. He can do without it and can make that quite evident in short order. He's keen on chastity and, if necessary, he can lead a sedentary, sexless life without caring too much about the fun others think he's missing. In short, you are liable to find him a first-class dud. He doesn't have much of an imagination; flights of fancy don't interest him. He is always correct and likes to be handled correctly. Almost everything about him is orderly. "There's a place for everything" is likely to be an adage he'll fall upon quite regularly.

He does have an honest-to-goodness heart, believe it or not. The Leo woman who finds herself strangely attracted to his cool, feet-flat-on-the-ground ways, will discover that his is a constant heart, not one that goes in for flings or sordid affairs. Virgos take an awfully long time to warm up to someone. A practical man, even in matters of the heart, he wants to know just what kind of a person you are before he takes a chance on you.

The impulsive Leo girl had better not make the mistake of kissing her Virgo friend on the street—even if it's only a peck on the cheek. He's not at all demonstrative and hates public displays of affection. Love, according to him, should be kept within the confines of one's home—with the curtains drawn. Once he believes that you are on the level with him as far as your love is concerned, you'll see how fast he can lose his cool. Virgos are considerate, gentle lovers. He'll spend a long time, though, getting to know you. He'll like you before he loves you.

A Leo-Virgo romance can be a sometime—or, rather, a one-time thing. If the bottom ever falls out, don't bother reaching for the adhesive tape. Nine times out of ten he won't care about patching up. He's a once-burnt-twice-shy guy. When he crosses your telephone number out of his address book, he's crossing you out of his life for good.

Neat as a pin, he's thumbs-down on what he considers "sloppy" housekeeping. An ashtray with just one stubbed-out cigarette in it can annoy him even if it's just two seconds old. Glassware should always sparkle and shine.

If you marry him, keep your kids spic-and-span, at least by the time he gets home from work. Train them to be kind and courteous.

LEO WOMAN
LIBRA MAN

If there's a Libran in your life, you are most likely a very happy woman. Men born under this sign have a way with women. You'll always feel at ease in a Libran's company; you can be yourself when you're with him.

Like you, he can be moody at times. His moodiness, though, is more puzzling. One moment he comes on hard and strong with declarations of his love, the next moment you find that he's left you like yesterday's mashed potatoes. He'll come back, though; don't worry. Librans are like that. Deep down inside he really knows what he wants even though he may not appear to.

You'll appreciate his admiration of beauty and harmony. If you're dressed to the teeth and never looked lovelier, you'll get a ready compliment—and one that's really deserved. Librans don't indulge in idle flattery. If they don't like something, they are tactful enough to remain silent.

Librans will go to great lengths to preserve peace and harmony—even tell a fat lie if necessary. They don't like show-downs or disagreeable confrontations. The frank Leo woman is all for getting whatever is bothering her off her chest and out into the open, even if it comes out all wrong. To the Libran, making a clean breast of everything seems like sheer folly sometimes.

You may lose your patience while waiting for your Libra friend to make up his mind. It takes him ages sometimes to make a decision. He weighs both sides carefully before committing himself to anything. You seldom dillydally—at least about small things—and so it's likely that you will find it difficult to see eye to eye with a hesitating Libra when it comes to decision-making methods.

All in all, though, he is kind, gentle, and fair. He is interested in the "real" truth; he'll try to balance everything out until he has all the correct answers. It is not difficult for him to see both sides of a story.

He's a peace-loving man. The sight of blood is apt to turn his stomach.

Librans are not showoffs. Generally, they are well-balanced people. Honest, wholesome, and affectionate, they are serious about every love encounter they have. If he should find that the girl he's dating is not really suited to him, he will end the relationship in such a tactful manner that no hard feelings will come about.

The Libra father is firm, gentle, and patient.

LEO WOMAN
SCORPIO MAN

Many people have a hard time understanding a man born under the sign of Scorpio. Few, however, are able to resist his fiery charm.

When angered, he can act like an overturned wasps' nest; his sting is capable of leaving an almost permanent mark. If you find yourself interested in a man born under this sign, you'd better learn how to keep on the good side of him. If he's in love with you, you'll know about it. Scorpio men let no one get in their way when they are out to win a certain heart. When it comes to romance, they never take "no" for an answer.

The Scorpio man can be quite blunt when he chooses; at times, he'll strike you as being a brute. His touchiness may get on your nerves after a while and if it does, you'd better tiptoe away from the scene rather than chance an explosive confrontation. He's capable of giving you a sounding-out that will make you pack your bags and go back to mother—for good.

You're the kind of woman who can put up with almost anything once you put your mind and heart to it. A stormy Scorpio relationship may be worth its ups and downs. Scorpio men are all quite perceptive and intelligent. In some respects, they know how to use their brains more effectively than others. They believe in winning in whatever they do—and in business, they usually achieve the position they want through drive and intellect.

He doesn't give a hoot for homelife, generally. He doesn't like being tied down. He would rather be out on the battlefield of life, belting away at what he feels is a just and worthy cause.

Many women are easily attracted to him. You are perhaps no exception. Know what you're getting into, before you go making any promises to him. Women who allow themselves to be swept off their feet by a Scorpio man, shortly find that they're dealing with a pepper pot of seething excitement. He's passion with a capital P, make no mistake about that.

Scorpios are straight to the point. They can be as sharp as a razor blade and just as cutting. Don't give him cause to find fault with you and you'll do just fine.

If you decide to marry him and take the bitter with the sweet, prepare yourself for a challenging relationship. Chances are you won't have as much time for your own interests as you'd like. Your Scorpio man may keep you at his beck and call.

In spite of the ins and outs of his difficult character, the Scorpio man makes an acceptable father.

LEO WOMAN
SAGITTARIUS MAN

If you've set your cap for a man born under the sign of Sagittarius, you may have to apply an awful lot of strategy before you can persuade him to get down on bended knee. Although some Sagittarians may be marriage-shy, they're not ones to skitter away from romance. You'll find a love relationship with a Sagittarian—whether a fling or "the real thing"—a very enjoyable experience.

As a rule, Sagittarians are bright, happy, and healthy people. They have a strong sense of fair play. Often they are a source of inspiration to others. They are full of drive and ideas.

You'll be taken by the Sagittarian's infectious grin and his light-hearted friendly nature. If you do wind up being the woman in his life, you'll find that he's apt to treat you more like a buddy than the love of his life. It's just his way. Sagittarians are often more chummy than romantic.

You'll admire his broadmindedness in most matters—including those of the heart. If, while dating you, he claims that he still wants to play the field, he'll expect you to enjoy the same liberty. Once he's promised to love, honor, and obey, however, he does just that. Marriage for him, once he's taken that big step, is very serious business.

The Sagittarius man is quick-witted. He has a genuine interest in equality. He hates prejudice and injustice. Generally, Sagittarians are good at sports. They love the great out-of-doors and respect wildlife in all its forms.

He's not much of a homebody. Quite often he's occupied with

far away places either in his daydreams or in reality. He enjoys being on-the-move. He's got ants in his pants and refuses to sit still for long stretches at a time. Humdrum routine—especially at home—bores him. At the drop of a hat, he may ask you to whip off your apron and dine out for a change. He likes surprising people. He'll take great pride in showing you off to his friends. He'll always be a considerate mate; he will never embarrass or disappoint you intentionally.

His friendly, sun-shiny nature is capable of attracting many people. Like you, he's very tolerant when it comes to friends and you'll most likely spend a great deal of time entertaining people.

Sagittarians are all thumbs when it comes to little shavers. They develop an interest in children as they get older and wiser.

LEO WOMAN
CAPRICORN MAN

A with-it girl like you is likely to find the average Capricorn man a bit of a drag. The man born under the sign of the Goat is often a closed person and difficult to get to know. Even if you do get to know him, you may not find him very interesting.

In romance, Capricorn men are a little on the rusty side. You'll probably have to make all the passes.

You may find his plodding manner, irritating, and his conservative, traditional ways downright maddening. He's not one to take chances on anything. "If it was good enough for my father, it's good enough for me" may be his motto. He follows a way that is tried and true.

Whenever adventure rears its tantalizing head, the Goat will turn the other way; he's just not interested.

He may be just as ambitious as you are—perhaps even more so—but his ways of accomplishing his aims are more subterranean or, at least, seem so. He operates from the background a good deal of the time. At a gathering you may never even notice him but he's there, taking in everything and sizing up everyone—planning his next careful move.

Although Capricorns may be intellectual to a degree, it is generally not the kind of intelligence you appreciate. He may not be as quick or as bright as you; it may take ages for him to understand a simple joke.

If you decide to take up with a man born under this sign, you ought to be pretty good in the "cheering up" department. The Capricorn man often acts as though he's constantly being followed by a cloud of gloom.

The Capricorn man is most himself when in the comfort and

privacy of his own home. The security possible within four walls can make him a happy man. He'll spend as much time as he can at home. If he is loaded down with extra work, he'll bring it home instead of working overtime at the office.

You'll most likely find yourself frequently confronted by his relatives. Family is very important to the Capricorn—*his* family that is. They had better take a pretty important place in your life, too, if you want to keep your home a happy one.

Although his caution in most matters may all but drive you up the wall, you'll find his concerned way with money justified most of the time. He'll plan everything right down to the last penny.

He can be quite a scold when it comes to disciplining children. You'll have to step in and soften things.

LEO WOMAN
AQUARIUS MAN

Aquarians love everybody—even their worst enemies, sometimes. Through your relationship with an Aquarian you'll find yourself running into all sorts of people, ranging from near-genius to down-right insane—and they're all friends of his.

As a rule, Aquarians are extremely friendly and open. Of all the signs, they are perhaps the most tolerant. In the thinking department, they are often miles ahead of others.

You'll most likely find your relationship with this man a challenging one. Your high respect for intelligence and imagination may be reason enough for you to settle your heart on a Water Bearer. You'll find that you can learn a lot from him.

In the holding-hands phase of your romance, you may find that your Water Bearing friend has cold feet. Aquarians take quite a bit of warming up before they are ready to come across with that first goodnight kiss. More than likely, he'll just want to be your pal in the beginning. For him, that's an important first step in any relationship—love, included. The "poetry and flowers" stage—if it ever comes—will be later. The Aquarian is all heart; still, when it comes to tying himself down to one person and for keeps, he is liable to hesitate. He may even try to get out of it if you breathe down his neck too heavily.

The Aquarius man is no Valentino and wouldn't want to be. The kind of love-life he's looking for is one that's made up mainly for companionship. Although he may not be very romantic, the memory of his first romance will always hold an important position in his heart. Sometimes Aquarians wind up marrying their childhood sweethearts.

You won't find it difficult to look up to a man born under the sign of the Water Bearer, but you may find the challenge of trying to keep up with him dizzying. He can pierce through the most complicated problem as if it were a matter of 2 + 2. You may find him a little too lofty and high-minded—but don't judge him too harshly if that's the case; he's way ahead of his time—your time, too, most likely.

If you marry this man, he'll stay true to you. Don't think that once the honeymoon is over, you'll be chained to the kitchen sink forever. Your Aquarius husband will encourage you to keep active in your own interests and affairs. You'll most likely have a minor tiff now and again but never anything serious.

Kids love him and vice-versa. He'll be as tolerant with them as he is with adults.

LEO WOMAN
PISCES MAN

The man born under Pisces is quite a dreamer. Sometimes he's so wrapped up in his dreams that he's difficult to reach. To the average ambitious woman, he may seem a little sluggish.

He's easy-going most of the time. He seems to take things in his stride. He'll entertain all kinds of views and opinions from just about anyone, nodding or smiling vaguely, giving the impression that he's with them one hundred percent while that may not be the case at all. His attitude may be "why bother" when he is confronted with someone wrong who thinks he's right. The Pisces man will seldom speak his mind if he thinks he'll be rigidly opposed.

The Pisces man is oversensitive at times—he's afraid of getting his feelings hurt. He'll sometimes imagine a personal injury when none's been made at all. Chances are you'll find this complex of his maddening; at times you may feel like giving him a swift kick where it hurts the most. It wouldn't do any good, though. It would just add fuel to the fire of his persecution complex.

One thing you will admire about this man is his concern for people who are sickly or troubled. He'll make his shoulder available to anyone in the mood for a good cry. He can listen to one hard-luck story after another without seeming to tire. When his advice is asked, he is capable of coming across with some pretty important words of wisdom. He often knows what is bugging someone before that person is aware of it himself. It's almost intuitive with Pisceans, it seems. Still, at the end of the day, he looks forward to some peace and quiet. If you've got a problem on your mind when he comes home, don't unload it in his lap. If you do, you're liable to find him short-tempered. He's a good listener, but he can only take so much.

Pisces men are not aimless although they may seem so at times. The positive sort of Pisces man is quite often successful in his profession and is likely to wind up rich and influential. Material gain, however, is not a direct goal for a man born under this sign.

The weaker Piscean is usually content to stay put on the level where he finds himself. He won't complain too much if the roof leaks and the fence is in need of repair. He'll just shrug it off as a minor inconvenience.

Because of their seemingly laissez-faire manner, people under this sign—needless to say—are immensely popular with children. For tots they play the double role of confidant and playmate. It will never enter his mind to discipline a child, no matter how spoiled or incorrigible that child becomes.

Man—Woman

LEO MAN
ARIES WOMAN

The Aries woman is quite a charmer. When she tugs at the strings of your heart, you'll know it. She's a woman who's in search of a knight in shining armor. She is a very particular person with very high ideals. She won't accept anyone but the man of her dreams.

The Aries woman never plays around with passion; she means business when it comes to love.

Don't get the idea that she's a dewy-eyed Miss. She isn't. In fact, she can be pretty practical and to-the-point when she wants. She's a girl with plenty of drive and ambition. With an Aries woman behind you, you are liable to go far in life. She knows how to help her man get ahead. She's full of wise advice; you only have to ask. In some cases, the Aries woman has a keen business sense; many of them become successful career women. There is nothing backward or retiring about her. She is equipped with a good brain and she knows how to use it.

Your union with her could be something strong, secure, and romantic. If both of you have your sights fixed in the same direction, there is almost nothing that you could not accomplish.

The Aries woman is proud and capable of being quite jealous. While you're with her, never cast your eye in another woman's direction. It could spell disaster for your relationship. The Aries woman won't put up with romantic nonsense when her heart is at stake.

If the Aries woman backs you up in your business affairs, you can be sure of succeeding. However, if she only is interested in advancing her own career and puts her interests before yours, she can be sure of rocking the boat. It will put a strain on the relationship. The over-ambitious Aries woman can be a pain in the neck and make you forget that you were in love with her once.

The cultivated Aries woman makes a wonderful wife and mother. She has a natural talent for home-making. With a pot of paint and some wallpaper, she can transform the dreariest domicile into an abode of beauty and snug comfort. The perfect hostess—even when friends just happen by —she knows how to make guests feel at home.

You'll also admire your Arien because she knows how to stand on her own two feet. Hers is of an independent nature. She won't break down and cry when things go wrong, but pick herself up and try to patch matters.

The Aries woman makes a fine, affectionate mother.

LEO MAN
TAURUS WOMAN

The woman born under the sign of Taurus may lack a little of the sparkle and bubble you often like to find in a woman. The Taurus woman is generally down-to-earth and never flighty. It's important to her that she keep both feet flat on the ground. She is not fond of bounding all over the place, especially if she's under the impression that there's no profit in it.

On the other hand, if you hit it off with a Taurus woman, you won't be disappointed at all in the romance area. The Taurus woman is all woman and proud of it, too. She can be very devoted and loving once she decides that her relationship with you is no fly-by-night romance. Basically, she's a passionate person. In sex, she's direct and to-the-point. If she really loves you, she'll let you know she's yours—and without reservations. Better not flirt with other women once you've committed yourself to her. She is capable of being jealous and possessive.

She'll stick by you through thick and thin. It's almost certain that if the going ever gets rough, she'll not go running home to her mother. She can adjust to hard times just as graciously as she can to the good times.

Taureans are, on the whole, pretty even-tempered. They like to be treated with kindness. Pretty things and soft things make them purr like kittens.

You may find her a little slow and deliberate. She likes to be safe and sure about everything. Let her plod along if she likes; don't coax her but just let her take her own sweet time. Everything she does is done thoroughly and, generally, without mistakes. Don't deride her for being a kind of slow-poke. It could lead to flying pots and pans and a fireworks display that would put Bastille Day to shame. The Taurus woman doesn't anger readily but when prodded often enough, she's capable of letting loose with a cyclone of ill-will. If you treat her with kindness and consideration, you'll have no cause for complaint.

The Taurean loves doing things for her man. She's a whiz in the kitchen and can whip up feasts fit for a king if she thinks they'll be royally appreciated. She may not fully understand you, but she'll adore you and be faithful to you if she feels you're worthy of it.

The woman born under Taurus will make a wonderful mother. She knows how to keep her children well-loved, cuddled, and warm. She may find them difficult to manage, however, when they reach the teenage stage.

LEO MAN
GEMINI WOMAN

You may find a romance with a woman born under the sign of the Twins a many-splendored thing. In her you can find the intellectual companionship you often look for in a friend or mate. A Gemini girl friend can appreciate your aims and desires because she travels pretty much the same road as you do intellectually —that is, at least part of the way. She may share your interest but she will lack your tenacity.

She suffers from itchy feet. She can be here, there . . . all over the place and at the same time, or so it would seem. Her eagerness to move about may make you dizzy; still you'll enjoy and appreciate her liveliness and mental agility.

Geminians often have sparkling personalities; you'll be attracted by her warmth and grace. While she's on your arm you'll probably notice that many male eyes are drawn to her—she may even return a gaze or two, but don't let that worry you. All women born under this sign have nothing against a harmless flirt once in a while. They enjoy this sort of attention; if she feels she is already spoken for, however, she will never let it get out of hand.

Although she may not be as handy as you'd like in the kitchen, you'll never go hungry for a filling and tasty meal. She's as much in a hurry as you are, and won't feel like she's cheating by breaking out the instant mashed potatoes or the frozen peas. She may not be much of a cook but she is clever; with a dash of this and a suggestion of that, she can make an uninteresting TV dinner taste like something out of a Jim Beard cookbook. Then, again, maybe you've struck it rich and have a Gemini girl friend who finds complicated recipes a challenge to her intellect. If so, you'll find every meal a tantalizing and mouth-watering surprise.

When you're beating your brains out over the Sunday crossword puzzle and find yourself stuck, just ask your Gemini girlie; she'll give you all the right answers without batting an eyelash.

Like you, she loves all kinds of people. You may even find that you're a bit more particular than she. Often all that a Geminian requires is that her friends be interesting . . . and stay interesting. One thing she's not able to abide is a dullard.

Leave the party-organizing to your Gemini sweetheart or mate and you'll never have a chance to know what a dull moment is. She'll bring the swinger out in you if you give her half a chance.

A Gemini mother enjoys her children. Like them, she's often restless, adventurous, and easily bored.

LEO MAN
CANCER WOMAN

If you fall in love with a Cancer woman, be prepared for anything. Cancerians are sometimes difficult to understand when it comes to love. In one hour, she can unravel a whole gamut of emotions that will leave you in a tizzy. She'll keep you guessing, that's for sure.

You may find her a little too uncertain and sensitive for your liking. You'll most likely spend a good deal of time encouraging her—helping her to erase her foolish fears. Tell her she's a living doll a dozen times a day and you'll be well loved in return.

Be careful of the jokes you make when in her company—don't let any of them revolve around her, her personal interests, or her family. If you do, you'll most likely reduce her to tears. She can't stand being made fun of. It will take bushels of roses and tons of chocolates—not to mention the apologies—to get her to come back out of her shell.

In matters of money-managing, she may not easily come around to your way of thinking. Money will never burn a hole in her pocket. You may get the notion that your Cancerian sweetheart or mate is a direct descendant of Scrooge. If she has her way, she'll hang onto that first dollar you earned. She's not only that way with money, but with everything right on up from bakery string to jelly jars. She's a saver; she never throws anything away, no matter how trivial.

Once she returns your "I love you", you'll find you have an affectionate, self-sacrificing, and devoted woman on your hands. Her love for you will never alter unless you want it to. She'll put you high upon a pedestal and will do everything—even if it's against your will—to keep you up there.

Cancer women love home life. For them, marriage is an easy step. They're domestic with a capital D. She'll do her best to make your home comfortable and cozy. She is more at ease at home than anywhere else. She makes an excellent hostess. The best in her comes out when she is in her own environment.

Cancer women make the best mothers of all the signs of the Zodiac. She'll consider every complaint of her child a major catastrophe. With her, children always come first. If you're lucky, you'll run a close second. You'll perhaps see her as too devoted to the children. You may have a hard time convincing her that her apron strings are a little too long.

LEO MAN
LEO WOMAN

If you can manage a girl who likes to kick up her heels every now and again, then the Leo woman was made for you. You'll have to learn to put away jealous fears—or at least forget about them—when you take up with a woman born under this sign, because she's often the kind that makes heads turn and tongues wag. You don't necessarily have to believe any of what you hear—it's most likely just jealous gossip. Take up with a Leo woman and you'll be taking off on a romance full of fire and ice; be prepared to take the good things with the bad—the bitter with the sweet.

The Leo girl has more than a fair share of grace and glamour. She is aware of her charms and knows how to put them to good use. Needless to say, other women in her vicinity turn green with envy and will try anything short of shoving her into the nearest lake, in order to put her out of commission.

If she's captured your heart and fancy, woo her full-force if your intention is to eventually win her. Shower her with expensive gifts and promise her the moon—if you're in a position to go that far—then you'll find her resistance beginning to weaken. It's not that she's such a difficult cookie—she'll probably make a lot over you once she's decided you're the man for her—but she does enjoy a lot of attention. What's more, she feels she's entitled to it. Her mild arrogance, though, is becoming. The Leo woman knows how to transform the crime of excessive pride into a very charming misdemeanor. It sweeps most men right off their feet. Those who do not succumb to her leonine charm are few and far between.

If you've got an important business deal to clinch and you have doubts as to whether or not it will go over, bring your Leo girl along to that business luncheon and it's a cinch that that contract will be yours. She won't have to do or say anything—just be there at your side. The grouchiest oil magnate can be transformed into a gushing, obedient schoolboy if there's a Leo woman in the room.

If you're rich and want to stay that way, don't give your Leo mate a free hand with the charge accounts and credit cards. If you're poor, the luxury-loving Leo will most likely never enter your life.

She makes a strict yet easy-going mother. She loves to pal around with her children.

LEO MAN
VIRGO WOMAN

The Virgo woman may be a little too difficult for you to understand at first. Her waters run deep. Even when you think you know her, don't take any bets on it. She's capable of keeping things hidden in the deep recesses of her womanly soul—things she'll only release when she's sure that you're the man she's been looking for. It may take her some time to come around to this decision. Virgo girls are finicky about almost everything; everything has to be letter-perfect before they're satisfied. Many of them have the idea that the only people who can do things correctly are Virgos.

Nothing offends a Virgo woman more than slovenly dress, sloppy character, or a careless display of affection. Make sure your tie is not crooked and your shoes sport a bright shine before you go calling on this lady. Keep your off-color jokes for the locker-room; she'll have none of that. Take her arm when crossing the street. Don't rush the romance. Trying to corner her in the back of a cab may be one way of striking out. Never criticize the way she looks; in fact, the best policy would be to agree with her as much as possible. Still, there's just so much a man can take; all those dos and don'ts you'll have to observe if you want to get to first base with a Virgo may be just a little too much to ask of you. After a few dates, you may come to the conclusion that she just isn't worth all that trouble. However, the Virgo woman is mysterious enough, generally speaking, to keep her men running back for more. Chances are you'll be intrigued by her airs and graces.

If love-making means a lot to you, you'll be disappointed at first in the cool ways of your Virgo girl. However, under her glacial facade there lies a hot cauldron of seething excitement. If you're patient and artful in your romantic approach, you'll find that all that caution was well worth the trouble. When Virgos love, they don't stint. It's all or nothing as far as they're concerned. Once they're convinced that they love you, they go all the way, right off the bat—tossing all cares to the wind.

One thing a Virgo woman can't stand in love is hypocrisy.

They don't give a hoot about what the neighbors say, if their hearts tell them, "go ahead". They're very concerned with human truths—so much so that if their hearts stumble upon another fancy, they're liable to be true to that new heart-throb and leave you standing in the rain.

She's honest to her heart and will be as true to you as you are with her, generally. Do her wrong once, however, and it's farewell.

She's both strict and tender with children. As a mother she'll try to bring out the best in her children.

LEO MAN
LIBRA WOMAN

You'll probably find that the girl born under the sign of Libra is worth more than her weight in gold. She's a woman after your own heart.

With her, you'll always come first—make no mistake about that. She'll always be behind you 100 percent, no matter what you do. When you ask her advice about almost anything, you'll most likely get a very balanced and realistic opinion. She is good at thinking things out and never lets her emotions run away with her when clear logic is called for.

As a homemaker she is hard to beat. She is very concerned with harmony and balance. You can be sure she'll make your house a joy to live in; she'll see to it that the house is tastefully furnished and decorated. A Libran cannot stand filth or disarray—it gives her goose-bumps. Anything that does not radiate harmony, in fact, runs against her orderly grain.

She is chock-full of charm and womanly ways. She can sweep just about any man off his feet with one winning smile. When it comes to using her brains, she can out-think almost anyone and, sometimes, with half the effort. She is diplomatic enough, though, never to let this become glaringly apparent. She may even turn the conversation around so that you think you were the one who did all the brain-work. She couldn't care less, really, just as long as you wind up doing what is right.

The Libra woman will put you up on a pretty high pedestal. You are her man and her idol. She'll leave all the decision-making, large or small, up to you. She's not interested in running things and will only offer her assistance if she feels you really need it.

Some find her approach to reason masculine; however, in the areas of love and affection the Libra woman is *all* woman. She'll literally shower you with love and kisses during your romance with her. She doesn't believe in holding out. You shouldn't, either, if you want to hang onto her.

She is the kind of girl who likes to snuggle up to you in front of the fire on chilly autumn nights—the kind of girl who will bring you breakfast in bed Sunday. She'll be very thoughtful about anything that concerns you. If anyone dares suggest you're not the grandest guy in the world, she'll give that person what-for. She'll defend you till her dying breath. The Libra woman will be everything you want her to be.

She'll be a sensitive and loving mother. Still, you'll always come before the children.

LEO MAN
SCORPIO WOMAN

The Scorpio woman can be a whirlwind of passion—perhaps too much passion to really suit you. When her temper flies, you'd better lock up the family heirlooms and take cover. When she chooses to be sweet, you're apt to think that butter wouldn't melt in her mouth—but, of course, it would.

The Scorpio woman can be as hot as a tamale or as cool as a cucumber, but whatever mood she's in, she's in it for real. She does not believe in posing or putting on airs.

The Scorpio woman is often sultry and seductive—her femme fatale charm can pierce through the hardest of hearts like a laser beam. She may not look like Mata Hari (quite often Scorpios resemble the tomboy next door) but once she's fixed you with her tantalizing eyes, you're a goner.

Life with the Scorpio woman will not be all smiles and smooth-sailing; when prompted, she can unleash a gale of venom. Generally, she'll have the good grace to keep family battles within the walls of your home. When company visits, she's apt to give the impression that married life with you is one great big joy-ride. It's just one of her ways of expressing her loyalty to you—at least in front of others. She may fight you tooth and nail in the confines of your livingroom, but at a ball or during an evening out, she'll hang onto your arm and have stars in her eyes.

Scorpio women are good at keeping secrets. She may even keep a few buried from you if she feels like it.

Never cross her up on even the smallest thing. When it comes to revenge, she's an eye-for-an-eye woman. She's not too keen on forgiveness—especially if she feels she's been wronged unfairly. You'd be well-advised not to give her any cause to be jealous, either. When the Scorpio woman sees green, your life will be made far from rosy. Once she's put you in the dog-house, you can be sure that you're going to stay there a while.

You may find life with a Scorpio woman too draining. Although she may be full of the old paprika, it's quite likely that she's not the kind of girl you'd like to spend the rest of your natural life with. You'd prefer someone gentler and not so hot-tempered; someone who can take the highs with the lows and not bellyache; someone who is flexible and understanding. A woman born under Scorpio can be heavenly, but she can also be the very devil when she chooses.

As a mother, a Scorpio is protective and encouraging.

LEO MAN
SAGITTARIUS WOMAN

You'll most likely never come across a more good-natured girl than the one born under the sign of Sagittarius. Generally, they're full of bounce and good cheer. Their sunny disposition seems almost permanent and can be relied upon even on the rainiest of days.

Women born under this sign are almost never malicious. If ever they seem to be it is only seeming. Sagittarians are often a little short on tact and say literally anything that comes into their pretty little heads—no matter what the occasion. Sometimes the words that tumble out of their mouths seem downright cutting and cruel. Still, no matter what she says, she means well. The Sagittarius woman is quite capable of losing some of her friends—and perhaps even some of yours—through a careless slip of the lip.

On the other hand, you are liable to appreciate her honesty and good intentions. To you, qualities of this sort play an important part in life. With a little patience and practice, you can probably help cure your Sagittarian of her loose tongue; in most cases, she'll give into your better judgement and try to follow your advice to the letter.

Chances are she'll be the outdoors type of girl friend. Long hikes, fishing trips, and white-water canoeing will most likely appeal to her. She's a busy person; no one could ever call her a slouch. She sets great store in mobility. Her feet are itchy and she won't sit still for a minute if she doesn't have to.

She is great company most of the time and, generally, lots of fun. Even if your buddies drop by for poker and beer, she won't have any trouble fitting in.

On the whole, she is a very kind and sympathetic woman. If she feels she's made a mistake, she'll be the first to call your attention to it. She's not afraid to own up to her faults and shortcomings.

You might lose your patience with her once or twice. After she's seen how upset her shortsightedness or tendency to blabbermouth has made you, she'll do her best to straighten up.

The Sagittarian woman is not the kind who will pry into your business affairs. But she'll always be there, ready to offer advice if you need it. If you come home with red stains on your collar and you say it's paint and not lipstick, she'll believe you.

She'll seldom be suspicious; your word will almost always be good enough for her.

She is a wonderful and loving friend to her children.

LEO MAN
CAPRICORN WOMAN

If you are not a successful businessman, or at least on your way to success, it's quite possible that a Capricorn woman will have no interest in entering your life. Generally speaking, she is a very security-minded female; she'll see to it that she invests her time only in sure things. Men who whittle away their time with one unsuccessful scheme or another, seldom attract a Capricorn. Men who are interested in getting somewhere in life and keep their noses close to the grindstone quite often have a Capricorn woman behind them, helping them to get ahead.

Although she is a kind of "climber" she is not what you could call cruel or hard-hearted. Beneath that cool, seemingly calculating, exterior, there's a warm and desirable woman. She just happens to think that it is just as easy to fall in love with a rich or ambitious man as it is with a poor or lazy one. She's practical.

The Capricorn woman may be keenly interested in rising to the top, but she'll never be aggressive about it. She'll seldom step on someone's feet or nudge competitors away with her elbows. She's quiet about her desires. She sits, waits, and watches. When an opening or opportunity does appear, she'll latch onto it lickety-split. For an on-the-move man, an ambitious Capricorn wife or girlfriend can be quite an asset. She can probably give you some very good advice about business matters. When you invite the boss and his wife for dinner, she'll charm them both right off the ground.

The Capricorn woman is thorough in whatever she does: cooking, cleaning, making a success out of life—Capricorns make excellent hostesses as well as guests. Generally, they are very well mannered and gracious, no matter what their backgrounds are. They seem to have a built-in sense of what is right. Crude behavior or a careless faux-pas can offend them no end.

If you should marry a woman born under Capricorn you need never worry about her going on a wild shopping spree. Capricorns are careful with every cent that comes into their hands. They understand the value of money better than most women and have no room in their lives for careless spending.

Capricorn girls are usually very fond of family—their own, that is. With them, family ties run very deep. Don't make jokes about her relatives; she won't stand for it. You'd better check her family out before you get down on bended knee; after your marriage you'll undoubtedly be seeing lots of them.

Capricorn mothers train their children to be polite and kind.

LEO MAN
AQUARIUS WOMAN

If you find that you've fallen head over heels for a woman born under the sign of the Water Bearer, you'd better fasten your safety belt. It may take you quite a while to actually discover what this girl is like—and even then, you may have nothing to go on but a string of vague hunches. The Aquarian is like a rainbow, full of bright and shining hues; she's like no other girl you've ever known. There is something elusive about her—something delightfully mysterious. You'll most likely never be able to put your finger on it. It's nothing calculated, either; Aquarians don't believe in phony charm.

There will never be a dull moment in your life with this Water Bearing woman; she seems to radiate adventure and magic. She'll most likely be the most open-minded and tolerant woman you've ever met. She has a strong dislike for injustice and prejudice. Narrow-mindedness runs against her grain.

She is very independent by nature and quite capable of shifting for herself if necessary. She may receive many proposals for marriage from all sorts of people without ever really taking them seriously. Marriage is a very big step for her; she wants to be sure she knows what she's getting into. If she thinks that it will seriously curb her independence and love of freedom, she's liable to shake her head and give the man his engagement ring back—if indeed she's let the romance get that far.

The line between friendship and romance is a pretty fuzzy one for an Aquarian. It's not difficult for her to remain buddy-buddy with an ex-lover. She's tolerant, remember? So, if you should see her on the arm of an old love, don't jump to any hasty conclusions.

She's not a jealous person herself and doesn't expect you to be, either. You'll find her pretty much of a free spirit most of the time. Just when you think you know her inside-out, you'll discover that you don't really know her at all.

She's a very sympathetic and warm person; she can be helpful to people in need of assistance and advice.

She'll seldom be suspicious even if she has every right to be. If the man she loves slips and allows himself a little fling, chances are she'll just turn her head the other way. Her tolerance does have its limits, however, and her man should never press his luck at hanky-panky.

She makes a big-hearted mother; her good qualities rub off on her children.

LEO MAN
PISCES WOMAN

Many a man dreams of a Piscean kind of a girl. You're perhaps no exception. She's soft and cuddly—very domestic. She'll let you be the brains of the family; she's contented to just lean on your shoulder and let you be the master of the household.

She can be very ladylike and proper. Your business associates and friends will be dazzled by her warmth and femininity. Although she's a charmer, there is a lot more to her than just a pretty face. There is a brain ticking away behind that soft, womanly facade. You may never become aware of it—that is, until you're married to her. It's no cause for alarm, however; she'll most likely never use it against you.

If she feels you're botching up your married life through careless behavior or if she feels you could be earning more money than you do, she'll tell you about it. But any wife would, really. She will never try to usurp your position as head of the family.

No one had better dare say one uncomplimentary word about you in her presence. It's liable to cause her to break into tears. Pisces women are usually very sensitive beings. Their reaction to adversity, frustration, or anger is just a plain, good, old-fashioned cry. They can weep buckets when inclined.

She'll have an extra-special dinner waiting for you when you come home from an important business meeting. Don't bother to go into any of the details about the meeting, though, at the dinner table; she doesn't have much of a head for business matters, usually, and is only too happy to leave that up to you.

She can do wonders with a house. She is very fond of soft and beautiful things. There will always be plenty of fresh-cut flowers around the house. She'll see that you always have plenty of socks and underwear in that top drawer of your dresser.

Treat her with tenderness and your relationship will be an enjoyable one. She's most likely fond of chocolates. A bunch of beautiful roses will never fail to make her eyes light up. See to it that you never forget her birthday or your anniversary. She won't.

If you are patient and kind, you can keep a Pisces woman happy for a lifetime. She is, however, not without her faults. Her "sensitivity" may get on your nerves after a while. You may find her lacking in imagination and zest. You may even feel that she only uses her tears as a method of getting her own way.

She makes a strong, self-sacrificing mother. She'll find it difficult to refuse her children anything.

VIRGO
August 22 — September 22

CHARACTER ANALYSIS

People born under the sign of Virgo are generally practical. They believe in doing things thoroughly; there is nothing slipshod or haphazard about the way they do things. They are precise and methodical. The man or woman born under this sixth sign of the Zodiac respects common sense and tries to be rational in his or her approach to tasks or problems.

The Virginian—as people under this sign are sometimes called—has excellent critical abilities; he knows how to analyze things. He is seldom fooled by superficialities.

The Virgo knows how to break things down to the minutest detail; he prefers to work on things piece by piece. Inwardly, he is afraid of being overwhelmed by things that seem larger than life. For this reason, one often finds the Virgo occupied with details. His powers of concentration are greatest when he can concentrate on small, manageable things.

The Virgo person believes in doing things correctly; he's thorough and precise. He's seldom carried away by fantasy; he believes in keeping his feet firmly on the ground. People who seem a bit flighty or impractical sometimes irritate him.

The Virgo knows how to criticize others. It is very easy for him to point out another's weaknesses or faults; he is seldom wrong. However, the Virgo is sometimes a bit sharp in making criticisms and often offends a good friend or acquaintance. At times, he is not very tactful and this can lead to considerable social discord. Quite often, the person born under this sign does not feel that he has done anything wrong by telling another of his faults. The cultivated Virgo, however, knows how to apply criticism tactfully. He is considerate of another's feelings.

The Virgo person believes in applying himself in a positive

manner to whatever task is set before him. He is a person full of purpose and goodwill. He is generally intelligent in his approach to work. He is seldom given to impulse, but works along steadily and constructively. Anything that isn't practical or scientific arouses his distrust. He is not very impressed by artistic or imaginative approaches to work. The Virgo person is usually intelligent, but frequently he does not like to be bothered with deep study. He likes his colleagues to be as well informed as he is, if not more. He has a deep respect for culture and intellect.

Usually, the Virgo takes in stride whatever comes into his life. Basically, he is an uncomplicated person, who views things clearly and sharply. He has a way of getting right down to the meat of the matter. Generally a serious-minded person, he believes in being reliable. He is not one who will take great risks in life as he has no interest in playing the hero or the idealist. The Virgo believes in doing what he can, but without flourishes.

Quite often he is a quiet, modest person. He believes that appearance is important and thus does his best to look well-groomed. He feels that being neat is important and dislikes untidiness in anything.

The Virgo man or woman likes to deal with life on a practical level and very seldom has the urge to look into the mystical side of existence.

Some Virgos are very talented in artistic matters. Others are great readers. They have a deep appreciation for the uncomplicated things of life.

On the whole, the Virgo person is even tempered. He does not allow himself to become angry easily. He knows how to take the bitter with the sweet. But if someone does him a wrong turn, he is not likely to forget it. His good nature is not to be abused.

Health

Many persons born under this sign are amazingly healthy. They frequently live to see a ripe old age. This longevity is generally due to the fact that people born under this sign take all things in moderation. The Virgo is not the type of person who burns the candle at both ends. He acknowledges his limits; he avoids excesses.

Frequently Virgos are small and neat featured. Virgo women are sometimes quite attractive in a sort of dry way. Both men and women of this sign have a youthful appearance throughout life. When young, Virgos are generally very active. However, as they reach middle age and beyond they have a tendency to put on a bit of weight.

The Virgo person usually enjoys good health, although some have a tendency to be overly concerned about it. They imagine ailments they do not really have. Still, they do manage to stay fit. Other Virgos see themselves as being rather strong and resourceful, even when they are ill; for that reason they seldom feel moved to feel sorry for another ailing Virgo. Actually, serious illnesses frighten the Virgo; he will do all he can to remain in good health.

The medicine cabinet of someone born under this sign is often filled with all sorts of pills, tablets, and ointments; most of them will never be used.

As a rule, the Virgo watches his diet. He stays away from foods that won't agree with him. He keeps a balanced diet and is moderate in his drinking habits. The Virgo person needs plenty of exercise to keep his body fit. Most Virgos do not have a particular liking for strenuous movement; however, the wise Virgo sees to it that his body gets a workout daily. Another thing that the person under this sign needs is rest; he should get at least eight hours sleep per day.

On the whole, the Virgo is a sensitive person. His nerves may be easily affected if he finds himself in a disagreeable situation. The stomach is another area of concern. When a Virgo becomes sick, this area is usually affected. Digestion complaints are not rare among persons born under this sign. Regular meals are important for the Virgo. Quick snacks and the like may play havoc with his digestive system. In spite of this particular weakness, the Virgo manages to lead a normal, healthy life. He should try to avoid becoming too concerned with his ups and downs; many of his illnesses may turn out to be imaginary.

Occupation

Virgos delight in keeping busy. They are not afraid of hard work. By nature, they are ambitious people and are happiest when they are putting their talents and abilities to good use. They can best be described as goal-directed; they never lose sight of their objective once committed. They are very thorough in whatever they undertake. Even routine work is something that they can do without finding fault. In fact, work that is scheduled—or that follows a definite pattern—is well suited to their steady natures. Virgos will put aside other things, if necessary, in order to attain a goal. They prefer to work under peaceful conditions, and will seldom do anything to irritate their superiors.

They learn well and are not afraid to undertake any kind of work—even the most menial—if it is necessary. Sometimes, however, they neglect their own conditions because they are so involved in their work. For this reason, Virgos occasionally fall ill or become a bit nervous. Any kind of work that allows them to make use of their talent for criticism will please them.

Virgo men and women usually shine as bookkeepers, accountants, teachers, and pharmacists. The cultivated Virgo person often turns to the world of science where he is likely to do well. Some great writers and poets have been born under this sixth sign of the Zodiac.

It is very important that the Virgo has the kind of work that is suited to his personality. It may take a while before he actually finds his niche in life, and he may have to struggle at times in order to make ends meet. But, because he is not afraid of work, he manages to come out on top.

The Virgo person is a perfectionist. He is always looking for ways to improve his work scheme or technique. He is never satisfied until things are working smoothly. He will even do more than his share in order to secure regularity and precision in a job he is doing. It is not unusual for the average Virgo to have various ideas about how to better the job he is doing, how to streamline things. He is an extremely resourceful person as far as energy is concerned. In most cases, he can work longer than others, without letting it show. Because the Virgo is so concerned with detail, he may seem a trifle slow to his co-workers.

The enterprising Virgo can go far in business if his partner is somewhat adventurous and enthusiastic—qualities which tend to balance those of the Virgo person. At times, the Virgo can be quite a worrier; battling problems large and small may prevent him from making the headway he feels is necessary in his work. A partner who knows how to cut the work and worries in half by taking advantage of shortcuts is someone the average Virgo businessman could learn to value. People enjoy working with Virgo men and women, generally, because they are so reliable and honest. They usually set a good example for others on the job.

If he is not careful, the ambitious Virgo can become the type of person who thinks about nothing else but his job. He is not afraid of taking on more than the average man; but sometimes he makes the mistake of expecting the same of others. This attitude can lead to conflict and unpleasantness. Generally, he does achieve what he sets out for, because he knows how to apply himself. He is seldom the envy of others because he is not the type of person who is easily noticed or recognized.

The Virgo is a quiet person. He enjoys working in peaceful and harmonious surroundings. Conflict at work is bound to upset him and affect his nerves. He works well under people. He is not against taking orders from those who prove themselves his superiors. Virgo women make excellent secretaries. On the whole, the man or woman born under this sign, does not like to be delegated with the full responsibility of a task or project; he or she would rather have a supporting or a subordinate role.

Virgo men frequently excel in a trade. They often make good metalsmiths and carpenters, or they like to take up wood carving or sheetmetal work as a hobby.

The Virgo person is one who is very concerned about security. Now and again he may have cause to worry about his financial position. On the whole, he is conscious of the value of money. He is a person who will never risk his securities by going out on a limb. He knows how to put money away for a rainy day. Many times he will scout about for new ways of increasing his savings. Bettering his financial situation is something that constantly concerns him. When he does invest, it usually turns out to his advantage. He generally makes sure that the investment he makes is a sure thing. He does not believe in gambling or taking big risks.

Sometimes the Virgo, because of his keen interest in money and profit, is the victim of a fraud. Dishonest people may try to take advantage of his interest in monetary gain. The well-off Virgo is extremely generous and enjoys looking after the needs of others. He sees to it that those he cares for live in comfort.

Not all Virgos are fortunate enough to become extremely wealthy, but all of them must work hard for what they achieve.

Home and Family

People born under this sign are generally homebodies. They like to spend as much time as possible surrounded by the things and the people they enjoy. They make excellent hosts and enjoy entertaining guests and visitors. It is important to the Virgo that the people around him be happy and content. He enjoys himself most in the company of others if their behavior is "correct," that is, if they are respectful of others and their property. He does not like people to take advantage of his hospitality and abuse what he considers to be a privilege. On the whole, he is easygoing; the demands he may make of his guests and family are usually reasonable.

A harmonious atmosphere at home is important to the person born under this sign. So long as this can be guaranteed, the Virgo person remains in good humor. He is the type of person who is likely to have a number of insurance policies on his home, family, and possessions. He believes that you can never be safe enough.

In spite of his love of home, the Virgo is likely to have a keen interest in travel. If he cannot make changes in his environment, then he is bound to make them in his home. The Virgo woman enjoys making changes in her house; she never tires of rearranging things. Generally speaking, she has a good sense of beauty and harmony. She knows how to make a room inviting and comfortable. Change is always of interest to the person born under this sign. He likes to read of faraway places, even if he never gets a chance to visit them. A new job or a new home address from time to time can brighten his spirits immeasurably.

The Virgo woman is as neat as a pin. Usually she is an excellent cook, and takes care that her kitchen never gets out of order or becomes untidy even while she is working in it. She believes that everything has its proper place and should be kept there. Because she is so careful with her possessions, they often appear brand new.

Others may feel that the Virgo man or woman, because of his or her cool, calm ways, is not especially cut out to be a good parent. But the opposite is true: Virgo people know how to bring up their offspring correctly. They generally pass on their positive qualities to their children without any trouble. They teach them that honesty and diligence are important; they instill them with an appreciation for common sense in all matters.

Although the Virgo father or mother may deeply love their children, they have a tendency to be rather strict. They are deeply concerned that their children turn out well. Sometimes they expect too much of them. Some of them are rather old-fashioned and believe that a child belongs in a child's place. They expect this not only of their own offspring but also of other people's children.

Social Relationships

The Virgo man or woman is particular about the friends he makes. He is fond of people who have a particular direction in life. He is inclined to avoid drifters or irresolute people. Those who have made their mark win his admiration. The Virgo likes intelligent people—those who are somewhat cultured in their interests. As a good friend, the Virgo person is invaluable; there is nothing he would not do to help someone in need. He stands by his friends even in their most difficult moments. The only demand he makes is that his interest in another's affairs be valued. He does not like to feel that his help is not appreciated. It is important to him that he be thanked for even the slightest favor.

Quite often people born under this sign are rather timid or at least retiring; they have to be drawn out by others. After the Virgo gets to know someone well, however, he blooms. In spite of his initial shyness, he does not enjoy being alone. He likes company; he likes to be reassured by the people around him. He prefers intelligent, informed people as companions. He is the type of person who can overlook negative qualities in a particular person if he feels that that person is basically sincere in his behavior toward others. The Virgo person needs friends. In his solitude, the average Virgo is apt to feel stranded or deserted. He enjoys having someone around who will make a fuss over him, no matter how small.

The Virgo person is a perfectionist; sometimes he criticizes others too strongly for their faults and as a result, he may not have as many friends as he would like.

LOVE AND MARRIAGE

In love matters, the person born under this sign is not inclined to be overly romantic. To his partner, he may seem rather reserved and inhibited. His practical nature prevails even in affairs of the heart. He is the person least likely to be swept off his feet when in love. Chances are he may flirt a bit in the beginning of a relationship, but soon thereafter he settles down to the serious side of love. His standards are very high and it may be some time before he finds someone who can measure up to them. As a consequence, the Virgo person frequently marries rather late in life.

It is important for the Virgo man or woman to find the right person because he is easily influenced by someone he loves. On the other hand, the Virgo has a protective side to his nature; when in love he will try to shield the object of his affection from the unpleasant things in life.

The person born under the sign of Virgo may be disappointed in love more than once. People whom he sets great store in may prove to be unsuitable. Sometimes it is the Virgo's own fault. He may be too critical of small weaknesses that his partner or lover has.

Some Virgos are rather prim and proper when it comes to romance. They would prefer to think that it was not absolutely necessary and that intellect is everything. It may take some doing to get such a Virgo to change this attitude. At any rate, he is not fond of being demonstrative as far as affection goes. He does not like to make a show of his love in front of others. If the Virgo's lover is too demanding or forceful in the relationship, he may feel inclined to break off the affair. The Virgo person appreciates gentleness and consideration in his love life. On the whole, he is not easy to approach. The person who finds him or her interesting will have to be very tactful and patient when trying to convince the Virgo of his love.

In married life, the person born under the sign of Virgo is apt to be very practical. He is interested in preserving the happiness he has found and will do everything in his power to keep the relationship alive. It is quite important that the Virgo man or woman marry someone with a similar outlook. Someone quite opposite may misinterpret his calm and cool manner as being unfeeling. The Virgo person makes a faithful mate. He can always be depended upon. He knows how to keep things in the home running smoothly. He will do what he can to preserve harmony as he dislikes discord and unpleasantness. A cooperative person, the Virgo is willing to make concessions if they seem necessary. In short, the Virgo person can make a success of marriage if he has had the good fortune to choose the right person.

Romance and the Virgo Woman

The Virgo woman is often a serious person. She knows what she wants out of life and what to expect from people. She is discriminating in her choice of men. It may take considerable time before she will admit to herself that she is in love. She is not afraid to wait in matters of romance; it is important to her that she select the right person. She may be more easily attracted to an intelligent man than to a handsome one. She values intellect more than physical attributes.

It is important for the Virgo woman to trust someone before she falls in love with him. She is apt to allow a relationship to develop into a love affair after she has gotten to know the man well on strictly a companionship basis.

The Virgo woman generally makes a good wife. She knows how to keep household matters in shipshape. She likes looking after people she loves. She is efficient and industrious. There is almost nothing she will not do for the man she loves. She is capable of deep affection and love, but must be allowed to express herself in her own way.

Some Virgo women have the opinion that sex is not altogether proper. A gentle and considerate man can persuade such a woman to give up her old-fashioned ideas.

As a mother, she is ideal. She trains her offspring well, teaches them to be polite and well-mannered. Sometimes she may be a bit too strict. However, she always has their best interests at heart.

Romance and the Virgo Man

The Virgo man, practical and analytical as he is in most matters, is rather cautious when it comes to love and romance. He is not what one would call romantic. He may be rather shy on the whole. It may be up to the female to begin the relationship. He may prefer not to begin a romance until he has known the girl as a companion first. He is particular. If the girl makes one false move, he is likely to dissolve the relationship. An understanding and patient woman, however, can help him to be a little more realistic and open in his approach to love.

He enjoys family life and does everything he can to keep his wife and children happy and secure. He may want to have a hand in running the household because he feels he is more efficient than his mate. He is a calm, steady, and faithful person.

As a father he could be a bit of a fuss. He may not know how to communicate with his children effectively in some matters. However, he is loving and responsible. He does what he can to see that they have a proper upbringing.

Woman—Man

**VIRGO WOMAN
ARIES MAN**

Although it's possible that you could find happiness with a man born under the sign of the Ram, it's uncertain as to how long that happiness would last.

An Arien who has made his mark in the world and is somewhat steadfast in his outlooks and attitudes could be quite a catch for you. On the other hand, men under this sign are often swift-footed and quick-minded; their industrious mannerisms may fail to impress you, especially if you feel that much of their get-up-and-go often leads nowhere.

When it comes to a fine romance, you want someone with a nice, broad shoulder to lean on. You are likely to find a relationship with someone who doesn't stay put for too long somewhat upsetting.

The Arien may have a little trouble in understanding you, too—at least, in the beginning of the relationship. He may find you a bit too shy and moody. An Arien tends to speak his mind; he's liable to criticize you at the drop of a hat.

You may find a man born under this sign too demanding. He may give you the impression that he expects you to be at his constant beck and call. You have a lot of patience at your disposal and he may try every last bit of it. He may not be as thorough as you in everything he does. In order to achieve success or a goal quickly, he is liable to overlook small but important details, and regret the oversight when it is far too late.

Being married to an Arien does not mean that you'll have a

secure and safe life as far as finances are concerned. Not all Ariens are rash with cash, but they lack the sound head you perhaps have for putting away something for that inevitable rainy day. He'll do his best, however, to see that you're adequately provided for, even though his efforts may leave something to be desired as far as you're concerned.

With an Aries man for a mate, you'll find yourself constantly among people. An Arien generally has many friends—and you may not heartily approve of them all. People born under the sign of the Ram are often more interested in "interesting" people than they are in influential ones. Although there may be a family squabble from time to time, you are stable enough to take it in your stride.

Aries men love children. They make wonderful fathers. Kids take to them like ducks to water. Their quick minds and behavior appeal to the young.

VIRGO WOMAN
TAURUS MAN

Some Taurus men are strong and silent. They do all they can to protect and provide for the women they love. In general, the Taurus man will never let you down. He's steady, sturdy, and reliable. He's pretty honest and practical, too. He says what he means and means what he says. He never indulges in deceit and will always put his cards on the table.

The Taurean is a very affectionate man. Being loved, appreciated and understood are very important for his well-being. Like you, he is also looking for peace and security in his life. If you both work toward these goals together, you'll find that they are easily attained.

If you should marry a Taurus man, you can be sure that the wolf will never darken your door. He is a notoriously good provider and will do everything he can to make his family comfortable and happy.

He'll appreciate the way you have of making a home warm and inviting. Slippers and pipe, and the evening papers are essential ingredients in making your Taurus husband happy at the end of the workday. Although he may be a big lug of a guy, you'll find that he's fond of gentleness and soft things. If you puff up his pillow and tuck him in at night, he won't complain.

You probably will like his friends. The Taurean tends to seek out those who are successful or prominent. You admire people, too, who work hard and achieve their goals.

The Taurus man doesn't care too much for change. He's a stay-at-home of the first order. Chances are that the house you move into after you're married will be the house you'll live in for the rest of your life.

You'll find that the man born under this sign is easy to get along with. It's unlikely that you'll have many quarrels or arguments.

Although he'll be gentle and tender with you, your Taurus man is far from being a sensitive type. He's a man's man. More than likely, he loves such sports as fishing and football. He can be earthy as well as down to earth.

Taureans love their children very much but do everything they can not to spoil them. They believe in children staying in their places. They make excellent disciplinarians. Your children will be polite and respectful.

VIRGO WOMAN
GEMINI MAN

The Gemini man is a good catch. Many a woman has set her cap for him and failed to bag him. Generally, Gemini men are intelligent, witty, and outgoing. Many of them tend to be versatile.

On the other hand, some of them seem to lack that sort of common sense that you set so much store in. Their tendency to start a half-dozen projects, then toss them up in the air out of boredom may do nothing more than exasperate you.

One thing that causes a Twin's mind and affection to wander is a bore, and it is unlikely that an active woman like you would ever allow herself to be accused of being one. The Gemini man who has caught your heart will admire you for your ideas and intellect, perhaps even more than for your homemaking talents and good looks.

A strong-willed woman could easily fill the role of rudder for her Gemini's ship-without-a-sail. The intelligent Gemini is often aware of his shortcomings and doesn't mind if someone with better bearings gives him a shove in the right direction—when it's needed. The average Gemini doesn't have serious ego-hangups and will even accept a well-deserved chewing out from his mate or girl friend gracefully.

A successful and serious-minded Gemini could make you a very happy woman, perhaps, if you gave him half a chance. Although he may give you the impression that he has a hole in his head, the Gemini man generally has a good head on his shoulders. Some Geminis, who have learned the art of being steadfast, have risen to great heights in their professions: President Kennedy, Thomas Mann, and William Butler Yeats.

Once you convince yourself that not all people born under the sign of the Twins are witless grasshoppers, you won't mind dating a few to test your newborn conviction. If you do wind up walking down the aisle with one, accept the fact that married life with him will mean your taking the bitter with the sweet.

Life with a Gemini man can be more fun than a barrel of clowns. You'll never be allowed to experience a dull moment. Don't leave money matters to him or you'll both wind up behind the eight ball.

Gemini men are always attractive to the opposite sex. You'll perhaps have to allow him an occasional harmless flirt; it will seldom amount to more than that if you're his proper mate.

The Gemini father is a pushover for children. See that you keep the young ones in line otherwise they'll be running the house.

VIRGO WOMAN
CANCER MAN

The man born under the sign of Cancer may very well be the man after your own heart. Generally, Cancerians are steady people. They are interested in security and practicality. Despite their seemingly grouchy exterior at times, men born under the sign of the Crab are rather sensitive and kind individuals. They are almost always hard workers and are very interested in making successes of themselves economically as well as socially. You'll find that their conservative outlook on many things often agrees with yours. They will be men on whom you can depend come rain or come shine. They will never shirk their responsibilities as providers; they will always see that their family never wants.

Your patience will come in handy if you decide it's a Cancerian you want for a mate. He isn't the type that rushes headlong into romance. He wants to be sure about love as you do. If, after the first couple of months of dating, he suggests that you take a walk with him down lovers' lane, don't jump to the conclusion that he's about to make his "great play." Chances are he'll only hold your hand and seriously observe the stars. Don't let his coolness fool you, though. Beneath his starched reserve lies a very warm heart. He's just not interested in showing off as far as affection is concerned. Don't think his interest is wandering if he doesn't kiss you goodnight at the front door; that just isn't his style. For him, affection should only be displayed for two sets of eyes—yours and his. He's passionate only in private.

He will never step out of line. He's too much of a gentleman for that. When you're alone with him and there's no chance of being disturbed or spied upon, he'll pull out an engagement ring (that used to belong to his grandmother) and slip it on your trembling finger.

Speaking of relatives, you'll have to get used to the fact that the Cancerian is overly fond of his mother. When he says his mother's the most wonderful woman in the world, you'd better agree with him, that is, if you want to become his wife.

He'll always be a faithful husband; a Cancerian never pussyfoots around after he has taken that marriage vow. He doesn't take marriage responsibilities lightly. He'll see that everything in the house runs smoothly and that bills are paid promptly. He's liable to take out all kinds of insurance policies on his family and property. He'll arrange it so that when retirement time rolls around, you'll both be very well off.

Men under this sign make patient and understanding fathers.

VIRGO WOMAN
LEO MAN

To know a man born under the sign of the Lion is not necessarily to love him, even though the temptation may be great. When he fixes most girls with his leonine double-whammy, it causes their hearts to pitter-patter and their minds to cloud over.

You are a little too sensible to allow yourself to be bowled over by a regal strut and a roar. Still, there's no denying that Leo has a way with women, even sensible women like yourself. Once he's swept a girl off her feet, it may be hard for her to scramble upright again. Still, you are no pushover for romantic charm, expecially if you feel it's all show.

He'll wine you and dine you in the fanciest places. He'll croon to you under the moon and shower you with diamonds if he can get a hold of them. Still, it would be wise to find out just how long that shower is going to last before consenting to be his wife.

Lions in love are hard to ignore, let alone brush off. Your no's will have a way of nudging him on until he feels he has you completely under his spell. Once mesmerized by this romantic powerhouse, you will probably find yourself doing things of which you never dreamed. Leos can be vain pussycats when involved romantically. They like to be cuddled, curried, and tickled under the chin. This may not be your cup of tea exactly. Still when you're romantically dealing with a man born under the sign of Leo, you'll find yourself doing all kinds of things to make him purr.

Although he may be big and magnanimous while trying to win you, he'll let out a bloodcurdling roar if he thinks he's not getting the tender love and care he feels is his due. If you keep him well supplied with affection, you can be sure his eyes will never look for someone else and his heart will never wander.

A Leo man often tends to be authoritarian; he can be depended upon to lord it over others in one way or another. If he is the top banana at his firm, he'll most likely do everything he can to stay on top. If he's not number one, he's probably working on it and will be sitting on the throne before long.

You'll have more security than you can use if he is in a position to support you in the manner to which he feels you should be accustomed. He is inclined to be too lavish, though—at least, by your standards.

You'll always have plenty of friends when you have a Leo for a mate. He's a natural-born friend-maker and entertainer. He loves to let his hair down at parties.

As fathers, Leos tend to spoil their children.

VIRGO WOMAN
VIRGO MAN

The Virgo man is all business or so he may seem to you. He is usually very cool, calm, and collected. He's perhaps too much of a fussbudget to arouse deep romantic interests in a woman like you. Torrid romancing to him is just so much sentimental mush. He can do without it and can make that quite evident in short order. He's keen on chastity and, if necessary, he can lead a sedentary, sexless life without caring very much about the fun others think he's missing. In short, you are liable to find him a first-class dud. He doesn't have much of an imagination; flights of fancy don't interest him. He is always correct and likes to be handled properly. Almost everything about him is orderly. "There's a place for everything . . ." is likely to be an adage he'll fall upon quite regularly.

He does have an honest-to-goodness heart, believe it or not. The woman who finds herself strangely attracted to his cool, feet-flat-on-the-ground ways, will discover that his is a constant heart, not one that goes in for flings or sordid affairs. A practical man, even in matters of the heart, he wants to know just what kind of person you are before he takes a chance on you.

The impulsive girl had better not make the mistake of kissing her Virgo friend on the street, even if it's only a peck on the cheek. He's not at all demonstrative and hates public displays of affection. Love, according to him, should be kept within the confines of one's home—with the curtains drawn. Once he believes that you are on the level with him as far as your love is concerned, you'll see how fast he can lose his cool. Virgos are considerate, gentle lovers. He'll spend a long time, though, getting to know you. He'll like you before he loves you.

A romance with a Virgo man can be a sometime or, rather, a one-time thing. If the bottom ever falls out, don't bother reaching for the adhesive tape. Nine times out of ten he won't care about patching up. He's a once-burnt-twice-shy guy. When he crosses your telephone number out of his address book, he's crossing you out of his life for good.

Neat as a pin, he's thumbs-down on what he considers "sloppy" housekeeping. An ashtray with just one stubbed out cigarette in it can annoy him even if it's only two seconds old. Glassware should always sparkle and shine if you want to keep him happy. If you marry him, keep your sunny-side up.

Your children should be kept as spotless as your house. Kids with dirty faces and hands displease him. Train them to be kind and courteous.

VIRGO WOMAN
LIBRA MAN

Men born under the sign of Libra are frequently too wrapped up in their own private dreams to be really interesting as far as love and romance are concerned. Many times, the Libra man is a difficult person to bring back down to earth; it is hard for him to face reality. Although he may be very cautious about weighing both sides of an argument, he may never really come to a reasonable decision about anything. Decision-making is something that often makes the Libra man uncomfortable; he'd rather leave that job to someone else. Don't ask him why, he probably doesn't know himself.

Qualities such as permanence and constancy are important to you in a love relationship. The Libra man may be an enigma to you. One moment he comes on hard and strong with declarations of his love; the next moment you find he's left you like yesterday's mashed potatoes. It does no good to wonder what went wrong. Chances are it was nothing on which you can put your finger. It's just one of Libra's strange ways.

He is not exactly what you would term an ambitious person; you are perhaps looking for a mate or friend with more drive and fidelity. You are the type of person who is interested in making some headway in the areas that interest you; the Libran is often contented to drift along. He does have drive, however, but it's not the long-range kind. It's not that he's shiftless or lazy; he's interested in material things and he appreciates luxuries, but he may not be willing to work hard enough to obtain them. Beauty and harmony interest him. He'll dedicate a lot of time to arranging things so that they are aesthetically pleasing. It would be difficult to call the Libra man practical; nine times out of ten, he isn't.

If you do begin a relationship with a man born under this sign, you will have to coax him now and again to face various situations in a realistic manner. You'll have your hands full, that's for sure. But if you love him, you'll undoubtedly do your best to understand him, no matter how difficult this may be.

If you become involved with a Libra man, either temporarily or permanently, you'd better take over the task of managing his money. Often he has little understanding of financial matters; he tends to spend without thinking, following his whims.

VIRGO WOMAN
SCORPIO MAN

Some people have a hard time understanding the man born under the sign of Scorpio; few, however, are able to resist his fiery charm. When angered, he can act like an overturned wasp's nest; his sting can leave an almost permanent mark. If you find yourself interested in the Scorpio man, you'd better learn how to keep on his good side.

The Scorpio man can be rather blunt when he chooses; at times, he may seem hardhearted. He can be touchy every now and then and this sensitiveness may get on your nerves after a while. When you feel as though you can't take it anymore, you'd better tiptoe away from the scene rather than chance an explosive confrontation. He's capable of giving you a sounding-out that will make you pack your bags and go back to Mother—for good.

If he finds fault with you, he'll let you know. He's liable to misinterpret your patience and think it a sign of indifference. But, you are the type of woman who can adapt to almost any sort of relationship or circumstance if you put your heart and mind to it.

Scorpio men are all very perceptive and intelligent. In some respects, they know how to use their brains more effectively than most. They believe in winning, in whatever they do; second-place holds no interest for them. In business, they usually achieve the position they want through a combination of drive and intellect.

Your interest in homelife probably won't be shared by him. No matter how comfortable you've managed to make the house, it will have very little influence on him with regard to making him aware of his family responsibilities. He does not like to be tied down, generally, and would rather be out on the battlefield of life, belting away at what he feels to be a just and worthy cause. Don't try to keep the homefires burning too brightly while you wait for him to come home from work—you may just run out of firewood.

The Scorpio man is passionate in all things, including love. Most women are easily attracted to him and you are perhaps no exception. Those who allow themselves to be swept off their feet by a Scorpio man, find out shortly thereafter that they're dealing with a carton of romantic fireworks. The Scorpio man is passionate with a capital P, make no mistake about that. Some women may find that he's just too love-happy, but that's their problem.

Scorpio men are straight to the point. They can be as sharp as a razor blade and just as cutting to anyone who crosses them.

Scorpio fathers like large families, generally.

VIRGO WOMAN
SAGITTARIUS MAN

The woman who has set her cap for a man born under the sign of

Sagittarius may have to use a great deal of strategy before she can get him to drop down on bended knee. Although some Sagittarians may be marriage-shy, they're not ones to skitter away from romance. A high-spirited woman may find a relationship with a Sagittarian, whether a fling or "the real thing," a very enjoyable experience.

As a rule, Sagittarians are bright, happy, and healthy people. They have a strong sense of fair play. Often they're a source of inspiration to others. They're full of ideas and drive.

You'll be taken by the Sagittarian's infectious grin and his lighthearted friendly nature. If you do wind up being the woman in his life, you'll find that he will treat you more like a buddy than the love of his life. It's his way.

You'll admire his broadmindedness in most matters, including that of the heart. If, while dating you, he claims that he still wants to play the field, he'll expect you to enjoy the same liberty. Once he's promised to love, honor, and obey, however, he does just that.

A woman who has a keen imagination and a great love of freedom will not be disappointed if she does marry a Sagittarian. The Sagittarius man is often quick-witted, and has a genuine interest in equality.

If he does insist on a night out with the boys once a week, he won't scowl if you decide to let him shift for himself in the kitchen once a week while you pursue some of your own interests. He believes in fairness.

The Sagittarian is not much of a homebody. Many times he's occupied with faraway places either in his dreams or in reality. He enjoys—just as you do—being on the go. Humdrum routine, especially at home, bores him. At the drop of a hat, he may ask you to whip off your apron and dine out for a change. He likes surprising people. He'll take great pride in showing you off to his friends. He'll always be a considerate mate; he will never embarrass or disappoint you intentionally. He's very tolerant when it comes to friends; you'll probably spend a lot of time entertaining people.

Sagittarians become interested in their children when they have passed through the baby stage.

VIRGO WOMAN
CAPRICORN MAN

The Capricorn man is frequently not the romantic lover that attracts most women. Still, with his reserve and calm, he is capable of giving his heart completely once he has found the right girl. The Capricorn man is thorough and deliberate in all that he does; he is slow and sure.

He doesn't believe in flirting and would never lead a heart on a merry chase just for the game of it. If you win his trust, he'll give you his heart on a platter. Many times, it is the woman who has to take the lead when romance is in the air. As long as he knows you're making the advances in earnest, he won't mind—in fact, he'll probably be grateful. Don't start thinking he's a cold fish; he isn't. While some Capricorns are indeed very capable of expressing passion, others often have difficulty in trying to display affection. He should have no trouble in this area, however, once he has found a patient and understanding girl.

The Capricorn man is very interested in getting ahead. He's quite ambitious and usually knows how to apply himself well to whatever task he undertakes. He certainly isn't a spendthrift. Like you, he knows how to handle money with extreme care. You, with your knack for putting away pennies for that rainy day, should have no difficulty understanding his way with money. The Capricorn man thinks in terms of future security. He wants to make sure that he and his wife have something to fall back on when they reach retirement age. There's nothing wrong with that; in fact, it's a plus quality.

The Capricorn man will want you to handle household matters efficiently. Most Capricorn-oriented women will have no trouble doing so. If he should check up on you from time to time, don't let it irritate you. Once you assure him that you can handle everything to his liking, he'll leave you alone.

Although he's a hard man to catch when it comes to marriage, once he's made that serious step, he's inclined to become possessive. The Capricorn man needs to know that he has the support of his wife in whatever he does, every step of the way.

The Capricorn man wants to be liked. He may seem dull to some, but underneath his reserve there is sometimes an adventurous streak that has never had a chance to express itself. He may be a real daredevil in his heart of hearts. The right woman, the affectionate, adoring woman can bring out that hidden zest in his nature.

He makes a loving, dutiful father, even though he may not understand his children completely.

VIRGO WOMAN
AQUARIUS MAN

You are liable to find the Aquarius man the most broadminded man you have ever met; on the other hand, you are also liable to find him the most impractical. Many times, he's more of a dreamer than a doer. If you don't mind putting up with a man whose heart and mind are as wide as the Missouri but whose head is almost always in the clouds, then start dating that Aquarian who has somehow captured your fancy. Maybe you, with your good sense, can bring him back down to earth when he gets too starry-eyed.

He's no dumbbell, make no mistake about that. He can be busy making some very complicated and idealistic plans when he's got that out-to-lunch look in his eyes. But more than likely, he'll never execute them. After he's shared one or two of his progressive ideas with you, you are liable to ask yourself, "Who is this nut?" But don't go jumping to conclusions. There's a saying that Aquarians are a half-century ahead of everybody else in the thinking department.

If you decide to answer "Yes" to his "Will you marry me?" you'll find out how right his zany whims are on or about your 50th anniversary. Maybe the waiting will be worth it. Could be that you have an Einstein on your hands and heart.

Life with an Aquarian won't be one of total despair if you can learn to temper his airiness with your down-to-earth practicality. He won't gripe if you do. The Aquarian always maintains an open mind; he'll entertain the ideas and opinions of everybody. But he may not agree with all of them.

Don't go tearing your hair out when you find that it's almost impossible to hold a normal conversation with your Aquarius friend at times. He's capable of answering your how-are-you-feeling with a rundown on the price of Arizona sugar beets. Always try to keep in mind that he means well.

His broadmindedness doesn't stop when it comes to you and your personal freedom. You won't have to give up any of your hobbies or projects after you're married; he'll encourage you to continue them.

He'll be a kind and generous husband. He'll never quibble over petty things. Keep track of the money you both spend. He can't. Money burns a hole in his pocket.

At times, you may feel like calling it quits. Chances are, though, that you'll always give him another chance.

He's a good family man. He understands and loves children.

VIRGO WOMAN
PISCES MAN

The man born under Pisces is quite a dreamer. Sometimes he's so wrapped up in his dreams that he's difficult to reach. To the average, active woman, he may seem a little sluggish.

He's easygoing most of the time. He seems to take things in his stride. He'll entertain all kinds of views and opinions from just about everyone, nodding or smiling vaguely, giving the impression that he's with them one hundred percent while that may not be the case at all. His attitude may be "why bother" when he's confronted with someone who is wrong but thinks he's right. The Pisces man will seldom speak his mind if he thinks he'll be rigidly opposed.

The Pisces man is oversensitive at times; he's afraid of getting his feelings hurt. He'll sometimes imagine a personal affront when none's been made. More than likely, you'll find this complex of his maddening; at times you may feel like giving him a swift kick where it hurts the most. It won't do any good, though.

One thing you'll admire about this man is his concern for people who are sickly or troubled. He'll make his shoulder available to anyone in the mood for a good cry. He can listen to one hard-luck story after another without seeming to tire. When his advice is asked, he can be depended upon to offer some wise counsel. He often knows what is bugging someone before that person is aware of it himself. Still, at the end of the day, this man will want some peace and quiet. If you've got a problem when he comes home, don't unload it in his lap. If you do, you are liable to find him short-tempered. He's a good listener but he can only take so much.

Pisceans are not aimless although they may seem so at times. The positive sort of Pisces man is often successful in his profession and is likely to become rich and influential. Material gain, however, is never a direct goal for a man born under this sign.

The weaker Pisces is usually content to stay on the level where he finds himself.

Because of their seemingly laissez-faire manner, people under this sign are immensely popular with children. For tots they play the double role of confidant and playmate. It will never enter their mind to discipline a child, no matter how spoiled or incorrigible that child becomes.

Man—Woman

VIRGO MAN
ARIES WOMAN

The Aries woman may be a little too bossy and busy for you. Generally speaking, the Arien is an ambitious creature. She can become a little impatient with people who are more thorough and deliberate than she is, especially if she feels they're taking too much time. The Aries woman is a fast worker. Sometimes she's so fast she forgets to look where she's going. When she stumbles or falls, it would be nice if you were there to catch her. But the Arien is a proud woman; she doesn't like to be told "I told you so" when she errs. Tongue lashings can turn her into a block of ice. Don't begin to think that the Aries woman frequently gets tripped up in her plans. Many times she is capable of taking aim and hitting the bull's-eye. You'll be flabbergasted by her accuracy as well as by her ambition. On the other hand, you're apt to spot a flaw in your Arien's plans before she does.

You are perhaps somewhat slower than the Arien in attaining your goals. Still, you are not inclined to make mistakes along the way; you're almost always well prepared.

The Aries woman is rather sensitive at times. She likes to be handled with gentleness and respect. Let her know that you love her for her brains as well as for her good looks. Never give her cause to become jealous. When your Aries date sees green, you'd better forget about sharing a rosy future together. Handle her with tender love and care and she's yours.

The Aries woman can be giving if she feels her partner is deserving. She is no iceberg; she responds to the proper masculine flame. She needs a man she can admire and of whom she can feel proud. She can cause you plenty of heartache if you've made up your mind about her but she hasn't made up hers about you. The Aries woman is very demanding at times. Some tend to be highstrung; they can be difficult if they feel their independence is being hampered.

The cultivated Aries woman makes a wonderful homemaker and hostess. You'll find she's very clever in decorating and using color. Your house will be tastefully furnished; she'll make sure that it radiates harmony. The Aries wife knows how to make guests feel at home.

Although the Aries woman may not be keen on burdensome responsibilities, she is fond of children and the joy they bring.

VIRGO MAN
TAURUS WOMAN

A Taurus woman could perhaps understand you better than most women. She is very considerate and loving. She is thorough and methodical in whatever she does. She is anxious to avoid mistakes.

Home is very important to the Taurus woman. She is an excellent homemaker. Although your home may not be a palace, it will become, under her care, a comfortable and happy abode. She'll love it when friends drop by for the evening. She is a good cook and enjoys feeding people well.

The Taurus woman is serious about love and affection. When she has taken a tumble for someone, she'll stay by him forever, if possible. She will try to be practical in romance, to some extent. When she decides she wants a certain man, she keeps after him until he's won her. Generally, the Taurus woman is a passionate lover, even though she may appear otherwise at first glance. She is on the lookout for someone who can return her affection fully. Taureans are sometimes given to fits of jealousy and possessiveness. They expect fair play in the area of marriage; when it doesn't come about, they can be bitingly sarcastic and mean.

The Taurus woman is usually an easygoing person, who is fond of keeping peace. She won't argue unless she must. She'll do her best to keep your love relationship on an even keel.

Marriage is generally a one-time thing for Taureans. Once they've taken the serious step, they seldom try to back out of it. They are fond of love and warmth and with the right man, they become ideal wives.

The Taurus woman will respect you for your steady ways; she'll have confidence in your common sense. Taurus women seldom put up with nonsense from their children. It is not that they are strict, but rather that they are concerned. They like their children to be well behaved and dutiful. Nothing pleases a Taurus mother more than a compliment from a neighbor or teacher about her child's behavior. Although some children may inwardly resent the iron hand of a Taurus mother, in later life they are often thankful that they were brought up in such an orderly and conscientious way.

VIRGO MAN
GEMINI WOMAN

You may find a romance with a woman born under the sign of the Twins a many-splendored thing. She will provide the intellectual companionship you often look for in a friend or mate. A Gemini girl friend can appreciate your aims and desires because she travels pretty much the same road as you do intellectually, that is, at least part of the way. She may share your interests but she will lack your tenacity.

She suffers from itchy feet. She can be here, there, all over the place. Her eagerness to move about may make you dizzy; still, you'll enjoy and appreciate her liveliness and mental agility.

The Gemini woman often has a sparkling personality; you'll be attracted to her warmth and grace. While she's on your arm you'll probably notice that many male eyes are drawn to her. She may even return a gaze or two, but don't let that worry you. All women born under this sign have nothing against a harmless flirt once in a while. But if she feels she is already spoken for, she will never let it get out of hand.

Although she may not be as handy as you'd like in the kitchen, you'll never go without a filling and tasty meal. The Gemini girl is always in a rush; she won't feel she's cheating by breaking out the instant mashed potatoes or the frozen peas. She may not be a good cook but she is clever; with a dash of this and a suggestion of that, she can make an uninteresting TV dinner taste like something out of a Jim Beard cookbook. Then, again, maybe you've struck it rich and have a Gemini girl friend who finds complicated recipes a challenge to her intellect. If so, you'll find every meal a tantalizing and mouthwatering surprise.

When you're beating your brains out over the Sunday crossword puzzle and find yourself stuck, just ask your Gemini woman; she'll give you all the right answers without batting an eyelash.

Just like you, she loves all kinds of people. You may even find that you're a bit more discriminating than she. Often all that a Geminian requires is that her friends be interesting and stay interesting. But one thing she's not able to abide is a dullard.

Leave the party-organizing to your Gemini sweetheart or mate and you'll never have a chance to know what a dull moment is. She'll bring out the swinger in you if you give her half the chance.

A Gemini mother enjoys her children. Like them, she's often restless, adventurous, and easily bored.

VIRGO MAN
CANCER WOMAN

The girl born under Cancer needs to be protected from the cold, cruel world. She'll love you for your masculine yet gentle manner; you make her feel safe and secure. You don't have to pull any he-man or heroic stunts to win her heart; that's not what interests her. She's more likely to be impressed by your sure, steady ways—that way you have of putting your arm around her and making her feel she's the only girl in the world. When she's feeling glum and tears begin to well up in her eyes, you have that knack of saying just the right thing—you know how to calm her fears, no matter how silly some of them may seem

The girl born under this sign is inclined to have her ups and downs. You have that talent for smoothing out the ruffles in her sea of life. She'll probably worship the ground you walk on or put you on a very high pedestal. Don't disappoint her if you can help it; she'll never disappoint you. The Cancer woman will take great pleasure in devoting the rest of her natural life to you. She'll darn your socks, mend your overalls, scrub floors, wash windows, shop, cook, and do just about anything in order to please you and let you know that she loves you. Sounds like that legendary good old-fashioned girl, doesn't it? Contrary to popular belief, there are still a good number of them around, and many of them are Cancerians.

Of all the signs of the Zodiac, the women under the Cancer sign are the most maternal. In caring for and bringing up children, they know just how to combine the right amount of tenderness with the proper dash of discipline. A child couldn't ask for a better mother. Cancer women are sympathetic, affectionate, and patient with their children.

While we're on the subject of motherhood, there's one thing you should be warned about: never be unkind to your mother-in-law. It will be the only golden rule your Cancerian wife will probably expect you to follow. No mother-in-law jokes in the presence of your Mrs., please. They'll go over like a lead balloon. Mother is something pretty special for her. She may be the crankiest, nosiest old bat this side of the Great Divide, but she's your wife's mother. You'd better treat her like she's one of the landed gentry. Sometimes this may be difficult to swallow, but if you want to keep your home together and your wife happy, learn to grin and bear it.

Treat your Cancer wife like a queen and she'll treat you royally.

VIRGO MAN
LEO WOMAN

The Leo woman can make most men roar like lions. If any woman in the Zodiac has that indefinable something that can make men lose their heads and find their hearts, it's the Leo woman.

She's got more than a fair share of charm and glamour and she knows how to make the most of her assets, especially when she's in the company of the opposite sex. Jealous men are apt to lose their cool or their sanity when trying to woo a woman born under the sign of the Lion. She likes to kick up her heels quite often and doesn't care who knows it. She frequently makes heads turn and tongues wag. You don't necessarily have to believe any of what you hear—it's probably jealous gossip or wishful thinking. Needless to say, other women in her vicinity turn green with envy and will try anything short of shoving her into the nearest lake in order to put her out of the running.

Although this vamp makes the blood rush to your head and makes you momentarily forget all the things you thought were important and necessary in your life, you may feel differently when you come back down to earth and the stars are out of your eyes. You may feel that she isn't the type of girl you planned to bring home to Mother. Not that your mother might disapprove of your choice, but *you* might after the shoes and rice are a thing of the past. Although the Leo woman may do her best to be a good wife for you, chances are she'll fall short of your idea of what a good wife should be like.

If you're planning on not going as far as the altar with the Leo woman you'd better be financially equipped for some very expensive dating. Be prepared to shower her with expensive gifts and to take her dining and dancing to the smartest spots in town. Promise her the moon if you're in a position to go that far. Luxury and glamour are two things that are bound to lower a Leo's resistance. She's got expensive tastes and you'll have to cater to them if you expect to get to first base with this femme.

If you've got an important business deal to clinch and you have doubts as to whether you can swing it or not, bring your Leo woman along to the business luncheon. More than likely, with her on your arm, you'll be able to win any business battle with both hands tied. She won't have to say or do anything, just be there at your side. The grouchiest oil magnate can be transformed into a gushing, obedient schoolboy if there's a charming Leo woman in the room.

Leo mothers are blind to the faults of their children. They make very loving and affectionate mothers and tend to spoil their offspring.

VIRGO MAN
VIRGO WOMAN

The Virgo woman may be a little too difficult for you to understand at first. Her waters run deep. Even when you think you know her, don't take any bets on it. She's capable of keeping things hidden in the deep recesses of her womanly soul—things she'll only release when she's sure that you're the man she wants. But it may take her some time to come around to this decision. Virgo girls are finicky about almost everything. Many of them have the idea that the only people who can do things correctly are Virgos.

Nothing offends a Virgo woman more than slovenly dress, sloppy character, or a careless display of affection. Make sure your tie is not crooked and your shoes sport a bright shine before you go calling on this lady. Keep your off-color jokes for the locker-room; she'll have none of that. Take her arm when crossing the street, but don't rush the romance. Trying to corner her in the back of a cab may be one way of striking out. Never criticize the way she looks. In fact, the best policy is to agree with her as much as possible. Still, there's just so much a man can take; all those dos and don'ts you have to observe if you want to get to first base with a Virgo may be just a little too much to ask of you. After a few dates, you may decide that she just isn't worth all that trouble. However, the Virgo woman is usually mysterious enough to keep her men running back for more. Chances are you'll be intrigued by her airs and graces.

If lovemaking means a great deal to you, you'll be disappointed at first in the cool ways of your Virgo woman. However, under her glacial facade there lies a hot cauldron of seething excitement. If you're patient and artful in your romantic approach, you'll find that all that caution was well worth the trouble. When Virgos love, it's all or nothing as far as they're concerned.

One thing a Virgo woman can't stand in love is hypocrisy. She doesn't care what the neighbors say, if her heart tells her "Go ahead." She is very concerned with human truths—if her heart stumbles upon another fancy, she is liable to be true to that new heartthrob and leave you standing in the rain.

She's honest to her heart and will be as true to you as you are with her, generally. Do her wrong once, however, and it's farewell.

She's both strict and tender with children. As a mother she'll try to bring out the best in her children.

VIRGO MAN
LIBRA WOMAN

The song goes: it's a woman's prerogative to change her mind. The lyricist must have had the Libra woman in his thoughts when he jotted this ditty out. Her changeability, in spite of its undeniable charm (sometimes) could actually drive even a man of your patience up the wall. She's capable of smothering you with love and kisses one day and on the next avoid you like the plague. If you think you're a man of steel nerves then perhaps you can tolerate these sudden changes without suffering too much. However, if you admit that you're only a mere mortal who can take so much, then you'd better fasten your attention on a girl who's somewhat more constant.

But don't get the wrong idea: a love affair with a Libran can have a lot of plusses to it. The Libra woman is soft, very feminine, and warm. She doesn't have to vamp all over the place in order to gain a man's attention. Her delicate presence is enough to warm the cockles of any man's heart. One smile and you're like a piece of putty in the palm of her hand.

She can be fluffy and affectionate, which you like in a girl. On the other hand, her indecision about which dress to wear, what to cook for dinner, or whether to redo the rumpus room or not could make you tear your hair out. What will perhaps be more exasperating is her flat denial to the accusation that she cannot make even the simplest decision. The trouble is that she wants to be fair or just in all matters; she'll spend hours weighing pros and cons. Don't make her rush into a decision; that will only irritate her.

The Libra woman likes to be surrounded by beautiful things. Money is no object when beauty is concerned. There will always be plenty of flowers in the house. She'll know how to arrange them tastefully, too. Women under this sign are fond of beautiful clothes and furnishings. They will run up bills without batting an eyelash, if given the chance.

Once she's involved with you, the Libra woman will do everything in her power to make you happy. She'll wait on you hand and foot when you're sick and bring you breakfast in bed Sundays. She'll be very thoughtful and devoted. If anyone dares suggest you're not the grandest man in the world, your Libra wife will give that person a good sounding-out.

The Libra woman works wonders with children. Gentle persuasion and affection are all she uses in bringing them up. It works.

VIRGO MAN
SCORPIO WOMAN

When the Scorpio woman chooses to be sweet, she's apt to give the impression that butter wouldn't melt in her mouth but, of course, it would. When her temper flies, so will everything else that isn't bolted down. She can be as hot as a *tamale* or as cool as a cucumber when she wants. Whatever mood she's in, you can be sure it's for real. She doesn't believe in poses or hypocrisy.

The Scorpio woman is often seductive and sultry. Her femme fatale charm can pierce through the hardest of hearts. The Scorpio woman can be a whirlwind of passion. Life with a girl born under this sign will not be all smiles and smooth sailing. If you think you can handle a woman who can purr like a pussycat when handled correctly but spits bullets once her fur is ruffled, then try your luck. Your stable and steady nature will probably have a calming effect on her. You're the kind of man she can trust and rely on. But never cross her, even on the smallest thing; if you do, you'd better tell Fido to make room for you in the doghouse.

Generally, the Scorpio woman will keep family battles within the walls of your home. When company visits, she can be depended upon to give the impression that married life with you is one big joy-ride. It's just her way of expressing her loyalty to you—at least, in front of others. The Scorpio woman will certainly see that others have a high opinion of you both. She'll support you in whatever it is you want to do. Although she's an individualist, after she has married, she'll put her own interests aside for those of the man she loves. With a woman like this behind you, you can't help but go far. She'll never try to take over your role as boss of the family and she'll give you all the support you need in order to fulfill that role. She won't complain if the going gets rough, for she is a courageous woman. She's as anxious as you to find that place in the sun for you both. She is as determined a person as you are.

Although the Scorpio woman may love her children, she may not be very affectionate toward them. She'll make a devoted mother, though and will encourage them to develop their talents. She'll teach the children to be courageous and steadfast.

VIRGO MAN
SAGITTARIUS WOMAN

You'll most likely never meet a more good-natured girl than the one under the sign of Sagittarius. Generally, she is full of bounce and good cheer. Her sunny disposition seems almost permanent and can be relied upon even on the rainiest of days.

The woman born under this sign is rarely malicious. The Sagittarian is often a little short on tact and says literally anything that comes into her pretty head, regardless of the occasion. Sometimes the words that tumble out of her mouth are downright cutting and cruel, but no matter what she says, she means well. Unfortunately, the Sagittarius woman is capable of losing some of her friends—and perhaps even some of yours—through such carelessness.

On the other hand, you are liable to appreciate her honesty and good intentions. To you, qualities of this sort play an important part in life. With a little patience and practice, you can probably help cure your Sagittarian of her loose tongue; in most cases, she'll give in to your better judgement and try to follow your advice to the letter.

Chances are, she'll be the outdoors type of girl friend. Long hikes, fishing trips, and white-water canoeing will probably appeal to her. She's a busy person, who sets great store in mobility. She won't sit still for one minute if it's not necessary.

She is great company most of the time, and even if your buddies drop by for poker and beer, she won't have any trouble fitting in.

On the whole, she is a very kind and sympathetic woman. If she feels she's made a mistake, she'll be the first to call your attention to it. She's not afraid to own up to her own faults and shortcomings.

You might lose your patience with her once or twice. After she's seen how upset her shortsightedness or tendency to blabbermouth has made you, she'll do her best to please you.

The Sagittarius woman is not the kind who will pry into your business affairs. But she'll always be there, ready to offer advice if you need it.

The Sagittarius woman is seldom suspicious. Your word will almost always be good enough for her.

She is a wonderful and loving friend to her children.

VIRGO MAN
CAPRICORN WOMAN

The Capricorn may not be the most romantic woman of the Zodiac, but she's certainly not frigid when she meets the right man. She believes in true love; she doesn't appreciate getting involved in flings. To her, they're just a waste of time. She's looking for a man who means "business"—in life as well as in love. Although she can be very affectionate with her boyfriend or mate, she tends to let her head govern her heart. That is not to say she is a cool, calculating cucumber. On the contrary, she just feels she can be more honest about love if she consults her brains first.

The Capricorn woman is faithful, dependable, and systematic in just about everything she undertakes. She is very concerned with security and makes sure that every penny she spends is spent wisely. She is very economical about using her time, too. She does not believe in whittling away her energy on a scheme that is bound not to pay off.

Ambitious herself, she is often attracted to the ambitious man—one who is interested in getting somewhere in life. If a man of this sort wins her heart, she'll stick by him and do all she can to help him get to the top.

The Capricorn woman is almost always diplomatic. She makes an excellent hostess. She can be very influential when your business acquaintances come to dinner.

The Capricorn woman is likely to be very concerned, if not extremely proud, of her family tree. Relatives are very important to her, particularly if they're socially prominent. Never say a cross word about her family members. She is likely to punish you by not talking to you for days.

As a rule, she's thorough in whatever she does. The Capricorn woman is well mannered and gracious, no matter what her background.

If you should marry a woman born under this sign, you need never worry about her going on a wild shopping spree. She understands the value of money better than most women. If you turn over your pay check to her at the end of the week, you can be sure that a good hunk of it will wind up in the bank.

The Capricorn mother is loving and correct.

VIRGO MAN
AQUARIUS WOMAN

If you find that you've fallen head over heels for a woman born under the sign of the Water Bearer, you'd better fasten your safety belt. It may take you quite a while to actually discover what this girl is like; even then, you may have nothing to go on but a series of vague hunches. The Aquarian is like a rainbow, full of bright and shining hues; she's like no other girl you've ever known. There is something elusive about her.

The Aquarius woman can be pretty odd and eccentric at times. Some say this is the source of her mysterious charm. You are liable to think she's just a plain screwball; you may be 50 percent right. The Aquarius woman often has her head full of dreams. By nature, she is often unconventional; she has her own thoughts about how the world should be run. Sometimes her ideas may seem weird, but chances are they're just a little too progressive. There is a saying that goes, "The way the Aquarian thinks, so will the world in 50 years."

She'll probably be the most tolerant and open-minded woman you've ever encountered.

If you find that she's too much mystery and charm for you to handle, tell her so and say that you think it would be best to call it quits. She'll probably give you a peck on the cheek and say, "Okay, but let's still be friends." The Aquarius woman is like that. Perhaps you'll both find it easier to get along in a friendship than in a romance.

The Aquarius woman is not a jealous person and, while you're romancing her, she won't expect you to be, either. You'll find her a free spirit most of the time. Just when you think you know her inside-out, you'll discover that you don't really know her at all.

She's a very sympathetic and warm person; she is often helpful to those in need of assistance and advice.

She'll seldom be suspicious even when she has every right to be. If the man she loves makes a little slip, she's inclined to forgive and forget it.

She makes a fine mother. Her positive and big-hearted qualities are easily transmitted to her offspring.

VIRGO MAN
PISCES WOMAN

Many a man dreams of a Piscean kind of a girl. She's soft, cuddly and very domestic. She'll let you be the brains of the family; she's content to just lean on your shoulder and let you be the master of the household.

She can be very ladylike and proper. Your business associates and friends will be dazzled by her warmth and femininity. Although she's a charmer, there is a lot more to her than just a pretty exterior. There is a brain ticking away behind that soft, womanly facade. But you may never become aware of it unless you're married to her.

If she feels you're botching up your married life through careless behavior or if she feels you could be earning more money than you do, she'll tell you so. But any wife would, really.

If anyone dares to say one uncomplimentary word about you in her presence, she is liable to break into tears. The Pisces woman is usually a very sensitive being. Her reaction to adversity, frustration, or anger is just a plain, good, old-fashioned cry.

She'll have an extra-special dinner prepared for you when you make a new conquest in your profession. Don't bother to go into details, though, at the dinner table; she doesn't have much of a head for business matters.

She can do wonders with a house. She is very fond of soft and beautiful things. There will always be plenty of fresh-cut flowers around the house. She'll see that you always have plenty of socks and underwear in that top drawer of your dresser.

Treat her with tenderness and your relationship will be an enjoyable one. She will probably appreciate a box of chocolates. A bunch of beautiful flowers will never fail to make her eyes light up. See that you never forget her birthday or your anniversary. These things are very important to her. If you let them slip your mind, you'll send her into a crying fit that could last a considerable length of time. If you are patient and kind, you can keep a Pisces woman happy for a lifetime. She, however, is not without her faults. Her "sensitivity" may get on your nerves after a while; you may find her lacking in imagination and zest; you may even feel that she uses her tears as a method of getting her own way.

She makes a strong, self-sacrificing mother.

LIBRA
September 23—October 22

CHARACTER ANALYSIS

People born under the sign of Libra are generally quite kind and sympathetic. They dislike seeing others suffer and do what they can to help those in dire straits. Another outstanding characteristic of a Libran is his love of harmony and beauty. He generally has a deep appreciation for all forms of art. He only feels comfortable in places that radiate harmony and beauty. He is often willing to make sacrifices in order to make his environment more suited.

Librans like people. They are often afraid of being alone. They love company. Others like them for their charm and gentle ways. They are happiest when with others.

His is a kind and gentle nature. He would never go out of his way to hurt someone. He is considerate of others' feelings. He will always keep up his end of a bargain. He is cooperative and courteous—sometimes to a fault.

The Libra man or woman is someone who is constantly weighing both sides of a problem. He is a difficult person to satisfy. He wants to make sure that he is right in all the decisions he makes. He may take his time before making a decision. He may even change his mind several times. Balance is important to someone born under this sign. Outwardly, the Libran is calm and intelligent.

Both men and women born under this sign are a bit soft in their dispositions. Sometimes others take advantage of this. The Libra person searches for a world where all things are beautiful and well-balanced—a place where harmony reigns. The Libran—because such a search would be useless in the real world—is given to daydreaming and flights of fancy.

He is a gentle, easy-going person. Librans seldom go where they know they are not wanted. Their interest in beauty and art leads them along the less troublesome and conflicting roads of life.

Libra women are often remarkably beautiful. They seldom have problems attracting the opposite sex. Their voices are generally soft and their eyes lively.

Even though the Libra man may not look terribly strong he is often capable of handling work that would exhaust someone who is bigger or seemingly more vigorous. They often know how to use what strength they have to effective advantage.

All in all, the Libra person is good-natured and easy-going. He may, however, become somewhat out of sorts if he is ill. Being sick tends to make him finicky and ill-humored. He likes sympathy when he is in this condition and when his whims are not satisfied he is likely to complain about being neglected or unloved.

Occupation

The Libra man or woman is usually pleasant to work with. He likes to cooperate with others. He will not oppose authority unless he feels that it is unjust. The Libran is flexible. It is not difficult for him to shift from one phase of an operation to another. Environment may have an uncommonly strong influence on the Libran; it may spur him on to greater heights or slow him down. Sometimes he needs to be inspired by the activities of those working in his immediate vicinity. He will sometimes look at the other fellow to see how he is working before he begins on his own.

The Libra person likes to work in pleasant surroundings. He abhors filth and disorder. He does what he can to bring about the working conditions that are best suited to his nature. Libra people are not attracted to work that is likely to be strenuous or untidy.

Libra people make good business partners. They are quite good at making the proper decisions at the right time. The person born under this sign knows how to weigh the pros and cons of an argument or problem. People often turn to him to make the right decision. Others find it easy to believe in his powers for reasoning. He seldom makes a wrong move. He can always be relied upon to do what is proper.

On the whole the Libran is rather moderate or conservative in most things; this stems from his desire to avoid extremes —especially if they are apt to bring about controversy. Secrets are safe with the Libran, especially if they might do someone some harm.

The Libran can often achieve what he wants through friendly persuasion. Because of his calm, others often find him a port in a storm. He will tell people what he knows they want to hear in order to bolster their confidence and to avoid unpleasantness. He is tactful and knows how to use his gentleness to his own advantage; others may try to take advantage of him, but when he has his wits about him, this is rather difficult. Even when others think they see through him, they find him a difficult nut to crack. He is so strong in his ways of persuasion that he is almost never undermined.

The Libra man or woman is even-tempered generally, but he can flare up when cornered. Still and all, he cools off quite rapidly and is willing to let bygones be bygones. The Libran understands others quite deeply because of his sympathetic nature; it is quite easy for him to put himself in another's place. He is considerate of other people's opinions no matter how wrong they may seem.

The Libran is fair-minded. He dislikes it when someone is mistreated or cheated out of a chance that is rightfully his. Injustice infuriates him. In all matters, he tries to make the right decision. He may take his time about coming to a conclusion.

In most social affairs, the Libran is quite popular and charming. People like him because of his pleasantness and easy-going ways. Most Librans have a lot of friends. All kinds of people attract him. He seldom makes preferences on a superficial basis.

Harmony plays an important part in the life of every Libran. He will try to preserve it at all costs. Harsh realities disturb the Libra man or woman so that he is at times given to lying in order to preserve peace and harmony.

Health

Librans are generally well-groomed and graceful. Their features, for the most part, are small. They are interested in maintaining good health and would never do anything that might encourage illness—even in a slight way. Quite often the man or woman born under this sign is not terribly vigorous and may require lots of rest in order to feel fit. Although he may never say no to a social obligation, the Libran often tires quickly as a result of them. If he does not have his proper rest, he is easily irritated.

Still, the Libran is built well and strongly. In spite of this, he is not what you could really call a strong person. His resistance is not always what it should be; often he falls ill before others when colds are going around. Still, he has remarkable powers of recovery and does not stay out of commission for very long. In spite of the fact that he is delicate, he is surprisingly resilient.

has the ability to reason well and to analyze. Philosophical argument does not frighten him and he can hold his own in almost any intellectual debate. He has a talent for objectivity; he can put himself in another's shoes quite easily. As a mediator he is excellent. People born under this sign also make good diplomats.

He can view things calmly when necessary. He is not easily swayed by his emotions if the truth or justice is at stake. He wants what is good for everybody concerned. He tends to look at things the way they are. He is not one to make a mountain out of a mole-hill. In moments of confusion, his mind is as clear as a bell. In law, the Libran can often be of service to many. He makes a competent judge or lawyer. He knows how to criticize without hurting and, therefore, he could do well as a reviewer of plays or books. Some Librans turn out to be admirable scientists and physicists.

Most Librans are good in creative matters. Anything to do with art or aesthetics appeals to them most of the time. Some of them make good painters, writers, or musicians. The person under this sign sometimes ignores surges of inspiration when they over-come him for fear of being too self-indulgent, but the strong Libran knows how to seize these moments to further his aims and interests. Some of the greatest painters in the world were born under the sign of Libra.

Because the Libra person is good at persuasion, he makes an invaluable salesman. He is in possession of so much charm that his customers often buy more than they originally intended. Because of their rare beauty, Libra women often do well in the field of modeling or acting.

The Libran is capable of spending more money than he actual-ly has. During his lifetime, great sums are apt to come into his hand. He does not care too much about money, though. He is gen-erous to a fault, and finds it hard to refuse people who claim they are in need. The Libran usually has expensive tastes. He finds it hard to save money. Because he likes people and a busy social life, the person born under this sign often spends considerable sums in entertainment. Luxuries are as important to him at times as ne-cessities are to someone else.

In spite of his light ways with money, the Libran is no fool. He knows well how to discourage someone who is only interested in him for his finances.

Home and Family

Home is important to the average Libran. It must be a place where he can relax and feel comfortable. It must radiate charm, beauty, and harmony. A popular person, the Libra man or woman loves to entertain. Nothing excites him more than company of good friends and acquaintances. He usually makes a good host; he knows how to put his guests at ease. People like to visit him be-cause of his charming and easy-going ways.

The furnishings in a Libran's home are usually of excellent taste. They like ornamental furnishings; things that are often a bit ostentatious. No Libra home is without its paintings or pieces of sculpture. The Libra woman is often excellent at interior decorat-ing. She may have a habit of changing the interior of her house quite often.

The Libra person is refined in nature and is not fond of getting his hands soiled. He'd rather leave the rough tasks for others to do. If he has money enough he'll see to it that someone comes to the house several times a week to clean up after him. There are always flowers and plants in the Libra home. In general, he is fond of light gardening.

There is usually a definite relationship between the Libra woman and her home. It usually complements or supplements her charm and personality.

The person born under this sign is generally a good parent. He or she does what he can to bring up the offspring properly. He never tries to influence his children unnecessarily. He lets them develop along natural lines, never forcing them into a mold he has designed. One thing a Libran respects in a child is originality and individuality. The Libran parent is far from strict, yet his children seldom turn out spoiled. The Libra mother or father will correct or punish whenever it is absolutely necessary. Most of the time, the children listen to him because of his calm sure way. They have faith in their Libra parent and usually respect his judgement. Children like being with Libra adults because in them they have a sympathetic friend—someone who can understand their point of view.

Librans as children are often happy and friendly. Parents find them ideal because they are so agreeable and cooperative. They never challenge their parents' authority and do what is expected of them most of the time. Libra children are often creative. Whenever they show signs of artistic ability they should be encouraged. Some of them are great daydreamers at school and have to be encouraged and inspired in order to do their best.

Social Relationships

The Libra man or woman usually makes a good friend because of his even disposition and easy-going ways. Others turn to him in time of need. He always is able to advise someone in a helpful manner. Generally he is honest and sincere in his dealings with his associates and friends. However, the Libra person may feel a bit envious if his friends have things that are nicer than his. Librans do not enjoy being alone and perhaps this is the reason they are so friendly. They enjoy being popular and well-liked. They seldom disappoint people who believe in them. All in all, they are quite cooperative and easy to get along with. They can be counted on to do the right thing at all times.

The person born under this sign usually becomes angry rather quickly. However, he quickly gets over it and is willing to kiss and make up within a short time after his explosion. Whatever he does he will try to avoid hurting someone else's feelings. He is not cruel or petty. That is not his nature.

The Libra person is a good conversationalist. Often at parties he's the center of attention. People generally have the impression that he is well-informed and rather aristocratic. At times he is upset or disturbed but does what he can not to let it show.

LOVE AND MARRIAGE

In matters of love and romance, the Libran is without equal. He is usually well up on everything that has to do with romance. Love is important to him. He is affectionate and gentle—considerate of his mate or lover.

At times, the Libra man or woman may be uncertain of his feelings. He may go through a series of love affairs before he really knows what he is looking for in a mate. He is rather fickle. He can be quite passionate in a love affair, then some days later break it off or lose interest for no apparent reason. It is just one of Libra's ways—difficult as it may be to understand.

He is easily attracted to members of the opposite sex and enjoys their company immensely. Others find his charm difficult to resist. Some people born under this seventh sign of the Zodiac are somewhat sentimental and are easily moved; this quality often appeals to their lovers or admirers. When he desires to transfer his affection he usually does so with much tact and consideration.

Librans are often passionate lovers in spite of their calm and gentle ways. Their calm fronts often hide a hot temperament. When in love he'll forsake his usual lamb-like ways for those of a lion.

The Libra woman expects to be handled with kid gloves by the man who professes to love her. She enjoys small courtesies and enjoys having things done for her.

Libra people are generally quite well suited for marriage or permanent love relationships. Although they may go from one romance to the other quite easily, what they are always in search of is permanent union. They are quite domestic by nature and enjoy setting up house and attending to family affairs. Some of them marry quite young. Although they may not be faithful at all times, they are honest in their intention of being steadfast.

The Libra person enjoys homelife. A place for entertaining and sharing the company of those he loves, the home is something rather special for him. He is usually a very considerate partner. His mate may find it a difficult task keeping up with him. His ease in social relationships is a quality that is rare to come by.

In spite of an occasional post-marital fling that he may find difficult to pass up from time to time, the Libran shuns all thoughts of divorce or separation. He does what he can to keep his marriage together and will try to keep his more serious faults to himself. He is not likely to be open about his indiscretions with his mate for fear of upsetting her and the relationship.

Romance and the Libra Woman

Libra women are quite passionate and affectionate. Most of them possess a mysterious charm which makes them much in demand with the opposite sex. The Libra woman is never short of admirers. She may have a difficult time trying to make up her mind about which one to settle down with, but she does what she can to enjoy herself during her state of indecision. She may go from one affair to the other without any regrets or misgivings. Others may accuse her of being a great flirt, but in all love relationships she is quite sincere. She is changeable though and impulsive and this makes it hard for her to be consistent in her affections at times.

The Libra woman adjusts to married life very well. When she has found the right man she is willing to do all she can to keep their life a peaceful and harmonious one. In spite of her inclination to flirt, the Libra woman usually remains faithful after she has married. At times, she may find herself strongly attracted to another man but she knows how to control herself and would do nothing that might jeopardize her marriage.

The Libra woman is usually poised and charming—in a rather standoffish way; underneath, however, she may be very passionate and loving. Her husband may find her more romantic than he expected. She is the kind of woman most men adore. There is something helpless yet seductive about her. She is not the sort of woman who would like to wear the pants in the family. She is only too glad to let someone else manage everything; she likes being taken care of.

Although she may seem terribly dependent and clinging, when the situations calls for her to take things over, she can do this quite ably. She's the kind of a woman who generally gets things her own way; her charm and beauty are indeed irresistible.

The Libra woman makes an ideal wife. She knows how to arrange things in a home so that they radiate peace, harmony, and beauty. When guests arrive, she knows how to make them feel comfortable immediately. She makes an excellent hostess. Her husband is apt to find her an invaluable companion. He can discuss things with her at his ease. The Libra woman is quite intelligent and has no difficulty in discussing matters that many women fail to understand or master.

She is a lover of a busy social life; however, she would be willing to give up all the glitter and laughter of party going if it interfered with her duties as a wife or mother.

The Libra woman makes an understanding mother. It is important to her that her children get a chance to develop their real personalities. She is quite persuasive in a gentle way.

Her tastes are rather expensive. She may run up bills without giving it much thought. If her husband can afford her extravagance, chances are he won't complain. He is apt to feel that his charming wife is worth the extra expense.

Romance and the Libra Man

Libra men have no trouble at all in attracting members of the opposite sex. Women find them charming and handsome. They are usually quite considerate of their women friends and know how to make them feel important and loved. The Libra man is quite a lover. He is not at a loss when it comes to romancing, for he finds love one of the most important things there is about life.

One fault, however, is the Libra man's ability to change from one love to another with appalling ease. He is always sincere in his love interests, but sometimes he finds it difficult to remain in love with the same person for a long period of time.

Women like him because he seems to know what is right; he never does the wrong thing, no matter what the occasion. His interest in the arts and such matters impress women. His sensitivity is another quality they often admire. The Libra man does not stint when it comes to demonstrating his affection for the woman he believes he loves; however, he is quite crestfallen if the woman should indicate that she is not ready to reciprocate.

Once he settles down, the Libra man makes a good husband and father. He is well suited to family life. Home is important to him. He likes to entertain close friends and relatives frequently. He is generally a very considerate and lively host. It is important that the Libra man find the right woman for his married life. If he has selected someone who finds it difficult to show the same interest in him that he shows in her, he will begin to look elsewhere for companionship. However, he is interested in having stability in his home and will do what he can to keep things in order.

He may be rather difficult to please at times, particularly if his wife does not share his refined tastes. If his wife has a practical mind, so much the better—for generally speaking, the Libran has a poor head for financial matters and is apt to let money slip through his fingers like water.

As a father he is quite considerate and encouraging. He is anxious to see his children express themselves as they desire; yet he will not tolerate spoiled behavior. Children understand him generally, and do what they can to please him.

Woman—Man

**LIBRA WOMAN
ARIES MAN**

In some ways, the Aries man resembles an intellectual mountain goat leaping from crag to crag. He has an insatiable thirst for knowledge. He's ambitious and is apt to have his finger in many pies. He can do with a woman like you—someone attractive, quickwitted, and smart.

He is not interested in a clinging-vine kind of wife, but someone who is there when he needs her; someone who listens and understands what he says; someone who can give advice if he should ever need it—which is not likely to be often. The Aries man wants a woman who will look good on his arm without hanging on it too heavily. He is looking for a woman who has both feet on the ground and yet is mysterious and enticing—a kind of domestic Helen of Troy whose face or fine dinner can launch a thousand business deals if need be. That woman he's in search of sounds a little like you, doesn't she? If the shoe fits, put it on. You won't regret it.

The Aries man makes a good husband. He is faithful and attentive. He is an affectionate kind of man. He'll make you feel needed and loved. Love is a serious matter for the Aries man. He does not believe in flirting or playing the field—especially after he's found the woman of his dreams. He'll expect you to be as constant in your affection as he is in his. He'll expect you to be one hundred percent his; he won't put up with any nonsense while romancing you.

The Aries man may be pretty progressive and modern about many things; however, when it comes to pants wearing, he's downright conventional: it's strictly male attire. The best position you can take in the relationship is a supporting one. He's the boss and that's that. Once you have learned to accept that, you'll find the going easy.

The Aries man, with his endless energy and drive, likes to relax in the comfort of his home at the end of the day. The good home-maker can be sure of holding his love. He's keen on slippers and pipe and a comfortable armchair. If you see to it that everything in the house is where he expects to find it, you'll have no difficulty keeping the relationship on an even keel.

Life and love with an Aries man may be just the medicine you need. He'll be a good provider. He'll spoil you if he's financially able.

He's young at heart and can get along with children easily. He'll spoil them every chance he gets.

LIBRA WOMAN
TAURUS MAN

If you've got your heart set on a man born under the sign of Tau-rus, you'll have to learn the art of being patient. Taureans take their time about everything—even love.

The steady and deliberate Taurus man is a little slow on the draw; it may take him quite a while before he gets around to pop-ping that question. For the woman who doesn't mind twiddling her thumbs, the waiting and anticipating almost always pays off in the end. Taurus men want to make sure that every step they take is a good one—particularly if they feel that the path they're on is one that leads to the altar.

If you are in the mood for a whirlwind romance, you had bet-ter cast your net in shallower waters. Moreover, most Taureans prefer to do the angling themselves. They are not keen on women taking the lead; once she does, he's liable to drop her like a dead fish. If you let yourself get caught on his terms, you'll find that he's fallen for you—hook, line and sinker.

The Taurus man is fond of a comfortable home life. It is very important to him. If you keep those home fires burning you will have no trouble keeping that flame in your Taurean's heart aglow. You have a talent for homemaking; use it. Your taste in furnish-ings is excellent. You know how to make a house come to life with colors and decorations.

Taurus, the strong, steady, and protective Bull may not be your idea of a man on the move; still he's reliable. Perhaps he could be the anchor for your dreams and plans. He could help you to ac-quire a more balanced outlook and approach to your life. If you're given to impulsiveness, he could help you to curb it. He's the man who is always there when you need him.

When you tie the knot with a man born under Taurus, you can put away fears about creditors pounding on the front door. Taureans are practical about everything including bill paying. When he carries you over that threshold, you can be certain that the entire house is paid for, not only the doorsill.

As a housewife, you won't have to worry about putting aside your many interests for the sake of back-breaking house chores. Your Taurus hubby will see to it that you have all the latest time-saving appliances and comforts.

Your children will be obedient and orderly. Your Taurus husband will see to that.

LIBRA WOMAN
GEMINI MAN

The Gemini man is quite a catch. Many a woman has set her cap for him and failed to bag him. Generally, Gemini men are intelligent, witty, and outgoing. Many of them tend to be rather versatile. The Gemini man could easily wind up being your better half.

One thing that causes a Twin's mind and affection to wander is a bore, and it is unlikely that an active woman like you would ever allow herself to be accused of being that. The Gemini man who has caught your heart will admire you for your ideas and intellect —perhaps even more than for your homemaking talents and good looks.

The woman who hitches up with a Twin needn't feel that once she's made her marriage vows that she'll have to store her interests and ambition in the attic somewhere. The Gemini man will admire you for your zeal and liveliness. He's the kind of guy who won't scowl if you let him shift for himself in the kitchen once in a while. In fact, he'll enjoy the challenge of wrestling with pots and pans himself for a change. Chances are, too, that he might turn out to be a better cook than you—that is, if he isn't already.

The man born under the sign of the Twins is a very active person. There aren't many women who have enough pep to keep up with him, but this should be no problem for a spry woman like you. The Gemini man is a dreamer, planner and idealist. A woman with a strong personality could easily fill the role of rudder for her Gemini's ship-without-a-sail. If you are a cultivated, purposeful woman, he won't mind it too much. The intelligent Twin is often aware of his shortcomings and doesn't resent it if someone with better bearings than himself gives him a shove in the right direction—when it's needed. The average Gemini does not have serious ego-hangups and will even accept a well-deserved chewing out from his mate quite good-naturedly.

When you team up with a Gemini man, you'll probably always have a houseful of people to entertain—interesting people, too; Geminis find it hard to tolerate sluggish minds and dispositions.

People born under Gemini generally have two sides to their natures, as different as night and day. It's very easy for them to be happy-go-lucky one minute, then down in the dumps the next. They hate to be bored and will generally do anything to make their lives interesting, vivid, and action-packed.

Gemini men are always attractive to the opposite sex. He'll flirt occasionally but it will never amount to anything serious.

As a father, he's a pushover; he loves children so much that he lets them do what they want.

LIBRA WOMAN
CANCER MAN

Chances are you won't hit it off too well with the man born under Cancer if your plans are love, but then, Cupid has been known to do some pretty unlikely things. The Cancer man is very sensitive—thin-skinned and occasionally moody. You've got to keep on your toes—and not step on his—if you're determined to make a go of the relationship.

The Cancer man may be lacking in some of the qualities you seek in a man, but when it comes to being faithful and being a good provider, he's hard to beat.

The perceptive woman will not mistake the Crab's quietness for sullenness or his thriftiness for pennypinching. In some respects, he is like that wise old owl out on a limb; he may look like he's dozing but actually he hasn't missed a thing. Cancer people often possess a well of knowledge about human behavior; they can come across with some pretty helpful advice to those in trouble or in need. He can certainly guide you in making investments both in time and money. He may not say much, but he's always got his wits about him.

The Crab may not be the match or catch for a woman like you; at times, you are likely to find him downright dull. True to his sign, he can be fairly cranky and crabby when handled the wrong way. He is perhaps more sensitive than he should be.

If you're smarter than your Cancer friend, be smart enough not to let him know. Never give him the idea that you think he's a little short on brain power. It would send him scurrying back into his shell—and all that ground lost in the relationship will perhaps never be recovered.

The Crab is most himself at home. Once settled down for the night or the weekend, wild horses couldn't drag him farther than the gatepost—that is, unless those wild horses were dispatched by his mother. The Crab is sometimes a Momma's boy. If his mate does not put her foot down, he will see to it that his mother always comes first. No self-respecting wife would ever allow herself to play second fiddle—even if it's to her old gray-haired mother-in-law. With a little bit of tact, however, she'll find that slipping into that number-one position is as easy as pie (that legendary one his mother used to bake).

If you pamper your Cancer man, you'll find that "Mother" turns up increasingly less—at the front door as well as in conversations.

Cancer men make protective, proud, and patient fathers.

LIBRA WOMAN
LEO MAN

For the woman who enjoys being swept off her feet in a romantic whirlwind fashion, Leo is the sign of love. When the Lion puts his mind to romancing, he doesn't stint. It's all wining and dining and dancing till the wee hours of the morning.

Leo is all heart and knows how to make his woman feel like a woman. The girl in constant search of a man she can look up to need go no farther: Leo is ten-feet tall—in spirit if not in stature. He's a man not only in full control of his faculties but in full control of just about any situation he finds himself in. He's a winner.

The Leo man may not look like Tarzan, but he knows how to roar and beat his chest if he has to. The woman who has had her fill of weak-kneed men, finds in a Leo someone she can at last lean upon. He can support you not only physically but spiritually as well. He's good at giving advice that pays off.

Leos are direct people. They don't believe in wasting time or effort. They almost never make unwise investments.

Many Leos rise to the top of their professions; through example, they often prove to be a source of great inspiration to others.

Although he's a ladies' man, the Leo man is very particular about his ladies. His standards are high when it comes to love interests. The idealistic and cultivated woman should have no trouble keeping her balance on the pedestal the Lion sets her on. Leo believes that romance should be played on a fair give-and-take basis. He won't stand for any monkey business in a love relationship. It's all or nothing.

You'll find him a frank, off-the-shoulder person; he generally says what is on his mind.

If you decide upon a Leo man for a mate, you must be prepared to stand behind him full-force. He expects it—and usually deserves it. He's the head of the house and can handle that position without a hitch. He knows how to go about breadwinning and, if he has his way (and most Leos do have their own way), he'll see to it that you'll have all the luxuries you crave and the comforts you need.

It's unlikely that the romance in your marriage will ever die out. Lions need love like flowers need sunshine. They're ever-amorous and generally expect like attention and affection from their mates. Leos are fond of going out on the town; they love to give parties, as well as go to them.

Leos make strict fathers, generally. They love their children but won't spoil them.

LIBRA WOMAN
VIRGO MAN

The Virgo man is all business—at least he may seem so to you. He is usually very cool, calm, and collected. He's perhaps too much of a fussbudget to wake up deep romantic interests in a woman like you. Torrid romancing to him is just so much sentimental mush. He can do without it and can make that quite evident in short order. He's keen on chastity and, if necessary, he can lead a sedentary, sexless life without caring too much about the fun others think he's missing. In short, you are liable to find him a first-class dud. He doesn't have much of an imagination; flights of fancy don't interest him. He is always correct and likes to be handled correctly. Almost everything about him is orderly. "There's a place for everything . . . " is likely to be an adage he'll fall back upon quite regularly.

He does have an honest-to-goodness heart, believe it or not. The woman who finds herself strangely attracted to his cool, feet-flat-on-the-ground ways, will discover that his is a constant heart, not one that goes in for flings or sordid affairs. Virgos take an awfully long time to warm up to someone. A practical man, even in matters of the heart, he wants to know just what kind of person you are before he takes a chance on you.

The impulsive girl had better not make the mistake of kissing her Virgo friend on the street—even if it's only a peck on the cheek. He's not at all demonstrative and hates public displays of affection. Love, according to him, should be kept within the confines of one's home—with the curtains drawn. Once he believes that you are on the level with him as far as your love is concerned, you'll see how fast he can lose his cool. Virgos are considerate, gentle lovers. He'll spend a long time, though, getting to know you. He'll like you before he loves you.

A romance with a Virgo man can be a sometime—or, rather, a onetime—thing. If the bottom ever falls out, don't bother reaching for the adhesive tape. Nine times out of ten he won't care about patching up. He's a once-burnt-twice-shy guy. When he crosses your telephone number out of his address book, he's crossing you out of his life—for good.

Neat as a pin, he's thumbs-down on what he considers "sloppy" housekeeping. An ashtray with just one stubbed out cigarette in it can annoy him even if it's only two seconds old. Glassware should always sparkle and shine if you want to keep him happy.

If you marry him, keep your sunny-side up.

Your children should be kept as spotless as your house. Kids with dirty faces and hands displease him. Train them to be kind and courteous.

LIBRA WOMAN
LIBRA MAN

If there's a Libra in your life, you are most likely a very happy woman. Men born under this sign have a way with women. You'll always feel at ease in a Libra's company; you can be yourself when you're with him.

The Libra man can be moody at times. His moodiness is often puzzling. One moment he comes on hard and strong with declarations of his love, the next moment you find that he's left you like yesterday's mashed potatoes. He'll come back, though; don't worry. Libras are like that. Deep down inside he really knows what he wants even though he may not appear to.

You'll appreciate his admiration of beauty and harmony. If you're dressed to the teeth and never looked lovelier, you'll get a ready compliment—and one that's really deserved. Libras don't indulge in idle flattery. If they don't like something, they are tactful enough to remain silent.

Libras will go to great lengths to preserve peace and harmony—even tell a fat lie if necessary. They don't like showdowns or disagreeable confrontations. The frank woman is all for getting whatever is bothering her off her chest and out into the open, even if it comes out all wrong. To the Libra man, making a clean breast of everything seems like sheer folly sometimes.

You may lose your patience while waiting for your Libra friend to make up his mind. It takes him ages sometimes to make a decision. He weighs both sides carefully before committing himself to anything. You seldom dillydally—at least about small things—and so it's likely that you will find it difficult to see eye to eye with a hesitating Libran when it comes to decision-making methods.

All in all, though, he is kind, considerate, and fair. He is interested in the "real" truth; he'll try to balance everything out until he has all the correct answers. It's not difficult for him to see both sides of a story.

He's a peace-loving man. The sight of blood is apt to turn his stomach.

Librans are not showoffs. Generally, they are well-balanced, modest people. Honest, wholesome, and affectionate, they are serious about every love encounter they have. If he should find that the girl he's dating is not really suited to him, he will end the relationship in such a tactful manner that no hard feelings will come about.

The Libra father is firm, gentle, and patient.

LIBRA WOMAN
SCORPIO MAN

Many find the Scorpio's sting a fate worse than death. When his anger breaks loose, you had better clear out of the vicinity.

The average Scorpio may strike you as a brute. He'll stick pins into the balloons of your plans and dreams if they don't line up with what he thinks is right. If you do anything to irritate him—just anything—you'll wish you hadn't. He'll give you a sounding out that would make you pack your bags and go back to mother—if you were that kind of a girl.

The Scorpio man hates being tied down to homelife—he would rather be out on the battlefield of life, belting away at whatever he feels is a just and worthy cause, instead of staying home nestled in a comfortable armchair with the evening paper. If you are a girl who has a homemaking streak—don't keep those home fires burning too brightly, too long; you may just run out of firewood.

As passionate as he is in business affairs and politics, the Scorpio man still has plenty of pep and ginger stored away for love-making.

Most women are easily attracted to him—perhaps you are no exception. Those who allow a man born under this sign to sweep them off their feet, shortly find that they are dealing with a cauldron of seething excitement. The Scorpio is passionate with a capital P, you can be sure of that. But he's capable of dishing out as much pain as pleasure. Damsels with fluttering hearts who, when in the embrace of a Scorpio, think "This is it," had better be in a position moments later to realize that "Perhaps this isn't it."

Scorpios are blunt. An insult is likely to whiz out of his mouth quicker than a compliment.

If you're the kind of woman who can keep a stiff upper lip, take it on the chin, turn a deaf ear, and all that, because you feel you are still under his love spell in spite of everything: lots of luck.

If you have decided to take the bitter with the sweet, prepare yourself for a lot of ups and downs. Chances are you won't have as much time for your own affairs and interests as you'd like. The Scorpio's love of power may cause you to be at his constant beck and call.

Scorpios like fathering large families. They love children but quite often they fail to live up to their responsibilities as a parent.

LIBRA WOMAN
SAGITTARIUS MAN

If you've set your cap for a man born under the sign of Sagittarius, you may have to apply an awful lot of strategy before you can persuade him to get down on bended knee. Although some Sagittarians may be marriage-shy, they're not ones to skitter away from romance. You'll find a love relationship with a Sagittarian—whether a fling or "the real thing"—a very enjoyable experience.

As a rule, Sagittarians are bright, happy, healthy people. They have a strong sense of fair play. Often they are a source of inspiration to others. They are full of drive and ideas.

You'll be taken by the Sagittarian's infectious grin and his lighthearted friendly nature. If you do wind up being the woman in his life, you'll find that he's apt to treat you more like a buddy than the love of his life. It's just his way. Sagittarians are often more chummy than romantic.

You'll admire his broadmindedness in most matters—including those of the heart. If, while dating you, he claims that he still wants to play the field, he'll expect you to enjoy the same liberty. Once he's promised to love, honor, and obey, however, he does just that. Marriage for him, once he's taken that big step, is very serious business.

The Sagittarius man is quick-witted. He has a genuine interest in equality. He hates prejudice and injustice. Generally, Sagittarians are good at sports. They love the great out-of-doors and respect wild life in all its forms.

He's not much of a homebody. Quite often he's occupied with faraway places either in his daydreams or in reality. He enjoys being on the move. He's got ants in his pants and refuses to sit still for long stretches at a time. Humdrum routine—especially at home—bores him.

At the drop of a hat, he may ask you to whip off your apron and dine out for a change. He likes to surprise people.

He'll take great pride in showing you off to his friends. He'll always be considerate where your feelings are concerned; he will never embarrass or disappoint you intentionally.

His friendly, sun-shiny nature is capable of attracting many people. Like you, he's very tolerant when it comes to friends. You will most likely spend a great deal of time helping him entertain people.

Sagittarians are all thumbs when it comes to tiny tots. They develop an interest in children when they grow older and wiser.

LIBRA WOMAN
CAPRICORN MAN

A with-it girl like you is likely to find the average Capricorn man a bit of a drag. The man born under the sign of the Goat is often a closed person and difficult to get to know. Even if you do get to know him, you may not find him very interesting.

In romance, Capricorn men are a little on the rusty side. You'll probably have to make all the passes.

You may find his plodding manner irritating and his conservative, traditional ways downright maddening. He's not one to take chances on anything. "If it was good enough for my father, it's good enough for me" may be his motto. He follows a way that is tried and true.

Whenever adventure rears its tantalizing head, the Goat will turn the other way; he's just not interested.

He may be just as ambitious as you are—perhaps even more so—but his ways of accomplishing his aims are more subterranean or, at least, seem so. He operates from the background a good deal of the time. At a gathering you may never even notice him, but he's there, taking in everything, sizing everyone up—planning his next careful move.

Although Capricorns may be intellectual to a degree, it is not generally the kind of intelligence you appreciate. He may not be as quick or as bright as you; it may take him ages to understand a simple joke.

If you do decide to take up with a man born under this sign, you ought to be pretty good in the "Cheering Up" department. The Capricorn man often acts as though he's constantly being followed by a cloud of gloom.

The Capricorn man is most himself when in the comfort and privacy of his own home. The security possible within four walls can make him a happy man. He'll spend as much time as he can at home. If he is loaded down with extra work, he'll bring it home instead of working overtime at the office.

You'll most likely find yourself frequently confronted by his relatives. Family is very important to the Capricorn—*his* family that is. They had better take a pretty important place in your life, too, if you want to keep your home a happy one.

Although his caution in most matters may all but drive you up the wall, you'll find that his concerned way with money is justified most of the time. He'll plan everything right down to the last penny.

He can be quite a scold with children. You'll have to step in and smooth things out.

LIBRA WOMAN
AQUARIUS MAN

Aquarians love everybody—even their worst enemies sometimes. Through your love relationship with an Aquarian you'll find yourself running into all sorts of people, ranging from near-genius to downright insane—and they're all friends of his.

As a rule, Aquarians are extremely friendly and open. Of all the signs, they are perhaps the most tolerant. In the thinking department, they are often miles ahead of others.

You'll most likely find your relationship with this man a challenging one. Your high respect for intelligence and imagination may be reason enough for you to set your heart on a Water-Bearer. You'll find that you can learn a lot from him.

In the holding-hands phase of your romance, you may find that your Water-Bearing friend has cold feet. Aquarians take quite a bit of warming up before they are ready to come across with that first goodnight kiss. More than likely, he'll just want to be your pal in the beginning. For him, that's an important first step in any relationship—love included. The "poetry and flowers" stage—if it ever comes—will come later. The Aquarian is all heart; still, when it comes to tying himself down to one person and for keeps, he is almost always sure to hesitate. He may even try to get out of it if you breathe down his neck too heavily.

The Aquarius man is no Valentino and wouldn't want to be. The kind of love life he's looking for is one that's made up mainly of companionship. Although he may not be very romantic, the memory of his first romance will always hold an important position in his heart. Some Aquarians wind up marrying their childhood sweethearts.

You won't find it difficult to look up to a man born under the sign of the Water-Bearer, but you may find the challenge of trying to keep up with him dizzying. He can pierce through the most complicated problem as if it were a matter of $2 + 2$. You may find him a little too lofty and high-minded, but don't judge him too harshly if that's the case; he's way ahead of his time—your time, too, most likely.

If you marry this man, he'll stay true to you. Don't think that once the honeymoon is over, you'll be chained to the kitchen sink forever. Your Aquarius husband will encourage you to keep active in your own interests and affairs. You'll most likely have a minor tiff now and again but never anything serious.

Kids love him and vice-versa. He'll be as tolerant with them as he is with adults.

LIBRA WOMAN
PISCES MAN

The man born under Pisces is quite a dreamer. Sometimes he's so wrapped up in his dreams that he's difficult to reach. To the average, ambitious woman, he may seem a little sluggish.

He's easy-going most of the time. He seems to take things in his stride. He'll entertain all kinds of views and opinions from just about anyone, nodding or smiling vaguely, giving the impression that he's with them 100 percent while that may not be the case at all. His attitude may be "why bother" when he is confronted with someone wrong who thinks he's right. The Pisces man will seldom speak his mind if he thinks he'll be rigidly opposed.

The Pisces man is oversensitive at times—he's afraid of getting his feelings hurt. He'll sometimes imagine a personal affront when none's been made. Chances are you'll find this complex of his maddening; at times, you may feel like giving him a swift kick where it hurts the most. It won't do any good, though. It would just add fuel to the fire of his complex.

One thing you will admire about this man is his concern for people who are sickly or troubled. He'll make his shoulder available to anyone in the mood for a good cry. He can listen to one hard-luck story after another without seeming to tire. When his advice is asked, he is capable of coming across with some pretty important words of wisdom. He often knows what's bugging someone before that person is aware of it himself. It's almost intuitive with Pisces, it seems. Still, at the end of the day, he looks forward to some peace and quiet. If you've got a problem on your mind, don't dump it into his lap at the end of the day. If you do, you're liable to find him short-tempered. He's a good listener but he can only take so much.

Pisces men are not aimless although they may seem so at times. The positive sort of Pisces man is quite often successful in his profession and is likely to wind up rich and influential. Material gain, however, is not a direct goal for a man born under this sign.

The weaker Pisces is usually content to stay put on the level where he happens to find himself. He won't complain too much if the roof leaks or the fence is in need of repair. He'll just shrug it off as a minor inconvenience. He's got more important things to think about, he'll say.

Because of their seemingly laissez-faire manner, people born under this sign are immensely popular with children. For tots they play the double role of confidant and playmate. It will never enter his mind to discipline a child, no matter how spoiled or incorrigible that child becomes.

Man—Woman

LIBRA MAN
ARIES WOMAN

The Aries woman may be a little too bossy and busy for you. Generally speaking, Aries women are ambitious creatures. They tend to lose their patience with thorough and deliberate people who take a lot of time to complete something. The Aries woman is a fast worker. Sometimes she's so fast she forgets to look where she's going. When she stumbles or falls, it would be nice if you were there to grab her. Aries women are proud. They don't like to be told "I told you so" when they err. Tongue-wagging can turn them into blocks of ice. However, don't begin to think that the Aries woman frequently gets tripped up in her plans. Quite often they are capable of taking aim and hitting the bull's-eye. You'll be flabbergasted at times by their accuracy as well as by their ambition.

You are perhaps somewhat slower than the Aries woman in attaining your goals. Still, you are not apt to make mistakes along the way; you're seldom ill-prepared.

The Aries woman is rather sensitive at times. She likes to be handled with gentleness and respect. Let her know that you love her for her brains as well as for her good looks. Never give her cause to become jealous. When your Aries woman sees green, you'd better forget about sharing a rosy future together. Handle her with tender love and care and she's yours.

The Aries woman can be giving if she feels her partner is deserving. She is no iceberg; she responds to the proper masculine flame. She needs a man she can look up to and feel proud of. If the shoe fits, put it on. If not, better put your sneakers back on and quietly tiptoe out of her sight. She can cause you plenty of heartache if you've made up your mind about her and she hasn't made up hers about you. Aries women are very demanding at times. Some of them tend to be high-strung. They can be difficult if they feel their independence is being hampered.

The cultivated Aries woman makes a wonderful homemaker and hostess. You'll find that she's very clever in decorating; she knows how to use colors. Your house will be tastefully furnished; she'll see to it that it radiates harmony. Friends and acquaintances will love your Aries wife. She knows how to make everyone feel at home and welcome.

Although the Aries woman may not be keen on burdensome responsibilities, she is fond of children and the joy they bring.

LIBRA MAN
TAURUS WOMAN

The woman born under the sign of Taurus may lack a little of the sparkle and bubble you often like to find in a woman. The Taurus woman is generally down-to-earth and never flighty. It's important to her that she keep both feet flat on the ground. She is not fond of bounding all over the place, especially if she's under the impression that there's no profit in it.

On the other hand, if you hit it off with a Taurus woman, you won't be disappointed in the romance area. The Taurus woman is all woman and proud of it, too. She can be very devoted and loving once she decides that her relationship with you is no fly-by-night romance. Basically, she's a passionate person. In sex, she's direct and to-the-point. If she really loves you, she'll let you know she's yours—and without reservations.

Better not flirt with other women once you've committed yourself to her. She's capable of being very jealous and possessive.

She'll stick by you through thick and thin. It's almost certain that if the going ever gets rough, she won't go running home to her mother. She can adjust to the hard times just as graciously as she can to the good times.

Taureans are, on the whole, pretty even-tempered. They like to be treated with kindness. Pretty things and soft objects make them purr like kittens.

You may find her a little slow and deliberate. She likes to be safe and sure about everything. Let her plod along if she likes;

don't coax her, but just let her take her own sweet time. Everything she does is done thoroughly and, generally, without mistakes.

Don't deride her for being a slowpoke. It could lead to flying pots and pans and a fireworks display that could put Bastille Day to shame. The Taurus woman doesn't anger readily but when prodded often enough, she's capable of letting loose with a cyclone of ill will. If you treat her with kindness and consideration, you'll have no cause for complaint.

The Taurean loves doing things for her man. She's a whiz in the kitchen and can whip up feasts fit for a king if she thinks they'll be royally appreciated. She may not fully understand you but she'll adore you and be faithful to you if she feels you're worthy of it.

The Taurus woman makes a wonderful mother. She knows how to keep her children well-loved, cuddled, and warm. She may have some difficult times with them when they reach adolescence, though.

LIBRA MAN
GEMINI WOMAN

You may find a romance with a woman born under the sign of the Twins a many-splendoured thing. In her you can find the intellectual companionship you often look for in a friend or mate. A Gemini girl friend can appreciate your aims and desires because she travels pretty much the same road as you do intellectually —that is, at least part of the way. She may share your interest but she will lack your tenacity.

She suffers from itchy feet. She can be here, there·. . . all over the place and at the same time, or so it would seem. Her eagerness to move about may make you dizzy, still you'll enjoy and appreciate her liveliness and mental agility.

Geminis often have sparkling personalities; you'll be attracted by her warmth and grace. While she's on your arm you'll probably notice that many male eyes are drawn to her—she may even return a gaze or two, but don't let that worry you. All women born under this sign have nothing against a harmless flirt once in a while. They enjoy this sort of attention; if she feels she is already spoken for, however, she will never let it get out of hand.

Although she may not be as handy as you'd like in the kitchen, you'll never go hungry for a filling and tasty meal. She's as much in a hurry as you are, and won't feel like she's cheating by breaking out the instant mashed potatoes or the frozen peas. She may not be much of a good cook but she is clever; with a dash of this and a suggestion of that, she can make an uninteresting TV dinner taste like something out of a Jim Beard cookbook. Then, again, maybe you've struck it rich and have a Gemini girl friend who finds complicated recipes a challenge to her intellect. If so, you'll find every meal a tantalizing and mouth-watering surprise.

When you're beating your brains out over the Sunday cross-word puzzle and find yourself stuck, just ask your Gemini girl; she'll give you all the right answers without batting an eyelash.

Like you, she loves all kinds of people. You may even find that you're a bit more particular than she. Often all that a Gemini re-quires is that her friends be interesting . . . and stay interesting. One thing she's not able to abide is a dullard.

Leave the party-organizing to your Gemini sweetheart or mate and you'll never have a chance to know what a dull moment is. She'll bring the swinger out in you if you give her half a chance.

A Gemini mother enjoys her children. Like them, she's often restless, adventurous, and easily bored.

LIBRA MAN
CANCER WOMAN

If you fall in love with a Cancer woman, be prepared for anything. They are sometimes difficult to understand when it comes to love. In one hour, she can unravel a whole gamut of emotions; it will leave you in a tizzy. She'll always keep you guessing, that's for sure.

You may find her a little too uncertain and sensitive for your liking. You'll most likely spend a good deal of time encouraging her—helping her to erase her foolish fears. Tell her she's a living doll a dozen times a day and you'll be well loved in return.

Be careful of the jokes you make when in her company—don't let any of them revolve around her, her personal interests, or her family. If you do, you'll most likely reduce her to tears. She can't stand being made fun of. It will take bushels of roses and tons of chocolates—not to mention the apologies—to get her to come back out of her shell.

In matters of money-managing, she may not easily come around to your way of thinking. Money will never burn a hole in her pocket book. You may get the notion that your Cancer sweet-heart or mate is a direct descendant of Scrooge. If she has her way, she'll hang onto the first dollar you earned. She's not only that way with money, but with everything right on up from bakery string to jelly jars. She's a saver; she never throws anything away, no matter how trivial.

Once she returns your "I love you," you'll find you have an affectionate, self-sacrificing, and devoted woman on your hands. Her love for you will never alter unless you want it to. She'll put you up on a high pedestal and will do everything—even if it's against your will—to keep you there.

Cancer women love homelife. For them, marriage is an easy step to make. They're domestic with a capital D. She'll do her best to make your home comfortable and cozy. The Cancer woman is more herself at home than in strange surroundings. She makes an excellent hostess. The best in her comes out when she's in her own environment.

Cancer women make the best mothers of all the signs of the Zodiac. She'll make every complaint of her child a major catastrophe. With her, children come first. If you're lucky, you'll run a close second. You'll perhaps see her as too devoted to the children. You may have a hard time convincing her that her apron strings are too long.

LIBRA MAN
LEO WOMAN

If you can manage a girl who likes to kick up her heels every now and again, then the Leo woman was made for you. You'll have to learn to put away jealous fears when you take up with a woman born under this sign, as she's often the kind that makes heads turn and tongues wag. You don't necessarily have to believe any of what you hear—it's most likely just jealous gossip or wishful thinking.

The Leo girl has more than a fair share of grace and glamour. She knows it, generally, and knows how to put it to good use. Needless to say, other women in her vicinity turn green with envy and will try anything, short of shoving her into the nearest lake, in order to put her out of the running.

If she's captured your heart and fancy, woo her full-force if your intention is to eventually win her. Shower her with expensive gifts and promise her the moon—if you're in a position to go that far—then you'll find her resistance beginning to weaken. It's not that she's such a difficult cookie—she'll probably make a lot over you once she's decided you're the man for her—but she does enjoy a lot of attention. What's more: she feels she's entitled to it. Her mild arrogance, however, is becoming. The Leo woman knows how to transform the crime of excessive pride into a very charming misdemeanor. It sweeps most men right off their feet—rather, all men. Those who do not succumb to her leonine charm are few and far between.

If you've got an important business deal to clinch and you have doubts as to whether you can bring it off as you should, take your Leo wife along to the business luncheon and it'll be a cinch that you'll have that contract—lock, stock, and barrel—in your pocket before the meeting is over. She won't have to say or do anything . . . just be there at your side. The grouchiest oil magnate can be transformed into a gushing, obedient schoolboy if there's a Leo woman in the room.

If you're rich and want to see to it that you stay that way, don't give your Leo spouse a free hand with the charge accounts and credit cards. When it comes to spending, Leos tend to overdo. If you're poor, you have no worries because the luxury-loving Leo will most likely never recognize your existence—let alone, consent to marry you.

As a mother, she's both strict and easy. She can pal around with her children and still see to it that they know their places. She won't spoil them but she'll be a loving and devoted parent.

LIBRA MAN
VIRGO WOMAN

The Virgo woman may be a little too difficult for you to understand at first. Her waters run deep. Even when you think you know her, don't take any bets on it. She's capable of keeping things hidden in the deep recesses of her womanly soul—things she'll only release when she's sure that you're the man she's been looking for. It may take her some time to come around to this decision. Virgo girls are finicky about almost everything; everything has to be letter-perfect before they're satisfied. Many of them have the idea that the only people who can do things correctly are Virgos.

Nothing offends a Virgo woman more than slovenly dress, sloppy character, or a careless display of affection. Make sure your tie is not crooked and your shoes sport a bright shine before you go calling on this lady. Keep your off-color jokes for the locker room; she'll have none of that. Take her arm when crossing the street. Don't rush the romance. Trying to corner her in the back of a cab may be one way of striking out. Never criticize the way she looks—in fact, the best policy would be to agree with her as much as possible. Still, there's just so much a man can take; all those dos and don'ts you'll have to observe if you want to get to first base with a Virgo may be just a little too much to ask of you. After a few dates, you may come to the conclusion that she just isn't worth all that trouble. However, the Virgo woman is mysterious enough, generally speaking, to keep her men running back for more. Chances are you'll be intrigued by her airs and graces.

If lovemaking means a lot to you, you'll be disappointed at first in the cool ways of your Virgo girl. However, under her glacial facade there lies a hot cauldron of seething excitement. If you're patient and artful in your romantic approach, you'll find that all that caution was well worth the trouble. When Virgos love, they don't stint. It's all or nothing as far as they're concerned. Once they're convinced that they love you, they go all the way, right off the bat—tossing all cares to the wind.

One thing a Virgo woman can't stand in love is hypocrisy. They don't give a hoot about what the neighbors say, if their hearts tell them "Go ahead." They're very concerned with human truths . . . so much so that if their hearts stumble upon another fancy, they're liable to be true to that new heartthrob and leave you standing in the rain.

She's honest to her heart and will be as true to you as you are with her, generally. Do her wrong once, however, and it's curtains.

She's both strict and tender with children. As a mother she'll try to bring out the best in her children.

LIBRA MAN
LIBRA WOMAN

You'll probably find that the girl born under the sign of Libra is worth more than her weight in gold. She's a woman after your own heart.

With her, you'll always come first—make no mistake about that. She'll always be behind you 100 percent, no matter what you do. When you ask her advice about almost anything, you'll most likely get a very balanced and realistic opinion. She is good at thinking things out and never lets her emotions run away with her when clear logic is called for.

As a homemaker she is hard to beat. She is very concerned with harmony and balance. You can be sure she'll make your house a joy to live in; she'll see to it that the house is tastefully furnished and decorated. A Libran cannot stand filth or disarray—it gives her goose-bumps. Anything that does not radiate harmony, in fact, runs against her orderly grain.

She is chock-full of charm and womanly ways. She can sweep just about any man off his feet with one winning smile. When it comes to using her brains, she can outthink almost anyone and, sometimes, with half the effort. She is diplomatic enough, though, never to let this become glaringly apparent. She may even turn the conversation around so that you think you were the one who did all the brainwork. She couldn't care less, really, just as long as you wind up doing what is right.

The Libra woman will put you up on a pretty high pedestal. You are her man and her idol. She'll leave all the decision-making—large or small—up to you. She's not interested in running things and will only offer her assistance if she feels you really need it.

Some find her approach to reason masculine; however, in the areas of love and affection the Libra woman is *all* woman. She'll literally shower you with love and kisses during your romance with her. She doesn't believe in holding out. You shouldn't either, if you want to hang on to her.

She is the kind of girl who likes to snuggle up to you in front of the fire on chilly autumn nights . . . the kind of girl who will bring you breakfast in bed Sunday. She'll be very thoughtful about anything that concerns you. If anyone dares suggest you're not the grandest guy in the world, she'll give that person what-for. She'll defend you till her dying breath. The Libra woman will be everything you want her to be.

She'll be a sensitive and loving mother. Still, you'll always come before the children.

LIBRA MAN
SCORPIO WOMAN

The Scorpio woman can be a whirlwind of passion—perhaps too much passion to really suit you. When her temper flies, you'd better lock up the family heirlooms and take cover. When she chooses to be sweet, you're apt to think that butter wouldn't melt in her mouth . . . but, of course, it would.

The Scorpio woman can be as hot as a tamale or as cool as a cucumber, but whatever mood she's in, she's in it for real. She does not believe in posing or putting on airs.

The Scorpio woman is often sultry and seductive—her femme-fatale charm can pierce through the hardest of hearts like a laser ray. She may not look like Mata Hari (quite often Scorpios resemble the tomboy next door) but once she's fixed you with her tantalizing eyes, you're a goner.

Life with the Scorpio woman will not be all smiles and smooth-sailing; when prompted, she can unleash a gale of venom. Generally, she'll have the good grace to keep family battles within the walls of your home. When company visits, she's apt to give the impression that married life with you is one great big joyride. It's just one of her ways of expressing her loyalty to you—at least in front of others. She may fight you tooth and nail in the confines of your living room, but at a ball or during an evening out, she'll hang onto your arm and have stars in her eyes.

Scorpio women are good at keeping secrets. She may even keep a few buried from you if she feels like it.

Never cross her up on even the smallest thing. When it comes to revenge, she's an eye-for-an-eye woman. She's not too keen on forgiveness—especially if she feels she's been wronged unfairly. You'd be well-advised not to give her any cause to be jealous, either. When the Scorpio woman sees green, your life will be made far from rosy. Once she's put you in the doghouse, you can be sure that you're going to stay there awhile.

You may find life with a Scorpio woman too draining. Although she may be full of the old paprika, it's quite likely that she's not the kind of girl you'd like to spend the rest of your natural life with. You'd prefer someone gentler and not so hot-tempered, someone who can take the highs with the lows and not bellyache, someone who is flexible and understanding. A woman born under Scorpio can be heavenly, but she can also be the very devil when she chooses.

As a mother, a Scorpio is protective and encouraging.

LIBRA MAN
SAGITTARIUS WOMAN

You'll most likely never come across a more good-natured girl than the one born under the sign of Sagittarius. Generally, they're full of bounce and good cheer. Their sunny disposition seems almost permanent and can be relied upon even on the rainiest of days.

Women born under this sign are almost never malicious. If ever they seem to be it is only seeming. Sagittarians are often a little short on tact and say literally anything that comes into their pretty little heads—no matter what the occasion. Sometimes the words that tumble out of their mouths seem downright cutting and cruel. Still, no matter what she says, she means well. The Sagittarius woman is quite capable of losing some of her friends—and perhaps even some of yours—through a careless slip of the lip.

On the other hand, you are liable to appreciate her honesty and good intentions. To you, qualities of this sort play an important part in life. With a little patience and practice, you can probably help cure your Sagittarian of her loose tongue; in most cases, she'll give in to your better judgement and try to follow your advice to the letter.

Chances are she'll be the outdoors type of girl friend. Long hikes, fishing trips, and white-water canoeing will most likely appeal to her. She's a busy person; no one could ever call her a slouch. She sets great store in mobility. Her feet are itchy and she won't sit still for a minute if she doesn't have to.

She is great company most of the time and, generally, lots of fun. Even if your buddies drop by for poker and beer, she won't have any trouble fitting in.

On the whole, she is a very kind and sympathetic woman. If she feels she's made a mistake, she'll be the first to call your attention to it. She's not afraid to own up to her faults and shortcomings.

You might lose your patience with her once or twice. After she's seen how upset her shortsightedness or tendency to blabber has made you, she'll do her best to straighten up.

The Sagittarian woman is not the kind who will pry into your business affairs. But she'll always be there, ready to offer advice if you need it. If you come home with red stains on your collar and you say it's paint and not lipstick, she'll believe you.

She'll seldom be suspicious; your word will almost always be good enough for her.

She is a wonderful and loving friend to her children.

LIBRA MAN
CAPRICORN WOMAN

If you are not a successful businessman or, at least, on your way to success, it's quite possible that a Capricorn woman will have no interest in entering your life. Generally speaking, she is a very security-minded female; she'll see to it that she invests her time only in sure things. Men who whittle away their time with one unsuccessful scheme or another, seldom attract a Capricorn. Men who are interested in getting somewhere in life and keep their noses close to the grindstone quite often have a Capricorn woman behind them, helping them to get ahead.

Although she is a kind of "climber" she is not what you could call cruel or hard-hearted. Beneath that cool, seemingly calculating, exterior, there's a warm and desirable woman. She just happens to think that it is just as easy to fall in love with a rich or ambitious man as it is with a poor or lazy one. She's practical.

The Capricorn woman may be keenly interested in rising to the top, but she'll never be aggressive about it. She'll seldom step on someone's feet or nudge competitors away with her elbows. She's quiet about her desires. She sits, waits, and watches. When an opening or opportunity does appear, she'll latch onto it lickety-split. For an on-the-move man, an ambitious Capricorn wife or girlfriend can be quite an asset. She can probably give you some very good advice about business matters. When you invite the boss and his wife for dinner, she'll charm them both right off the ground.

The Capricorn woman is thorough in whatever she does: cooking, cleaning, making a success out of life . . . Capricorns make excellent hostesses as well as guests. Generally, they are very well mannered and gracious, no matter what their backgrounds are. They seem to have a built-in sense of what is proper. Crude behavior or a careless faux pas can offend them no end.

If you should marry a woman born under Capricorn you need never worry about her going on a wild shopping spree. Capricorns are careful with every cent that comes into their hands. They understand the value of money better than most women and have no room in their lives for careless spending.

Capricorn girls are usually very fond of family—their own, that is. With them, family ties run very deep. Don't make jokes about her relatives; she won't stand for it. You'd better check her family out before you get down on bended knee; after your marriage you'll undoubtedly be seeing lots of them.

Capricorn women make loving mothers. They train their children to be polite and respectful.

LIBRA MAN
AQUARIUS WOMAN

If you find that you've fallen head over heels for a woman born under the sign of the Water-Bearer, you'd better fasten your safety belt. It may take you quite a while to actually discover what this girl is like—and even then, you may have nothing to go on but a string of vague hunches. The Aquarian is like a rainbow, full of bright and shining hues; she's like no other girl you've ever known. There is something elusive about her—something delightfully mysterious. You'll most likely never be able to put your finger on it. It's nothing calculated, either; Aquarians don't believe in phony charm.

There will never be a dull moment in your life with this Water-Bearing woman; she seems to radiate adventure and magic. She'll most likely be the most open-minded and tolerant woman you've ever met. She has a strong dislike for injustice and prejudice. Narrow-mindedness runs against her grain.

She is very independent by nature and quite capable of shifting for herself if necessary. She may receive many proposals for marriage from all sorts of people without ever really taking them seriously. Marriage is a very big step for her; she wants to be sure she knows what she's getting into. If she thinks that it will seriously curb her independence and love of freedom, she's liable to shake her head and give the man his engagement ring back—if indeed she's let the romance get that far.

The line between friendship and romance is a pretty fuzzy one for an Aquarian. It's not difficult for her to remain buddy-buddy with an ex-lover. She's tolerant, remember? So, if you should see her on the arm of an old love, don't jump to any hasty conclusions.

She's not a jealous person herself and doesn't expect you to be, either. You'll find her pretty much of a free spirit most of the time. Just when you think you know her inside-out, you'll discover that you don't really know her at all.

She's a very sympathetic and warm person; she can be helpful to people in need of assistance and advice.

She'll seldom be suspicious even if she has every right to be. If she loves a man, she'll forgive him just about anything. If he allows himself a little fling, chances are she'll just turn her head the other way. Her tolerance does have its limits, however, and her man should never press his luck at hanky-panky.

She makes a big-hearted mother; her good qualities rub off on her children.

LIBRA MAN
PISCES WOMAN

Many a man dreams of a Pisces kind of a girl. You're perhaps no exception. She's soft and cuddly—very domestic. She'll let you be the brains of the family; she's contented to just lean on your shoulder and let you be the master of the household.

She can be very ladylike and proper. Your business associates and friends will be dazzled by her warmth and femininity. Although she's a charmer, there is a lot more to her than just a pretty face. There is a brain ticking away behind that soft, womanly facade. You may never become aware of it—that is, until you're married to her. It's no cause for alarm, however; she'll most likely never use it against you.

If she feels you're botching up your married life through careless behavior or if she feels you could be earning more money than you do, she'll tell you about it. But any wife would, really. She will never try to usurp your position as head of the family.

No one had better dare say one uncomplimentary word about you in her presence. It's liable to cause her to break into tears. Pisces women are usually very sensitive beings. Their reaction to adversity, frustration, or anger is just a plain, good, old-fashioned cry. They can weep buckets when inclined.

She'll have an extra-special dinner waiting for you when you come home from an important business meeting. Don't bother to go into any of the details about the meeting, though, at the dinner table; she doesn't have much of a head for business matters, usually, and is only too happy to leave that up to you.

She can do wonders with a house. She is very fond of soft and beautiful things. There will always be plenty of fresh-cut flowers around the house. She'll see that you always have plenty of socks and underwear in that top drawer of your dresser.

Treat her with tenderness and your relationship will be an enjoyable one. She's most likely fond of chocolates. A bunch of beautiful roses will never fail to make her eyes light up. See to it that you never forget her birthday or your anniversary. She won't. If you are patient and kind, you can keep a Pisces woman happy for a lifetime. She is, however, not without her faults. Her "sensitivity" may get on your nerves after a while. You may find her lacking in imagination and zest. You may even feel that she only uses her tears as a method of getting her own way.

She makes a strong, self-sacrificing mother. She'll find it difficult to refuse her children anything.

SCORPIO
October 23—November 22

CHARACTER
ANALYSIS

People born under the sign of Scorpio are usually gifted with a very strong personality. Of all the signs, they are perhaps the most goal-directed and relentless. Often they are quite dominating. Some people find them hard to like or appreciate. Scorpio people are not afraid of being disliked. They just do not want to be ignored. They know what they want, generally speaking, and do not give up the struggle until they have it.

He has his own way of doing things—his own laws to follow. As long as he is true to himself, he is happy; he seldom dances to someone else's tune. The Scorpio is a person who perseveres.

The person born under this sign often sees life as one big fight. Often he controls himself like a soldier. He is willing to undergo self-discipline in order to win out. He trains himself so that he is bound to be the victor. Defeat is something the Scorpio man or woman cannot accept. They do their best to see to it that it never comes about. People born under this eighth sign of the Zodiac are fighters. Generally, they are gifted with brains and know how to put them to use. They can be clever and shrewd when the occasion calls for it. The Scorpion could hardly be called sensitive. Most of the time he is not terribly interested in how others might feel or react to his behavior. His nature is not a soft one; he can't be buttered up and sugared over.

Many people find it difficult to understand the personality of the person born under the sign of Scorpio. It is rather a subtle combination of intelligence and ruthlessness. Quite often people of this sign are seized by profound and revealing thoughts that are too complex to express. At such moments, the Scorpio is likely to draw within himself and remain silent. He may spend most of his quiet moments within his own private world—a realm with its own rules and regulations. He is quite interested in the mysteries of life.

Scorpios tend to be consistent in all that they do. They never do things halfway. They are not afraid of conflict situations or emergencies. Under duress they can be relied upon to handle things in a calm manner. He is generally constructive and positive in the way he channels his forces. He is against waste and feels committed to make every gesture—every action—count.

In spite of his good sense of purpose and direction, the person born under the sign of Scorpio is sometimes the victim of his conflicting moods. He may contradict himself several times a day without feeling that he is being untrue to himself and his beliefs. He believes that every moment has its own truth. He feels his moods strongly and believes that it is necessary to obey them in order to remain the person he is. The Scorpio is an organizer. He likes to have things his own way or not at all. On the whole, he is what you would call a principled person. He holds fast to his ideals.

His understanding of life is sometimes remarkable. He is not short on insight and often can analyze a human situation accurately long before others. His knowledge of things in general is often superior to that of others. In spite of the intelligence he has at his disposal he is not the kind of person to take the easy way toward a goal. He seems to have a penchant for argumentation. In some instances, he seems to bring about quarrels just for the enjoyment he derives from crossing swords.

The Scorpio's ability to fly into a rage is considerable. People sometimes wind up disliking him intensely after having witnessed one of his fits of temper. This does not bother him, however. If he loses a friend or two along his way in life he is not apt to let it upset him. He keeps moving on—his ultimate goal always in sight. He is capable of being angry at someone quite abruptly but it never lasts very long. He has more important things to do in life besides holding grudges.

He does not believe in using fancy or complicated language; he is to the point—not really caring how blunt he may sound to sensitive ears. Power—and how to get it—is what is most important to him in life; he does not try to hide this fact.

In spite of his being straight-off-the-shoulder in most of his dealings, the Scorpio man or woman is capable of holding back a fact or two—especially if it is to his or her advantage.

Health

On the whole, the person born under this sign is quite healthy. His constitution is generally strong; he seldom has to worry about common ailments. He is capable of great spurts of energy. He can apply himself to a strenuous task for a long period of time without tiring. The Scorpio person rather enjoys stress and strain; it proves his mettle. As has already been mentioned, the Scorpio man or woman is seldom bothered by illnesses; their resistance is remarkably strong. When, however, he does become ill—really ill—he has to give in in order to recuperate. Illness is a sort of weakness or frailty to him. He is ashamed of himself when he is sick and does all he can to quickly recover. If he tries to fight it—that is, act as if he weren't incapacitated—he often winds up worse off than when he began. It is difficult at times for the Scorpio to realize that even he has limits.

In spite of the fact that he can take on a lot, it is also important that the person born under the sign of Scorpio learn how to relax. Often, Scorpio people push themselves to the limit—and sometimes there are serious consequences to pay. Overworked Scorpios are highly susceptible to breakdowns of various sorts. It is the cultivated Scorpio man or woman who knows when and how to relax. Because of their serious attitude toward most things, the Scorpio when young often seems much older than what he really is.

The Scorpio man or woman is often sturdily built. There is usually something massive about them—they are often largeboned and have deep set interesting eyes. In general, they could best be described as sensuous in their appearance and behavior. Scorpio women are often beautiful in a seductive way. Their voices are sometimes husky and rather sexy.

The weakest part of the Scorpio's anatomy is his digestive system. Whenever he becomes ill this is the area usually affected. The sensible person born under this sign pays attention to minor warnings of an oncoming illness and does something about it while there is still time. Some people born under this sign pick up infections rather easily.

Occupation

The Scorpio man or woman is a very industrious person. He enjoys keeping busy and he always finishes what he starts. He does not believe in turning out slipshod work; he's a professional. The Scorpio is not a person lacking in push or energy. He takes his work seriously and does what he can to be recognized for his deeds.

Quite often the person born under the sign of Scorpio dislikes heavy work. He would much rather leave that to someone else. He is goal-directed. It is important for him to achieve what he desires . . . in some instances, it does not matter how. When he sets his mind to it—and he usually does—he can accomplish almost anything he wishes. Obstacles do not frighten him; in fact, the threat of opposition seems to spur him on. He is no quitter. He'll hang on until the bitter end. His never-say-die attitude helps him to scan heights that would frighten others. He's confident of himself and of the moves he makes.

The Scorpio person is ambitious. He can make work even when there isn't any—just to keep busy. Idleness tends to bore him and make him disagreeable. He is fascinated by difficult tasks. He enjoys figuring out ways of how to attack a project or a chore. He doesn't always choose the easiest route—but the most challenging. In short he's a fighter.

His intellectual ability is quite superior. There is almost no subject that would stump him. He is not afraid of learning something new and is quite capable of applying himself to new or different trains of thought if he feels they will help him achieve his ends.

Generally speaking Scorpio people prefer to work for themselves—they don't like to share tasks, but will if it is absolutely necessary. People who work with them are not apt to find this relationship an enjoyable one, for the Scorpio is always ready to bring about a quarrel or argument if things are not going exactly the way he likes.

Often people born under this sign do extremely well in the field of medicine or science. They have a deep interest in exploration of all sorts and are willing to devote their whole lives to something that is somewhat elusive and mysterious. The Scorpio has an open mind and this helps him to succeed in the things he does. He likes to make tests; to prove things through experimentation. He isn't afraid of taking risks. He is always sure of himself—sure that he'll come out a winner. Some people born under the sign of Scorpio make good detectives and lawyers.

The Scorpio person feels deeply whenever he is engaged socially. He can either hate someone or love them; there is no middle of the road. He cannot afford to be indifferent. He'll admire someone if he feels that person deserves to be admired. He makes a strong leader. The people working under him may dislike him rather intensely but they will not try to usurp his authority. He won't put up with any nonsense from his subordinates and he lets them know that right from the start.

In whatever he undertakes, he forges ahead with no thought of quitting until the goal has been reached. His powers of concentration are amazingly strong. He seldom allows himself to be distracted from the path he has chosen. He expects the people working under him to have the same sort of devotion to purpose that he has. He can be quite a driver at times. If others are not up to his standards, he won't waste time by pampering them—he'll simply discard them and take on new people.

Some Scorpios have a bit of the genius in them. They are quite perceptive and often can accurately guess what someone else is thinking—particularly in a conflict situation.

People born under this sign are basically materialists. They are quite fond of money and what it can do and make no effort to disguise their interest. They are extremely power-oriented. Money seldom presents a problem to them. One way or another, they almost always come by the finances they feel they need or deserve. They are fond of luxuries as well, of course; and are sometimes deeply involved in such power-games as "keeping up with the Joneses;" in most instances the Joneses wind up trying to keep up with them.

The Scorpio person is careful in the way he handles his finances. He doesn't believe in waste, although at times he is given to being extravagant. When he is wealthy, he can be a bit of a show-off about it. He can easily detect a false friend—someone who associates with him for the gain he is likely to derive from the relationship.

Home and Family

In general, the person born under the sign of Scorpio is not terribly interested in an intense domestic life. He does not like to feel tied down by home and family. However, he is adaptable and will be willing to sacrifice some of his freedoms for the comforts and conveniences a home life can provide. Routine, though, bores him and is apt to put him in a bad mood. He enjoys a home life that has a surprise in it now and again. Day-in day-out monotony is something he refuses to tolerate.

He is as efficient and forceful in his homemaking as he is in other things. He likes to see to it that everything runs well. His home may be quite glamorous in an ostentatious way. He is fond of a show of luxury. His tastes in furnishings is likely to be somewhat outspoken. It is likely to offend someone who has refined or cultivated taste.

The Scorpio man is proud. He enjoys showing off his possessions. His family is important to him. He likes his wife and children to support him in his interests and attitudes. Keeping his home attractive and luxurious is a full-time activity for many

Scorpios. They are interested in having the latest appliances and the best trademark.

The Scorpio person likes to rule his own roost. His mate had better not try to take the head position. He wears the pants in the family and is apt to make that unmistakably clear before the marriage has taken place. All of the major decisions must be made by him. He'll listen to another's point of view but will hardly take it into consideration when making up his mind.

Luxury helps the Scorpio man or woman to feel successful. It has definite psychological influence. The Scorpio in shabby surroundings is apt to be quite difficult to get along with. A show of affluence brightens his spirits and helps him to feel that he is on the right road.

The Scorpio person is often fond of large families. He may not be as responsible as he should be in caring for them. Quite often he is a strict parent and tolerates no misbehavior from his offspring. The children may resent his iron hand—especially when they are young—but as they reach adulthood they are likely to be thankful for his firmness. The Scorpio is only concerned with instilling those values in his children which will help them to go far in the battlefield of life. He can be quite a disciplinarian. Some of them are quite possessive of their children.

Scorpios as children are often very affectionate. As a rule, they are sensitive children and should be handled in a considerate and loving way. Emotionally, they may not be as strong as children born under other signs. The observant and sensitive parent should have no trouble in bringing him up in such a way that he is able to develop his personality along natural lines as he reaches a stage of independence.

At times the Scorpio child may be difficult to manage. He may be delinquent at times and cause some trouble at school. In spite of this, he is apt to show strong creative or artistic talent during his growing-up period. The wise parent or guardian will do what he can to foster this interest in such a way that it develops along satisfactory lines.

Social Relationships

Scorpio people are deeply interested in sex. They enjoy being physically involved with the people they feel themselves attracted to. They are often given to experimentation in sex; they are curious and want to know all there is to discover. They are, by and large, intensely passionate and intensely emotional. Life without love is difficult for them to imagine. It is important to them that their sex life is well arranged and interesting. They may spend a great deal of time getting involved sexually with all kinds of people before they are satisfied and can concentrate their attention on just one person.

LOVE AND MARRIAGE

The Scorpio can be quite a flirt. He may have quite a number of affairs before he thinks about settling down. In every romantic adventure he is quite sincere. He does not believe in being false or untrue when involved with someone. However, his interest may dissolve after he feels he has discovered everything there was to find out about a particular person. He is not very interested in light romances. He means business when it comes to love. He expects his lover to be as honest in his affections as he is.

The Scorpio is in need of someone who is as passionate and understanding as he is. His romances may be rather violent at times; an element of struggle may be quite definite in them—in fact, it is this quality that will perhaps keep his interest alive in a love affair. He likes to be admired and complimented by his partner. He hates criticism and is apt to become rather difficult if his lover finds fault with him.

He does what he can to make his loved one comfortable and happy. He can be rather generous when in love and is never without a gift or some token of his affection. He likes to impress his loved one with a show of luxury. Often his gifts are quite expensive.

It is important to the Scorpio person that the object of his affections be true during the relationship. He is very jealous and possessive. If he suspects deceit, he can be violent.

The best partner for a Scorpio person is one who can compliment his character. Someone who does not mind being agreeable and supportive. Someone who does not mind letting him make all of the decisions both large and small. A quiet, retiring sort of person sometimes makes the ideal mate for the man or woman born under Scorpio. Two Scorpios often clash; however, if they are cultivated and understand themselves well, they can go far together—helping each other out in various ways.

When the Scorpio man or woman sets his sights on someone he generally wins them. He can be quite demonstrative when dealing with someone who tries to stand between him and his loved one. He will do everything in his power to win the person who interests him. Some people born under this sign will stop at nothing in order to eliminate competition. Others are rather jealous and suspicious when they really have no cause to be.

In married life, the Scorpio person seldom gives himself completely—even though he may expect this of his partner. There is always a corner of himself which he does not give away. In general, the person born under this sign is faithful to his mate. However, if home life is rather dull, he will do what he can not to spend too much time there. He'll see to it that outside interests keep him occupied as much as possible.

The Scorpio person marries for keeps. He is not the kind of person who shouts "divorce!" as soon as something goes wrong. Marriage is important to him and he is willing to do whatever is necessary to keep the relationship alive and fruitful.

Romance and the Scorpio Woman

The Scorpio woman is generally quite attractive and is often sought after by the opposite sex. Her attractiveness is sometimes more suggestive than real. Her voice is rather rough and mellow— her mannerisms not without charm. She can be quite passionate when in love. She may be too much to handle for the man of moderate romantic interests. She does what she can to make a success of her love life. When in love, she does not hold back her affections. She expects the same honesty from her partner.

She is always serious when in love. She may have a great number of affairs before actually settling down. Romance is important to her. But more important is that she find a man that is compatible to her interests and needs. The man she desires, she usually wins. She is sure of herself in matters of the heart and can be very persuasive when necessary. Men find her difficult to ignore or resist. She may be rather jealous and possessive. If she suspects her lover of not being true, she can become quite angry and vindictive.

She is usually accurate when sizing up someone who interests her. She seldom choses the wrong man. She is usually very faithful when married. She does all she can to help her man get ahead in his career. She supports him in all his interests and often is able to supply him with some very good advice. She will never let her husband down even in difficult times. She will fight for her husband if it is necessary.

The Scorpio woman is a bit old-fashioned when it comes to attitudes about marriage. She is often contented with her role as housewife and mother. She does everything she can to keep the household in order.

Although others may not think her suitable material for a mother because of her emotional and sometimes explosive outbursts, she does what she can to bring up her children correctly. She is rather strict, especially when they are young. They understand her better though, as they grow older.

Romance and the Scorpio Man

The Scorpio man is often popular with women. There is something magnetic about his charm. He is protective and adventurous. His passionate way in love often sweeps women off their feet. Love—in each affair—is a matter of life and death. He does not believe in being lighthearted.

As a rule, he is warm and generous. He knows how to make a woman feel loved and wanted. He expects his loved one to be as demonstrative as he is in expressing her love. By nature, he is possessive and resents another's interest in his woman. He can easily become jealous. His anger can be quite frightening to a sensitive woman.

The Scorpio man makes a good husband and father. He is a good provider, most often, and sees to it that his family has everything it needs. His married life is apt to be full of ups and downs. He is affectionate though and true in his desire to be a good husband; this sometimes makes it easier for his wife to accept his changeable nature. He is faithful. Once settled down he is apt to stay true to his wife. The cultivated Scorpio man is often successful in marriage. He knows how to withhold his negative traits so that they do not seriously affect the relationship.

He is fond of large families. Even though he may father one himself, he may not have enough interest in his offspring—especially when they are young—to make them feel secure and well loved. As the children grow older, however, and reach an adult stage, his interest is likely to increase considerably. At any rate, he will always see to it that they never want for anything.

Woman—Man

SCORPIO WOMAN
ARIES MAN

Although it's possible that you could find happiness with a man born under the sign of the Ram, it's uncertain as to how long that happiness would last.

An Aries who has made his mark in the world and is somewhat

steadfast in his outlooks and attitudes could be quite a catch for you. On the other hand, men under this sign are often swift-footed and quick-minded; their industrious mannerisms may fail to impress you, especially if you feel that much of their get-up-and-go often leads nowhere.

When it comes to a fine romance, you want someone with a nice, broad shoulder to lean on. You are likely to find a relationship with someone who doesn't like to stay put for too long somewhat upsetting.

The Aries man may have a little trouble in understanding you, too . . . at least, in the beginning of the relationship. He may find you a bit too shy and moody. Aries men tend to speak their minds; he's liable to criticize you at the drop of a hat.

You may find a man born under this sign too demanding. He may give you the impression that he expects you to be at his beck and call. You have a lot of patience at your disposal and he may try every last bit of it. He is apt to be not as thorough as you in everything he does. In order to achieve success or a goal quickly, he is liable to overlook small but important details—and regret it when it is too late.

Being married to an Aries does not mean that you'll have a secure and safe life as far as finances are concerned. Not all Aries are rash with cash, but they lack the sound head you perhaps have for putting away something for that inevitable rainy day. He'll do his best, however, to see that you're adequately provided for—even though his efforts may leave something to be desired as far as you're concerned.

With an Aries man for a mate, you'll find yourself constantly among people. Aries people generally have many friends—and you may not heartily approve of them all. People born under this sign are often more interested in "interesting" people than they are in influential ones. Although there may be a family squabble from time to time, you are stable enough to be able to take it in your stride.

Aries men love children. They make wonderful fathers. Kids take to them like ducks to water. Their quick minds and behavior appeal to the young.

SCORPIO WOMAN
TAURUS MAN

If you've got your heart set on a man born under the sign of Taurus, you'll have to learn the art of being patient. Taureans take their time about everything—even love.

The steady and deliberate Taurus man is a little slow on the draw; it may take him quite a while before he gets around to pop-ping that question. For the woman who doesn't mind twiddling her thumbs, the waiting and anticipating almost always pays off. Tau-rus men want to make sure that every step they take is a good one —particularly if they feel that the path they're on leads to the al-tar.

If you are in the mood for a whirlwind romance, you had bet-ter cast your net in shallower waters. Moreover, most Taureans prefer to do the angling themselves. They are not keen on women taking the lead; once she does, he's liable to drop her like a dead fish. If you let yourself get caught on his terms, you'll find that he's fallen for you—hook, line, and sinker.

The Taurus man is fond of a comfortable homelife. It is very important to him. If you keep those home fires burning you will have no trouble keeping that flame in your Taurean's heart aglow. You have a talent for homemaking; use it. Your taste in furnish-ings is excellent. You know how to make a house come to life with colors and decorations.

Taurus, the strong, steady, and protective Bull may not be your idea of a man on the move; still he's reliable. Perhaps he could be the anchor for your dreams and plans. He could help you to ac-quire a more balanced outlook and approach to your life. If you're given to impulsiveness, he could help you to curb it. He's the man who is always there when you need him.

When you tie the knot with a man born under Taurus, you can put away fears about creditors pounding on the door. Taureans are practical about everything including bill-paying. When he carries you over that threshold, you can be certain that the entire house is paid for, not only the doorsill.

As a housewife, you won't have to worry about putting aside your many interests for the sake of back-breaking house chores. Your Taurus hubby will see to it that you have all the latest time-saving appliances and comforts.

Your children will be obedient and orderly. Your Taurus hus-band will see to that.

SCORPIO WOMAN
GEMINI MAN

Gemini men, in spite of their charm and dashing manner, may make your skin crawl. They may seem to lack the sort of common sense you set so much store in. Their tendency to start something then, out of boredom, never finish it, may do nothing more than exasperate you.

You may be inclined to interpret a Gemini's jumping around

from here to there as childish if not downright neurotic. A man born under this sign will seldom stay put and if you should take it upon yourself to try and make him sit still, he's liable to resent it strongly.

On the other hand, the Gemini man is liable to think you're an old slowpoke—someone far too interested in security and material things. He's attracted to things that sparkle and dazzle; you, with your practical way of looking at things most of the time, are likely to seem a little dull and uninteresting to this gadabout. If you're looking for a life of security and permanence, you'd better look elsewhere for your Mr. Right.

Chances are you'll be taken by his charming ways and facile wit—few women can resist Gemini magic—but after you've seen through his live-for-today, gossamer facade, you'll most likely be very happy to turn your attention to someone more stable, even if he is not as interesting. You want a man who is there when you need him. You need someone on whom you can fully rely. Keeping track of a Gemini's movements will make you dizzy. Still, if you are a patient woman, you should be able to put up with someone contrary—especially if you feel the experience may be well worth the effort.

A successful and serious Gemini could make you a very happy woman, perhaps if you gave him half a chance. Although you may think he's got bats in his belfry, the Gemini man generally has a good brain and can make good use of it when he wants. Some Geminis who have learned the importance of being diligent have risen to great heights, professionally. President Kennedy was a Gemini as was Thomas Mann and William Butler Yeats. Once you can convince yourself that not all people born under the sign of the Twins are witless grasshoppers, you'll find that you've come a long way in trying to understand them.

Life with a Gemini man can be more fun than a barrel of clowns. You'll never experience a dull moment. He's always the life of the party. He's a little scatterbrained when it comes to handling money most of the time. You'd better handle the budgeting and bookkeeping.

In ways, he's like a child and perhaps that is why he can get along so well with the younger generation.

SCORPIO WOMAN
CANCER MAN

The man born under the sign of Cancer may very well be the man after your own heart. Generally, Cancer people are steady. They are interested in security and practicality. Despite their seemingly grouchy exterior, men born under the sign of the Crab are rather sensitive and kind individuals. They are amost always hard workers and are very interested in becoming successful in business as well as in society. You'll find that his conservative outlook on many things often agrees with yours. He'll be a man on whom you can depend come rain or shine. He'll never shirk his responsibilities as a provider and he'll always see to it that his wife and family never want.

Your patience will come in handy if you decide it's a Cancer man you want for a mate. He isn't the type that rushes headlong into romance. He wants to be sure about love as you do. If after the first couple of months of dating, he suggests that you take a walk with him down lovers' lane, don't jump to the conclusion that he's about to make his "great play." Chances are he'll only hold your hand and seriously observe the stars. Don't let his coolness fool you, though. Beneath his starched reserve lies a very warm heart. He's just not interested in showing off as far as affection is concerned. Don't think his interest is wandering if he doesn't kiss you goodnight at the front door; that just isn't his style. For him, affection should only be displayed for two sets of eyes—yours and his. He's passionate only in private.

He will never step out of line. He's too much of a gentleman for that. When you're alone with him and there's no chance of you being disturbed or spied upon, he'll pull out an engagement ring (that used to belong to his grandmother) and slip it on your trembling finger.

Speaking of relatives, you'll have to get pretty much used to the fact that Cancer men are overly fond of their mothers. When he says his mother is the most wonderful woman in the world, you'd better agree with him—that is, if you want to become his wife.

He'll always be a faithful husband; Cancer men never play around after they've taken that marriage vow. They don't take marriage responsibilities lightly. He'll see to it that everything in the house runs smoothly and that bills are paid promptly—never put aside. He's liable to take all kinds of insurance policies out on his family and property. He'll arrange it so that when retirement time rolls around, you'll both be very well off.

Men under this sign make patient and understanding fathers.

SCORPIO WOMAN
LEO MAN

To know a man born under the sign of the Lion is not necessarily to love him—even though the temptation may be great. When he fixes most girls with his leonine double-whammy, it causes their hearts to pitter-pat and their minds to cloud over.

You are a little too sensible to allow yourself to be bowled over by a regal strut and a roar. Still, there's no denying that Leo has a way with women—even sensible women like yourself. Once he's swept a girl off her feet, it may be hard for her to scramble upright again. However, you are no pushover for romantic charm—especially if you feel it's all show.

He'll wine you and dine you in the fanciest places. He'll croon to you under the moon and shower you with diamonds if he can get a hold of them . . . but, it would be wise to find out just how long that shower is going to last before consenting to be his wife.

Lions in love are hard to ignore, let alone brush off. Your no's will have a way of nudging him on until he feels he has you completely under his spell. Once mesmerized by this romantic power-house, you will most likely find yourself doing things you never dreamed of. Leos can be like vain pussycats when involved romantically. They like to be cuddled, curried, and tickled under the chin. This may not be your cup of tea exactly, still when you're romantically dealing with a man born under the sign of Leo, you'll find yourself doing all kinds of things to make him purr.

Although he may be big and magnanimous while trying to win you, he'll let out a blood-curdling roar if he thinks he's not getting the tender love and care he feels is his due. If you keep him well supplied with affection, you can be sure his eyes will never look for someone else and his heart will never wander.

Leo men often tend to be authoritarian—they are born to lord it over others in one way or another, it seems. If he is the top banana at his firm, he'll most likely do everything he can to stay on top. If he's not number one, he's most likely working on it and will be sitting on the throne before long.

You'll have more security than you can use if he is in a position to support you in the manner to which he feels you should be accustomed. He is apt to be too lavish, at least by your standards.

You'll always have plenty of friends when you have a Leo for a mate. He's a natural-born friend-maker and entertainer. He loves to kick up his heels at a party.

As fathers, Leos tend to spoil their children no end.

SCORPIO WOMAN
VIRGO MAN

Although the Virgo man may be a bit of a fuss-budget at times, his seriousness and dedication to common sense may help you to overlook his tendency to sometimes be overcritical about minor things.

Virgo men are often quiet, respectable types who set great store in conservative behavior and level-headedness. He'll admire you for your practicality and tenacity—perhaps even more than for your good looks. He's seldom bowled over by a glamour-puss. When he gets his courage up, he turns to a serious and reliable girl for romance. He'll be far from a Valentino while dating. In fact, you may wind up making all the passes. Once he does get his motor running, however, he can be a warm and wonderful fellow—to the right girl.

He's gradual about love. Chances are your romance with him will most likely start out looking like an ordinary friendship. Once he's sure you're no fly-by-night flirt and have no plans of taking him for a ride, he'll open up and rain sunshine all over your heart.

Virgo men tend to marry late in life. He believes in holding out until he's met the right girl. He may not have many names in his little black book; in fact, he may not even have a black book. He's not interested in playing the field; leave that to men of the more flamboyant signs. The Virgo man is so particular that he may remain romantically inactive for a long period. His girl has to be perfect or it's no go. If you find yourself feeling weak-kneed for a Virgo man, do your best to convince him that perfection is not so important when it comes to love; help him to realize that he's missing out on a great deal by not considering the near-perfect or whatever it is you consider yourself to be. With your sure-fire perseverance, you will most likely be able to make him listen to reason and he'll wind up reciprocating your romantic interests.

The Virgo man is no block of ice. He'll respond to what he feels to be the right feminine flame. Once your love-life with a Virgo man starts to bubble, don't give it a chance to fall flat. You may never have a second chance at winning his heart.

If you should ever have a falling out with him, forget about patching up. He'd prefer to let the pieces lie scattered. Once married, though, he'll stay that way—even if it hurts. He's too conscientious to try to back out of a legal deal of any sort.

The Virgo man is as neat as a pin. He's thumbs down on sloppy housekeeping. Keep everything bright, neat, and shiny . . . and that goes for the children, too, at least by the time he gets home from work. Chocolate-coated kisses from Daddy's little girl go over like a lead balloon with him.

SCORPIO WOMAN
LIBRA MAN

You are apt to find men born under the sign of Libra too wrapped up in their own private dreams to be really interesting as far as love and romance are concerned. Quite often, he is a difficult person to bring back down to earth; it is hard for him to face reality at times. Although he may be very cautious about weighing both sides of an argument, he may never really come to a reasonable decision about anything. Decision-making is something that often makes the Libra man uncomfortable; he'd rather leave that job to someone else. Don't ask him why for he probably doesn't know himself.

Qualities such as permanance and constancy are important to you in a love relationship. The Libra man may be quite a puzzle for you. One moment he comes on hard and strong with declarations of his love; the next moment you find he's left you like yesterday's mashed potatoes. It does no good to wonder what went wrong. Chances are: nothing, really. It's just one of Libra's strange ways.

He is not exactly what you would call an ambitious person; you are perhaps looking for a mate or friend with more drive and fidelity. You are the sort of person who is interested in getting ahead—in making some headway in the areas that interest you; the Libran is often contented just to drift along. He does have drive, however, but it's not the long-range kind. It is not that he's shiftless or lazy. He's interested in material things; he appreciates luxuries and the like, but he may not be willing to work hard enough to obtain them. Beauty and harmony interest him. He'll dedicate a lot of time arranging things so that they are aesthetically pleasing. It would be difficult to accuse the Libra man of being practical; nine times out of ten, he isn't.

If you do begin a relationship with a man born under this sign, you will have to coax him now and again to face various situations in a realistic manner. You'll have your hands full, that's for sure. But if you love him, you'll undoubtedly do your best to understand him—no matter how difficult this may be.

If you take up with a Libra man, either temporarily or permanently, you'd better take over the task of managing his money. Often he has little understanding of financial matters; he tends to spend without thinking, following his whims.

SCORPIO WOMAN
SCORPIO MAN

Many find the Scorpio's sting a fate worse than death. When his anger breaks loose, you had better clear out of the vicinity.

The average Scorpio may strike you as a brute. He'll stick pins into the balloons of your plans and dreams if they don't line up with what he thinks is right. If you do anything to irritate him—

just anything—you'll wish you hadn't. He'll give you a sounding out that would make you pack your bags and go back to Mother—if you were that kind of a girl.

The Scorpio man hates being tied down to home life—he would rather be out on the battlefield of life, belting away at whatever he feels is a just and worthy cause, instead of staying home nestled in a comfortable armchair with the evening paper. If you are a girl who has a homemaking streak—don't keep those home fires burning too brightly too long; you may just run out of firewood.

As passionate as he is in business affairs and politics, the Scorpio man still has plenty of pep and ginger stored away for lovemaking.

Most women are easily attracted to him—perhaps you are no exception. Those who allow a man born under this sign to sweep them off their feet, shortly find that they're dealing with a pepper pot of seething excitement. The Scorpio man is passionate with a capital P, you can be sure of that. But he's capable of dishing out as much pain as pleasure. Damsels with fluttering hearts who, when in the embrace of a Scorpio, think "This is it," had better be in a position moments later to realize that "Perhaps this isn't it."

Scorpios are blunt. An insult is likely to whiz out of his mouth quicker than a compliment.

If you're the kind of woman who can keep a stiff upper lip, take it on the chin, turn a deaf ear, and all of that, because you feel you are still under his love spell in spite of everything: lots of luck.

If you have decided to take the bitter with the sweet, prepare yourself for a lot of ups and downs. Chances are you won't have as much time for your own affairs and interests as you'd like. The Scorpio's love of power may cause you to be at his constant beck and call.

Scorpios like fathering large families. They love children but quite often they fail to live up to their responsibilities as a parent.

SCORPIO WOMAN
SAGITTARIUS MAN

Sagittarius men are not easy to catch. They get cold feet whenever visions of the altar enter the romance. You'll most likely be attracted to the Sagittarian because of his sunny nature. He's lots of laughs and easy to get along with, but as soon as the relationship begins to take on a serious hue, you may feel yourself a little letdown.

Sagittarians are full of bounce; perhaps too much bounce to suit you. They are often hard to pin down; they dislike staying put. If he ever has a chance to be on-the-move, he'll latch onto it without so much as a how-do-you-do. Sagittarians are quick people—both in mind and spirit. If ever they do make mistakes, it's because of their zip; they leap before they look.

If you offer him good advice, he most likely won't follow it. Saigittarians like to rely on their own wits and ways.

His up-and-at-'em manner about most things is likely to drive you up the wall. He's likely to find you a little too slow and deliberate. "Get the lead out of your shoes," he's liable to tease when you're accompanying him on a stroll or jogging through the park with him on Sunday morning. He can't abide a slowpoke.

At times you'll find him too much like a kid—too breezy. Don't mistake his youthful zest for premature senility. Sagittarians are equipped with first-class brain power and know how to use it. They are often full of good ideas and drive. Generally, they are very broadminded people and very much concerned with fair play and equality.

In the romance department, he's quite capable of loving you wholeheartedly while treating you like a good pal. His hail-fellow-well-met manner in the arena of love is likely to scare off a dainty damsel. However, a woman who knows that his heart is in the right place won't mind it too much if, once in a while, he slaps her (lightly) on the back instead of giving her a gentle embrace.

He's not so much of a homebody. He's got ants in his pants and enjoys being on the move. Humdrum routine—especially at home—bores him silly. At the drop of a hat, he may ask you to whip off your apron and dine out for a change. He's a past-master in the instant surprise department. He'll love to keep you guessing. His friendly, candid nature will win him many friends. He'll expect his friends to be yours, and vice-versa.

Sagittarians make good fathers when the children become older; with little shavers, they feel all thumbs.

SCORPIO WOMAN
CAPRICORN MAN

The Capricorn man is quite often not the romantic kind of lover that attracts most women. Still, with his reserve and calm, he is capable of giving his heart completely once he has found the right girl. The Capricorn man is thorough and deliberate in all that he does; he is slow and sure.

He doesn't believe in flirting and would never lead a heart on a merry chase just for the game of it. If you win his trust, he'll give you his heart on a platter. Quite often, it is the woman who has to take the lead when romance is in the air. As long as he knows you're making the advances in earnest, he won't mind—in fact, he'll probably be grateful. Don't get to thinking he's all cold fish; he isn't. While some Capricorns are indeed quite capable of expressing passion, others often have difficulty in trying to display affection. He should have no trouble in this area, however, once he has found a patient and understanding girl.

The Capricorn man is very interested in getting ahead. He's quite ambitious and usually knows how to apply himself well to whatever task he undertakes. He's far from being a spendthrift. Like you, he knows how to handle money with extreme care. You, with your knack for putting away pennies for that rainy day, should have no difficulty understanding his way with money. The Capricorn man thinks in terms of future security. He wants to make sure that he and his wife have something to fall back on when they reach retirement. There's nothing wrong with that; in fact, it's a plus quality.

The Capricorn man will want you to handle household matters efficiently. Most Capricorn-oriented women will have no trouble in doing this. If he should check up on you from time to time, don't let it irritate you. Once you assure him that you can handle it all to his liking, he'll leave you alone.

The Capricorn man likes to be liked. He may seem dull to some, but underneath his reserve there is sometimes an adventurous streak that has never had a chance to express itself. He may be a real daredevil in his heart of hearts. The right woman—the affectionate, adoring woman can bring out that hidden zest in his nature.

He makes a loving, dutiful father, even though he may not understand his children completely.

SCORPIO WOMAN
AQUARIUS MAN

You are liable to find the Aquarius man the most broadminded man you have ever met; on the other hand, you are also liable to find him the most impractical. Oftentimes, he's more of a dreamer than a doer. If you don't mind putting up with a man whose heart and mind are as wide as the Missouri but whose head is almost always up in the clouds, then start dating that Aquarian who has somehow captured your fancy.

He's no dumbbell; make no mistake about that. He can be busy making some very complicated and idealistic plans when he's got that out-to-lunch look in his eyes. But more than likely, he'll never execute them. After he's shared one or two of his progressive ideas with you, you are liable to ask yourself, "Who is this nut?" But don't go jumping to conclusions. There's a saying that Aquarians are a half-century ahead of everybody else in the thinking department.

If you decide to answer "Yes" to his "Will you marry me?", you'll find out how right his zany whims are on or about your 50th anniversary. Maybe the waiting will be worth it. Could be that you have an Einstein on your hands—and heart.

Life with an Aquarian won't be one of total dispair if you can learn to temper his airiness. The Aquarian always maintains an open mind; he'll entertain the ideas and opinions of everybody although he may not agree with all of them.

His broadmindedness doesn't stop when it comes to you and your personal freedom. You won't have to give up any of your hobbies or projects after you're married; he'll encourage you to continue in your interests.

He'll be a kind and generous husband. He'll never quibble over petty things. Keep track of the money you both spend. He can't. Money burns a hole in his pockets.

At times, you may feel like calling it quits because he fails to satisfy your intense feelings. Chances are, though, that you'll always give him another chance.

He's a good family man. He understands children as much as he loves them.

SCORPIO WOMAN
PISCES MAN

The Pisces man could be the man you've looked for high and low and thought never existed. He's terribly sensitive and terribly romantic. Still, he has a very strong individual character and is well aware that the moon is not made of green cheese. He'll be very considerate of your every wish and will do his best to see to it that your relationship is a happy one.

The Pisces man is great for showering the object of his affection with all kinds of little gifts and tokens of his love.

He's just the right mixture of dreamer and realist; he's capable of pleasing most women's hearts. When it comes to earning bread and butter, the strong Pisces will do all right in the world. Quite often they are capable of rising to the very top. Some do extremely well as writers or psychiatrists. He'll be as patient and understanding with you as you will undoubtedly be with him. One thing a Pisces man dislikes is pettiness; anyone who delights in running another into the ground is almost immediately crossed off his list of possible mates. If you have any small grievances with your girl-friends, don't tell him. He couldn't care less and will think less of you if you do.

If you fall in love with a weak kind of Piscean, don't give up your job at the office before you get married. Better hang onto it until a good time after the honeymoon; you may still need it. A funny thing about the man born under this sign is that he can be content almost anywhere. This is perhaps because he is quite inner-directed and places little value on material things. In a shack or a palace, the Pisces man is capable of making the best of all possible adjustments. He won't kick up a fuss if the roof leaks and if the fence is in sad need of repair, he's liable just to shrug his shoulders. He's got more important things on his mind, he'll tell you. At this point, you'll most likely feel like giving him a piece of your mind. Still and all, the Pisces man is not shiftless or aimless; it is important to understand that material gain is never a direct goal for someone born under this sign.

Pisces men have a way with the sick and troubled. He can listen to one hard-luck story after another without seeming to tire. He often knows what's bothering someone before that someone knows it himself.

As a lover, he'll be quite attentive. You'll never have cause to doubt his intentions or sincerity. Everything will be above-board in his romantic dealings with you.

Children are delighted with Pisces men because of their permissiveness.

Man—Woman

SCORPIO MAN
ARIES WOMAN

The Aries woman may be a little too bossy and busy for you. Generally speaking, Aries are ambitious creatures. They can become a little impatient with people who are more thorough and deliberate than they are—especially if they feel they're taking too much time. The Aries woman is a fast worker. Sometimes she's so fast she forgets to look where she's going. When she stumbles or falls, it would be nice if you were there to catch her. Aries are proud women. They don't like to be told "I told you so" when they err. Tongue lashings can turn them into blocks of ice. Don't begin to think that the Aries woman frequently gets tripped up in her plans. Quite often they are capable of taking aim and hitting the bull's-eye. You'll be flabbergasted at times by their accuracy as well as by their ambition. On the other hand, you're apt to spot a flaw in the Aries woman's plans before she does.

You are perhaps somewhat slower than the Aries in attaining your goals. Still, you are not apt to make mistakes along the way; you're almost always well prepared.

The Aries woman is rather sensitive. She likes to be handled with gentleness and respect. Let her know that you love her for her brains as well as for her good looks. Never give her cause to become jealous. Handle her with tender love and care and she's yours.

The Aries woman can be giving if she feels her partner is deserving. She is no iceberg; she responds to the proper masculine flame. She needs a man she can look up to and feel proud of. If the shoe fits, put it on. If not, better put your sneakers back on and quietly tiptoe out of her sight. She can cause you plenty of heartache if you've made up your mind about her but she hasn't made up hers about you. Aries women are at times very demanding. Some of them tend to be high-strung; they can be difficult if they feel their independence is being hampered.

The cultivated Aries woman makes a wonderful homemaker and hostess. You'll find she's very clever in decorating and using color. Your house will be tastefully furnished; she'll see to it that it radiates harmony. The Aries wife knows how to make guests feel at home.

Although the Aries woman may not be keen on burdensome responsibilities, she is fond of children and the joy they bring.

SCORPIO MAN
TAURUS WOMAN

The woman born under the sign of Taurus may lack a little of the sparkle and bubble you often like to find in a woman. The Taurus woman is generally down-to-earth and never flighty. It's important to her that she keep both feet flat on the ground. She is not fond of bounding all over the place, especially if she's under the impression that there's no profit in it.

On the other hand, if you hit it off with a Taurus woman, you won't be disappointed in romance. The Taurus woman is all woman and proud of it too. She can be very devoted and loving once she decides that her relationship with you is no fly-by-night romance. Basically, she's a passionate person. In sex, she's direct and to-the-point. If she really loves you, she'll let you know she's yours—and without reservations. Better not flirt with other women once you've committed yourself to her. She is capable of being jealous and possessive.

She'll stick by you through thick and thin. It's almost certain that if the going ever gets rough, she'll not go running home to her mother. She can adjust to hard times just as graciously as she can to the good times.

Taureans are, on the whole, even-tempered. They like to be treated with kindness. Pretty things and soft things make them purr like kittens.

You may find her a little slow and deliberate. She likes to be safe and sure about everything. Let her plod along if she likes; don't coax her but just let her take her own sweet time. Everything she does is done thoroughly and, generally, without mistakes. Don't ride her for being a slowpoke. It could lead to flying pots and pans and a fireworks display that would put Bastille Day to shame. The Taurus woman doesn't anger readily but when prodded enough, she's capable of letting loose with a cyclone of anger. If you treat her with kindness and consideration, you'll have no cause for complaint.

The Taurean loves doing things for her man. She's a whiz in the kitchen and can whip up feasts fit for a king if she thinks they'll be royally appreciated. She may not fully understand you, but she'll adore you and be faithful to you if she feels you're worthy of it.

The woman born under Taurus will make a wonderful mother. She knows how to keep her children well-loved, cuddled, and warm. She may find them difficult to manage, however, when they are teen-agers.

SCORPIO MAN
GEMINI WOMAN

The Gemini woman may be too much of a flirt to ever strike your heart seriously. Then again, it depends on what kind of mood she's in. Gemini women can change from hot to cold quicker than a cat can wink its eye. Chances are her fluctuations will tire you, and you'll pick up your heart—if it's not already broken into small pieces—and go elsewhere. Women born under the sign of the Twins have the talent of being able to change their moods and attitudes as frequently as they change their party dresses.

Sometimes, Gemini girls like to whoop it up. Some of them are good-time girls who love burning the candle at both ends. You'll see them at parties and gatherings, surrounded by men of all types, laughing gaily and kicking up their heels. Wallflowers, they're not. The next day you may bump into the same girl at the neighborhood library and you'll hardly recognize her for her "sensible" attire. She'll probably have five or six books under her arm—on five or six different subjects. In fact, she may even work there. If you think you've met the twin sister of Dr. Jekyll and Mr. Hyde, you're most likely right.

You'll probably find her a dazzling and fascinating creature— for a time, at any rate. Most men do. But when it comes to being serious about love you may find that that sparkling Eve leaves quite a bit to be desired. It's not that she has anything against being serious, it's just that she might find it difficult trying to be serious with you.

At one moment, she'll be capable of praising you for your steadfast and patient ways; the next moment she'll tell you in a cutting way that you're an impossible stick in the mud.

Don't even begin to fathom the depths of her mercurial soul— it's full of false bottoms. She'll resent close investigation, anyway, and will make you rue the day you ever took it into your head to try to learn more about her than she feels is necessary. Better keep the relationship full of fun and fancy free until she gives you the go-ahead. Take as much of her as she is willing to give; don't ask for more. If she does take a serious interest in you, then she'll come across with the goods.

There will come a time when the Gemini girl will realize that she can't spend her entire life at the ball and that the security and warmth you have to offer is just what she needs to be a happy, complete woman.

As a mother, she's easy-going with her children. She likes to spoil them as much as she can.

SCORPIO MAN
CANCER WOMAN

The girl born under Cancer needs to be protected from the cold, cruel world. She'll love you for your masculine yet gentle manner; you make her feel safe and secure. You don't have to pull any he-man or heroic stunts to win her heart; that's not what interests her. She's more likely to be impressed by your sure, steady ways— that way you have of putting your arm around her and making her feel that she's the only girl in the world. When she's feeling glum and tears begin to well up in her eyes, you have that knack of saying just the right thing—you know how to calm her fears, no matter how silly some of them may seem.

The girl born under this sign is inclined to have her ups and downs. You have that talent for smoothing out the ruffles in her sea of life. She'll most likely worship the ground you walk on or put you on a terribly high pedestal. Don't disappoint her if you can help it. She'll never disappoint you. This is the kind of woman who will take great pleasure in devoting the rest of her natural life to you. She'll darn your socks, mend your overalls, scrub floors, wash windows, shop, cook, and do just about anything short of murder in order to please you and to let you know that she loves you. Sounds like that legendary good old-fashioned girl, doesn't it? Contrary to popular belief, there are still a good number of them around—and many of them are Cancer people.

Of all the signs of the Zodiac, the women under the Cancer sign are the most maternal. In caring for and bringing up children, they know just how to combine the right amount of tenderness with the proper dash of discipline. A child couldn't ask for a better mother. Cancer women are sympathetic, affectionate, and patient with their children.

While we're on the subject of motherhood, there's one thing you should be warned about: never be unkind to your mother-in-law. It will be the only golden rule your Cancer wife will probably expect you to live up to. No mother-in-law jokes in the presence of your wife, please. With her, they'll go over like a lead balloon. Mother is something pretty special for her. She may be the crankiest, noisiest old bat this side of the Great Divide, still she's your wife's mother; you'd better treat her like she's one of the landed gentry. Sometimes this may be difficult to swallow, but if you want to keep your home together and your wife happy, you'd better learn to grin and bear it.

Treat your Cancer wife like a queen and she'll treat you royally.

SCORPIO MAN
LEO WOMAN

If you can manage a girl who likes to kick up her heels every now and again, then the Leo woman was made for you. You'll have to learn to put away jealous fears—or at least forget about them—when you take up with a woman born under this sign, because she's often the kind that makes heads turn and tongues wag. You don't necessarily have to believe any of what you hear—it's most likely just jealous gossip or wishful thinking. Take up with a Leo woman and you'll be taking off on a romance full of fire and ice; be prepared to take the good things with the bad—the bitter with the sweet.

The Leo girl has more than a fair share of grace and glamor. She is aware of her charms and knows how to put them to good use. Needless to say, other women in her vicinity turn green with envy and will try anything short of shoving her into the nearest lake, in order to put her out of commission.

If she's captured your heart and fancy, woo her intensely if your intention is to eventually win her. Shower her with expensive gifts and promise her the moon—if you're in a position to go that far—then you'll find her resistance beginning to weaken. It's not that she's difficult, she'll probably make a fuss over you once she's decided you're the man for her, but she does enjoy a lot of attention. What's more: she feels she's entitled to it. Her mild arrogance, though, is becoming. The Leo woman knows how to transform the crime of excessive pride into a very charming misdemeanor. It sweeps most men right off their feet. Those who do not succumb to her leonine charm are few and far between.

If you've got an important business deal to clinch and you have doubts as to whether or not it will go over well, bring your Leo girl along to that business luncheon and it's a cinch that that contract will be yours. She won't have to do or say anything—just be there, at your side. The grouchiest oil magnate can be transformed into a gushing, obedient schoolboy if there's a Leo woman in the room.

If you're rich and want to stay that way, don't give your Leo mate a free hand with the charge accounts and credit cards. If you're poor, the luxury-loving Leo will most likely never enter your life.

She makes a strict yet easy-going mother. She loves to pal around with her children.

SCORPIO MAN
VIRGO WOMAN

The Virgo woman may be a little too difficult for you to understand at first. Her waters run deep. Even when you think you know her, don't take any bets on it. She's capable of keeping things hidden in the deep recesses of her womanly soul—things she'll only release when she's sure that you're the man she's been looking for. It may take her some time to come around to this decision. Virgo girls are finicky about almost everything; everything has to be letter-perfect before they're satisfied. Many of them have the idea that the only people who can do things right are Virgos.

Nothing offends a Virgo woman more than slovenly dress, sloppy character, or a careless display of affection. Make sure your tie is not crooked and your shoes sport a bright shine before you go calling on this lady. Keep your off-color jokes for the locker-room, she'll have none of that. Take her arm when crossing the street. Don't rush the romance. Trying to corner her in the back of a cab may be one way of striking out. Never criticize the way she looks—in fact, the best policy would be to agree with her as much as possible. Still, there's just so much a man can take; all those dos and don'ts you'll have to follow if you want to get to first base. After a few dates, you may come to the conclusion that she just isn't worth all that trouble. However, the Virgo woman is mysterious enough generally speaking, to keep her men running back for more. Chances are you'll be intrigued by her airs and graces.

If love-making means a lot to you, you'll be disappointed at first in the cool ways of your Virgo woman. However, under her glacial facade there lies a caldron of seething excitement. If you're patient and artful in your romantic approach, you'll find that all that caution was well worth the trouble. When Virgos love, they don't stint. It's all or nothing as far as they're concerned. Once they're convinced that they love you, they go all the way, right off the bat—tossing caution to the wind.

One thing a Virgo woman can't stand in love is hypocrisy. They don't give a hoot about what the neighbors say, if their hearts tell them "Go ahead!" They're very concerned with human truths . . . so much so that if their hearts stumble upon another fancy, they're liable to be true to that new heart-throb and leave you standing in the rain. She's honest to her heart and will be as true to you as you are with her, generally. Do her wrong once, however, and it's farewell.

Both strict and tender, she tries to bring out the best in her children.

SCORPIO MAN
LIBRA WOMAN

As the old saying goes: It's a woman's prerogative to change her mind. Whoever said it must have had the Libra woman in mind. Her changeability, in spite of its undeniable charm (sometimes) could actually drive even a man of your patience up the wall. She's capable of smothering you with love and kisses one day and on the next, avoid you like the plague. If you think you're a man of steel nerves then perhaps you can tolerate her sometime-ness without suffering too much. However, if you own up to the fact that you're only a mere mortal who can only take so much, then you'd better fasten your attention on a girl who's somewhat more constant.

But don't get the wrong idea: a love affair with a Libra is not bad at all. In fact, it can have an awful lot of plusses to it. Libra women are soft, very feminine, and warm. She doesn't have to vamp all over the place in order to gain a man's attention. Her delicate presence is enough to warm the cockles of any man's heart. One smile and you're like a piece of putty in the palm of her hand.

She can be fluffy and affectionate—things you like in a girl. On the other hand, her indecision about which dress to wear, what to cook for dinner, or whether to redo the rumpus room or not could make you tear your hair out. What will perhaps be more exasperating is her flat denial to the accusation that she cannot make even the simplest decision. The trouble is that she wants to be fair or just in all matters; she'll spend hours weighing pros and cons. Don't make her rush into a decision; that will only irritate her.

The Libra woman likes to be surrounded by beautiful things. Money is no object where beauty is concerned. There will always be plenty of flowers in the house. She'll know how to arrange them tastefully, too. Women under this sign are fond of beautiful clothes and furnishings. They will run up bills without batting an eye—if given the chance.

Once she's cottoned to you, the Libra woman will do everything in her power to make you happy. She'll wait on you hand and foot when you're sick and bring you breakfast in bed on Sundays. She'll be very thoughtful and devoted. If anyone dares suggest you're not the grandest man in the world, your Libra wife will give that person a piece of her mind.

Libras work wonders with children. Gentle persuasion and affection are all she uses in bringing them up. It works.

SCORPIO MAN
SCORPIO WOMAN

The Scorpio woman can be a whirlwind of passion—perhaps too much passion to really suit you. When her temper flies, you'd better lock up the family heirlooms and take cover. When she chooses to be sweet, you're apt to think that butter wouldn't melt in her mouth—but, of course, it would.

The Scorpio woman can be as hot as a tamale or as cool as a cucumber, but whatever mood she's in, she's in it for real. She does not believe in posing or putting on airs.

The Scorpio woman is often sultry and seductive—her femme fatale charm can pierce through the hardest of hearts like a laser ray. She may not look like Mata Hari (quite often Scorpios resemble the tomboy next door) but once she's fixed you with her tantalizing eyes, you're a goner.

Life with the Scorpio woman will not be all smiles and smooth-sailing; when prompted, she can unleash a gale of venom. Generally, she'll have the good grace to keep family battles within the walls of your home. When company visits, she's apt to give the impression that married life with you is one great big joyride. It's just one of her ways of expressing her loyalty to you—at least in front of others. She may fight you tooth and nail in the confines of your living room, but at a ball or during an evening out, she'll hang onto your arm and have stars in her eyes.

Scorpio women are good at keeping secrets. She may even keep a few buried from you.

Never cross her on even the smallest thing. When it comes to revenge, she's an eye-for-an-eye woman. She's not too keen on forgiveness—especially if she feels she's been wronged unfairly. You'd be well advised not to give her any cause to be jealous, either. When the Scorpio woman sees green, your life will be made far from rosy. Once she's put you in the doghouse, you can be sure that you're going to stay there a while.

You may find life with a Scorpio woman too draining. Although she may be full of the old paprika, it's quite likely that she's not the kind of girl you'd like to spend the rest of your natural life with. You'd prefer someone gentler and not so hot-tempered . . . someone who can take the highs with the lows and not bellyache . . . someone who is flexible and understanding. A woman born under Scorpio can be heavenly, but she can also be the very devil when she chooses.

As a mother, a Scorpio is protective and encouraging.

SCORPIO MAN
SAGITTARIUS WOMAN

The Sagittarius woman is hard to keep track of: first she's here, then she's there. She's a woman with a severe case of itchy feet. She's got to keep on the move.

People generally like her because of her hail-fellow-well-met manner and breezy charm. She is constantly good-natured and almost never cross. She is the kind of girl you're likely to strike up a palsy-walsy relationship with; you might not be interested in letting it go any farther. She probably won't sulk if you leave it on a friendly basis, either. Treat her like a kid sister and she'll eat it up like candy.

She'll probably be attracted to you because of your restful, self-assured manner. She'll need a friend like you to help her over the rough spots in her life; she'll most likely turn to you for advice.

There is nothing malicious about a girl born under this sign. She is full of bounce and good cheer. Her sunshiny disposition can be relied upon on even the rainiest of days. No matter what she says or does, you'll always know that she means well. Sagittarians are sometimes short on tact. Some of them say anything that comes into their pretty little heads, no matter what the occasion. Sometimes the words that tumble out of their mouths seem downright cutting and cruel; they mean well but often everything they say comes out wrong. She's quite capable of losing her friends—and perhaps even yours—through a careless slip of the lip. Always remember that she is full of good intentions. Stick with her if you like her and try to help her mend her ways.

She's not a girl that you'd most likely be interested in marrying, but she'll certainly be lots of fun to pal around with. Quite often, Sagittarius women are outdoor types. They're crazy about things like fishing, camping, and mountain climbing. They love the wide open spaces. They are fond of all kinds of animals. Make no mistake about it: this busy little lady is no slouch. She's full of pep and ginger.

She's great company most of the time; she's more fun than a three-ring circus when she's in the right company. You'll like her for her candid and direct manner. On the whole, Sagittarians are very kind and sympathetic women.

If you do wind up marrying this girl-next-door type, you'd better see to it that you handle all of the financial matters. Sagittarians often let money run through their fingers like sand.

As a mother, she'll smother her children with love and give them all of the freedom *they* think they need.

SCORPIO MAN
CAPRICORN WOMAN

The Capricorn may not be the most romantic woman of the Zodiac, but she's far from frigid when she meets the right man. She believes in true love; she doesn't appreciate getting involved in flings. To her, they're just a waste of time. She's looking for a man who means "business'—in life as well as in love. Although she can be very affectionate with her boyfriend or mate, she tends to let her head govern her heart. That is not to say she is a cool, calculating cucumber. On the contrary, she just feels she can be more honest about love if she consults her brains first. She wants to size-up the situation before throwing her heart in the ring. She wants to make sure it won't get stepped on.

The Capricorn woman is faithful, dependable, and systematic in just about everything she undertakes. She is quite concerned with security and sees to it that every penny she spends is spent wisely. She is very economical about using her time, too. She does not believe in whittling away her energy on a scheme that is not going to pay off.

Ambitious themselves, they are quite often attracted to ambitious men—men who are interested in getting somewhere in life. If a man of this sort wins her heart, she'll stick by him and do all she can to help him get to the top.

The Capricorn woman is almost always diplomatic. She makes an excellent hostess. She can be very influential when your business acquaintances come to dinner.

The Capricorn woman is likely to be very concerned, if not downright proud, about her family tree. Relatives are pretty important to her, particularly if they're socially prominent. Never say a cross word about one of her family. That can really go against her grain and she'll punish you by not talking to you for days.

She's generally thorough in whatever she does. Capricorn women are well-mannered and gracious, no matter what their backgrounds. They seem to have it in their natures to always behave properly.

If you should marry a woman born under this sign, you need never worry about her going on a wild shopping spree. They understand the value of money better than most women. If you turn over your paycheck to her at the end of the week, you can be sure that a good hunk of it will wind up in the bank.

The Capricorn mother is loving and correct.

SCORPIO MAN
AQUARIUS WOMAN

If you find that you've fallen head over heels for a woman born under the sign of the Water Bearer, you'd better fasten your safety belt. It may take you quite a while to actually discover what this girl is like—and even then, you may have nothing to go on but a string of vague hunches. The Aquarian is like a rainbow, full of bright and shining hues; she's like no other girl you've ever known. There is something elusive about her—something delightfully mysterious. You'll most likely never be able to put your finger on it. It's nothing calculated, either; Aquarians don't believe in phony charm.

There will never be a dull moment in your life with this Water Bearing woman; she seems to radiate adventure and magic. She'll most likely be the most open-minded and tolerant woman you've ever met. She has a strong dislike for injustice and prejudice. Narrow-mindedness runs against her grain.

She is very independent by nature and quite capable of shifting for herself if necessary. She may receive many proposals for marriage from all sorts of people without ever really taking them seriously. Marriage is a very big step for her; she wants to be sure she knows what she's getting into. If she thinks that it will seriously curb her independence and love of freedom, she's liable to shake her head and give the man his engagement ring back—if indeed she's let the romance get that far.

The line between friendship and romance is a pretty fuzzy one for an Aquarian. It's not difficult for her to remain buddy-buddy with an ex-lover. She's tolerant, remember? So, if you should see her on the arm of an old love, don't jump to any hasty conclusions.

She's not a jealous person herself and doesn't expect you to be, either. You'll find her pretty much of a free spirit most of the time. Just when you think you know her inside-out, you'll discover that you don't really know her at all.

She's a very sympathetic and warm person; she can be helpful to people in need of assistance and advice.

She'll seldom be suspicious even if she has every right to be. If the man she loves slips and allows himself a little fling, chances are she'll just turn her head the other way. Her tolerance does have its limits, however, and her man should never press his luck at hanky-panky.

She makes a big-hearted mother; her good qualities rub off on her children.

SCORPIO MAN
PISCES WOMAN

The Pisces woman places great value on love and romance. She's gentle, kind, and romantic. Perhaps she's that girl you've been dreaming about all these years. Like you, she has very high ideals; she will only give her heart to a man who she feels can live up to her expectations.

She will never try to wear the pants in the family. She's a staunch believer in the man being the head of the house. Quite often Pisces women are soft and cuddly. They have a feminine, domestic charm that can win the heart of just about any man.

Generally, there's a lot more to her than just a pretty exterior and womanly ways. There's a brain ticking behind that gentle face. You may not become aware of it—that is, until you've married her. It's no cause for alarm, however; she'll most likely never use it against you. But if she feels you're botching up your married life through careless behavior or if she feels you could be earning more money than you do, she'll tell you about it. But any wife would, really. She'll never try to usurp your position as head and breadwinner of the family. She'll admire you for your ambition and drive. If anyone says anything against you in her presence, she'll probably break out into tears. Pisces women are usually very sensitive and their reaction to frustration or anger is often just a plain good old-fashioned cry. They can weep buckets when inclined.

She'll prepare an extra-special dinner for you when you've made a new conquest in your profession. Don't bother to go into the details though at the dinner table; she doesn't have much of a head for business matters, usually, and is only too happy to leave that up to you.

She is a wizard in decorating a home. She's fond of soft and beautiful things. There will always be a vase of fresh flowers on the dining room table. She'll see to it that you always have plenty of socks and underwear in the top dresser drawer.

Treat her with tenderness and your relationship will be an enjoyable one. Pisces women are generally fond of sweets, so keep her in chocolates (and flowers, of course) and you'll have a happy wife. Never forget birthdays or anniversaries; she won't.

If you have a talent for patience and gentleness, it will certainly pay off in your relationship with a Pisces woman. Chances are she'll never make you regret that you placed that band of gold on her finger.

There is usually a strong bond between a Pisces mother and her children. She'll try to give them things she never had as a child and is apt to spoil them as a result.

SAGITTARIUS
November 23 — December 20

CHARACTER ANALYSIS

People born under this ninth sign of the Zodiac are quite often self-reliant and intelligent. Generally, they are quite philosophical in their outlook on life. They know how to make practical use of their imagination.

There is seldom anything narrow about a Sagittarian. He is generally very tolerant and considerate. He would never consciously do anything that would hurt another's feelings. He is gifted with a good sense of humor and believes in being honest in his relationships with others. At times he is a little short of tact. He is so intent on telling the truth that sometimes he is a bit blunt. At any rate, he means well, and people who enjoy their relationship with him are often willing to overlook this flaw.

The person born under this sign is often positive and optimistic. He likes life. He often helps others to snap out of an ill mood. His joie de vivre is often infectious. People enjoy being around the Sagittarian because he is almost always in a good mood. Quite often people born under the sign of Sagittarius are fond of the outdoors. They enjoy sporting events and often excel in them. Many of them are fond of animals—especially horses. Generally speaking they are healthy—in mind and limb. They have pluck; they enjoy the simple things of life. Fresh air and good comradeship are important to them. On the other hand, they are fond of developing their minds. Many Sagittarians cannot read or study enough. They like to keep abreast of things.

It is important to the person born under this sign that justice prevails. They dislike seeing anyone treated unfairly. If the Sagittarian feels that the old laws are out-of-date or unrealistic he will fight to have them changed. At times he can be quite a rebel. It is important to him that law is carried out impartially In matters of law, he often excels.

Sagittarians are almost always fond of travel. It seems to be imbedded in their natures. At times, they feel impelled to get away from familiar surroundings and people. Far away places have a magical attraction for someone born under this sign. They enjoy reading about foreign lands and strange customs. Many people who are Sagittarians are not terribly fond of living in big cities; they prefer the quiet and greenery of the countryside. Of all the signs of the Zodiac the Sign of Sagittarius is closest to mother nature. They can usually build a trusting relationship with animals.

The Sagittarian is quite clever in conversation. He has a definite way with words. He is fond of a good argument. He knows how to phrase things exactly; his sense of humor often has a cheerful effect on his manner of speech. He is seldom without a joke of some sort. At times he is apt to hurt others with his wit, but this is never done intentionally. A slip of the tongue sometimes gets him into social difficulties. The person born under this sign often angers quite easily; however, they cool down quickly and are not given to holding grudges. They are willing to forgive and forget.

On the whole, the Sagittarian is good-natured and fun-loving. He finds it easy to take up with people of all sorts. In most cases, his social circle is rather large. People enjoy his company. Many of his friends share his interest in outdoor life and intellectual pursuits.

At times, he can be rather impulsive. He is not afraid of risk; on the contrary, at times he can be rather foolhardy in the way he courts danger. However, he is very sporting in all that he does, and if he should wind up the loser, he is not apt to waste much time grieving about it. He can be fairly optimistic—he believes in good luck.

Health

Often people born under the sign of Sagittarius are quite athletic. They are healthy-looking—quite striking in a robust way. Often they are rather tall and well-built. They are enthusiastic people and like being active or involved. Exercise may interest them a great deal. The Sagittarian cannot stand not being active. He has to be on the go. As he grows older, he seems to increase his strength and physical ability. At times he may have worries, but he never allows them to affect his humor or health.

It is important to the Sagittarian to remain physically sound. He is usually very physically fit, but his nervous system may be somewhat sensitive. Too much activity—even while he finds action attractive—may put a severe strain upon him after a time. The Sagittarian should try to concentrate his energies on as few objects as possible. However, usually he has his projects scattered here and there, and as a result he is easily exhausted. At times illnesses fall upon him rather suddenly. Some Sagittarians are accident-prone. They are not afraid of taking risks and as a result are sometimes careless in the way they do things. Injuries often come to them by way of sports or other vigorous activities.

At times, people of this sign try to ignore signs of illness —especially if they are engaged in some activity that has captured their interest. This results in a severe setback at times.

In later life, the Sagittarian sometimes suffers from stomach disorders. High blood pressure is another ailment that might affect him; he should also be on guard for signs of arthritis and sciatica. In spite of these possible dangers, the average Sagittarian manages to stay quite youthful and alert through his interest in life.

Occupation

The Sagittarian is someone who can be relied upon in a work situation. He is loyal and dependable. He is an energetic worker, anxious to please his superiors. He is forward-looking by nature and enjoys working in modern surroundings and toward progressive goals. Challenges do not frighten him. He is rather flexible and can work in confining situations even though he may not enjoy it. Work which gives him a chance to move about and meet new people is well suited to his character. If he has to stay in one locale he is apt to become sad and ill-humored. He can take orders but he would rather be in a situation where he does not have to. He is difficult to please at times, and may hop from job to job before feeling that it is really time to settle down. He does his best work when he is allowed to work on his own.

The Sagittarian is interested in expressing himself in the work he does. If he occupies a position which does not allow him to do this, he will seek outside activities that give him a chance to develop in a direction which interests him.

Some Sagittarians do well in the field of journalism; others make good teachers and public speakers. They are generally quite flexible and would do well in many different positions. Some excel as foreign ministers or in music; others do well in government work or in publishing.

The person born under this sign is often more intelligent than the average man. The cultivated Sagittarian knows how to employ his intellectual gifts to their best advantage. In politics and religion, the Sagittarian often displays considerable brilliance.

He is generally pleasant to work with; he is considerate of his colleagues and would do nothing that might upset their working relationship. Because he is so self-reliant he often inspires others. He likes to work with detail. His ideas are often quite practical and intelligent. The Sagittarian is curious by nature and is always looking for ways of increasing his knowledge.

The people born under this sign are almost always generous. They rarely refuse someone in need, but are always willing to share what they have. Whether he is up or down, the Sagittarian can always be relied upon to help someone in dire straits. His attitude toward life may be happy-go-lucky in general. He is difficult to depress no matter what his situation. He is optimistic and forward-looking. Money always seems to fall into his hands; it's seldom a problem for him.

The average Sagittarian is interested in expansion and promotion. Sometimes these concerns weaken his projects rather than strengthen them.

He is interested in large profit and is sometimes willing to take risks to secure it. In the long run he is successful. He has a flair for carrying off business deals well. It is the cultivated Sagittarian who prepares himself well in business matters so that he is well-supported in his interests by knowledge, as well as by experience.

The average person born under this sign is more interested in contentment and joy than in material gain. However he will do his best to make the most of profit when it comes his way.

Home and Family

Not all Sagittarians are very interested in home life. Many of them set great store in being mobile. Their activities outside the home may attract them more than those inside the home. Not exactly homebodies, Sagittarians, however, can adjust themselves to a stable domestic life if they put their minds to it.

People born under this sign are not keen on luxuries and other displays of wealth. They prefer the simple things. Anyone entering their home should be able to discern this. They are generally neat; they like a place that has plenty of space—not too cluttered with imposing furniture.

Even when he settles down, the Sagittarian likes to keep a small corner of his life just for himself; independence is important to him. If necessary, he'll insist upon it, no matter what the situation. He likes a certain amount of beauty in his home, but he may not be too interested in keeping things looking nice—his interests lead him elsewhere. Housekeeping may bore him to distraction. If he is forced to stick to a domestic routine he is liable to become somewhat disagreeable.

Children bring him a great deal of happiness. He is fond of family life. Friends generally drop in any old time to visit a Sagittarian for they know they will always be welcomed and properly entertained. The Sagittarian's love of his fellow man is well known.

When children are small, he may not understand them too well, even though he tries. He may feel he is a bit too clumsy to handle them properly—although this may be far from the case. As they begin to grow up and develop definite personalities, the Sagittarian's interest grows. There is always a strong tie between children and the Sagittarian parent.

Children are especially drawn to Sagittarians because they seem to understand them better than other adults.

One is apt to find children born under this sign a little restless and disorganized at times. They are usually quite independent in their ways and may ask for quite a bit of freedom while still young. They don't like being fussed over by adults. They like to feel that their parents believe in them and trust them on their own.

Social Relationships

The Sagittarian enjoys having people around. It is not difficult for him to make friends. He is very sociable by nature. Most of the friends he makes, he keeps for life. As a rule, the person born under this sign is rather broadminded; he is apt to have all sorts of friends. He appreciates people for their good qualities, however few they may have. He is not quick to judge and is often very forgiving. He is not impressed by what a friend has in the way of material goods.

The Sagittarian is generally quite popular. He is much in demand socially; people like him for his easy disposition and his good humor. His friendship is valued by others. Quite often in spite of his chumminess, the Sagittarian is rather serious; light conversation may be somewhat difficult for him.

He believes in speaking his mind—in saying what he feels—yet at times, he can appear rather quiet and retiring. It all depends on his mood. Others may feel that there are two sides to his personality because of this quirk in his nature; for this reason it may be difficult for some people to get to know him. In some instances, he employs his silence as a sort of protection. When people pierce through however and don't leave him in peace, he can become rather angry.

On the whole, he is a kind and considerate person. His nature is gentle and unassuming. With the wrong people though, he can become somewhat disagreeable. He can become angry quite easily at times; however, he cools down quickly and is willing to let bygones be bygones. He never holds a grudge against anyone. Companionship and harmony in all social relationships is quite necessary for the Sagittarian; he is willing to make some sacrifices for it. The partner for someone born under this sign must be a good listener. There are times when the Sagittarian feels it is necessary to pour his heart out. He is willing to listen to another's problems, too. His mate or loved one should be able to take an interest in his hobbies and such. If not, the Sagittarian may be tempted to go his own way even more.

The Sagittarian says what he means; he doesn't beat around the bush. Being direct is one of his strongest qualities. Sometimes it pays off; sometimes it doesn't. He is often forgetful that the one he loves may be more sensitive than she allows herself to appear—even to him. He has a tendency to put his foot in his mouth at times. However, his mate should be able to overlook this flaw in his character or else try to correct it in some subtle way. At times, when joking broadly he has the ability to strike a sensitive chord in his loved one and this may result in a serious misunderstanding. The cultivated Sagittarian learns his boundaries; he knows when not to go too far. Understanding his partner's viewpoint is also an important thing for someone born under this sign to learn.

LOVE AND MARRIAGE

Sagittarians are faithful to their loved ones. They are affectionate in nature and not at all possessive. Love is important for them spiritually as well as physically. For some people born under this sign, romance is a chance to escape reality—it is a chance for adventure. Quite often, the Sagittarian's mate finds it difficult to keep up with him—he is so active and energetic. When Sagittarians fall in love, however, they are quite easy to handle.

Sagittarians do like having freedom. They will make concessions in a steady relationship; still there will be a part of themselves that they keep from others. He or she is very keen on preserving his individual rights, no matter what sort of relationship he is engaged in. The Sagittarian's ideals are generally high and they are important to him. He is looking for someone with similar standards, not someone too lax or conventional.

In love, the Sagittarian may be a bit childlike at times. As a result of this he is apt to encounter various disappointments before he has found the one meant for him. At times he or she says things he really shouldn't and this causes the end of a romantic relationship. The person born under this sign may have many love affairs before he feels he is ready to settle down with just one person. If the person he loves does not exactly measure up to his standards, the Sagittarian is apt to overlook this—depending on how strong his love is—and accept the person for what that person is.

On the whole, the Sagittarian is not an envious person. He is willing to allow his or her partner needed freedoms—within reason. The Sagittarian does this so that he will not have to jeopardize his own liberties. Live and let live could easily be his motto. If his ideals and freedom are threatened, the Sagittarian fights hard to protect what he believes is just and fair.

He does not want to make any mistakes in love, so he takes his time when choosing someone to settle down with. He is direct and positive when he meets the right one; he does not waste time.

The average Sagittarian may be a bit altar-shy. It may take a bit of convincing before Sagittarians agree that married life is right for them. This is generally because they do not want to lose their freedom. The Sagittarian is an active person who enjoys being around a lot of other people. Sitting quietly at home does not interest him at all. At times it may seem that he or she wants to have things his own way, even in marriage. It may take some doing to get him to realize that in marriage, as in other things, give and take plays a great role.

Romance and the Sagittarius Woman

The Sagittarian woman is often kind and gentle. Most of the time she is very considerate of others and enjoys being of help in some way to her friends. She can be quite active and, as a result, be rather difficult to catch. On the whole, she is optimistic and friendly. She believes in looking on the bright side of things. She knows how to make the best of situations that others feel are not worth salvaging. She has plenty of pluck.

Men generally like her because of her easy-going manner. Quite often she becomes friends with a man before venturing on to romance. There is something about her that makes her more of a companion than a lover. She can best be described as sporting and broad-minded.

She is almost never possessive; she enjoys her own freedom too much to want to make demands on that of another person.

She is always youthful in her disposition. She may seem rather guileless at times. Generally it takes her longer really to mature than it does others. She tends to be impulsive and may easily jump from one thing to another. If she has an unfortunate experience in love early in life, she may shy away from fast or intimate contacts for a while. She is usually very popular. Not all the men who are attracted to her see her as a possible lover, but more as a friend or companion.

The woman born under this sign generally believes in true love. She may have several romances before she decides to settle down. For her there is no particular rush. She is willing to have a long romantic relationship with the man she loves before making marriage plans.

The Sagittarius woman is often the outdoors type and has a strong liking for animals—especially dogs and horses. Quite often she excels in sports. She is not generally someone who is content to stay at home and cook and take care of the house. She would rather be out attending to her other interests. When she does household work, however, she does it well.

She makes a good companion as well as a wife. She usually enjoys participating with her husband in his various interests and affairs. Her sunny disposition often brightens up the dull moments of a love affair.

At times her temper may flare, but she is herself again after a few moments. She would never butt into her husband's business affairs, but she does enjoy being asked for her opinion from time to time. Generally she is up to date on all that her husband is doing and can offer him some pretty sound advice.

The Sagittarius woman is seldom jealous of her husband's interest in other people—even if some of them are of the opposite sex. If she has no reason to doubt his love, she never questions it.

She makes a loving and sympathetic mother. Quite often she will play with her children. Her cheerful manner makes her an invaluable playmate.

Romance and the Sagittarius Man

The Sagittarius man is often an adventurer. He likes taking chances in love as well as in life. He may hop around quite a bit—from one romance to another—before really thinking about settling down. Many men born under this sign feel that marriage would mean the end of their freedom—so they avoid it as much as possible. Whenever a romance becomes too serious, they move on. Many Sagittarians are rather impulsive in love. Early marriages for some often end unpleasantly. The Sagittarian is not a very mature person—even at an age when most others are. He takes a bit more time. He may not always make a wise choice in a love partner.

He is affectionate and loving but not at all possessive. Because he is rather lighthearted in love, he sometimes gets into trouble.

Most Sagittarius men find romance an exciting adventure. They make attentive lovers and are never cool or indifferent. Love should also have a bit of fun in it for him too. He likes to keep things light and gay. Romance without humor—at times—is difficult for him to accept. The woman he loves should also be a good sport. She should have as open and fun-loving a disposition as he has—if she is to understand him properly.

He wants his mate to share his interest in the outdoor life and animals. If she is good at sports, she is likely to win his heart, for the average Sagittarian generally has an interest in athletics of various sorts—from bicycling to baseball.

His mate must also be a good intellectual companion; someone who can easily discuss those matters which interest her Sagittarian. Physical love is important to him—but so is spiritual love. A good romance will contain these in balance.

His sense of humor may sometimes seem a little unkind to someone who is not used to being laughed at. He enjoys playing jokes now and again; it is the child in his nature that remains a part of his character even when he grows old and gray.

He is not a homebody. He is responsible, however, and will do what is necessary to keep a home together. Still and all, the best wife for him is one who can manage household matters single-handedly if need be.

He loves children—especially as they grow older and begin to take on definite personalities.

Woman—Man

SAGITTARIUS WOMAN
ARIES MAN

In some ways, the Aries man resembles an intellectual mountain goat leaping from crag to crag. He has an insatiable thirst for knowledge. He's ambitious and is apt to have his finger in many pies. He can do with a woman like you—someone attractive, quick-witted, and smart.

He is not interested in a clinging vine kind of wife, but someone who is there when he needs her; someone who listens and understands what he says; someone who can give advice if he should ever need it . . . which is not likely to be often. The Aries man wants a woman who will look good on his arm without hanging on it too heavily. He is looking for a woman who has both feet on the ground and yet is mysterious and enticing . . . a kind of domestic Helen of Troy whose face or fine dinner can launch a thousand business deals if need be. That woman he's in search of sounds a little like you, doesn't she? If the shoe fits, put it on. You won't regret it.

The Aries man makes a good husband. He is faithful and attentive. He is an affectionate kind of man. He'll make you feel needed and loved. Love is a serious matter for the Aries man. He does not believe in flirting or playing the field—especially after he's found the woman of his dreams. He'll expect you to be as constant in your affection as he is in his. He'll expect you to be one hundred percent his; he won't put up with any nonsense while romancing you.

The Aries man may be pretty progressive and modern about many things; however, when it comes to pants wearing, he's down-right conventional: it's strictly male attire. The best position you can take in the relationship is a supporting one. He's the boss and that's that. Once you have learned to accept that, you'll find the going easy.

The Aries man, with his endless energy and drive, likes to relax in the comfort of his home at the end of the day. The good homemaker can be sure of holding his love. He's keen on slippers and pipe and a comfortable armchair. If you see to it that everything in the house is where he expects to find it, you'll have no difficulty keeping the relationship on an even keel.

Life and love with an Aries man may be just the medicine you need. He'll be a good provider. He'll spoil you if he's financially able.

He's young at heart and can get along with children easily. He'll spoil them every chance he gets.

SAGITTARIUS WOMAN
TAURUS MAN

If you've got your heart set on a man born under the sign of Taurus, you'll have to learn the art of being patient. Taureans take their time about everything—even love.

The steady and deliberate Taurus man is a little slow on the draw; it may take him quite a while before he gets around to popping that question. For the woman who doesn't mind twiddling her thumbs, the waiting and anticipating almost always pays off in the end. Taurus men want to make sure that every step they take is a good one—particularly, if they feel that the path they're on is one that leads to the altar.

If you are in the mood for a whirlwind romance, you had better cast your net in shallower waters. Moreover, most Taureans prefer to do the angling themselves. They are not keen on a woman taking the lead; once she does, they are liable to drop her like a dead fish. If you let yourself get caught on a Taurean's terms, you'll find that he's fallen for you—hook, line, and sinker.

The Taurus man is fond of a comfortable homelife. It is very important to him. If you keep those home fires burning you will have no trouble keeping that flame in your Taurean's heart aglow. You have a talent for homemaking; use it. Your taste in furnishings is excellent. You know how to make a house come to life with colors and decorations.

Taurus, the strong, steady, and protective Bull may not be your idea of a man on the move; still he's reliable. Perhaps he could be the anchor for your dreams and plans. He could help you to acquire a more balanced outlook and approach to your life. If you're given to impulsiveness, he could help you to curb it. He's the man who is always there when you need him.

When you tie the knot with a man born under Taurus, you can put away fears about creditors pounding on the front door. Taureans are practical about everything including bill-paying. When he carries you over that threshold, you can be certain that the entire house is paid for, not only the doorsill.

As a housewife, you won't have to worry about putting aside your many interests for the sake of back-breaking house chores. Your Taurus husband will see to it that you have all the latest time-saving appliances and comforts.

Your children will be obedient and orderly. Your Taurus husband will see to that.

SAGITTARIUS WOMAN
GEMINI MAN

The Gemini man is quite a catch. Many a woman has set her cap for him and failed to bag him. Generally, Gemini men are intelligent, witty, and outgoing. Many of them tend to be versatile.

On the other hand, some of them seem to lack that sort of common sense that you set so much store in. Their tendency to start a half-dozen projects, then toss them up in the air out of boredom may do nothing more than exasperate you.

One thing that causes a Twin's mind and affection to wander is a bore, but it is unlikely that an active woman like you would ever allow herself to be accused of dullness. The Gemini man who has caught your heart will admire you for your ideas and intellect—perhaps even more than for your homemaking talents and good looks.

A strong willed woman could easily fill the role of rudder for her Gemini's ship-without-a-sail. The intelligent Gemini is often aware of his shortcomings and doesn't mind if someone with better bearings gives him a shove in the right direction—when it's needed. The average Gemini doesn't have serious ego-hangups and will even accept a well-deserved chewing out from his mate or girlfriend gracefully.

A successful and serious-minded Gemini could make you a very happy woman, perhaps, if you gave him half the chance. Although he may give you the impression that he has a hole in his head, the Gemini man generally has a good head on his shoulders and can make efficient use of it when he wants. Some of them, who have learned the art of being steadfast, have risen to great heights in their professions. President Kennedy was a Gemini as was

Thomas Mann and William Butler Yeats.

Once you convince yourself that not all people born under the sign of the Twins are witless grasshoppers, you won't mind dating a few—to test your newborn conviction. If you do wind up walking down the aisle with one, accept the fact that married life with him will mean your taking the bitter with the sweet.

Life with a Gemini man can be more fun than a barrel of clowns. You'll never be allowed to experience a dull moment. But don't leave money matters to him or you'll both wind up behind the eight ball.

Gemini men are always attractive to the opposite sex. You'll perhaps have to allow him an occasional harmless flirt—it will seldom amount to more than that if you're his proper mate.

The Gemini father is a pushover for children. See to it that you keep them in line; otherwise they'll be running the house.

SAGITTARIUS WOMAN
CANCER MAN

Chances are you won't hit it off too well with the man born under Cancer if your plans concern love, but then, Cupid has been known to do some pretty unlikely things. The Cancerian is a very sensitive man—thin-skinned and occasionally moody. You've got to keep on your toes—and not step on his—if you're determined to make a go of the relationship.

The Cancer man may be lacking in some of the qualities you seek in a man, but when it comes to being faithful and being a good provider, he's hard to beat.

The perceptive woman will not mistake the Crab's quietness for sullenness or his thriftiness for penny-pinching. In some respects, he is like that wise old owl out on a limb; he may look like he's dozing but actually he hasn't missed a thing. Cancerians often possess a well of knowledge about human behavior; they can come across with some pretty helpful advice to those in trouble or in need. He can certainly guide you in making investments both in time and money. He may not say much, but he's always got his wits about him.

The Crab may not be the match or catch for a woman like you; at times, you are likely to find him downright dull. True to his sign, he can be fairly cranky and crabby when handled the wrong way. He is perhaps more sensitive than he should be.

If you're smarter than your Cancer friend, be smart enough

not to let him know. Never give him the idea that you think he's a little short on brain power. It would send him scurrying back into his shell—and all that ground lost in the relationship will perhaps never be recovered.

The Crab is most content at home. Once settled down for the night or the weekend, wild horses couldn't drag him any farther than the gatepost—that is, unless those wild horses were dispatched by his mother. The Crab is sometimes a Momma's boy. If his mate does not put her foot down, he will see to it that his mother always comes first. No self-respecting wife would ever allow herself to play second fiddle—even if it's to her old gray-haired mother-in-law. With a little bit of tact, however, she'll find that slipping into that number-one position is as easy as pie (that legendary one his mother used to bake).

If you pamper your Cancer man, you'll find that "Mother" turns up increasingly less—at the front door as well as in conversations.

Cancerians make protective, proud, and patient fathers.

SAGITTARIUS WOMAN
LEO MAN

For the woman who enjoys being swept off her feet in a romantic whirlwind fashion, Leo is the sign of such love. When the Lion puts his mind to romancing, he doesn't stint. It's all wining and dining and dancing till the wee hours of the morning.

Leo is all heart and knows how to make his woman feel like a woman. The girl in constant search of a man she can look up to need go no farther: Leo is ten-feet tall—in spirit if not in stature. He's a man not only in full control of his faculties but in full control of just about any situation he finds himself in. He's a winner.

The Leo man may not look like Tarzan, but he knows how to roar and beat his chest if he has to. The woman who has had her fill of weak-kneed men finds in a Leo someone she can at last lean upon. He can support you not only physically but spiritually as well. He's good at giving advice that pays off.

Leos are direct people. They don't believe in wasting time or effort. They almost never make unwise investments.

Many Leos rise to the top of their professions; through example, they often prove to be a source of great inspiration to others.

Although he's a ladies' man, the Leo man is very particular about his ladies. His standards are high when it comes to love interests. The idealistic and cultivated woman should have no trouble keeping her balance on the pedestal the Lion sets her on. Leo believes that romance should be played on a fair give-and-take basis. He won't stand for any monkey business in a love relationship. It's all or nothing.

You'll find him a frank, off-the-shoulder person; he generally says what is on his mind.

If you decide upon a Leo man for a mate, you must be prepared to stand behind him full-force. He expects it—and usually deserves it. He's the head of the house and can handle that position without a hitch. He knows how to go about breadwinning and, if he has his way (and most Leos do have their own way), he'll see to it that you'll have all the luxuries you crave and the comforts you need.

It's unlikely that the romance in your marriage will ever die out. Lions need love like flowers need sunshine. They're ever amorous and generally expect similar attention and affection from their mates. Leos are fond of going out on the town; they love to give parties, as well as to go to them.

Leos make strict fathers, generally. They love their children but won't spoil them.

SAGITTARIUS WOMAN
VIRGO MAN

Although the Virgo man may be a bit of a fussbudget at times, his seriousness and dedication to common sense may help you to overlook his tendency to sometimes be overcritical about minor things.

Virgo men are often quiet, respectable types who set great store in conservative behavior and levelheadedness. He'll admire you for your practicality and tenacity . . . perhaps even more than for your good looks. He's seldom bowled over by a glamour-puss. When he gets his courage up, he turns to a serious and reliable girl for romance. He'll be far from a Valentino while dating. In fact, you may wind up making all the passes. Once he does get his motor running, however, he can be a warm and wonderful fellow—to the right girl.

He's gradual about love. Chances are your romance with him will start out looking like an ordinary friendship. Once he's sure you're no fly-by-night flirt and have no plans of taking him for a ride, he'll open up and rain sunshine all over your heart.

Virgo men tend to marry late in life. The Virgo believes in holding out until he's met the right girl. He may not have many names in his little black book; in fact, he may not even have a black book. He's not interested in playing the field; leave that to men of the more flamboyant signs. The Virgo man is so particular that he may remain romantically inactive for a long period. His girl has to be perfect or it's no go. If you find yourself feeling weak-kneed for a Virgo, do your best to convince him that perfect is not so important when it comes to love; help him to realize that he's missing out on a great deal by not considering the near perfect or whatever it is you consider yourself to be. With your surefire perseverance, you will most likely be able to make him listen to reason and he'll wind up reciprocating your romantic interests.

The Virgo man is no block of ice. He'll respond to what he feels to be the right feminine flame. Once your love-life with a Virgo man starts to bubble, don't give it a chance to fall flat. You may never have a second chance at winning his heart.

If you should ever have a falling out with him, forget about patching it up. He'd prefer to let the pieces lie scattered. Once married, though, he'll stay that way—even if it hurts. He's too conscientious to try to back out of a legal deal of any sort.

The Virgo man is as neat as a pin. He's thumbs down on sloppy housekeeping. Keep everything bright, neat, and shiny . . . and that goes for the children, too, at least by the time he gets home from work. Chocolate-coated kisses from Daddy's little girl go over like a lead balloon with him.

SAGITTARIUS WOMAN
LIBRA MAN

If there's a Libran in your life, you are most likely a very happy woman. Men born under this sign have a way with women. You'll always feel at ease in a Libran's company; you can be yourself when you're with him.

The Libra man can be moody at times. His moodiness is often puzzling. One moment he comes on hard and strong with declarations of his love, the next moment you find that he's left you like yesterday's mashed potatoes. He'll come back, though; don't worry. Librans are like that. Deep down inside he really knows what he wants even though he may not appear to.

You'll appreciate his admiration of beauty and harmony. If you're dressed to the teeth and never looked lovelier, you'll get a ready compliment—and one that's really deserved. Librans don't indulge in idle flattery. If they don't like something, they are tactful enough to remain silent.

Librans will go to great lengths to preserve peace and harmony—they will even tell a fat lie if necessary. They don't like showdowns or disagreeable confrontations. The frank woman is all for getting whatever is bothering her off her chest and out into the open, even if it comes out all wrong. To the Libran, making a clean breast of everything seems like sheer folly sometimes.

You may lose your patience while waiting for your Libra friend to make up his mind. It takes him ages sometimes to make a decision. He weighs both sides carefully before comitting himself to anything. You seldom dillydally—at least about small things—and so it's likely that you will find it difficult to see eye to eye with a hesitating Libran when it comes to decision-making methods.

All in all, though, he is kind, considerate, and fair. He is interested in the "real" truth; he'll try to balance everything out until he has all the correct answers. It's not difficult for him to see both sides of a story.

He's a peace-loving man. The sight of blood is apt to turn his stomach.

Librans are not show-offs. Generally, they are well-balanced, modest people. Honest, wholesome, and affectionate, they are serious about every love encounter they have. If one should find that the girl he's dating is not really suited to him, he will end the relationship in such a tactful manner that no hard feelings will come about.

The Libra father is firm, gentle, and patient.

SAGITTARIUS WOMAN
SCORPIO MAN

Many find the Scorpio's sting a fate worse than death. When his anger breaks loose, you had better clear out of the vicinity.

The average Scorpio may strike you as a brute. He'll stick pins into the balloons of your plans and dreams if they don't line up with what he thinks is right. If you do anything to irritate him—just anything—you'll wish you hadn't. He'll give you a sounding out that would make you pack your bags and go back to Mother—if you were that kind of a girl.

The Scorpio man hates being tied down to homelife—he would rather be out on the battlefield of life, belting away at whatever he feels is a just and worthy cause, instead of staying home nestled in a comfortable armchair with the evening paper. If you are a girl who has a homemaking streak—don't keep those home fires burning too brightly too long; you may just run out of firewood.

As passionate as he is in business affairs and politics, the Scorpio man still has plenty of pep and ginger stored away for lovemaking.

Most women are easily attracted to him—perhaps you are no exception. Those who allow a man born under this sign to sweep them off their feet, shortly find that they're dealing with a pepper pot of seething excitement. The Scorpio man is passionate with a capital P, you can be sure of that. But he's capable of dishing out as much pain as pleasure. Damsels with fluttering hearts who, when in the embrace of a Scorpio, think "This is it," had better be in a position moments later to realize that "Perhaps this isn't it."

Scorpios are blunt. An insult is likely to whiz out of their mouths quicker than a compliment.

If you're the kind of woman who can keep a stiff upper lip, take it on the chin, turn a deaf ear, and all of that, because you feel you are still under his love spell in spite of everything: lots of luck.

If you have decided to take the bitter with the sweet, prepare yourself for a lot of ups and downs. Chances are you won't have as much time for your own affairs and interests as you'd like. The Scorpio's love of power may cause you to be at his constant beck and call.

Scorpios like fathering large families. They love children but quite often they fail to live up to their responsibilities as a parent.

SAGITTARIUS WOMAN
SAGITTARIUS MAN

The woman who has set her cap for a man born under the sign of Sagittarius may have to apply an awful amount of strategy before she can get him to drop down on bended knee. Although some Sagittarians may be marriage-shy, they're not ones to skitter away from romance. A high-spirited woman may find a relationship with a Sagittarian—whether a fling or "the real thing"—a very enjoyable experience.

As a rule, Sagittarians are bright, happy, and healthy people. They have a strong sense of fair play. Often they're a source of inspiration to others. They're full of ideas and drive.

You'll be taken by the Sagittarian's infectious grin and his lighthearted friendly nature. If you do wind up being the woman in his life, you'll find that he's apt to treat you more like a buddy than the love of his life. It's just his way. Sagittarians are often chummy instead of romantic.

You'll admire his broadmindedness in most matters—including those of the heart. If, while dating you, he claims that he still wants to play the field, he'll expect you to enjoy the same liberty. Once he's promised to love, honor, and obey, however, he does just that. Marriage for him, once he's taken that big step, is very serious business.

A woman who has a keen imagination and a great love of freedom will not be disappointed if she does tie up with a Sagittarian. The Sagittarius man is often quick-witted. Men of this sign have a genuine interest in equality. They hate prejudice and injustice.

If he does insist on a night out with the boys once a week, he won't scowl if you decide to let him shift for himself in the kitchen once a week while you pursue some of your own interests. He believes in fairness.

He's not much of a homebody. Quite often he's occupied with faraway places either in his dreams or in reality. He enjoys—just as you do—being on the go or on the move. He's got ants in his pants and refuses to sit still for long stretches at a time. Humdrum routine—especially at home—bores him. At the drop of a hat, he may ask you to whip off your apron and dine out for a change. He likes surprising people. He'll take great pride in showing you off to his friends. He'll always be a considerate mate; he will never embarrass or disappoint you intentionally.

He's very tolerant when it comes to friends and you'll most likely spend a lot of time entertaining people.

Sagittarians become interested in their children when the children are out of the baby stage.

SAGITTARIUS WOMAN
CAPRICORN MAN

A with-it girl like you is likely to find the average Capricorn man a bit of a drag. The man born under this sign is often a closed up person and difficult to get to know. Even if you do get to know him, you may not find him very interesting.

In romance, Capricorn men are a little on the rusty side. You'll probably have to make all the passes.

You may find his plodding manner irritating and his conservative, traditional ways downright maddening. He's not one to take a chance on anything. "If it was good enough for my father, it's good enough for me" may be his motto. He follows a way that is tried and true.

Whenever adventure rears its tantalizing head, the Goat will turn the other way; he's just not interested.

He may be just as ambitious as you are—perhaps even more so—but his ways of accomplishing his aims are more subterranean or, at least, seem so. He operates from the background a good deal of the time. At a gathering you may never even notice him, but he's there, taking everything in, sizing everyone up, planning his next careful move.

Although Capricorns may be intellectual to a degree, it is not generally the kind of intelligence you appreciate. He may not be as quick or as bright as you; it may take him ages to understand a simple joke.

If you do decide to take up with a man born under this sign of the Goat, you ought to be pretty good in the "Cheering Up" department. The Capricorn man often acts as though he's constantly being followed by a cloud of gloom.

The Capricorn man is most himself when in the comfort and privacy of his own home. The security possible within four walls can make him a happy man. He'll spend as much time as he can at home. If he is loaded down with extra work, he'll bring it home instead of finishing it up at the office.

You'll most likely find yourself frequently confronted by his relatives. Family is very important to the Capricorn—*his* family that is. They had better take an important place in your life, too, if you want to keep your home a happy one.

Although his caution in most matters may all but drive you up the wall, you'll find that his concerned way with money is justified most of the time. He'll plan everything right down to the last penny.

He can be quite a scolder with children. You'll have to step in and smooth things out.

SAGITTARIUS WOMAN
AQUARIUS MAN

Aquarians love everybody—even their worst enemies sometimes. Through your love relationship with an Aquarian you'll find yourself running into all sorts of people, ranging from near-genius to downright insane . . . and they're all friends of his.

As a rule, Aquarians are extremely friendly and open. Of all the signs, they are perhaps the most tolerant. In the thinking department, they are often miles ahead of others.

You'll most likely find your relationship with this man a challenging one. Your high respect for intelligence and imagination may be reason enough for you to set your heart on a Water Bearer. You'll find that you can learn a lot from him.

In the holding-hands phase of your romance, you may find that your Water Bearing friend has cold feet. Aquarians take quite a bit of warming up before they are ready to come across with that first goodnight kiss. More than likely, he'll just want to be your pal in the beginning. For him, that's an important first step in any relationship—love, included. The "poetry and flowers" stage—if it ever comes—will come later. The Aquarian is all heart; still, when it comes to tying himself down to one person and for keeps, he is almost always sure to hesitate. He may even try to get out of it if you breathe down his neck too heavily.

The Aquarius man is no Valentino and wouldn't want to be. The kind of love-life he's looking for is one that's made up mainly of companionship. Although he may not be very romantic, the memory of his first romance will always hold an important position in his heart. Some Aquarians wind up marrying their childhood sweethearts.

You won't find it difficult to look up to a man born under the sign of the Water Bearer, but you may find the challenge of trying to keep up with him dizzying. He can pierce through the most complicated problem as if it were a matter of 2 + 2. You may find him a little too lofty and high-minded—but don't judge him too harshly if that's the case; he's way ahead of his time—your time, too, most likely.

If you marry this man, he'll stay true to you. Don't think that once the honeymoon is over, you'll be chained to the kitchen sink forever. Your Aquarius husband will encourage you to keep active in your own interests and affairs. You'll most likely have a minor tiff now and again but never anything serious.

Kids love him and vice-versa. He'll be as tolerant with them as he is with adults.

SAGITTARIUS WOMAN
PISCES MAN

The man born under Pisces is quite a dreamer. Sometimes he's so wrapped up in his dreams that he's difficult to reach. To the average, active woman, he may seem a little sluggish.

He's easygoing most of the time. He seems to take things in his stride. He'll entertain all kinds of views and opinions from just about everyone, nodding or smiling vaguely, giving the impression that he's with them one hundred percent while that may not be the case at all. His attitude may be "why bother" when he's confronted with someone wrong who thinks he's right. The Pisces man will seldom speak his mind if he thinks he'll be rigidly opposed.

The Pisces man is oversensitive at times—he's afraid of getting his feelings hurt. He'll sometimes imagine a personal affront when none's been made. Chances are you'll find this complex of his maddening; at times you may feel like giving him a swift kick where it hurts the most. It wouldn't do any good, though. It would just add fuel to the fire of his complex.

One thing you'll admire about this man is his concern for people who are sickly or troubled. He'll make his shoulder available to anyone in the mood for a good cry. He can listen to one hard-luck story after another without seeming to tire. When his advice is asked, he is capable of coming across with some words of wisdom. He often knows what is bugging someone before that person is aware of it himself. It's almost intuitive with Pisceans, it seems.

Still, at the end of the day, this man will want some peace and quiet. If you've got a problem when he comes home, don't unload it in his lap. If you do, you are liable to find him short-tempered. He's a good listener but he can only take so much.

Pisceans are not aimless although they may seem so at times. The positive sort of Pisces man is quite often successful in his profession and is likely to wind up rich and influential. Material gain, however, is never a direct goal for a man born under this sign.

The weaker Pisces are usually content to stay on the level where they find themselves. They won't complain too much if the roof leaks or if the fence is in need of repair.

Because of their seemingly laissez-faire manner, people under this sign—needless to say—are immensely popular with children. For tots they play the double role of confidant and playmate. It will never enter the mind of a Pisces to discipline a child, no matter how spoiled or incorrigible that child becomes.

Man—Woman

SAGITTARIUS MAN
ARIES WOMAN

The Aries woman is quite a charmer. When she tugs at the strings of your heart, you'll know it. She's a woman who's in search of a knight in shining armor. She is a very particular person with very high ideals. She won't accept anyone but the man of her dreams.

The Aries woman never plays around with passion; she means business when it comes to love.

Don't get the idea that she's a dewy-eyed Miss. She isn't. In fact, she can be pretty practical and to-the-point when she wants. She's a girl with plenty of drive and ambition. With an Aries woman behind you, you are liable to go far in life. She knows how to help her man get ahead. She's full of wise advice; you only have to ask. In some cases, the Aries woman has a keen business sense; many of them become successful career women. There is nothing backward or retiring about her. She is equipped with a good brain and she knows how to use it.

Your union with her could be something strong, secure, and romantic. If both of you have your sights fixed in the same direction, there is almost nothing that you could not accomplish.

The Aries woman is proud and capable of being quite jealous. While you're with her, never cast your eye in another woman's direction. It could spell disaster for your relationship. The Aries woman won't put up with romantic nonsense when her heart is at stake.

If the Aries woman backs you up in your business affairs, you can be sure of succeeding. However, if she only is interested in advancing her own career and puts her interests before yours, she can be sure to rock the boat. It will put a strain on the relationship. The over-ambitious Aries woman can be a pain in the neck and make you forget that you were in love with her once.

The cultivated Aries woman makes a wonderful wife and mother. She has a natural talent for homemaking. With a pot of paint and some wallpaper, she can transform the dreariest domicile into an abode of beauty and snug comfort. The perfect hostess—even when friends just happen by—she knows how to make guests feel at home.

You'll also admire your Arien because she knows how to stand on her own two feet. Hers is an independent nature. She won't break down and cry when things go wrong, but will pick herself up and try to patch up matters.

The Aries woman makes a fine, affectionate mother.

SAGITTARIUS MAN
TAURUS WOMAN

The woman born under the sign of Taurus may lack a little of the sparkle and bubble you often like to find in a woman. The Taurus woman is generally down-to-earth and never flighty. It's important to her that she keep both feet flat on the ground. She is not fond of bounding all over the place, especially if she's under the impression that there's no profit in it.

On the other hand, if you hit it off with a Taurus woman, you won't be disappointed in the romance area. The Taurus woman is all woman and proud of it, too. She can be very devoted and loving once she decides that her relationship with you is no fly-by-night romance. Basically, she's a passionate person. In sex, she's direct and to-the-point. If she really loves you, she'll let you know she's yours—and without reservations.

Better not flirt with other women once you've committed yourself to her. She's capable of being very jealous and possessive.

She'll stick by you through thick and thin. It's almost certain that if the going ever gets rough, she won't go running home to her mother. She can adjust to the hard times just as graciously as she can to the good times.

Taureans are, on the whole, pretty even-tempered. They like to be treated with kindness. Pretty things and soft objects make them purr like kittens.

You may find her a little slow and deliberate. She likes to be safe and sure about everything. Let her plod along if she likes;

don't coax her, but just let her take her own sweet time. Everything she does is done thoroughly and, generally, without mistakes.

Don't deride her for being a slow-poke. It could lead to flying pots and pans and a fireworks display that could put Bastille Day to shame. The Taurus woman doesn't anger readily but when prodded often enough, she's capable of letting loose with a cyclone of ill-will. If you treat her with kindness and consideration, you'll have no cause for complaint.

The Taurean loves doing things for her man. She's a whiz in the kitchen and can whip up feasts fit for a king if she thinks they'll be royally appreciated. She may not fully understand you, but she'll adore you and be faithful to you if she feels you're worthy of it.

The Taurus woman makes a wonderful mother. She knows how to keep her children well-loved, cuddled, and warm. She may have some difficult times with them when they reach adolescence, though.

SAGITTARIUS MAN
GEMINI WOMAN

You may find a romance with a woman born under the sign of the Twins a many splendored thing. In her you can find the intellectual companionship you often look for in a friend or mate. A Gemini girl friend can appreciate your aims and desires because she travels pretty much the same road as you do intellectually . . . that is, at least part of the way. She may share your interests but she will lack your tenacity.

She suffers from itchy feet. She can be here, there . . . all over the place and at the same time, or so it would seem. Her eagerness to move about may make you dizzy; still you'll enjoy and appreciate her liveliness and mental agility.

Geminians often have sparkling personalities; you'll be attracted by her warmth and grace. While she's on your arm you'll probably notice that many male eyes are drawn to her—she may even return a gaze or two, but don't let that worry you. All women born under this sign have nothing against a harmless flirt once in a while. They enjoy this sort of attention; if the Gemini feels she is already spoken for, however, she will never let such attention get out of hand.

Although she may not be as handy as you'd like in the kitchen, you'll never go hungry for a filling and tasty meal. The Gemini girl is always in a rush; she won't feel like she's cheating by breaking out the instant mashed potatoes or the frozen peas. She may not be much of a good cook but she is clever; with a dash of this and a suggestion of that, she can make an uninteresting TV dinner taste like something out of a Jim Beard cookbook. Then, again, maybe you've struck it rich and have a Gemini girl friend who finds complicated recipes a challenge to her intellect. If so, you'll find every meal a tantalizing and mouth-watering surprise.

When you're beating your brains out over the Sunday crossword puzzle and find yourself stuck, just ask your Gemini girl; she'll give you all the right answers without batting an eyelash.

Like you, she loves all kinds of people. You may even find that you're a bit more particular than she. Often all that a Geminian requires is that her friends be interesting . . . and stay interesting. One thing she's not able to abide is a dullard.

Leave the party-organizing to your Gemini sweetheart or mate and you'll never have a chance to know a dull moment. She'll bring out the swinger in you if you give her half the chance.

A Gemini mother enjoys her children. Like them, she's often restless, adventurous, and easily bored.

SAGITTARIUS MAN
CANCER WOMAN

If you fall in love with a Cancer woman, be prepared for anything. The Cancerian is sometimes difficult to understand when it comes to love. In one hour, she can unravel a whole gamut of emotions that will leave you in a tizzy. She'll undoubtedly keep you guessing.

You may find her a little too uncertain and sensitive for your liking. You'll most likely spend a good deal of time encouraging her—helping her to erase her foolish fears. Tell her she's a living doll a dozen times a day and you'll be well loved in return.

Be careful of the jokes you make when in her company—don't let any of them revolve around her, her personal interests, or her family. If you do, you'll most likely reduce her to tears. She can't stand being made fun of. It will take bushels of roses and tons of chocolates—not to mention the apologies—to get her to come back out of her shell.

In matters of money-managing, she may not easily come around to your way of thinking. Money will never burn a hole in her pocket. You may get the notion that your Cancerian sweetheart or mate is a direct descendent of Scrooge. If she has her way, she'll hang onto that first dollar you earned. She's not only that way with money, but with everything right on up from bakery string to jelly jars. She's a saver; she never throws anything away, no matter how trivial.

Once she returns your "I love you," you'll find you have an affectionate, self-sacrificing, and devoted woman on your hands. Her love for you will never alter unless you want it to. She'll put you high upon a pedestal and will do everything—even if it's against your will—to keep you up there.

Cancer women love homelife. For them, marriage is an easy step. They're domestic with a capital D. The Cancerian will do her best to make your home comfortable and cozy. She, herself, is more at ease at home than anywhere else. She makes an excellent hostess. The best in her comes out when she is in her own environment.

Cancer women make the best mothers. Each will consider every complaint of her child a major catastrophe. With her, children always come first. If you're lucky, you'll run a close second. You'll perhaps see her as too devoted to the children. You may have a hard time convincing her that her apron strings are a little too tight.

SAGITTARIUS MAN
LEO WOMAN

If you can manage a girl who likes to kick up her heels every now and again, then the Leo woman was made for you. You'll have to learn to put away jealous fears when you take up with a woman born under this sign, as she's often the kind that makes heads turn and tongues wag. You don't necessarily have to believe any of what you hear—it's most likely just jealous gossip or wishful thinking.

The Leo girl has more than a fair share of grace and glamour. She knows it, generally, and knows how to put it to good use. Needless to say, other women in her vicinity turn green with envy and will try anything short of shoving her into the nearest lake in order to put her out of the running.

If she's captured your heart and fancy, woo her full-force—if your intention is eventually to win her. Shower her with expensive gifts and promise her the moon—if you're in a position to go that far—then you'll find her resistance beginning to weaken. It's not that she's such a difficult cookie—she'll probably make a lot over you once she's decided you're the man for her—but she does enjoy a lot of attention. What's more, she feels she's entitled to it. Her mild arrogance, however, is becoming. The Leo woman knows how to transform the crime of excessive pride into a very charming misdemeanor. It sweeps most men—or rather, all men—right off their feet. Those who do not succumb to her leonine charm are few and far between.

If you've got an important business deal to clinch and you have doubts as to whether you can bring it off as you should, take your Leo wife along to the business luncheon and it'll be a cinch that you'll have that contract—lock, stock, and barrel—in your pocket before the meeting is over. She won't have to say or do anything . . . just be there at your side. The grouchiest oil magnate can be transformed into a gushing, obedient schoolboy if there's a Leo woman in the room.'

If you're rich and want to see to it that you stay that way, don't give your Leo spouse a free hand with the charge accounts and credit cards. When it comes to spending, Leo tend to overdo. If you're poor, you have no worries because the luxury-loving Leo will most likely never recognize your existence—let alone, consent to marry you.

As a mother, she's both strict and easy. She can pal around with her children and still see to it that they know their places. She won't spoil them but she'll be a loving and devoted parent.

SAGITTARIUS MAN
VIRGO WOMAN

The Virgo woman may be a little too difficult for you to understand at first. Her waters run deep. Even when you think you know her, don't take any bets on it. She's capable of keeping things hidden in the deep recesses of her womanly soul—things she'll only release when she's sure that you're the man she's been looking for. It may take her some time to come around to this decision. Virgo girls are finicky about almost everything; everything has to be letter-perfect before they're satisfied. Many of them have the idea that the only people who can do things right are Virgos.

Nothing offends a Virgo woman more than slovenly dress, sloppy character, or a careless display of affection. Make sure your tie is not crooked and that your shoes sport a bright shine before you go calling on this lady. Keep your off-color jokes for the locker room; she'll have none of that. Take her arm when crossing the street. Don't rush the romance. Trying to corner her in the back of a cab may be one way of striking out. Never criticize the way she looks—in fact, the best policy would be to agree with her as much as possible. Still, there's just so much a man can take; all those dos and don'ts you'll have to observe if you want to get to first base with a Virgo may be just a little too much to ask of you. After a few dates, you may come to the conclusion that she just isn't worth all that trouble. However, the Virgo woman is mysterious enough, generally speaking, to keep her men running back for more. Chances are you'll be intrigued by her airs and graces.

If lovemaking means a lot to you, you'll be disappointed at first in the cool ways of your Virgo girl. However, under her gla-

cial facade there lies a hot cauldron of seething excitement. If
you're patient and artful in your romantic approach, you'll find
that all that caution was well worth the trouble. When Virgos love,
they don't stint. It's all or nothing as far as they're concerned.
Once they're convinced that they love you, they go all the way
right off the bat—tossing all cares to the wind.

One thing a Virgo woman can't stand in love is hypocrisy.
They don't give a hoot about what the neighbors say if their hearts
tell them "Go ahead!" They're very concerned with human
truths—so much so that if their hearts stumble upon another fancy, they're liable to be true to that new heartthrob and leave you
standing in the rain. She's honest to her heart and will be as true
to you as you are with her, generally. Do her wrong once, however,
and it's farewell.

Both strict and tender, she tries to bring out the best in her children.

SAGITTARIUS MAN
LIBRA WOMAN

You'll probably find that the girl born under the sign of Libra is
worth more than her weight in gold. She's a woman after your
own heart.

With her, you'll always come first—make no mistake about
that. She'll always be behind you 100 percent, no matter what you
do. When you ask her advice about almost anything, you are likely
to get a very balanced and realistic opinion. She is good at thinking things out and never lets her emotions run away with her when
clear logic is called for.

As a homemaker she is hard to beat. She is very concerned
with harmony and balance. You can be sure she'll make your
house a joy to live in; she'll see to it that the home is tastefully
furnished and decorated. A Libran cannot stand filth or
disarray—it gives her goose-bumps. Anything that does not radiate harmony, in fact, runs against her orderly grain.

She is chock-full of charm and womanly ways. She can sweep
just about any man off his feet with one winning smile. When it
comes to using her brains, she can out-think almost anyone and,
sometimes, with half the effort. She is diplomatic enough, though,
never to let this become glaringly apparent. She may even turn the
conversation around so that you think you were the one who did
all the brain-work. She couldn't care less, really, just as long as
you wind up doing what is right.

The Libra woman will put you up on a pretty high pedestal.
You are her man and her idol. She'll leave all the decision-mak-

ing—large or small—up to you. She's not interested in running things and will only offer her assistance if she feels you really need it.

Some find her approach to reason masculine; however, in the areas of love and affection the Libra woman is *all* woman. She'll literally shower you with love and kisses during your romance with her. She doesn't believe in holding out. You shouldn't, either, if you want to hang onto her.

She is the kind of girl who likes to snuggle up to you in front of the fire on chilly autumn nights . . . the kind of girl who will bring you breakfast in bed on Sunday. She'll be very thoughtful about anything that concerns you. If anyone dares suggest you're not the grandest guy in the world, she'll give that person what-for. She'll defend you till her dying breath. The Libra woman will be everything you want her to be.

She'll be a sensitive and loving mother. Still, you'll always come before the children.

SAGITTARIUS MAN
SCORPIO WOMAN

The Scorpio woman can be a whirlwind of passion—perhaps too much passion to really suit you. When her temper flies, you'd better lock up the family heirlooms and take cover. When she chooses to be sweet, you're apt to think that butter wouldn't melt in her mouth . . . but, of course, it would.

The Scorpio woman can be as hot as a *tamale* or as cool as a cucumber, but whatever mood she's in, she's in it for real. She does not believe in posing or putting on airs.

The Scorpio woman is often sultry and seductive—her femme fatale charme can pierce through the hardest of hearts like a laser ray. She may not look like Mata Hari (quite often Scorpios resemble the tomboy next door) but once she's fixed you with her tantalizing eyes, you're a goner.

Life with the Scorpio woman will not be all smiles and smooth-sailing; when prompted, she can unleash a gale of venom. Generally, she'll have the good grace to keep family battles within the walls of your home. When company visits, she's apt to give the impression that married life with you is one great big joy-ride. It's just one of her ways of expressing her loyalty to you—at least in front of others. She may fight you tooth and nail in the confines of your living room, but at a ball or during an evening out, she'll hang onto your arm and have stars in her eyes.

Scorpio women are good at keeping secrets. She may even keep a few buried from you if she feels like it.

Never cross her up on even the smallest thing. When it comes to revenge, she's an eye-for-an-eye woman. She's not too keen on forgiveness—especially if she feels she's been wronged unfairly. You'd be well-advised not to give her any cause to be jealous, either. When the Scorpio woman sees green, your life will be made far from rosy. Once she's put you in the doghouse, you can be sure that you're going to stay there a while.

You may find life with a Scorpio woman too draining. Although she may be full of the old paprika, it's quite likely that she's not the kind of girl you'd like to spend the rest of your natural life with. You'd prefer someone gentler and not so hot-tempered . . . someone who can take the highs with the lows and not complain . . . someone who is flexible and understanding. A woman born under Scorpio can be heavenly, but she can also be the very devil when she chooses.

As a mother, a Scorpio is protective and encouraging.

SAGITTARIUS MAN
SAGITTARIUS WOMAN

You'll most likely never come across a more good-natured girl than the one born under the sign of Sagittarius. Generally, they're full of bounce and good cheer. Their sunny dispositions seem almost permanent and can be relied upon even on the rainiest of days.

Women born under this sign are almost never malicious. If ever they seem to be, it is only seeming. Sagittarians are often a little short on tact and say literally anything that comes into their pretty little heads—no matter what the occasion. Sometimes the words that tumble out of their mouths seem downright cutting and cruel. Still, no matter what the Sagittarian says, she means well. The Sagittarius woman is quite capable of losing some of her friends—and perhaps even some of yours—through a careless slip of the lip.

On the other hand, you are liable to appreciate her honesty and good intentions. To you, qualities of this sort play an important part in life. With a little patience and practice, you can probably help cure your Sagittarian of her loose tongue; in most cases, she'll give in to your better judgement and try to follow your advice to the letter.

Chances are, she'll be the outdoors type of girlfriend. Long hikes, fishing trips, and white-water canoeing will most likely appeal to her. She's a busy person; no one could ever call her a slouch. She sets great store in mobility. She won't sit still for one minute if she doesn't have to.

She is great company most of the time and, generally, lots of fun. Even if your buddies drop by for poker and beer, she won't have any trouble fitting in.

On the whole, she is a very kind and sympathetic woman. If she feels she's made a mistake, she'll be the first to call your attention to it. She's not afraid to own up to her own faults and shortcomings.

You might lose your patience with her once or twice. After she's seen how upset her shortsightedness or tendency to blabbermouth has made you, she'll do her best to straighten up.

The Sagittarius woman is not the kind who will pry into your business affairs. But she'll always be there, ready to offer advice if you need it.

The Sagittarius woman is seldom suspicious. Your word will almost always be good enough for her.

She is a wonderful and loving friend to her children.

SAGITTARIUS MAN
CAPRICORN WOMAN

If you are not a successful businessman or, at least, on your way to success, it's quite possible that a Capricorn woman will have no interest in entering your life. Generally speaking, she is a very security-minded female; she'll see to it that she invests her time only in sure things. Men who whittle away their time with one unsuccessful scheme or another, seldom attract a Capricorn. Men who are interested in getting somewhere in life and keep their noses close to the grindstone quite often have a Capricorn woman behind them, helping them to get ahead.

Although she is a kind of "climber," she is not what you could call cruel or hard-hearted. Beneath that cool, seemingly calculating, exterior, there's a warm and desirable woman. She just happens to think that it is just as easy to fall in love with a rich or ambitious man as it is with a poor or lazy one. She's practical.

The Capricorn woman may be keenly interested in rising to the top, but she'll never be aggressive about it. She'll seldom step on someone's feet or nudge competitors away with her elbows. She's quiet about her desires. She sits, waits, and watches. When an opening or opportunity does appear, she'll latch onto it licketysplit. For an on-the-move man, an ambitious Capricorn wife or girlfriend can be quite an asset. She can probably give you some very good advice about business matters. When you invite the boss and his wife for dinner, she'll charm them both right off the ground.

The Capricorn woman is thorough in whatever she does: cooking, cleaning, making a success out of life . . . Capricorns make excellent hostesses as well as guests. Generally, they are very well-mannered and gracious, no matter what their backgrounds are. They seem to have a built-in sense of what is right. Crude behavior or a careless faux-pas can offend them no end.

If you should marry a woman born under Capricorn, you need never worry about her going on a wild shopping spree. Capricorns are careful with every cent that comes into their hands. They understand the value of money better than most women and have no room in their lives for careless spending.

The Capricorn girl is usually very fond of family—her own, that is. With her, family ties run very deep. Don't make jokes about her relatives; she won't stand for it. You'd better check her family out before you get down on bended knee; after your marriage you'll undoubtedly be seeing a lot of them.

Capricorn mothers train their children to be polite and kind.

SAGITTARIUS MAN
AQUARIUS-WOMAN

If you find that you've fallen head over heels for a woman born under the sign of the Water Bearer, you'd better fasten your safety belt. It may take you quite a while actually to discover what this girl is like—and even then, you may have nothing to go on but a string of vague hunches. The Aquarian is like a rainbow, full of bright and shining hues; she's like no other girl you've ever known. There is something elusive about her—something delightfully mysterious. You'll most likely never be able to put your finger on it. It's nothing calculated, either; Aquarians don't believe in phony charm.

There will never be a dull moment in your life with this Water Bearing woman; she seems to radiate adventure and magic. She'll most likely be the most open-minded and tolerant woman you've ever met. She has a strong dislike for injustice and prejudice. Narrow-mindedness runs against her grain.

She is very independent by nature and quite capable of shifting for herself if necessary. She may receive many proposals of marriage from all sorts of people without ever really taking them seriously. Marriage is a very big step for her; she wants to be sure she knows what she's getting into. If she thinks that it will seriously curb her independence and love of freedom, she's liable to shake her head and give the man his engagement ring back—if indeed she's let the romance get that far.

The line between friendship and romance is a pretty fuzzy one for an Aquarian. It's not difficult for her to remain buddy-buddy with an ex-lover. She's tolerant, remember? So, if you should see her on the arm of an old love, don't jump to any hasty conclusions.

She's not a jealous person herself and doesn't expect you to be, either. You'll find her pretty much of a free spirit most of the time. Just when you think you know her inside-out, you'll discover that you don't really know her at all, though.

She's a very sympathetic and warm person; she can be helpful to people in need of assistance and advice.

She'll seldom be suspicious even if she has every right to be. If she loves a man, she'll forgive him just about anything. If he allows himself a little fling, chances are she'll just turn her head the other way. Her tolerance does have its limits, however, and her man should never press his luck at hanky-panky.

She makes a big-hearted mother; her good qualities rub off on her children.

SAGITTARIUS MAN
PISCES WOMAN

Many a man dreams of a Piscean kind of girl. You're perhaps no exception. She's soft and cuddly—and very domestic. She'll let you be the brains of the family; she's contented to just lean on your shoulder and let you be the master of the household.

She can be very ladylike and proper. Your business associates and friends will be dazzled by her warmth and femininity. Although she's a charmer, there is a lot more to her than just a pretty exterior. There is a brain ticking away behind that soft, womanly facade. You may never become aware of it—that is, until you're married to her. It's no cause for alarm, however; she'll most likely never use it against you.

If she feels you're botching up your married life through careless behavior or if she feels you could be earning more money than you do, she'll tell you about it. But any wife would, really. She will never try to usurp your position as head and breadwinner of the family.

No one had better dare say an uncomplimentary word about you in her presence. It's liable to cause her to break into tears. Pisces women are usually very sensitive beings. Their reaction to adversity, frustration, or anger is just a plain, good, old-fashioned cry. They can weep buckets when so inclined.

She'll have an extra-special dinner prepared for you when you make a new conquest in your profession. Don't bother to go into details, though, at the dinner table; she doesn't have much of a head for business matters usually, and is only too happy to leave that up to you.

She can do wonders with a house. She is very fond of soft and beautiful things. There will always be plenty of fresh-cut flowers around the house. She'll see that you always have plenty of socks and underwear in that top drawer of your dresser.

Treat her with tenderness and generosity and your relationship will be an enjoyable one. She's most likely fond of chocolates. A bunch of beautiful flowers will never fail to make her eyes light up. See to it that you never forget her birthday or your anniversary. These things are very important to her. If you let them slip your mind, you'll send her into a crying fit that could last a considerable length of time. If you are patient and kind, you can keep a Pisces woman happy for a lifetime. She, however, is not without her faults. Her "sensitivity" may get on your nerves after a while; you may find her lacking in imagination and zest; you may even feel that she uses her tears as a method of getting her own way.

She makes a strong, self-sacrificing mother.

CAPRICORN
December 21—January 19

CHARACTER ANALYSIS

People born under this tenth sign of the Zodiac are generally strong-willed and goal-directed. They seldom do anything without a purpose. They tend to be quite ambitious; they hammer away at something until they have made their point. The Capricornian knows what he wants out of life. Through perseverance and patience, he generally achieves it. There is almost nothing he can not attain once he makes up his mind. He is interested in progress, in making things better. When he believes in something, he puts himself behind it totally. He does not believe in acting in a half-hearted fashion. The mountain goat is the symbol of the Capricornian. Like the goat he climbs, always slowly and surely, holding his balance even under the most unstable circumstances. At times, for the sake of getting ahead, the Capricornian will make use of others in his company. He is not mercenary, however, for the people he uses are also likely to gain through his manipulation. He inspires confidence and trust. He always admires in others those qualities he himself lacks. The Capricornian is not a person to sit idly by while others are in action. He can be quite shrewd in his own quiet way.

When the Capricornian likes or believes in someone, he will stick by that person for the rest of his life. In short, he is loyal. He believes in being constant. He seldom wavers once he has committed himself to an ideal or person. He can always be depended upon to speak up for something or someone he believes in. Often he wins others over by his charm. At times he is somewhat aloof and proud.

People born under this sign are often in possession of clear minds. They are not necessarily brilliant, but they are capable of concentrating on what interests them in an effective manner. They believe in doing things right; never half-way. Generally, the Capri-

311

cornian is exact and accurate. He prides himself on doing his work correctly. He is conscientious and careful; he can always be counted on to hold up his end of a bargain. He tends to be stiff when it comes to making judgements. He is more interested in justice than forgiveness. In spite of this, one could never accuse him of not being fair-minded in most things. He makes a point of it.

The Capricornian could hardly be called soft-hearted. He can be quite harsh at times in the way he handles others, especially if he thinks he's right. Others are likely to find him cold and callous. Honor and pride are important to him. Although he may not be exceedingly intelligent, he is bound to have some intellectual pretensions. He knows how to put things together—how to organize and arrange things.

Capricornians who are a bit weak in character are apt to feel they are a cut above others and will do what they can to let this be felt. Often they suffer from a feeling of inadequacy. He may not know how to rid himself of this complex exactly and this may have an adverse effect on his disposition. He is often depressed and insecure. For these reasons, others are apt to find him difficult to get along with. If he is too conscious of the qualities he lacks and can't assume, he may ruin his chances to attain the ends he desires. Some Capricornians of this caliber find it difficult to settle down; they roam from one thing to another, never satisfied. Their cleverness may become rather mean and cutting. They may be destructive rather than constructive and positive. He may be afraid to forge ahead. The future frightens him and increases his feeling of insecurity. He may strike out at people whom he suspects are laughing at him behind his back. He is likely to overrate his own importance, and when confronted with the reality of his own worth is likely to become rather angry and disagreeable. The weak Capricornian is not an easy person to get along with. Others may be afraid to be truthful with him. This sort of Capricorn is likely to be rather narrow-minded and conservative. He clings desperately to the past, a bit afraid of moving on. He thinks more of himself than of others and may abuse friends and acquaintances.

He may be lacking in a healthy sense of humor. A harmless joke may make him suspicious and aggressive if he thinks that it was secretly directed at him. He is not the kind of person who can laugh at himself when he pulls a boner. If someone criticizes him even in a helpful way, it can spell the end of a friendship.

Some Capricorns are rather careful with their money. As a rule, however, they tend to be on the generous side. They would never refuse someone in need. They will, at times, go out of their way to help someone in trouble. They do not expect or insist that the favor be returned; a word of thanks is good enough for them. The Capricornian is very grateful when someone offers to lend him a helping hand. He never forgets a favor. Although he may find it difficult to express his thanks at times, he does appreciate help that is given to him.

Health

During childhood, the Capricorns may not be too strong or sturdy. Often they are subject to a series of childhood diseases. As they grow older, however, they become stronger. An adult Capricorn often has a strong resistance to diseases. He is a fighter. He never wants to lose in anything, not even illness. Many people born under this sign live a long life. They are generally very active people and have a store of energy at their disposal. The weak areas of a Capricorn person's body are his knees and joints. When he has an accident these areas are often involved. Some Capricornians have rather poor teeth; this may be the result of insufficient calcium in the system. Skin troubles often plague him; in later life he may become the victim of an arthritic disease.

Being a practical sort of person, a Capricorn generally sees to it that he eats sensibly. A balanced diet is important to him. He needs plenty of fresh fruits and vegetables in order to remain fit. Hard work and exercise help him to maintain his good constitution. He is a strong person and his strength is seldom undermined.

His moods may have a bad effect on his health. He is given to depressed feelings and melancholy. He can easily fall into the bad habit of worrying about small things. His worries can drain him of his energy and may make him prey to a variety of illnesses. Plenty of fresh air, sunshine, and exercise, may help him to keep a healthy disposition and a happy frame of mind. The people he associates with will also play a great role in his health. He gets along best with those who are youthful, positive and energetic.

Occupation

The Capricorn man or woman is very much interested in being successful in life. He will work hard to win, at whatever it is he does. Reputation means a lot to him. He will fight to advance and to hold his position. He likes a job that carries a bit of prestige with it. Having others respect him is very important to the Capricorn. He enjoys being in a position of authority. Money, of course, has a great attraction for the person born under this sign. When accepting a job, salary usually plays an important part. He would not take a job just for the glory or prestige alone. It has to have its financial advantages.

There are people born under this sign who believe that the only way to win is to stick to something that is regular, or routine. They don't mind plodding along, if they are sure that they will get that pot of gold at the end of the rainbow. Still and all, the strong Capricorn, while seeing the advantages of routine work, does not allow himself to become a robot or slave to a humdrum work schedule. He tries to move along with the times. He keeps abreast of new developments in his field, applying new techniques to his work where he sees fit.

Hard work does not frighten the man or woman born under the sign of Capricorn. They are willing to put in long and hard hours, if they feel the benefits they are to receive are indeed worth their efforts. They are usually conscientious and loyal in their work. Many of them start at the bottom and slowly work their way up. Although they are interested in being successful, some of them tend to become a bit depressed if it seems to take them longer than others. But they are willing to bide their time. They hold no rosy view of the future. They know that they will really have to apply themselves to their tasks in order to attain their goals. It is the idea of winning that keeps Capricorn on the go. He never falters once he has made up his mind to get ahead in the world. Some of them never attain what they're after until very late in life. But they are not afraid of pushing ahead, making small gains here and there, as long as they seem to be on the right road.

Politics is an area where someone born under this sign usually excels. Capricorn has a diplomatic way about him. He is interested in justice and being fair. Some Capricornians make good researchers. They are not afraid to put in long hours when involved in investigation. They are reliable and steady. In a position that gives him a chance to organize or arrange things, he could do very well. Authoritarian positions hold a particular attraction for him. He enjoys the challenge of this sort of position, also the respect it generally commands. Having people under his control, sometimes makes him respect himself more; makes him more sure of his own worth. In crafts and sciences, they often do well, too.

The Capricorn man or woman—as has already been stated—is very success oriented. He or she will let no one stand in the way. At times, the Capricorn person can be quite brutal and heartless in his methods for getting to the top. Needless to say, the pushy sort born under this sign has no trouble in making himself unpopular with others. He is always on the look out for an opportunity to get ahead. If necessary, he will step on another's toes in order to make a gain, no matter how small it is. He is good at what he does—thorough. There are seldom any complaints about his work. His employers are generally satisfied with his job-performance because they know he is accurate and professional.

Money is important to the Capricorn person. He'll work hard to build up his financial resources. If he winds up rich, it's not because of luck, generally, but because he has earned it. He is an open opportunist, and he will not try to disguise this. Capricorn is no hypocrite. He's direct in his actions, even if he does not talk about them. Of all the signs, that of Capricorn is the most interested in gain and profit. Security is something he must have. It drives him on; it motivates him. During difficult moments, he may feel a bit discouraged or depressed. Still, there is that interest in the ultimate goal that keeps him going.

The Capricorn person is generally thrifty. He believes in saving. Waste disgusts him. For the most part he is quite conservative in the way he handles his finances. Although he may be given to moods in which he feels rather expansive or generous, on the whole, he manages to keep tight control of his money. He can be trusted with the money of others.

During his youth, the Capricornian may impress others as being rather penny-pinching. He is cautious in the way he manages his finances. Generally, he can account for every cent he spends. His eye always on the future, he thinks about that inevitable rainy day, and prepares himself for it. However, once he has gained quite a bit and feels himself financially secure, his attitudes are likely to change. He becomes generous and charitable. He is very helpful to those in need, especially if their background is similar to his own.

Home and Family

The average Capricornian enjoys the security of home life. Still, it generally does not appeal to him in the same way as it does others. He may not marry for love or companionship alone. He may think of marriage and domesticity as a practical means for realizing his material goals. The person born under this sign sometimes marries for position or money. Not that they are all that cold-hearted and calculating; but the Capricornian finds it just as easy to fall in love with a socially-prominent and wealthy person as it is to become romantically involved with a poor person. His occupation is apt to play the center role in his life, with family coming in second. Many people born under this sign are not fond of large families.

Parenthood can be something of a burden for the average Capricorn. He takes his responsibilities toward his family very seriously. Family ties are strong for him. However, he may seem a bit distant even to those who love him. He is capable of great affection from time to time, but he is apt to be more demonstrative when managing or organizing household affairs. It is important for him that everything connected with his home life run smoothly. The children of a Capricorn parent may find him rather cold and aloof. They may even secretly dislike him. However, as the children become older and wiser, they generally realize that their Capricorn mother or father has always acted in their best interests. As they mature, they will respect and love their Capricorn mother or father for the security that he or she gave them while growing up.

It is important to the Capricorn that his family make him feel needed, even if he himself is not too demonstrative in showing his affections. Once he is settled, he is interested in improving or expanding his home life in various ways.

The average Capricorn person generally feels he is lacking in some quality or characteristic. It is generally this feeling of inadequacy that drives him in romance; he wants to find someone who has what he himself lacks. A harmonious family often gives him the feeling of being a complete person.

The Capricorn husband or wife will often do what he or she can to make his home harmonious and tasteful. He generally has a great interest in all that is beautiful and cultural. Some Capricorns are fond of music and a piano in the home is a must. The home of a Capricorn person generally radiates good taste and beauty. It may be a bit on the luxurious side—if he can afford it—but never in an ostentatious way. His home is usually peaceful and harmonious. He feels that it is important that everything in the household run on some regular basis: a special time for meals, for sleeping, for entertaining. His home is a comfortable place and it is usually easy for someone to feel at his ease while visiting a Capricorn friend.

He is proud of his home and property. He is a responsible member of the community and will do what is necessary to fulfill his duties as a neighbor. However, he likes to keep his home life to himself. He values his privacy. His home is usually well kept and attractive. He likes to be respected and highly thought of because of his possessions. Prestige in the community is important to him. A materialistic duel with the Joneses is not beneath him. He will always try to do his neighbors one better if he can afford it.

Children bring joy into the Capricorn's life. He may not be very fond of a large family. Still, he will give the necessary love and attention to the few children he has. He is interested in them as individuals and enjoys seeing them grow up. His hope is, of course, that they will be a credit to him and will reflect the good upbringing he has given them. At times, he may seem a bit unsympathetic, especially if they misbehave.

Social Relationships

The Capricorn man or woman is not what one could accurately describe as being romantic. His feelings however generally run deep; he is quite emotional. However his respect for intellect and convention may prevent him from expressing himself in a demonstrative manner when it comes to love and affection. He is very considerate for the most part. His approach to courtship and romance are conventional. He would never do anything that might injure the feelings or sensibilities of the person he is romantically interested in. Doing the right thing at the right time is important. The Capricornian is seldom incorrect in his romantic behavior. He doesn't let his affections run rampant. His mind reigns over his emotions. Flirting has little or no appeal for him. When in love, he is serious. Even if a love relationship does not end up in a permanent union, it is important to him and he takes it seriously. He is not the kind of person who runs from one love affair to the other—or enjoys several romances at the same time. He is constant. He is not the kind of person who will give his heart right out. He is likely to begin by just being friends. If his love interest encourages him or indicates that she has the same feelings, he will then allow the relationship to enter a more intimate phase. He does not want to be deceived or made a fool of, and will take steps to guard himself against that.

As has already been mentioned, the Capricorn person's greatly driven by ambition. In love, too, he is apt to direct his affections toward someone who can help him get ahead in his career. He is not the kind of person who could totally lose his head when in love. He knows what he's about. This will not say that he is insincere at all in his approach to love; he is just practical. He would never deceive someone he felt warmly about. Still he may not say everything he feels until he is sure that the other person is in a position to accept it in a positive way. The person who falls under his charm—and he has this aplenty—may find it difficult to understand him at times. His hesitation may seem to be without reason. He may seem somewhat secretive. Although he may build up a love affair slowly, he will end it quickly if he feels it is a waste of time. When disappointed, he is direct and to the point.

LOVE AND MARRIAGE

When in love the Capricorn is usually quite possessive. He can be jealous at times. His loved one may find him very difficult to understand—especially when he feels he has been wronged. At those moments, he retires into himself and says little. Someone who does not understand him may find this behavior unreasonable or childish.

He is faithful to the person he loves. Always loyal, he is capable of making great sacrifices in order to keep a love relationship going.

The cultivated or strong Capricornian tries to improve himself when in love so that his relationship will be a lasting one. He admits his faults readily and does what he can to be more affectionate and open. An exciting, impulsive person is sometimes the ideal mate for someone born under this sign.

Romance and the Capricorn Woman

The Capricorn woman is very serious when it comes to love and courtship. She is correct. When her loved one offends her sensibilities she lets him know in short order. She can be quite affectionate when with the right man. On the whole, however, she is rather inhibited. A warm and understanding man can teach her how to be more demonstrative in her affection.

She is not fond of flirting. A man who tries to win her with his charm, may not have much of a chance. She is interested in someone who is serious on whom she can depend. Respect also plays an important part when she selects a lover or partner. A man who abuses her affections is quickly dismissed. She will never take the lead in a love affair, yet she is not fond of people who "move fast." She likes to take her time in learning someone. Whirlwind romance has very little appeal to a woman of this sort.

She is a perfectionist to some extent. She wants a man she can look up to and respect. Someone who is in a position to provide a good home and the necessary securities is more important and interesting to her than someone who is amorous and charming.

The Capricorn woman needs someone who is warm and affectionate even though she may not show or indicate it. She needs someone who is what she is not. She may spend a great deal of time looking for the right person. She is not someone who will settle for something short of her ideals. Some women under this sign marry rather late in life, as a result. The cultivated Capricorn woman, however, knows how to take the bitter with the sweet. If she meets someone who lines up with her ideals basically but is not perfect, she will settle for him and try to make the most of it.

The Capricorn wife runs her home in a very efficient manner. She is faithful and systematic. She enjoys taking care of her family and sees to it that everything runs smoothly. She may not be very romantic, even after marriage. However, the right man can help her to develop a deeper interest in love and companionship as the marriage grows.

She is a correct mother. Her children never want. She may not be too loving or sympathetic, but she is responsible and protective. Children's love for her grows as they grow older.

Romance and the Capricorn Man

The Capricorn man is no Lothario. He will never be swept off his feet by romance. He's more intellectual than romantic. He is fond of affection but may find it difficult to express affection toward the one he is interested in.

He is capable of great passion—yet passion that is lacking in affection. His loved one is apt to find him difficult to understand at times. He is honest in his love relationships. He would never lead a woman astray; flirting has no interest for him. He believes in steady, gradual relationships. He likes to know his partner well as a person before going on to romance or love. He may seem casual at first in the way he demonstrates his interest. As he wins the woman's trust, however, he will begin to unwind and reveal his feelings for what they are.

A woman who can help him gain those things in life that interest him holds a great attraction for him. He is not a fortune-hunter, but if the woman he is interested in has some money or social background, so much the better. He can be practical, even when in love.

He is an idealist. He has a dream woman running around in his head and he won't give up his search until he has found her—or someone like her. He is faithful in marriage. And does what he can to provide well for his family. He can be depended on to fulfill his role as father and husband to the letter.

He always tries to do what is best for his children. He may not be the most affectionate father, but he is dutiful and responsible. The feelings a Capricorn father has for his offspring generally intensify as they grow up.

Woman—Man

CAPRICORN WOMAN
ARIES MAN

In some ways, the Aries man resembles an intellectual mountain goat leaping from crag to crag. He has an insatiable thirst for knowledge. He's ambitious and is apt to have his finger in many pies. He can do with a woman like you—someone attractive, quickwitted, and smart.

He is not interested in a clinging vine kind of wife, but someone who is there when he needs her; someone who can give advice if he should ever need it, which is not likely to be often. The Aries man wants a woman who will look good on his arm without hanging on it too heavily. He is looking for a woman who has both feet on the ground and yet is mysterious and enticing, a kind of domestic Helen of Troy whose face or fine dinner can launch a thousand business deals if need be. That woman he's in search of sounds a little like you, doesn't she? If the shoe fits, put it on. You won't regret it. The Aries man makes a good husband. He is faithful and attentive. He is an affectionate kind of man. He'll make you feel needed and loved. Love is a serious matter for the Aries man. He does not believe in flirting or playing the field—especially after he's found the woman of his dreams. He'll expect you to be as constant in your affection as he is in his. He'll expect you to be one hundred percent his; he won't put up with any nonsense while romancing you.

The Aries man may be pretty progressive and modern about many things; however, when it comes to pants wearing, he's the boss and that's that. Once you have learned to accept that, you'll find the going easy.

The Aries man, with his endless energy and drive, likes to relax in the comfort of his home at the end of the day. The good homemaker can be sure of holding his love. He's keen on slippers and pipe and a comfortable armchair. If you see to it that everything in the house is where he expects to find it, you'll have no difficulty keeping the relationship on an even keel.

Life and love with an Aries man may be just the medicine you need. He'll be a good provider. He'll spoil you if he's financially able.

He's young at heart and can get along with children easily. He'll spoil them every chance he gets.

CAPRICORN WOMAN
TAURUS MAN

Some Taurus men are strong and silent. They do all they can to protect and provide for the women they love. The Taurus man will never let you down. He's steady, sturdy, and reliable. He's pretty honest and practical, too. He says what he means and means what he says. He never indulges in deceit and will always put his cards on the table.

The Taurean is a very affectionate man. Being loved, appreciated and understood are very important for his well-being. Like you, he is also looking for peace and security in his life. If you both work toward these goals together, you'll find that they are easily attained.

If you should marry a Taurus man, you can be sure that the wolf will never darken your door. They are notoriously good providers and do everything they can to make their families comfortable and happy.

He'll appreciate the way you have of making a home warm and inviting. Slippers and pipe, and the evening papers are essential ingredients in making your Taurus husband happy at the end of the workday. Although he may be a big lug of a guy, you'll find that he's pretty fond of gentleness and soft things. If you puff up his pillow and tuck him in at night, he won't complain. He'll eat it up and ask for more.

You probably won't complain about his friends. The Taurean tends to seek out friends who are successful or prominent. You admire people, too, who work hard and achieve what they set out for.

The Taurus man doesn't care too much for change. He's the original stay-at-home. Chances are that the house you move into after you're married will be the house you'll live in for the rest of your life.

You'll find that the man born under this sign is easy to get along with. It's unlikely that you'll have many quarrels or arguments.

Although he'll be gentle and tender with you, your Taurus man is far from being a sensitive type. He's a man's man. Chances are he loves sports like fishing and football. He can be earthy as well as down-to-earth.

Taureans love their children very much but do everything they can not to spoil them. They believe in children staying in their places. They make excellent disciplinarians. Your children will be polite and respectful.

CAPRICORN WOMAN
GEMINI MAN

Gemini men, in spite of their charm and dashing manner, may make your skin crawl. They may seem to lack the sort of common sense you set so much store in. Their tendency to start something, then—out of boredom—never finish it, may exasperate you.

You may interpret a Gemini's jumping around from here to there as childish, if not downright neurotic. A man born under this sign will seldom stay put and if you should take it upon yourself to try and make him sit still, he's liable to resent it strongly.

On the other hand, the Gemini man is liable to think you're an old slowpoke—someone far too interested in security and material things. He's attracted to things that sparkle and dazzle; you, with your practical way of looking at things most of the time, are likely to seem a little dull and uninteresting to this gadabout. If you're looking for a life of security and permanence, you'd better look elsewhere for your Mr. Right.

Chances are you'll be taken by his charming ways and facile wit—few women can resist Gemini magic. But after you've seen through his live-for-today, gossamer facade, you'll most likely be very happy to turn your attention to someone more stable, even if he is not as interesting. You want a man who is there when you need him. You need someone on whom you can fully rely. Keeping track of a Gemini's movements will make you dizzy. Still, if you are a patient woman, you should be able to put up with someone contrary—especially if you feel the experience may be worth the effort.

A successful and serious Gemini could make you a very happy woman, if you gave him half a chance. Although you may think he's got bats in his belfry, the Gemini man generally has a good brain and can make good use of it when it wants. Some Geminis who have learned the importance of being consequent have risen to great heights, professionally. President Kennedy was a Gemini, as was Thomas Mann and William Butler Yeats. Once you can convince yourself that not all people born under the sign of the Twins are witless grasshoppers, you'll find that you've come a long way in trying to understand them.

Life with a Gemini man can be more fun than a barrel of clowns. You'll never have a chance to experience a dull moment. He's always the life of the party. He's a little scatterbrained when it comes to handling money most of the time. You'd better handle the budgeting and bookkeeping.

In ways, he's like a child and perhaps that is why he can get along so well with the younger generation.

CAPRICORN WOMAN
CANCER MAN

If your plans are love, chances are you won't hit it off too well with the man born under Cancer. But then, Cupid has been known to do some pretty unlikely things. The Cancerian is a very sensitive man—thin-skinned and moody. You've got to keep on your toes not to step on his.

Cancer may be lacking in some of the qualities you seek in a man, but when it comes to being faithful and being a good provider, he's hard to beat.

The perceptive woman will not mistake the Crab's quietness for sullenness or his thriftiness for penny-pinching. In some respects, he is like that wise old owl out on a limb; he may look like he's dozing but actually he hasn't missed a thing. Cancers often possess a well of knowledge about human behavior; they can come across with some pretty helpful advice to those in trouble or in need. He can certainly guide you in making investments both in time and money. He may not say much, but he's always got his wits about him.

The Crab may not be the match or catch for a woman like you; at times, you are likely to find him downright dull. True to his sign, he can be fairly cranky and crabby when handled the wrong way.

If you're smarter than your Cancer friend, be smart enough not to let him know. Never give him the idea that you think he's a little short on brain-power. It would send him scurrying back into his shell, and all that lost ground will never be recovered.

The Crab is most comfortable at home. Settled down for the night or the weekend, wild horses couldn't drag him any further than the gatepost—that is, unless those wild horses were dispatched by his mother. The Crab is sometimes a Mama's boy. If his mate does not put her foot down, he will see to it that his mother always comes first. No self-respecting wife would ever allow herself to play second fiddle—even if it's to her old gray-haired mother-in-law. With a little bit of tact, however, she'll find that slipping into that number-one position is as easy as pie (that legendary one his mother used to bake).

If you pamper your Cancer man, you'll find that "Mother" turns up less and less—at the front door as well as in conversations.

Cancers make protective, proud, and patient fathers.

CAPRICORN WOMAN
LEO MAN

To know a man born under the sign of the Lion is not necessarily to love him—even though the temptation may be great. When he fixes most girls with his leonine double-whammy, it causes their hearts to pitter-pat and their minds to cloud over.

You are a little too sensible to allow yourself to be bowled over by a regal strut and a roar. Still, there's no denying that Leo has a way with women—even sensible women like yourself. Once he's swept a girl off her feet, it may be hard for her to scramble upright again. Still, you are no pushover for romantic charm—especially if you feel it's all show.

He'll wine you and dine you in the fanciest places. He'll croon to you under the moon and shower you with diamonds if he can get a hold of them . . . still, it would be wise to find out just how long that shower is going to last before consenting to be his wife.

Lions in love are hard to ignore, let alone brush off. Your no's will have a way of nudging him on until he feels he has you completely under his spell. Once mesmerized by this romantic powerhouse, you will most likely find yourself doing things you never dreamed of. Leos can be like vain pussycats when involved romantically. They like to be cuddled, curried, and tickled under the chin. This may not be your cup of tea exactly, still when you're romantically dealing with a man born under the sign of Leo, you'll find yourself doing all kinds of things to make him purr.

Although he may be big and magnanimous while trying to win you, he'll let out a blood-curdling roar if he thinks he's not getting the tender love and care he feels is his due. If you keep him well supplied with affection, you can be sure his eyes will never look for someone else and his heart will never wander.

Leo men often tend to be authoritarian—they are bound to lord it over others in one way or another it seems. If he is the top banana at his firm, he'll most likely do everything he can to stay on top. If he's not number one, he's most likely working on it and will be sitting on the throne before long.

You'll have more security than you can use if he is in a position to support you in the manner to which he feels you should be accustomed. He is apt to be too lavish, though—at least, by your standards.

You'll always have plenty of friends when you have a Leo for a mate. He's a natural-born friend-maker and entertainer. He loves to let his hair down at parties.

As fathers, Leos tend to spoil their children no end.

CAPRICORN WOMAN
VIRGO MAN

Although the Virgo man may be a bit of a fuss-budget at times, his seriousness and dedication to common sense may help you to overlook his tendency to sometimes be overcritical about minor things.

Virgo men are often quiet, respectable types who set great store in conservative behavior and level-headedness. He'll admire you for your practicality and tenacity, perhaps even more than for your good looks. He's seldom bowled over by a glamor-puss. When he gets his courage up, he turns to a serious and reliable girl for romance. He'll be far from a Valentino while dating. In fact, you may wind up making all the passes. Once he does get his motor running, however, he can be a warm and wonderful fellow—to the right girl.

He's gradual about love. Chances are your romance with him will most likely start out looking like an ordinary friendship. Once he's sure you're no fly-by-night flirt and have no plans of taking him for a ride. he'll open up and rain sunshine all over your heart.

Virgo men tend to marry late in life. He believes in holding out until he's met the right girl. He may not have many names in his little black book; in fact, he may not even have a black book. He's not interested in playing the field; leave that to men of the more flamboyant signs. The Virgo man is so particular that he may remain romantically inactive for a long period. His girl has to be perfect or it's no go. If you find yourself feeling weak-kneed for a Virgo, do your best to convince him that perfect is not so important when it comes to love. Help him realize that he's missing out on a great deal by not considering the near-perfect or whatever it is you consider yourself to be. With your sure-fire perseverance, you will most likely to able to make him listen to reason and he'll wind up reciprocating your romantic interests.

The Virgo man is no block of ice. He'll respond to what he feels to be the right flame. Once your love life with a Virgo man starts to bubble, don't give it a chance to fall flat. You may never have a second chance at winning his heart.

If you should ever have a falling out with him, forget about patching up. He'd prefer to let the pieces lie scattered. Once married, though, he'll stay that way—even if it hurts. He's too conscientious to try to back out of a legal deal of any sort.

The Virgo man is as neat as a pin. He's thumbs down on sloppy housekeeping. Keep everything bright, neat, and shiny. And that goes for the children, too, at least by the time he gets home from work. Chocolate-coated kisses from Daddy's little girl go over like a lead balloon with him.

CAPRICORN WOMAN
LIBRA MAN

If there's a Libran in your life, you are most likely a very happy woman. Men born under this sign have a way with women. You'll always feel at ease in a Libran's company; you can be yourself when you're with him.

The Libra man can be moody at times. His moodiness is often puzzling. One moment he comes on hard and strong with declarations of his love, the next moment you find that he's left you like yesterday's mashed potatoes. He'll come back, though; don't worry. Librans are like that. Deep down inside he really knows what he wants even though he may not appear to.

You'll appreciate his admiration of beauty and harmony. If you're dressed to the teeth and never looked lovelier, you'll get a ready compliment—and one that's really deserved. Librans don't indulge in idle flattery. If they don't like something, however, they are tactful enough to remain silent.

Librans will go to great lengths to preserve peace and harmony—even tell a fat lie if necessary. They don't like show-downs or disagreeable confrontations. The frank woman is all for getting whatever is bothering her off her chest and out into the open, even if it comes out all wrong. To the Libran, making a clean breast of everything seems like sheer folly sometimes.

You may lose your patience while waiting for your Libra friend to make up his mind. It takes him ages sometimes to make a decision. He weighs both sides carefully before committing himself to anything. You seldom dillydally—at least about small things—and so it's likely that you will find it difficult to see eye to eye with a hesitating Libran when it comes to decision-making methods.

All in all, though, he is kind, considerate, and fair. He is interested in the "real" truth; he'll try to balance everything out until he has all the correct answers. It's not difficult for him to see both sides of a story.

He's a peace-loving man. The sight of blood is apt to turn his stomach.

Librans are not show-offs. Generally, they are well-balanced, modest people. Honest, wholesome, and affectionate, they are serious about every love encounter they have. If he should find that the girl he's dating is not really suited to him, he will end the relationship in such a tactful manner that no hard feelings will come about.

The Libran father is firm, gentle, and patient.

CAPRICORN WOMAN
SCORPIO MAN

Some people have a hard time understanding the man born under the sign of Scorpio; few, however, are able to resist his fiery charm. When angered, he can act like an overturned wasps' nest; his sting can leave an almost permanent mark. If you find yourself interested in the Scorpio man, you'd better learn how to keep on his good side.

The Scorpio man can be quite blunt when he chooses; at times, he may seem rather hard-hearted. He can be touchy every now and then and this is apt to get on your nerves after a while. When you feel like you can't take it anymore, you'd better tiptoe away from the scene rather than chance an explosive confrontation. He's capable of giving you a sounding-out that will make you pack your bags and go back to Mother—for good.

If he finds fault with you, he'll let you know. He's liable to misinterpret your patience and think it a sign of indifference. Still and all, you are the kind of woman who can adapt to almost any sort of relationship or circumstance if you put your heart and mind to it.

Scorpio men are all quite perceptive and intelligent. In some respects, they know how to use their brains more effectively than most. They believe in winning at whatever they do; second-place holds no interest for them. In business, they usually achieve the position they want through drive and use of intellect.

Your interest in home-life is not likely to be shared by him. No matter how comfortable you've managed to make the house, it will have very little influence on him with regards to making him aware of his family responsibilities. He does not like to be tied down, generally, and would rather be out on the battlefield of life, belting away at what he feels to be a just and worthy cause. Don't try to keep the homefires burning too brightly while you wait for him to come home from work: you may just run out of firewood.

The Scorpio man is passionate in all things—including love. Most women are easily attracted to him and you are perhaps no exception. Those who allow themselves to be swept off their feet by a Scorpio man, shortly find that they're dealing with a carton of romantic fireworks. The Scorpio man is passionate with a capital P, make no mistake about that. Some women may find that he's just too love-happy, but that's their problem.

Scorpio men are straight to the point. They can be as sharp as a razor blade and just as cutting to anyone that crosses them.

Scorpio fathers generally like large families.

CAPRICORN WOMAN
SAGITTARIUS MAN

Sagittarius men are not easy to catch. They get cold feet whenever visions of the altar enter the romance. You'll most likely be attracted to the Sagittarian because of his sunny nature. He's lots of laughs and easy to get along with, but as soon as the relationship begins to take on a serious hue, you may feel yourself a little let-down.

Sagittarians are full of bounce; perhaps too much bounce to suit you. They are often hard to pin down; they dislike staying put. If he ever has a chance to be on-the-move, he'll latch onto it without so much as a how-do-you-do. Sagittarians are quick people— both in mind and spirit. If ever they do make mistakes, it's because of their zip; they leap before they look.

If you offer him good advice, he most likely won't follow it. Sagittarians like to rely on their own wits and ways whenever possible.

His up-and-at-'em manner about most things is likely to drive you up the wall at times. He's likely to find you a little too slow and deliberate. "Get the lead out of your shoes," he's liable to tease when you're accompanying him on a stroll or jogging through the park with him on Sunday morning. He can't abide a slow-poke.

At times you'll find him too much like a kid—too breezy. Don't mistake his youthful zest for premature senility. Sagittarians are equipped with first-class brain power and know how to use it. They are often full of good ideas and drive. Generally, they are very broadminded people and very much concerned with fair play and equality.

In the romance department, he's quite capable of loving you wholeheartedly while treating you like a good pal. His hail-fellow-well-met manner in the arena of love is likely to scare off a dainty damsel. However, a woman who knows that his heart is in the right place won't mind it too much if, once in a while, he slaps her (lightly) on the back instead of giving her a gentle embrace.

He's not so much of a homebody. He's got ants in his pants

and enjoys being on the move. Humdrum routine—especially at home—bores him silly. At the drop of a hat, he may ask you to whip off your apron and dine out for a change. He's a past-master in the instant surprise department. He'll love to keep you guessing. His friendly, candid nature will win him many friends. He'll expect his friends to be yours, and vice-versa.

Sagittarians make good fathers when the children become older; with little shavers, they feel all thumbs.

CAPRICORN WOMAN
CAPRICORN MAN

The Capricorn man is quite often not the romantic kind of lover that attracts most women. Still, with his reserve and calm, he is capable of giving his heart completely once he has found the right girl. The Capricorn man is thorough and deliberate in all that he does; he is slow and sure.

He doesn't believe in flirting and would never lead a heart on a merry chase just for the game. If you win his trust, he'll give you his heart on a platter. Quite often, the woman has to take the lead when romance is in the air. As long as he knows you're making the advances in earnest, he won't mind—in fact, he'll probably be grateful. Don't get to thinking he's all cold fish; he isn't. While some Capricorns are indeed quite capable of expressing passion, others often have difficulty in trying to display affection. He should have no trouble in this area, however, once he has found a patient and understanding girl.

The Capricorn man is very interested in getting ahead. He's quite ambitious and usually knows how to apply himself well to whatever task he undertakes. He's far from being a spendthrift. Like you, he knows how to handle money with extreme care. You, with your knack for putting away pennies for that rainy day, should have no difficulty understanding his way with money. The Capricorn man thinks in terms of future security. He wants to make sure that he and his wife have something to fall back on when they reach retirement age. There's nothing wrong with that; in fact, it's a plus quality.

The Capricorn man will want to handle household matters efficiently. Most Capricorn-oriented women will have no trouble in doing this. If he should check up on you from time to time, don't let it irritate you. Once you assure him that you can handle it all to his liking, he'll leave you alone.

Although he's a hard man to catch when it comes to marriage, once he's made that serious step, he's quite likely to become possessive. Capricorns need to know that they have the support of their wives in whatever they do—every step of the way.

The Capricorn man needs to be liked. He may seem dull to some, but underneath his reserve there is sometimes an adventurous streak that has never had a chance to express itself. He may be a real dare-devil in his heart of hearts. The right woman—the affectionate, adoring woman can bring out that hidden zest in his nature.

He makes a loving, dutiful father, even though he may not understand his children completely.

CAPRICORN WOMAN
AQUARIUS MAN

You are liable to find the Aquarius man the most broadminded man you have ever met; on the other hand, you are also liable to find him the most impractical. Oftentimes, he's more of a dreamer than a doer. If you don't mind putting up with a man whose heart and mind are as wide as the Missouri but whose head is almost always up in the clouds, then start dating that Aquarian who has somehow captured your fancy. Maybe you, with your good sense, can bring him back down to earth when he gets too starry-eyed.

He's no dumb-bell; make no mistake about that. He can be busy making some very complicated and idealistic plans when he's got that out-to-lunch look in his eyes. But more than likely, he'll never execute them. After he's shared one or two of his progressive ideas with you, you are liable to ask yourself, "Who is this nut?" But don't go jumping to conclusions. There's a saying that Aquarians are a half-century ahead of everybody else in the thinking department.

If you decide to answer "Yes" to his "Will you marry me?" you'll find out how right his zany whims are on or about your 50th anniversary. Maybe the wait will be worth it. Could be that you have an Einstein on your hands—and heart.

Life with an Aquarian won't be one of total despair if you can learn to temper his airiness with your down-to-earth practicality. He won't gripe if you do. The Aquarian always maintains an open mind; he'll entertain the ideas and opinions of everybody. He may not agree with all of them.

Don't go tearing your hair out when you find that it's almost impossible to hold a normal conversation with your Aquarius friend at times. He's capable of answering your how-are-you-feeling with a run-down on the price of Arizona sugar beets. Always try to keep in mind that he means well.

His broadmindedness doesn't stop when it comes to you and your personal freedom. You won't have to give up any of your hobbies or projects after you're married; he'll encourage you to continue in your interests.

He'll be a kind and generous husband. He'll never quibble over petty things. Keep track of the money you both spend. He can't. Money burns a hole in his pocket.

At times, you may feel like calling it quits. Chances are, though, that you'll always give him another chance.

He's a good family man. He understands children as much as he loves them.

CAPRICORN WOMAN
PISCES MAN

Pisces could be the man you've looked for high and low and thought never existed. He's terribly sensitive and terribly romantic. Still, he has a very strong individual character and is well aware that the moon is not made of green cheese. He'll be very considerate of your every wish and will do his best to see to it that your relationship is a happy one.

The Pisces man is great for showering the object of his affection with all kinds of little gifts and tokens of his love.

He's just the right mixture of dreamer and realist; he's capable of pleasing most women. When it comes to earning bread and butter, the strong Pisces will do all right in the world. Quite often they are capable of rising to the very top. Some do extremely well as writers or psychiatrists. He'll be as patient and understanding with you as you undoubtedly will be with him. One thing a Pisces man dislikes is pettiness; anyone who delights in running another into the ground is almost immediately crossed off his list of possible mates. If you have any small grievances with your girlfriends, don't tell him. He couldn't care less and will think less of you if you do.

If you fall in love with a weak kind of Piscean, don't give up your job at the office before you get married. Better hang onto it until a good time after the honeymoon; you may still need it. A funny thing about the man born under this sign is that he can be content almost anywhere. This is perhaps because he is quite inner-directed and places little value on material things. In a shack or a palace, the Pisces man is capable of making the best of all possible adjustments. He won't kick up a fuss if the roof leaks and if the fence is in sad need of repair, he's liable just to shrug his shoulders. He's got more important things on his mind, he'll tell you. At this point, you'll most likely feel like giving him a piece of your mind. Still and all, the Pisces man is not shiftless or aimless; it is important to understand that material gain is never a direct goal for someone born under this sign.

Pisces men have a way with the sick and troubled. He can listen to one hard-luck story after another without seeming to tire. He often knows what's bothering someone before that someone knows it himself.

As a lover, he'll be quite attentive. You'll never have cause to doubt his intentions or sincerity. Everything will be above-board in his romantic dealings with you.

Children are delighted with Pisces men because of their permissiveness.

Man—Woman

CAPRICORN MAN
ARIES WOMAN

The Aries woman may be a little too bossy and busy for you. Generally speaking, Ariens are ambitious creatures. They tend to lose their patience with thorough and deliberate people who take a lot of time to complete something. The Aries woman is a fast worker. Sometimes she's so fast she forgets to look where she's going. When she stumbles or falls, it would be nice if you were there to grab her. Ariens are proud. They don't like to be told "I told you so" when they err. Tongue-wagging can turn them into blocks of ice. However, don't begin to think that the Aries woman frequently gets tripped up in her plans. Quite often they are capable of taking aim and hitting the bull's-eye. You'll be flabbergasted at times by their accuracy as well as by their ambition.

You are perhaps somewhat slower than the Arien in attaining your goals. Still, you are not apt to make mistakes along the way; you're seldom ill-prepared.

The Aries woman is rather sensitive at times. She likes to be handled with gentleness and respect. Let her know that you love her for her brains as well as for her good looks. Never give her cause to become jealous. When your Aries woman sees green, you'd better forget about sharing a rosy future together. Handle her with tender love and care and she's yours.

The Aries woman can be giving if she feels her partner is deserving. She is no iceberg; she responds to the proper masculine flame. She needs a man she can look up to and feel proud of. If the shoe fits, put it on. If not, better put your sneakers back on and quietly tiptoe out of her sight. She can cause you plenty of heartache if you've made up your mind about her and she hasn't made up hers about you. Aries women are very demanding at times.

Some of them tend to be high-strung. They can be difficult if they feel their independence is being hampered.

The cultivated Aries woman makes a wonderful homemaker and hostess. You'll find that she's very clever in decorating; she knows how to use colors. Your house will be tastefully furnished; she'll see to it that it radiates harmony. Friends and acquaintances will love your Aries wife. She knows how to make everyone feel at home and welcome.

Although the Aries woman may not be keen on burdensome responsibilities, she is fond of children and the joy they bring.

CAPRICORN MAN
TAURUS WOMAN

A Taurus woman could perhaps understand you better than most women. She is very considerate and loving. She is thorough and methodical in whatever she does. She knows how to take her time in doing things; she is anxious to avoid mistakes. She is a careful person. She never skips over things that may seem unimportant, she goes over everything with a fine-tooth comb.

Home is very important to the Taurus woman. She is an excellent homemaker. Although your home may not be a palace, it will become, under her care, a comfortable and happy abode. She'll love it when friends drop by for the evening. She is a good cook and enjoys feeding people well. No one will ever go away from your house with an empty stomach.

The Taurus woman is serious about love and affection. When she has taken a tumble for someone, she'll stay by him—for good, if possible. She will try to be practical in romance, to some extent. When she sets her cap for a man, she keeps after him until he's won her. Generally, the Taurus woman is a passionate lover, even though she may appear otherwise at first glance. She is on the look-out for someone who can return her affection fully. Taureans are sometimes given to fits of jealousy and possessiveness. They expect fair play in the area of marriage; when it doesn't come about, they can be bitingly sarcastic and mean.

The Taurus woman is generally an easy-going person. She's fond of keeping peace. She won't argue unless she has to. She'll do her best to maintain your love relationship on an even keel.

Marriage is generally a one-time thing for Taureans. Once they've made the serious step, they seldom try to back out of it. Marriage is for keeps. They are fond of love and warmth. With the right man, they turn out to be ideal wives.

The Taurus woman will respect you for your steady ways; she'll have confidence in your common sense.

Taurus women seldom put up with nonsense from their children. They are not so much strict as concerned. They like their children to be well-behaved and dutiful. Nothing pleases a Taurus mother more than a compliment from a neighbor or teacher about her child's behavior. Although some children may inwardly resent the iron hand of a Taurus mother, in later life they are often thankful that they were brought up in such an orderly and conscientious way.

CAPRICORN MAN
GEMINI WOMAN

The Gemini woman may be too much of a flirt for you. Then again, it depends on what kind of mood she's in. Gemini women can change from hot to cold quicker than a cat can wink its eye. Chances are her fluctuations will tire you after a time, and you'll pick up your heart—if it's not already broken into small pieces—and go elsewhere. Women born under the sign of the Twins have the talent of being able to change their moods and attitudes as frequently as they change their party dresses.

Sometimes, Gemini girls like to whoop it up. Some of them are good-time girls who love burning the candle to the wick. You'll see them at parties and gatherings, surrounded by men of all types, laughing gaily or kicking up their heels at every opportunity. The next day you may bump into the same girl at the neighborhood library and you'll hardly recognize her for her "sensible" attire. She'll probably have five or six books under her arm—on five or six different subjects. In fact, she may even work there. If you think you've met the twin sister of Dr. Jekyll and Mr. Hyde, you're most likely right.

You'll probably find her a dazzling and fascinating creature—for a time, at any rate. Most men do. But when it comes to being serious about love you may find that that sparkling Eve leaves quite a bit to be desired. It's not that she has anything against being serious, it's just that she might find it difficult trying to be serious with you.

At one moment, she'll be capable of praising you for your steadfast and patient ways; the next moment she'll tell you in a cutting way that you're an impossible stick in the mud.

Don't even begin to fathom the depths of her mercurial soul—it's full of false bottoms. She'll resent close investigation, anyway, and will make you rue the day you ever took it into your head to try to learn more about her than she feels is necessary. Better keep the relationship full of fun and fancy free until she gives you the go-ahead sign. Take as much of her as she is willing to give; don't ask for more. If she does take a serious interest in you, then she'll come across with the goods.

There will come a time when the Gemini girl will realize that she can't spend her entire life at the ball and that the security and warmth you have to offer is just what she needs to be a happy, complete woman.

As a mother, she's easy-going with her children. She likes to spoil them as much as she can.

CAPRICORN MAN
CANCER WOMAN

If you fall in love with a Cancer woman, be prepared for anything. Cancerians are sometimes difficult to understand when it comes to love. In one hour, she can unravel a whole gamut of emotions; it will leave you in a tizzy. She'll always keep you guessing, that's for sure.

You may find her a little too uncertain and sensitive for your liking. You'll most likely spend a good deal of time encouraging her—helping her to erase her foolish fears. Tell her she's a living doll a dozen times a day and you'll be well loved in return.

Be careful of the jokes you make when in her company—don't let any of them revolve around her, her personal interests, or her family. If you do, you'll most likely reduce her to tears. She can't stand being made fun of. It will take bushels of roses and tons of chocolates—not to mention the apologies—to get her to come back out of her shell.

In matters of money-managing, she may not easily come around to your way of thinking. You may get the notion that your Cancerian sweetheart or mate is a direct descendant of Scrooge. If she has her way, she'll hang onto that first dollar you earned. She's not only that way with money, but with everything right on up from bakery string to jelly jars. She's a saver; she never throws anything away, no matter how trivial.

Once she returns your "I love you," you'll find you have an affectionate, self-sacrificing, and devoted woman on your hands. Her love for you will never alter unless you want it to. She'll put you up on a high pedestal and will do everything—even if it's against your will—to keep you there.

Cancer women love homelife. For them, marriage is an easy step to make. They're domestic with a capital D. She'll do her best to make your home comfortable and cozy. The Cancer woman is happiest in her own home. She makes an excellent hostess. The best in her comes out when she's in her own environment.

Of all the signs of the Zodiac, Cancer women make the best

mothers. She'll treat every complaint of her child as a major catastrophe. With her, children come first. If you're lucky, you'll run a close second. You may think she's too devoted to the children. You may have a hard time convincing her to cut her apron strings.

CAPRICORN MAN
LEO WOMAN

The Leo woman can make most men roar like lions. If any woman in the Zodiac has that indefinable something that can make men lose their heads and find their hearts, it's the Leo woman.

She's got more than a fair share of charm and glamor and she knows how to make the most of her assets, especially when she's in the company of the opposite sex. Jealous men are apt to lose their cool or their sanity when trying to woo a woman born under the sign of the Lion. She likes to kick up her heels quite often and doesn't care who knows it. She often makes heads turn and tongues wag. You don't necessarily have to believe any of what you hear—it's most likely jealous gossip or wishful thinking. Needless to say, other women in her vicinity turn green with envy and will try anything short of shoving her into the nearest lake in order to put her out of the running.

Although this vamp makes the blood rush to your head and makes you momentarily forget all the things you thought were important and necessary in your life, you may feel differently when you come back down to earth and the stars are out of your eyes. You may feel that she isn't the kind of girl you planned to bring home to Mother. Not that your mother might disapprove of your choice—but *you* might after the shoes and rice are a thing of the past. Although the Leo woman may do her best to be a good wife for you, chances are she'll fall short of your idea of what a good wife should be like.

If you're planning on not going as far as the altar with that Leo woman who has you flipping your lid, you'd better be financially equipped for some very expensive dating. Be prepared to shower her with expensive gifts and to take her dining and dancing in the smartest spots in town. Promise her the moon if you're in a position to deliver. Luxury and glamor are two things that are bound to lower a Leo's resistance. She's got expensive tastes and you'd better cater to them if you expect to get to first base with this lady.

If you've got an important business deal to clinch and you have doubts as to whether you can swing it or not, bring your Leo girlfriend along to the luncheon. Chances are that with her on your arm, you'll be able to win any business battle. She won't have to say or do anything—just be there at your side. The grouchiest oil magnate can be transformed into a gushing, obedient schoolboy if there's a charming Leo woman in the room.

Leo mothers are blind to the faults of their children. They make very loving and affectionate mothers and tend to spoil their offspring.

CAPRICORN MAN
VIRGO WOMAN

The Virgo woman may be a little too difficult for you to understand at first. Her waters run deep. Even when you think you know her, don't take any bets on it. She's capable of keeping things hidden in the deep recesses of her womanly soul—things she'll only release when she's sure that you're the man she's been looking for. It may take her some time to come around to this decision. Virgo girls are finicky about almost everything; everything has to be letter-perfect before they're satisfied. Many of them have the idea that the only people who can do things right are Virgos.

Nothing offends a Virgo woman more than slovenly dress, sloppy character, or a careless display of affection. Make sure your tie is not crooked and your shoes sport a bright shine before you go calling on this lady. Keep your off-color jokes for the locker-room; she'll have none of that. Take her arm when crossing the street. Don't rush the romance. Trying to corner her in the back of a cab may be the one way of striking out. Never criticize the way she looks—in fact, the best policy would be to agree with her as much as possible. Still, there's just so much a man can take; all those do's and don'ts you'll have to observe if you want to get to first base with a Virgo may be just a little too much to ask of you. After a few dates, you may come to the conclusion that she just isn't worth all that trouble. However, the Virgo woman is mysterious enough generally speaking, to keep her men running back for more. Chances are you'll be intrigued by her airs and graces.

If love-making means a lot to you, you'll be disappointed at first in the cool ways of your Virgo friend. However, under her glacial facade there lies a hot cauldron of seething excitement. If you're patient and artful in your romantic approach, you'll find that all that caution was well worth the trouble. When Virgos love, they don't stint. It's all or nothing as far as they're concerned. Once they're convinced that they love you, they go all the way, tossing all cares to the wind.

One thing a Virgo woman can't stand in love is hypocrisy. They don't give a hoot about what the neighbors say, if their hearts tell them "Go ahead!" They're very concerned with human truths . . . So much so that if their hearts stumble upon another fancy, they're liable to be true to that new heart-throb and leave you standing in the rain. She's honest to her heart and will be as true to you as you are with her, generally. Do her wrong once, however, and it's farewell.

Both strict and tender, she tries to bring out the best in her children.

CAPRICORN MAN
LIBRA WOMAN

The song goes: It's a woman's prerogative to change her mind. The lyricist must have had the Libra woman in his thoughts when he jotted this ditty out. Her changeability, in spite of its undeniable charm (sometimes) could actually drive even a man of your patience up the wall. She's capable of smothering you with love and kisses one day and on the next, avoid you like the plague. If you think you're a man of steel nerves then perhaps you can tolerate her sometime-ness without suffering too much. However, if you own up to the fact that you're only a mere mortal who can only take so much, then you'd better fasten your attention on a girl who's somewhat more constant.

But don't get the wrong idea: a love affair with a Libran is not bad at all. In fact, it can have an awful lot of plusses to it. Libra women are soft, very feminine, and warm. She doesn't have to vamp all over the place in order to gain a man's attention. Her delicate presence is enough to warm the cockles of any man's heart. One smile and you're like a piece of putty in the palm of her hand.

She can be fluffy and affectionate—things you like in a girl. On the other hand, her indecision about which dress to wear, what to cook for dinner, or whether to redo the rumpus room or not could make you tear your hair out. What will perhaps be more exasperating is her flat denial to the accusation that she cannot make even the simplest decision. The trouble is that she wants to be fair or just in all matters; she'll spend hours weighing pros and cons. Don't make her rush into a decision; that will only irritate her.

The Libra woman likes to be surrounded by beautiful things. Money is no object when beauty is concerned. There will always be plenty of flowers in the house. She'll know how to arrange them tastefully, too. Women under this sign are fond of beautiful clothes and furnishings. They will run up bills without batting an eye—if given the chance.

Once she's cottoned to you, the Libra woman will do everything in her power to make you happy. She'll wait on you hand

and foot when you're sick and bring you breakfast in bed Sundays. She'll be very thoughtful and devoted. If anyone dares suggest you're not the grandest man in the world, your Libra wife will tell that person where to get off—and in no uncertain terms.

Librans work wonders with children. Gentle persuasion and affection are all a Libra mother uses in bringing them up. It works.

CAPRICORN MAN
SCORPIO WOMAN

When the Scorpio woman chooses to be sweet, she's apt to give the impression that butter wouldn't melt in her mouth . . . but, of course, it would. When her temper flies, so will everything else that isn't bolted down. She can be as hot as a *tamale* or as cool as a cucumber when she wants. Whatever mood she's in, you can be sure it's for real. She doesn't believe in poses or hypocrisy.

The Scorpio woman is often seductive and sultry. Her *femme fatale* charm can pierce the hardest hearts like a laser ray. She doesn't have to look like Mata Hari (many of them resemble the tomboy next door) but once you've looked into those tantalizing eyes, you're a goner.

The Scorpio woman can be a whirlwind of passion. Life with a girl born under this sign will not be all smiles and smooth-sailing. If you think you can handle a woman who can purr like a pussycat when handled correctly but spit bullets once her fur is ruffled, then try your luck. Your stable and steady nature will most likely have a calming effect on her. You're the kind of man she can trust and rely on. But never cross her—even in the smallest thing; if you do, you'd better tell Fido to make room for you in the dog-house— you'll be his guest for the next couple of days.

Generally, the Scorpio woman will keep family battles within the walls of your home. When company visits, she's apt to give the impression that married life with you is one big joy-ride. It's just her way of expressing her loyalty to you—at least, in front of others. She believes that family matters are and should stay private. She'll certainly see to it that others have a high opinion of you both. She'll be right behind you in whatever it is you want to do. Although she's an individualist, after she has married, she'll put her own interests aside for those of the man she loves. With a woman like this backing you up, you can't help but go far. She'll never try to take over your role as boss of the family. She'll give you all the support you need in order to fulfill that role. She won't complain if the going gets rough. She is a courageous woman. She's as anxious as you to find that place in the sun for you both. She's as determined a person as you are.

Although she may love her children, she may not be very affectionate toward them. She'll make a devoted mother, though. She'll be anxious to see them develop their talents. She'll teach the children to be courageous and steadfast.

CAPRICORN MAN
SAGITTARIUS WOMAN

The Sagittarius woman is hard to keep track of: first she's here, then she's there . . . She's a woman with a severe case of itchy feet. She's got to keep on the move.

People generally like her because of her hail-fellow-well-met manner and breezy charm. She is constantly good-natured and almost never cross. She is the kind of girl you're likely to strike up a palsywalsy relationship with; you might not be interested in letting it go any farther. She probably won't sulk if you leave it on a friendly basis, either. Treat her like a kid sister and she'll eat it up like candy.

She'll probably be attracted to you because of your restful, self-assured manner. She'll need a friend like you to help her over the rough spots in her life; she'll most likely turn to you for advice frequently.

There is nothing malicious about a girl born under this sign. She is full of bounce and good cheer. Her sun-shiny disposition can be relied upon on even the rainiest of days. No matter what she says or does, you'll always know that she means well. Sagittarians are sometimes short on tact. Some of them say anything that comes into their pretty little heads, no matter what the occasion. Sometimes the words that tumble out of their mouths seem downright cutting and cruel; they mean well but often everything they say comes out wrong. She's quite capable of losing her friends —and perhaps even yours—through a careless slip of the lip. Always remember that she is full of good intentions. Stick with her if you like her and try to help her mend her ways.

She's not a girl that you'd most likely be interested in marrying, but she'll certainly be lots of fun to pal around with. Quite often, Sagittarius women are outdoor types. They're crazy about things like fishing, camping, and mountain climbing. They love the wide open spaces. They are fond of all kinds of animals. Make no mistake about it: this busy little lady is no slouch. She's full of pep and ginger.

She's great company most of the time; she's more fun than a three-ring circus when she's in the right company. You'll like her for her candid and direct manner. On the whole, Sagittarians are very kind and sympathetic women.

If you do wind up marrying this girl-next-door type, you'd better see to it that you handle all of the financial matters. Sagittarians often let money run through their fingers like sand.

As a mother, she'll smother her children with love and give them all the freedom *they* think they need.

CAPRICORN MAN
CAPRICORN WOMAN

The Capricorn may not be the most romantic woman of the Zodiac, but she's far from frigid when she meets the right man. She believes in true love; she doesn't appreciate getting involved in flings. To her, they're just a waste of time. She's looking for a man who means "business"—in life as well as in love. Although she can be very affectionate with her boyfriend or mate, she tends to let her head govern her heart. That is not to say she is a cool, calculating cucumber. On the contrary, she just feels she can be more honest about love if she consults her brains first. She wants to size-up the situation before throwing her heart in the ring. She wants to make sure it won't get stepped on.

The Capricorn woman is faithful, dependable, and systematic in just about everything she undertakes. She is quite concerned with security and sees to it that every penny she spends is spent wisely. She is very economical about using her time, too. She does not believe in whittling away her energy on a scheme that is bound not to pay off.

Ambitious themselves, they are quite often attracted to ambitious men—men who are interested in getting somewhere in life. If a man of this sort wins her heart, she'll stick by him and do all she can to help him get to the top.

The Capricorn woman is almost always diplomatic. She makes an excellent hostess. She can be very influential when your business acquaintances come to dinner.

The Capricorn woman is likely to be very concerned, if not downright proud, about her family tree. Relatives are pretty important to her, particularly if they're socially prominent. Never say a cross word about her family members. That can really go against her grain and she'll punish you by not talking to you for days.

She's generally thorough in whatever she does. Capricorn women are well-mannered and gracious, no matter what their backgrounds. They seem to have it in their natures to always behave properly.

If you should marry a woman born under this sign, you need never worry about her going on a wild shopping spree. They understand the value of money better than most women. If you turn over your paycheck to her at the end of the week, you can be sure that a good hunk of it will wind up in the bank.

The Capricorn mother is loving and correct.

CAPRICORN MAN
AQUARIUS WOMAN

If you find that you've fallen head over heels for a woman born under the sign of the Water Bearer, you'd better fasten your safety belt. It may take you quite a while to actually discover what this girl is like—and even then, you may have nothing to go on but a string of vague hunches. The Aquarian is like a rainbow, full of bright and shining hues; she's like no other girl you've ever known. There is something elusive about her . . . something difficult to put your finger on.

The Aquarius woman can be pretty odd and eccentric at times. Some say this is the source of her mysterious charm. You are liable to think she's just a plain screwball; you may be 50 per cent right.

Aquarius women often have their heads full of dreams. By nature, they're often unconventional; they have their own ideas about how the world should be run. Sometimes their ideas may seem pretty weird—chances are they're just a little bit too progressive. They say that the Aquarian is about fifty years ahead of the rest of the world in her thinking. She'll most likely be the most tolerant and open-minded woman you've ever encountered.

If you find that she's too much mystery and charm for you to handle, just talk it out with her and say that you think it would be better to call it quits. She'll most likely give you a peck on the cheek and say, "Okay, but let's still be friends." Aquarius women are like that. Perhaps you'll both find it easier to get along in a friendship than in a romance.

It is not difficult for her to remain buddy-buddy with an ex-lover. For many Aquarians, the line between friendship and romance is a pretty fuzzy one.

She is not a jealous person, and while you're romancing her, she won't expect you to be, either. You'll find her a pretty free spirit most of the time. Just when you think you know her inside-out, you'll discover that you don't really know her at all.

She's a very sympathetic and warm person; she is often helpful to those in need of assistance and advice.

She'll seldom be suspicious even when she has every right to be. If the man she loves makes a little slip, she's liable to forgive and forget it.

She makes a fine mother. Her positive and big-hearted qualities are easily transmitted to her offspring.

CAPRICORN MAN
PISCES WOMAN

The Pisces woman places great value on love and romance. She's gentle, kind, and romantic. Perhaps she's that girl you've been dreaming about all these years. Like you, she has very high ideals; she will only give her heart to a man who she feels can live up to her expectations.

She will never try to wear the pants in the family. She's a staunch believer in the man being the head of the house. Quite often Pisces women are soft and cuddly. They have a feminine, domestic charm that can win the heart of just about any man.

Generally, there's a lot more to her than just a pretty exterior and womanly ways. There's a brain ticking behind that gentle face. You may not become aware of it—that is, until you've married her. It's no cause for alarm, however; she'll most likely never use it against you. But if she feels you're botching up your married life through careless behavior or if she feels you could be earning more money than you do, she'll tell you about it. But any wife would, really. She'll never try to usurp your position as head and breadwinner of the family. She'll admire you for your ambition and drive. If anyone says anything against you in her presence, she'll probably break into tears. Pisces women are usually very sensitive and their reaction to frustration or anger is often just a plain good old-fashioned cry. They can weep buckets when inclined.

She'll prepare an extra-special dinner for you when you've made a new conquest in your profession. Don't bother to go into the details though at the dinner table; she doesn't have much of a head for business matters, usually, and is only too happy to leave that up to you.

She is a wizard in decorating a home. She's fond of soft and beautiful things. There will always be a vase of fresh flowers on the dining room table. She'll see to it that you always have plenty of socks and underwear in the top drawer of your dresser.

Treat her with tenderness and your relationship will be an enjoyable one. Pisces women are generally fond of sweets, so keep her in chocolates (and flowers, of course) and you'll have a happy wife. Never forget birthdays or anniversaries; she won't.

There is usually a strong bond between a Pisces mother and her children. She'll try to give them things she never had as a child and is apt to spoil them as a result.

AQUARIUS
January 20 — February 18

CHARACTER
ANALYSIS

Of all the signs of the Zodiac, Aquarius is perhaps the most progressive. People born under this sign are usually quite tolerant and broadminded. There is a saying that most Aquarians are 50 years ahead of their time. As a rule they are unselfish and peace-loving. They are often more interested in helping others than they are in helping themselves. They think of mankind on a very broad scale

The Aquarian does not believe in hanging onto old, useless values. He is for progress; for moving ahead and making a better world. It is important to him that peace and harmony exist

Anything connected with the betterment of mankind interests him. He is also likely to have a useful hobby. In short, he is a person with a purpose in mind. General education methods and sociology are usually things that interest him greatly. He does not believe that mankind should be divided into rich and poor. He feels that everyone should be entitled to the same privileges no matter what his background. More often than not, people born under the sign of Aquarius have an intellectual nature. They usually know a lot about many things and they are sure of what they know.

As has already been mentioned, the Aquarian is years ahead of time in his way of thinking. Others often find it hard to keep up with him. He is not afraid of change; on the contrary, he welcomes it. New ways of living are always of interest to him. The person born under this eleventh sign of the zodiac is eager to develop along creative lines—he is keen on new forms of organization or thought. Even in love matters, he tends to be creative.

The Aquarian is interested in groups—how they are structured, their behavioral patterns and so on. He enjoys bringing people together. He wants to see everyone living in peace and harmony.

The individual holds little interest for him. He thinks in terms of masses of people. For him, this is life.

He surprises many people. The Aquarian always keeps others guessing. At times, he does not even know himself what his next step in life will be.

At times he may seem rather detached, disengaged. Others may feel he is sizing up everyone around him and making mental notes. The Aquarian believes in live and let live as an all-around way of getting on in the world. He would never try to dominate another; he respects the other man for his individuality. He believes in letting others express themselves as they want. He does not feel he has the right to direct another's life style. Others often find it difficult placing an Aquarian; he seems so full of contradictions at times—it's difficult to say he is one thing or the other.

The person born under this sign usually has his own set of laws to live by. Conventional rules and regulations, he feels, need not apply to him. He has his own rights and wrongs. To the average person he may seem downright unconventional. Others may think he is just trying to gain attention by shocking his neighbors, but this is far from the truth. The Aquarian does not believe in poses; he believes in what he does. The customs and dress of the average person say little to him. He may find it quite necessary to develop his own way of behaving and dressing in order to express the "real" him. He is an individualist. Original modes of behavior and thinking are something he cannot do without.

His head is generally full of plans and ideas. Because he is so often busy turning things over in his head, he is apt to seem a bit dreamy and "out of it" to others. At times, the Aquarian shoots his hopes too high and has to pay the consequences of being too unrealistic.

Health

On the whole, people born under the sign of Aquarius are good to look at. They may be slight of build, yet they are strong in a wiry sort of way. They have a strong resistance against illnesses, generally. They are healthy, for the most part, and know how to take care of themselves. They are usually interested in hygiene and take all sorts of precautions so that disease never has a chance to strike them. Physically they have little to worry about; their constitutions are strong and healthy.

Tensions and pressure, however, can cause them to become depressed, and this often has a bad effect on their overall health. But this is generally rare, for the Aquarian has the ability to remove himself from things that are disturbing. He can look at things in an objective way so that they do not really affect his spiritual balance.

It is important for the person born under this sign to oppose people who try to dominate him or drive him into a corner. He is not the kind of person who can allow someone to encroach upon his freedom. The strain of someone bearing down on him can have a bad influence on his well-being. At times, he may be downright nervous due to disturbing conditions. It is important that the Aquarian see to it that he has the proper amount of vitamins and minerals to help counteract his nervousness. He should try to see to it that his diet is well-balanced with plenty of fresh fruit and vegetables. He also needs peace and quiet and plenty of fresh air. A country place where he can retreat when the going gets rough would be ideal. Harmonious surroundings are important to him.

Still and all, he is not the kind of person who will hold his tongue if someone criticizes his ideals. He'll stand up for what he believes. His objective manner will protect him from injury to some extent.

The mind is important to the Aquarian. He can train himself to control it so that when he meets with minor setbacks or disturbances they do not really affect him.

The weak parts of his body are his ankles and calves. If he has an accident, quite often these areas are affected. Nervous and circulatory disorders sometimes bother him. The Aquarian who is not careful may become the victim of low blood pressure and anemia. By taking the proper vitamins and eating the proper food, he can prevent these ailments.

Occupation

The kind of occupation that generally interests someone born under the sign of Aquarius is work that has a bit of idealism to it—a job that has a philosophical outlook. It is important to someone born under this sign that he has a job suited to his particular talents and character. If it is not exactly his kind of work then it must be open-ended enough so that he can mold it to fit his particular need. He has to be creative in his work. Suggestions and new techniques are important to him. Quite often his place of business profits through his being allowed to approach the duties of his position in a creative manner.

He is a person who enjoys keeping busy. He believes in rolling up his sleeves and getting down to brass tacks immediately. He doesn't like to waste time when working. Quite often he is quicker than the people he works with and can finish his job in half the time it takes others to do it. He is energetic and enthusiastic about what he does. Many of the suggestions he has for improvements on the job are helpful. He is usually a great source of inspiration for his co-workers. Responsibility does not frighten him, but he would rather not take orders from someone else.

Quite often the mind of the Aquarian is turning over new plans and ideas, even while he is busy at work. His thoughts never rest. He is inventive in his way of thinking. Quite often the results of his mental endeavors benefit everyone. He is intrigued by things that are new and different. He is not afraid to try out a new work technique or method. He believes in modern ideas. Routine work is not apt to hold his interest for very long. He likes unusual chores; things that give him a chance to do something on his own. If he is tied down to a humdrum kind of job, he is not likely to be interested in doing his best. Employers may find him a bit trying and unreliable. Routine chores hold little interest for him; he is apt to work at them in spurts, but his attention will be easily distracted. If his work is dull, he is apt to begin with a bang (in an attempt to get it out of the way as soon as possible), but later his energy is likely to peter out and he may even allow himself to become careless.

If the people he works with are rather slow and unimaginative, the Aquarian is apt to become restless and impatient. If he feels that they do not make an effort to better themselves, he is likely to become a bit scornful.

Social work is an occupation well suited to someone born under this sign. He is more concerned for others than he is for himself. His self-sacrificing way is a feather in his cap, and the people he deals with are apt to put themselves in his hands completely, trusting him to do what is best for them. The Aquarian does well in rehabilitation work. He likes to help people help themselves. He is the kind of person who is cut out for service work.

Some Aquarians make good writers and journalists. They have sharp, acute minds and know how to translate their thoughts on paper so that others can benefit from them.

Art and all things related to culture attract the average Aquarian. Some of them make good painters and musicians. They know how to be critical in a constructive way. Often they make good art or music critics.

It is important that the Aquarian put his heart and soul into his creative work if he wants to attain the high goals he sets for himself. He can do well in any job where he is allowed to make use of his rich imagination. In strict business matters, he may not be able to function very well due to a tendency to dream. Some people born under this sign, in spite of their good intentions, only plan during their lives and never get around to putting their ideas into action. Then when things get to be too much for them, they allow their plans to slide.

Money to the average Aquarian is nice to have for what it can do. Money in itself has little interest for him. He is neither a splurger or a pennypincher. He generally makes use of his finances in what he feels is a practical way. He may use some of it to make progress for himself and others easier.

Some Aquarians come by money through their inventions or discoveries. They may work night and day for a long period of time before coming up with the answer or solution of a problem. However, this sort of research or investigatory work generally intrigues them.

The Aquarian is the kind of person who will work hard for success, but he is more pleased if it comes as a surprise.

Home and Family

The Aquarian is generally a very sociable person. He or she feels it is important to have a nice home—one where it is pleasant to entertain friends and associates. His taste is generally modern —although he may have a respect for old things. He is bound to have all the latest fixtures and appliances in his home. As soon as something becomes out-of-date or non-functional, he is likely to throw it out and get something that is in keeping with the times. Appliances that save on housework are a must for the Aquarian woman. She has more important things to do than attending to the drudgery of housekeeping.

Although the Aquarian is fond of having a lot of people about, he does have his moments when he has to be alone. He wants peace and quiet so he can think things out without being interrupted. Chances are he is a member of many kinds of clubs and organizations. He likes people of all kinds. But he also likes his privacy to be respected. When he feels that it is necessary to withdraw from the hubbub of the crowd, he does not appreciate others who try to prevent this.

Although he loves his home and family, he does not like them to play a dominating role in his life. He'll own up to his responsibilities but he does not want to have his duties shoved under his nose constantly. In short, he does not want to feel that he is tied down. He needs love and affection, as everyone does, but he needs to be independent too. At times, these may conflict with each other.

With children, the Aquarian is likely to get along very well. He does not treat them as his inferiors, but is apt to handle them as little people. He knows how to talk and reason with them just as he would someone his own age. Children, in turn, generally respect him for treating them as individuals. He does not oppress children but encourages them to develop their natural talents and to express their own personalities.

The Aquarian, at times, enjoys the direct and honest company of children to that of so-called adults. He knows how to keep children entertained with stories and games. In spite of his ability to be permissive, the average Aquarian makes it clear to the child that he will tolerate no nonsense from them. Children, understanding this, never misbehave while in the company of an Aquarian adult.

Social Relationships

The average Aquarian is cheerful and outgoing when around people. At home he may be rather quiet and pensive. Few people understand this sort of person very well, even though they may feel they do. Some Aquarians withdraw so often from social situations that it becomes a permanent habit. Some famous recluses were born under this eleventh sign of the zodiac.

Because he sometimes keeps himself apart, he seems rather standoffish and critical to those who do not understand him. The Aquarian is apt to make many friends in his life, but his quality for being unconsciously aloof may make it difficult for others to get to know him. His close friendships may be few.

He is optimistic by nature and always tends to look on the positive or bright side of social situations. This outlook makes it possible for him to get along well with all kinds of people—even if only for a limited amount of time. Some of his friends and acquaintances may seem rather strange and eccentric to others. His collection of friends is likely to encompass many extremes in personality types.

The Aquarian makes a good friend because of his many nice qualities and his tolerant disposition. He does well with business associates as a rule and with his loved ones.

The average Aquarian enjoys observing mankind in all its forms and variations. He is never quick to judge another. For him, no one is totally bad or good. He is willing to make excuses for others if he really feels that they mean well. At times, this works against him; people may take advantage of his tolerant ways and play him for the fool. He does not always learn from his mistakes. He is easily moved by hard-luck stories. He is always willing to give another the benefit of a doubt.

He is the kind of person who sticks by his friends and acquaintances. Many of the friends he makes he keeps for life. He is loyal and dependable. When friends are in trouble, they can always depend on him. He likes them to respect his individuality as much as he respects theirs. He is never apt to meddle in their private affairs but will lend a helping hand if asked.

LOVE AND MARRIAGE

The average Aquarian may not be as interested in love for himself, that is, on a person to person basis, as he is in love on a universal basis. When he or she does fall in love with someone it is usually because of some intellectual attraction he feels rather than for some physical or superficial quality the person of the opposite sex may have.

Love to the Aquarian is serious business. He is faithful. When looking for a mate or partner, he will be more interested in the person's intellectual capacities and emotional depths than in what his personality may seem to be like. If the person that interests him does not measure up to his standards, he ends the relationship then and there—often without an explanation.

Although the average Aquarian may be deeply interested in love and romance, he or she may occasionally seem rather cool. He is difficult to understand in the battlefield of love. As with other things, he has his particular rules which he feels he must follow. The Aquarian's lover may have a hard time trying to pin him down. He won't allow himself to be totally possessed. He believes in holding onto his sense of liberty and freedom. He would never make excessive demands of his loved one's freedom; he expects the same consideration. In spite of this attitude, he is generally quite affectionate and loving.

In love, Aquarians do not always know what they want. They may have a good many love affairs before they decide to settle down. The *idea* of love may mean more to an Aquarian than the *act* of loving.

When he or she does marry, the Aquarian is faithful and considerate, and enjoys family life, the peace and quiet of home. Aquarians' love may waver at times, but it will never stray.

Romance and the Aquarius Woman

Some Aquarian women may seem rather cool and aloof, on the one hand, while exuding a sort of sexual warmth and charm, on the other. They may not be particularly interested in sex. They are more often than not attracted to the mental capacities of a man. The purely physical attributes, no matter how attractive they may be, hold little interest for them. When she does fall in love, it is usually with a man who is her intellectual equal or superior. She makes a faithful wife or lover. The man to whom she gives her affection must live up to her expectations. If he does not, she is likely to drop him rather quickly.

Many men are apt to find this kind of woman both attractive and cold. She is not a very affectionate person as a rule. A possessive man is apt to be in for a lot of frustration while courting her. She has her own laws to live by. She will not submit to a man who wants to fashion her to fit his own needs. Freedom and privacy are important to her even after marriage. If the man she loves respects her for her individuality and allows her what she feels are her God-given rights, everything will run smoothly in their relationship. She is in need of warmth and affection. The right man can help her to develop her interest in these qualities. Although she is no flirt, she may have a good many romantic adventures behind her before she consents to marry and settle down.

She makes an excellent companion, spiritually and intellectually. She makes a faithful and devoted wife. It is important to her that she have all the latest household appliances—especially those that save time—for she is not very domestically inclined. Chances are that after marriage she will want to continue her career or interests outside the home.

She is loving when dealing with her family. She must have peace and harmony in her home. She will put her foot down if things upset her. Her husband or children must not make excessive demands of her. Home may tie her down more than she desires; at times she may feel the need to get out and do something for others. Her family may see this as a kind of neglectful behavior although it is not. She holds that her family is more than just a husband and children; she relates to the community in which she lives and feels that she has obligations to it. She is very conscientious in her relationships.

As a mother, she is ideal. She understands her children and treats them as equals. She is not a scold but her children would never step out of line, anyway. They respect her too much for that.

Romance and the Aquarius Man

The Aquarius man is generally quite broad-minded. His interests extend to the farthest horizons. Humanity means a lot to him. He is in love with people; this is more important to him, sometimes, than being in love with just one person.

He is the kind of a lover who can win a woman over by his intellectual charm. He is usually witty and a good conversationalist. His joy of life usually impresses members of the opposite sex. Liberty is important to him. He will take up with the woman he loves but never try to strap her down with dos and don'ts. He wants his loved one to respect his right to express himself as he desires. If she understands his deep interest in personal freedom, and accepts it, the relationship is bound to be an enjoyable one. If she becomes too possessive, he is apt to break the relationship without giving an explanation.

Chances are he will have quite a number of love affairs in his life before he thinks of marrying. Sometimes he is impulsive about love and falls for a woman rather quickly and without reason; later he may regret it. He is unpredictable in love. Some Aquarian men marry their loved ones after a relatively unhappy love affair and make good husbands. They may disappoint their loved ones while courting, but after they settle down they do their best to set matters right.

He is generally affectionate, although he may not be very demonstrative. He is kind and considerate; he would never take advantage of another's feelings. Every time he is in love he is serious—even if the affair is short-lived.

He is fair in all things. He is likely to treat strangers with the same courtesy and kindness as he treats his family. Everyone is equal to him. He won't act one way with one person, another way with another. He's honest and always the same as far as his personality is concerned.

He is a faithful husband and a responsible parent. His interests outside may take him away from home affairs quite often, however, he will never neglect his basic duties as a provider. He may have to be coaxed to stay home more often, from time to time.

Children love him. He is tolerant with them and enjoys seeing them developing their own personalities. He is not a disciplinarian; he does not have to be. He guides his offspring with ease.

Woman—Man
AQUARIUS WOMAN
ARIES MAN
In some ways, the Aries man resembles an intellectual mountain goat leaping from crag to crag. He has an insatiable thirst for knowledge. He's ambitious and is apt to have his finger in many pies. He can go far with a woman like you—someone attractive, quickwitted, and smart.

He is not interested in a clinging vine kind of wife, but someone who is there when he needs her, someone who listens and understands what he says, someone who can give advice if he should ever need it . . . which is not likely to be often. The Aries man wants a woman who will look good on his arm without hanging on it too heavily. He is looking for a woman who has both feet on the ground and yet is mysterious and enticing—a kind of domestic Helen of Troy whose face or fine dinner can launch a thousand business deals if need be. That woman he's in search of sounds a little like you, doesn't she? If the shoe fits, put it on. You won't regret it.

The Aries man makes a good husband. He is faithful and attentive. He is an affectionate kind of man. He'll make you feel needed and loved. Love is a serious matter for the Aries man. He does not believe in flirting or playing the field, especially after he's found the woman of his dreams. He'll expect you to be as constant in your affection as he is in his. He'll expect you to be one hundred percent his; he won't put up with any nonsense while romancing you.

The Aries man may be pretty progressive and modern about many things; however, when it comes to pants wearing, he's downright conventional: it's strictly male attire. The best position you can take in the relationship is a supporting one. He's the boss and that's that. Once you have learned to accept that, you'll find the going easy.

The Aries man, with his endless energy and drive, likes to relax in the comfort of his home at the end of the day. The good homemaker can be sure of holding his love. He's keen on slippers and pipe and a comfortable armchair. If you see to it that everything in the house is where he expects to find it, you'll have no difficulty keeping the relationship on an even keel.

Life and love with an Aries man may be just the medicine you need. He'll be a good provider. He'll spoil you if he's financially able.

He's young at heart and can get along with children easily. He'll spoil them every chance he gets.

AQUARIUS WOMAN
TAURUS MAN

If you've got your heart set on a man born under the sign of Taurus, you'll have to learn the art of being patient. Taureans take their time about everything—even love.

The steady and deliberate Taurus man is a little slow on the draw; it may take him quite a while before he gets around to popping that question. For the woman who doesn't mind twiddling her thumbs, the waiting and anticipating almost always pays off in the end. Taurus men want to make sure that every step they take is a good one—particularly, if they feel that the path they're on is one that leads to the altar.

If you are in the mood for a whirlwind romance, you had better cast your net in shallower waters. Moreover, most Taureans prefer to do the angling themselves. They are not keen on women taking the lead; once she does, he's liable to drop her like a dead fish. If you let yourself get caught on his terms, you'll find that he's fallen for you—hook, line, and sinker.

The Taurus man is fond of a comfortable home life. It is very important to him. If you keep those home fires burning you will have no trouble keeping that flame in your Taurean's heart aglow. You have a talent for homemaking; use it. Your taste in furnishings is excellent. You know how to make a house come to life with colors and decorations.

Taurus, the strong, steady, and protective Bull may not be your idea of a man on the move; still, he's reliable. Perhaps he could be the anchor for your dreams and plans. He could help you to acquire a more balanced outlook and approach to your life. If you're given to impulsiveness, he could help you to curb it. He's the man who is always there when you need him.

When you tie the knot with a man born under Taurus, you can put away fears about creditors pounding on the front door. Taureans are practical about everything including bill-paying. When he carries you over that threshold, you can be certain that the entire house is paid for, not only the doorsill.

As a housewife, you won't have to worry about putting aside your many interests for the sake of back-breaking household chores. Your Taurus hubby will see to it that you have all the latest time-saving appliances and comforts.

Your children will be obedient and orderly. Your Taurus husband will see to that.

AQUARIUS WOMAN
GEMINI MAN

The Gemini man is quite a catch. Many a woman has set her cap for him and failed to bag him. Generally, Gemini men are intelligent, witty, and outgoing. Many of them tend to be rather versatile. The Gemini man could easily wind up being your better half.

One thing that causes a Twin's mind and affection to wander is a bore, and it is unlikely that an active woman like you would ever allow herself to be accused of being that. The Gemini man who has caught your heart will admire you for your ideas and intellect—perhaps even more than for your homemaking talents and good looks.

The woman who hitches up with a Twin needn't feel that once she's made her marriage vows that she'll have to store her interests and ambition in the attic somewhere. The Gemini man will admire you for your zeal and liveliness. He's the kind of guy who won't scowl if you let him shift for himself in the kitchen once in a while. In fact, he'll enjoy the challenge of wrestling with pots and pans himself for a change. Chances are, too, that he might turn out to be a better cook than you—that is, if he isn't already.

The man born under the sign of the Twins is a very active person. There aren't many women who have enough pep to keep up with him, but this should be no problem for a spry woman like you. The Gemini man is a dreamer, planner, and idealist. A woman with a strong personality could easily fill the role of rudder for her Gemini's ship-without-a-sail. If you are a cultivated, purposeful woman, he won't mind it too much. The intelligent Twin is often aware of his shortcomings and doesn't resent it if someone with better bearings than himself gives him a shove in the right direction—when it's needed. The average Gemini does not have serious ego-hangups and will even accept a well-deserved chewing out from his mate quite good-naturedly.

When you team up with a Gemini man, you'll probably always have a houseful of people to entertain—interesting people, too; Geminians find it hard to tolerate sluggish minds and dispositions.

People born under Gemini generally have two sides to their natures, as different as night and day. It's very easy for them to be happy-go-lucky one minute, then down in the dumps the next. They hate to be bored and will generally do anything to make their lives interesting, vivid, and action-packed.

Gemini men are always attractive to the opposite sex. He'll flirt occasionally, but it will never amount to anything serious.

As a father, he's a pushover; he loves children so much that he lets them do what they want.

AQUARIUS WOMAN
CANCER MAN

Chances are you won't hit it off too well with the man born under Cancer if your plans are love, but then, Cupid has been known to do some pretty unlikely things. The Cancerian is a very sensitive man—thin-skinned and occasionally moody. You've got to keep on your toes—and not step on his—if you're determined to make a go of the relationship.

The Cancer man may be lacking in some of the qualities you seek in a man, but when it comes to being faithful and being a good provider, he's hard to beat.

The perceptive woman will not mistake the Crab's quietness for sullenness or his thriftiness for pennypinching. In some respects, he is like that wise old owl out on a limb; he may look like he's dozing but actually he hasn't missed a thing. Cancerians often possess a well of knowledge about human behavior; they can come across with some pretty helpful advice to those in trouble or in need. He can certainly guide you in making investments both in time and money. He may not say much, but he's always got his wits about him.

The Crab may not be the match or catch for a woman like you; at times, you are likely to find him downright dull. True to his sign, he can be fairly cranky and crabby when handled the wrong way. He is perhaps more sensitive than he should be.

If you're smarter than your Cancer friend, be smart enough not to let him know. Never give him the idea that you think he's a little short on brain power. It would send him scurrying back into his shell—and all that ground lost in the relationship will perhaps never be recovered.

The Crab is happiest at home. Once settled down for the night or the weekend, wild horses couldn't drag him any farther than the gatepost—that is, unless those wild horses were dispatched by his mother. The Crab is sometimes a Momma's boy. If his mate does not put her foot down, he will see to it that his mother always comes first. No self-respecting wife would ever allow herself to play second fiddle—even if it's to her old gray-haired mother-in-law. With a little bit of tact, however, she'll find that slipping into that number-one position is as easy as pie (that legendary one his mother used to bake).

If you pamper your Cancer man, you'll find that "Mother" turns up increasingly less—at the front door as well as in conversations.

Cancerians make protective, proud, and patient fathers.

AQUARIUS WOMAN
LEO MAN

To know a man born under the sign of the Lion is not necessarily to love him—even though the temptation may be great. When he fixes most girls with his leonine double-whammy, it causes their hearts to pitter-pat and their minds to cloud over.

You are a little too sensible to allow yourself to be bowled over by a regal strut and a roar. Still, there's no denying that Leo has a way with women—even sensible women like yourself. Once he's swept a girl off her feet, it may be hard for her to scramble upright again. Still, you are no pushover for romantic charm, especially if you feel it's all show.

He'll wine you and dine you in the fanciest places. He'll croon to you under the moon and shower you with diamonds if he can get a hold of them . . . still, it would be wise to find out just how long that shower is going to last before consenting to be his wife.

Lions in love are hard to ignore, let alone brush off. Your no's will have a way of nudging him on until he feels he has you completely under his spell. Once mesmerized by this romantic power-house, you will most likely find yourself doing things you never dreamed of. Leos can be like vain pussycats when involved romantically. They like to be cuddled, curried, and tickled under the chin. This may not be your cup of tea exactly, still when you're romantically dealing with a man born under the sign of Leo, you'll find yourself doing all kinds of things to make him purr.

Although he may be big and magnanimous while trying to win you, he'll let out a blood-curdling roar if he thinks he's not getting the tender love and care he feels is his due. If you keep him well supplied with affection, you can be sure his eyes will never look for someone else and his heart will never wander.

Leo men often tend to be authoritarian—they are born to lord it over others in one way or another, it seems. If he is the top banana at his firm, he'll most likely do everything he can to stay on top. If he's not number one, he's most likely working on it and will be sitting on the throne before long.

You'll have more security than you can use if he is in a position to support you in the manner to which he feels you should be accustomed. He is apt to be too lavish, though—at least, by your standards.

You'll always have plenty of friends when you have a Leo for a mate. He's a natural-born friendmaker and entertainer. He loves to kick up his heels at a party.

As fathers, Leos tend to spoil their children no end.

AQUARIUS WOMAN
VIRGO MAN

The Virgo man is all business—at least he may seem so to you. He is usually very cool, calm, and collected. He's perhaps too much of a fuss-budget to wake up deep romantic interests in a woman like you. Torrid romancing to him is just so much sentimental mush. He can do without it and can make that quite evident in short order. He's keen on chastity and, if necessary, he can lead a sedentary, sexless life without caring too much about the fun others think he's missing. In short, you are liable to find him a first-class dud. He doesn't have much of an imagination; flights of fancy don't interest him. He is always correct and likes to be handled correctly. Almost everything about him is orderly. "There's a place for everything..." is likely to be an adage he'll fall back upon quite regularly.

He does have an honest-to-goodness heart, believe it or not. The woman who finds herself strangely attracted to his cool, feet-flat-on-the-ground ways, will discover that his is a constant heart, not one that goes in for flings or sordid affairs. Virgos take an awfully long time to warm up to someone. A practical man, even in matters of the heart, he wants to know just what kind of person you are before he takes a chance on you.

The impulsive girl had better not make the mistake of kissing her Virgo friend on the street—even if it's only a peck on the cheek. He's not at all demonstrative and hates public displays of affection. Love, according to him, should be kept within the confines of one's home—with the curtains drawn. Once he believes that you are on the level with him as far as your love is concerned, you'll see how fast he can lose his cool. Virgos are considerate, gentle lovers. He'll spend a long time, though, getting to know you. He'll like you before he loves you.

A romance with a Virgo man can be a sometime—or, rather, a one-time—thing. If the bottom ever falls out, don't bother reaching for the adhesive tape. Nine times out of ten he won't care about patching up. He's a once-burnt twice-shy guy. When he crosses your telephone number out of his address book, he's crossing you out of his life for good.

Neat as a pin, he's thumbs-down on what he considers "sloppy" housekeeping. An ashtray with just one stubbed out cigarette in it can annoy him even if it's only two seconds old. Glassware should always sparkle and shine if you want to keep him happy.

If you marry him, keep your sunny-side up.

Your children should be kept as spotless as your house. Kids with dirty faces and hands displease him. Train them to be kind and courteous.

AQUARIUS WOMAN
LIBRA MAN

If there's a Libran in your life, you are most likely a very happy woman. Men born under this sign have a way with women. You'll always feel at ease in a Libran's company; you can be yourself when you're with him.

The Libra man can be moody at times. His moodiness is often puzzling. One moment he comes on hard and strong with declarations of his love, the next moment you find that he's left you like yesterday's mashed potatoes. He'll come back, though; don't worry. Librans are like that. Deep down inside he really knows what he wants, even though he may not appear to.

You'll appreciate his admiration of beauty and harmony. If

you're dressed to the teeth and never looked lovelier, you'll get a ready compliment—and one that's really meant. Librans don't indulge in idle flattery. If they don't like something, they are tactful enough to remain silent.

Librans will go to great lengths to preserve peace and harmony, even by telling a fat lie if necessary. They don't like showdowns or disagreeable confrontations. The frank woman is all for getting whatever is bothering her off her chest and out into the open, even if it comes out all wrong. To the Libran, making a clean breast of everything seems like sheer folly sometimes.

You may lose your patience while waiting for your Libra friend to make up his mind. It takes him ages sometimes to make a decision. He weighs both sides carefully before committing himself to anything. You seldom dillydally—at least about small things—and so it's likely that you will find it difficult to see eye to eye with a hesitating Libran when it comes to decision-making methods.

All in all, though, he is kind, considerate, and fair. He is interested in the "real" truth; he'll try to balance everything out until he has all the correct answers. It's not difficult for him to see both sides of a story.

He's a peace-loving man. The sight of blood is apt to turn his stomach.

Librans are not showoffs. Generally, they are well-balanced, modest people. Honest, wholesome, and affectionate, they are serious about every love encounter they have. If he should find that the girl he's dating is not really suited to him, he will end the relationship in such a tactful manner that no hard feelings will come about.

The Libra father is firm, gentle, and patient.

AQUARIUS WOMAN
SCORPIO MAN

Many find the Scorpio's sting a fate worse than death. When his anger breaks loose, you had better clear out of the vicinity.

The average Scorpio may strike you as a brute. He'll stick pins into the balloons of your plans and dreams if they don't line up with what he thinks is right. If you do anything to irritate him—just anything—you'll wish you hadn't. He'll give you a sounding out that would make you pack your bags and go back to Mother—if you were that kind of a girl.

The Scorpio man hates being tied down to home life—he would rather be out on the battlefield of life, belting away at whatever he feels is a just and worthy cause, instead of staying home nestled in a comfortable armchair with the evening paper. If you are a girl who has a homemaking streak, don't keep those home fires burning too brightly too long; you may just run out of firewood.

As passionate as he is in business affairs and politics, the Scorpio man still has plenty of pep and ginger stored away for lovemaking.

Most women are easily attracted to him—perhaps you are no exception. Those who allow a man born under this sign to sweep them off their feet, shortly find that they're dealing with a pepper pot of seething excitement. The Scorpio man is passionate with a capital P, you can be sure of that. But he's capable of dishing out as much pain as pleasure. Damsels with fluttering hearts who, when in the embrace of a Scorpio, think "This is it," had better be in a position moments later to realize that "Perhaps this isn't it."

Scorpios are blunt. An insult is likely to whiz out of his mouth quicker than a compliment.

If you're the kind of woman who can keep a stiff upper lip, take it on the chin, turn a deaf ear, and all of that, because you feel you are still under his love-spell in spite of everything: lots of luck.

If you have decided to take the bitter with the sweet, prepare yourself for a lot of ups and downs. Chances are you won't have as much time for your own affairs and interests as you'd like. The Scorpio's love of power may cause you to be at his constant beck and call.

Scorpios like fathering large families. They love children, but quite often they fail to live up to their responsibilities as a parent.

AQUARIUS WOMAN
SAGITTARIUS MAN

If you've set your cap for a man born under the sign of Sagittarius, you may have to apply an awful lot of strategy before you can persuade him to get down on bended knee. Although some Sagittarians may be marriage-shy, they're not ones to skitter away from romance. You'll find a love relationship with a Sagittarian—whether a fling or "the real thing"—a very enjoyable experience.

As a rule, Sagittarians are bright, happy, healthy people. They have a strong sense of fair play. Often they are a source of inspiration to others. They are full of drive and ideas.

You'll be taken by the Sagittarian's infectious grin and his light-hearted friendly nature. If you do wind up being the woman in his life, you'll find that he's apt to treat you more like a buddy than the love of his life. It's just his way. Sagittarians are often more chummy than romantic.

You'll admire his broadmindedness in most matters, including those of the heart. If, while dating you, he claims that he still wants to play the field, he'll expect you to enjoy the same liberty. Once he's promised to love, honor, and obey, however, he does just that. Marriage for him, once he's taken that big step, is very serious business.

The Sagittarius man is quick-witted. He has a genuine interest in equality. He hates prejudice and injustice. Generally, Sagittarians are good at sports. They love the great out-of-doors and respect wild life in all its forms.

He's not much of a homebody. Quite often he's occupied with far away places either in his daydreams or in reality. He enjoys being on the move. He's got ants in his pants and refuses to sit still for long stretches at a time. Humdrum routine—especially at home—bores him.

At the drop of a hat, he may ask you to whip off your apron and dine out for a change. He likes to surprise people.

He'll take great pride in showing you off to his friends. He'll always be considerate where your feelings are concerned; he will never embarrass or disappoint you intentionally.

His friendly, sun-shiny nature is capable of attracting many people. Like you, he's very tolerant when it comes to friends. You will most likely spend a great deal of time helping him entertain people.

Sagittarians are all thumbs when it comes to tiny tots. They develop an interest in children when they grow older and wiser.

AQUARIUS WOMAN
CAPRICORN MAN

A with-it girl like you is likely to find the average Capricorn man a bit of a drag. The man born under the sign of the Goat is often a closed person and difficult to get to know. Even if you do get to know him, you may not find him very interesting.

In romance, Capricorn men are a little on the rusty side. You'll probably have to make all the passes.

You may find his plodding manner irritating and his conservative, traditional ways downright maddening. He's not one to take chances on anything. "If it was good enough for my father, it's good enough for me" may be his motto. He follows a way that is tried and true.

Whenever adventure rears its tantalizing head, the Goat will turn the other way; he's just not interested.

He may be just as ambitious as you are—perhaps even more so—but his ways of accomplishing his aims are more subterranean or, at least, seem so. He operates from the background a good deal of the time. At a gathering you may never even notice him, but he's there, taking in everything, sizing everyone up, planning his next careful move.

Although Capricorns may be intellectual to a degree, it is not generally the kind of intelligence you appreciate. He may not be as quick or as bright as you; it may take him ages to understand a simple joke.

If you do decide to take up with a man born under this sign, you ought to be pretty good in the "cheering up" department. The Capricorn man often acts as though he's constantly being followed by a cloud of gloom.

The Capricorn man is happiest when in the comfort and privacy of his own home. The security possible within four walls can make him a happy man. He'll spend as much time as he can at home. If he is loaded down with extra work, he'll bring it home instead of working overtime at the office.

You'll most likely find yourself frequently confronted by his relatives. Family is very important to the Capricorn—*his* family that is. They had better take a pretty important place in your life, too, if you want to keep your home a happy one.

Although his caution in most matters may all but drive you up the wall, you'll find his concerned way with money is justified most of the time. He'll plan everything right down to the last penny.

He can be quite a scold with children. You'll have to step in and smooth things out.

AQUARIUS WOMAN
AQUARIUS MAN

Aquarians are extremely friendly and open, even with other Aquarians. Of all the signs, they are perhaps the most tolerant. In the thinking department they are often miles ahead of others, and with very little effort, it seems. As an Aquarian yourself, you will most likely find your Aquarian friend intriguing, and the relationship between two Aquarians is likely to be twice as challenging. Your own high respect for intelligence and fair play may be reason enough to settle your heart on another Water Bearer.

Aquarians love everybody, even their worst enemies— sometimes. Through your relationship with another Aquarian, you'll find yourself running into all sorts of people, ranging from near-genius to downright insane—and these are all friends that you'll share in common.

In the holding hands stage of your romance you may find that your Water Bearing friend has cold feet that may take quite a bit of warming up. More than likely, he'll just want to be your pal in the beginning. For him—as for you, that's an important step in any relationship—even love. The "poetry and flowers" stage will come later, perhaps some years later.

The Aquarian is all heart; still, when it comes to tying himself down to one person and for keeps, he is liable to hesitate. He may even try to get out of it if you give him half a chance—and as an Aquarian, you may be inclined to do just that. He's no Valentino and wouldn't want to be, but then, a Valentino isn't quite what you're looking for either. In fact, as an Aquarian yourself, you are bound to understand his hesitation—more or less. You are also likely to be more attracted by his broadmindedness and high moral standards than by his abilities to romance.

You won't find it difficult to look up to a man born under your sign, and the challenge is certain to be exciting. He can pierce through the most complicated problem as if it were a matter of two plus two. Others may find him too lofty or high-minded, but you're pretty much that way yourself.

In marriage you need never be afraid that his affection will wander. It stays put once he's hitched. He'll certainly admire you for your intelligence, and don't think that you have to stick close to the kitchen. Once you're married, he'll want you to pursue whatever you want in your quest for knowledge. You'll most likely have a minor squabble with him now and then, but never anything serious.

Still, even you may find his forgetfulness (added to your own) a little bothersome. His head is so full of ideas and plans that sometimes he seems like the absent-minded professor. Kids love him and vice versa. He's tolerant and open-minded with everybody, from the very young to the very old.

AQUARIUS WOMAN
PISCES MAN

The man born under Pisces is quite a dreamer. Sometime he's so wrapped up in his dreams that he's difficult to reach. To the average, ambitious woman, he may seem a little sluggish.

He's easy-going most of the time. He seems to take things in his stride. He'll entertain all kinds of views and opinions from just about anyone, nodding or smiling vaguely, giving the impression that he's with them one hundred percent while that may not be the case at all. His attitude may be "why bother" when he is confronted with someone wrong who thinks he's right. The Pisces man will seldom speak his mind if he thinks he'll be rigidly opposed.

The Pisces man is oversensitive at times—he's afraid of getting his feelings hurt. He'll sometimes imagine a personal affront when none's been made. Chances are you'll find this complex of his maddening; at times, you may feel like giving him a swift kick where it hurts the most. It won't do any good, though. It would just add fuel to the fire of his complex.

One thing you will admire about this man is his concern for people who are sickly or troubled. He'll make his shoulder available to anyone in the mood for a good cry. He can listen to one hard-luck story after another without seeming to tire. When his advice is asked, he is capable of coming across with some pretty important words of wisdom. He often knows what's bugging someone before that person is aware of it himself. It's almost intuitive with Pisceans, it seems. Still, at the end of the day, he looks forward to some peace and quiet. If you've got a problem on your mind, don't dump it into his lap at the end of the day. If you do, you're liable to find him short-tempered. He's a good listener but he can only take so much.

Pisces men are not aimless although they may seem so at times. The positive sort of Pisces man is quite often successful in his profession and is likely to wind up rich and influential. Material gain, however, is not a direct goal for a man born under this sign.

The weaker Piscean is usually content to stay put on the level where he happens to find himself. He won't complain too much if the roof leaks or the fence is in need of repair. He'll just shrug it off as a minor inconvenience. He's got more important things to think about, he'll say.

Because of their seemingly laissez-faire manner, people born under this sign are immensely popular with children. For tots they play the double role of confidant and playmate. It will never enter his mind to discipline a child, no matter how spoiled or incorrigible that child becomes.

Man—Woman

AQUARIUS MAN
ARIES WOMAN

The Aries woman is quite a charmer. When she tugs at the strings of your heart, you'll know it. She's a woman who's in search of a knight in shining armor. She is a very particular person with very high ideals. She won't accept anyone but the man of her dreams.

The Aries woman never plays around with passion; she means business when it comes to love.

Don't get the idea that she's a dewy-eyed miss. She isn't. In fact, she can be pretty practical and to-the-point when she wants. She's a girl with plenty of drive and ambition. With an Aries woman behind you, you are liable to go far in life. She knows how to help her man get ahead. She's full of wise advice; you only have to ask. In some cases, the Aries woman has a keen business sense; many of them become successful career women. There is nothing backward or retiring about her. She is equipped with a good brain and she knows how to use it.

Your union with her could be something strong, secure, and romantic. If both of you have your sights fixed in the same direction, there is almost nothing that you could not accomplish.

The Aries woman is proud and capable of being quite jealous. While you're with her, never cast your eye in another woman's direction. It could spell disaster for your relationship. The Aries woman won't put up with romantic nonsense when her heart is at stake.

If the Aries woman backs you up in your business affairs, you can be sure of succeeding. However, if she only is interested in advancing her own career and puts her interests before yours, she can be sure of rocking the boat. It will put a strain on the relationship. The over-ambitious Aries woman can be a pain in the neck and make you forget that you were once in love with her.

The cultivated Aries woman makes a wonderful wife and mother. She has a natural talent for homemaking. With a pot of paint and some wallpaper, she can transform the dreariest domicile into an abode of beauty and snug comfort. The perfect hostess—even when friends just happen by—she knows how to make guests feel at home.

You'll also admire your Arien because she knows how to stand on her own two feet. Hers is an independent nature. She won't break down and cry when things go wrong, but pick herself up and try to patch up matters.

The Aries woman makes a fine, affectionate mother.

AQUARIUS MAN
TAURUS WOMAN

The woman born under the sign of Taurus may lack a little of the sparkle and bubble you often like to find in a woman. The Taurus woman is generally down-to-earth and never flighty. It's important to her that she keep both feet flat on the ground. She is not fond of bounding all over the place, especially if she's under the impression that there's no profit in it.

On the other hand, if you hit if off with a Taurus woman, you won't be disappointed at all in the romance area. The Taurus woman is all woman and proud of it, too. She can be very devoted and loving once she decides that her relationship with you is no fly-by-night romance. Basically, she's a passionate person. In sex, she's direct and to-the-point. If she really loves you, she'll let you know she's yours—and without reservations. Better not flirt with other women once you've committed yourself to her. She is capable of being jealous and possessive.

She'll stick by you through thick and thin. It's almost certain that if the going ever gets rough, she'll not go running home to her mother. She can adjust to hard times just as graciously as she can to the good times.

Taureans are, on the whole, pretty even-tempered. They like to be treated with kindness. Pretty things and soft things make them purr like kittens.

You may find her a little slow and deliberate. She likes to be safe and sure about everything. Let her plod along if she likes; don't coax her but just let her take her own sweet time. Everything she does is done thoroughly and, generally, without mistakes. Don't deride her for being a kind of slow-poke. It could lead to flying pots and pans and a fireworks display that would put Bastille Day to shame. The Taurus woman doesn't anger readily but when prodded often enough, she's capable of letting loose with a cyclone of ill-will. If you treat her with kindness and consideration, you'll have no cause for complaint.

The Taurean loves doing things for her man. She's a whiz in the kitchen and can whip up feasts fit for a king if she thinks they'll be royally appreciated. She may not fully understand you, but she'll adore you and be faithful to you if she feels you're worthy of it.

The woman born under Taurus will make a wonderful mother. She knows how to keep her children well-loved, cuddled, and warm. She may find them difficult to manage, however, when they reach the teenage stage.

AQUARIUS MAN
GEMINI WOMAN

You may find a romance with a woman born under the sign of the Twins a many-splendored thing. In her you can find the intellectual companionship you often look for in a friend or mate. A

Gemini girl friend can appreciate your aims and desires because she travels pretty much the same road as you do intellectually —that is, at least part of the way. She may share your interest but she will lack your tenacity.

She suffers from itchy feet. She can be here, there all over the place and at the same time, or so it would seem. Her eagerness to move about may make you dizzy; still you'll enjoy and appreciate her liveliness and mental agility.

Geminians often have sparkling personalities; you'll be attracted by her warmth and grace. While she's on your arm you'll probably notice that many male eyes are drawn to her—she may even return a gaze or two, but don't let that worry you. All women born under this sign have nothing against a harmless flirt once in a while. They enjoy this sort of attention; if she feels she is already spoken for, however, she will never let it get out of hand.

Although she may not be as handy as you'd like in the kitchen, you'll never go hungry for a filling and tasty meal. She's as much in a hurry as you are, and won't feel like she's cheating by breaking out the instant mashed potatoes or the frozen peas. She may not be much of a good cook but she is clever; with a dash of this and a suggestion of that, she can make an uninteresting TV dinner taste like something out of a James Beard cookbook. Then, again, maybe you've struck it rich and have a Gemini girl friend who finds complicated recipes a challenge to her intellect. If so, you'll find every meal a tantalizing and mouth-watering surprise.

When you're beating your brains out over the Sunday crossword puzzle and find yourself stuck, just ask your Gemini girlie; she'll give you all the right answers without batting an eyelash.

Like you, she loves all kinds of people. You may even find that you're a bit more particular than she. Often all that a Geminian requires is that her friends be interesting—and stay interesting. One thing she's not able to abide is a dullard.

Leave the party-organizing to your Gemini sweetheart or mate, and you'll never have a chance to know what a dull moment is. She'll bring the swinger out in you if you give her half a chance.

A Gemini mother enjoys her children. Like them, she's often restless, adventurous, and easily bored.

AQUARIUS MAN
CANCER WOMAN

If you fall in love with a Cancer woman, be prepared for anything. Cancerians are sometimes difficult to understand when it comes to love. In one hour, she can unravel a whole gamut of emotions that will leave you in a tizzy. She'll keep you guessing, that's for sure.

You may find her a little too uncertain and sensitive for your liking. You'll most likely spend a good deal of time encouraging her—helping her to erase her foolish fears. Tell her she's a living doll a dozen times a day and you'll be well loved in return.

Be careful of the jokes you make when in her company. Don't let any of them revolve around her, her personal interests, or her family. If you do, you'll most likely reduce her to tears. She can't stand being made fun of. It will take bushels of roses and tons of chocolates—not to mention the apologies—to get her to come back out of her shell.

In matters of money-managing she may not easily come around to your way of thinking. Money will never burn a hole in her pocket. You may get the notion that your Cancerian sweetheart or mate is a direct descendent of Scrooge. If she has her way, she'll hang onto that first dollar you earned. She's not only that way with money, but with everything right on up from bakery string to jelly jars. She's a saver; she never throws anything away, no matter how trivial.

Once she returns your "I love you," you'll find you have an affectionate, self-sacrificing, and devoted woman on your hands. Her love for you will never alter unless you want it to. She'll put you high upon a pedestal and will do everything—even if it's against your will—to keep you up there.

Cancer women love home life. For them, marriage is an easy step. They're domestic with a capital D. She'll do her best to make your home comfortable and cozy. She, herself, is more at ease at home then anywhere else. She makes an excellent hostess. The best in her comes out when she is in her own environment.

Cancer women make the best mothers of all the signs of the zodiac. She'll consider every complaint of her child a major catastrophe. With her, children always come first. If you're lucky, you'll run a close second. You'll perhaps see her as too devoted to the children. You may have a hard time convincing her that her apron strings are a little too long.

AQUARIUS MAN
LEO WOMAN

If you can manage a girl who likes to kick up her heels every now and again, then the Leo woman was made for you. You'll have to learn to put away jealous fears—or at least forget about them—when you take up with a woman born under this sign, because she's often the kind that makes heads turn and tongues wag. You don't necessarily have to believe any of what you hear—it's most likely just jealous gossip or wishful thinking. Take up with a

Leo woman and you'll be taking off on a romance full of fire and ice; be prepared to take the good things with the bad—the bitter with the sweet.

The Leo girl has more than a fair share of grace and glamour. She is aware of her charms and knows how to put them to good use. Needless to say, other women in her vicinity turn green with envy and will try anything short of shoving her into the nearest lake, in order to put her out of commission.

If she's captured your heart and fancy, woo her full-force if your intention is to eventually win her. Shower her with expensive gifts and promise her the moon—if you're in a position to go that far—then you'll find her resistance beginning to weaken. It's not that she's such a difficult cookie—she'll probably make a big fuss over you once she's decided you're the man for her—but she does enjoy a lot of attention. What's more, she feels she's entitled to it. Her mild arrogance, though, is becoming. The Leo woman knows how to transform the crime of excessive pride into a very charming misdemeanor. It sweeps most men right off their feet . . . rather, all men. Those who do not succumb to her leonine charm are few and far between.

If you've got an important business deal to clinch and you have doubts as to whether or not it will go over well, bring your Leo girl along to that business luncheon and it's a cinch that contract will be yours. She won't have to do or say anything—just be there, at your side. The grouchiest oil magnate can be transformed into a gushing, obedient schoolboy if there's a Leo woman in the room.

If you're rich and want to stay that way, don't give your Leo mate a free hand with the charge accounts and credit cards. If you're poor, the luxury-loving Leo will most likely never enter your life.

She makes a strict yet easy-going mother. She loves to pal around with her children.

AQUARIUS MAN
VIRGO WOMAN

The Virgo woman may be a little too difficult for you to understand at first. Her waters run deep. Even when you think you know her, don't take any bets on it. She's capable of keeping things hidden in the deep recesses of her womanly soul—things she'll only release when she's sure that you're the man she's been looking for. It may take her some time to come around to this decision. Virgo girls are finicky about almost everything; everything has to be letter-perfect before they're satisfied. Many of them have the idea that the only people who can do things correctly are Virgos.

Nothing offends a Virgo woman more than slovenly dress, sloppy character, or a careless display of affection. Make sure your tie is not crooked and your shoes sport a bright shine before you go calling on this lady. Keep your off-color jokes for the locker-room; she'll have none of that. Take her arm when crossing the street. Don't rush the romance. Trying to corner her in the back of a cab may be one way of striking out. Never criticize the way she looks—in fact, the best policy would be to agree with her as much as possible. Still, there's just so much a man can take; all those dos and don'ts you'll have to observe if you want to get to first base with a Virgo may be just a little too much to ask of you. After a few dates, you may come to the conclusion that she just isn't worth all that trouble. However, the Virgo woman is mysterious enough, generally speaking, to keep her men running back for more. Chances are you'll be intrigued by her airs and graces.

If love-making means a lot to you, you'll be disappointed at first in the cool ways of your Virgo girlie. However, under her glacial facade there lies a hot cauldron of seething excitement. If you're patient and artful in your romantic approach, you'll find that all that caution was well worth the trouble. When Virgos love, they don't stint. It's all or nothing as far as they're concerned. Once they're convinced that they love you, they go all the way right off the bat, tossing all cares to the wind.

One thing a Virgo woman can't stand in love is hypocrisy. They don't give a hoot about what the neighbors say, if their hearts tell them "Go ahead." They're very concerned with human truths—so much so that if their hearts stumble upon another fancy, they're liable to be true to that new heart-throb and leave you standing in the rain.

She's honest to her heart and will be as true to you as you are with her, generally. Do her wrong once, however, and it's farewell.

She's both strict and tender with children. As a mother she'll try to bring out the best in her children.

AQUARIUS MAN
LIBRA WOMAN

You'll probably find that the girl born under the sign of Libra is worth more than her weight in gold. She's a woman after your own heart.

With her, you'll always come first—make no mistake about that. She'll always be behind you 100 percent, no matter what you do. When you ask her advice about almost anything, you'll most likely get a very balanced and realistic opinion. She is good at thinking things out and never lets her emotions run away with her when clear logic is called for.

As a homemaker she is hard to beat. She is very concerned with harmony and balance. You can be sure she'll make your house a joy to live in; she'll see to it that the house is tastefully furnished and decorated. A Libran cannot stand filth or disarray—it gives her goose-bumps. Anything that does not radiate harmony, in fact, runs against her orderly grain.

She is chock-full of charm and womanly ways. She can sweep just about any man off his feet with one winning smile. When it comes to using her brains, she can out-think almost anyone and, sometimes, with half the effort. She is diplomatic enough, though, never to let this become glaringly apparent. She may even turn the conversation around so that you think you were the one who did all the brain-work. She couldn't care less, really, just as long as you wind up doing what is right.

The Libra woman will put you up on a pretty high pedestal. You are her man and her idol. She'll leave all the decision-making—large or small—up to you. She's not interested in running things and will only offer her assistance if she feels you really need it.

Some find her approach to reason masculine; however, in the areas of love and affection the Libra woman is *all* woman. She'll literally shower you with love and kisses during your romance with her. She doesn't believe in holding out. You shouldn't, either, if you want to hang onto her.

She is the kind of girl who likes to snuggle up to you in front of the fire on chilly autumn nights—the kind of girl who will bring you breakfast in bed on Sunday. She'll be very thoughtful about anything that concerns you. If anyone dares suggest you're not the grandest guy in the world, she'll give that person what-for. She'll defend you with her dying breath. The Libra woman will be everything you want her to be.

She'll be a sensitive and loving mother. Still, you'll always come before the children.

AQUARIUS MAN
SCORPIO WOMAN

The Scorpio woman can be a whirlwind of passion—perhaps too much passion to really suit you. When her temper flies, you'd better lock up the family heirlooms and take cover. When she chooses to be sweet, you're apt to think that butter wouldn't melt in her mouth . . . but, of course, it would.

The Scorpio woman can be as hot as a *tamale* or as cool as a cucumber, but whatever mood she's in, she's in it for real. She does not believe in poses or putting on airs.

The Scorpio woman is often sultry and seductive—her femme fatale charm can pierce through the hardest of hearts like a laser ray. She may not look like Mata Hari (quite often Scorpios resemble the tomboy next door) but once she's fixed you with her tantalizing eyes, you're a goner.

Life with the Scorpio woman will not be all smiles and smooth-sailing; when prompted she can unleash a gale of venom. Generally, she'll have the good grace to keep family battles within the walls of your home. When company visits, she's apt to give the impression that married life with you is one great big joy-ride. It's just one of her ways of expressing her loyalty to you, at least in front of others. She may fight you tooth and nail in the confines of your living room, but at a ball or during an evening out, she'll hang on your arm and have stars in her eyes.

Scorpio woman are good at keeping secrets. She may even keep a few buried from you if she feels like it.

Never cross her on even the smallest thing. When it comes to revenge, she's an eye-for-an-eye woman. She's not too keen on forgiveness, especially when she feels she's been wronged unjustly. You'd be well-advised not to give her any cause to be jealous, either. When the Scorpio woman sees green, your life will be made far from rosy. Once she's put you in the dog-house, you can be sure that you'll stay there a long time.

You may find life with the Scorpio woman too draining. Although she may be full of the old paprika, it's quite likely that she's not the kind of girl you'd like to spend the rest of your natural life with. You'd prefer someone gentler and not so hot-tempered, someone who can take the highs with the lows and not bellyache, someone who is flexible and understanding. If you've got your sights set on a shapely Scorpio, forget about that sweet girl of your dreams. A woman born under Scorpio can be heavenly, but she can also be the very devil when she chooses.

As a mother, a Scorpio woman is protective and encouraging.

AQUARIUS MAN
SAGITTARIUS WOMAN

You'll most likely never come across a more good-natured girl than the one born under the sign of Sagittarius. Generally, they're full of bounce and good cheer. Their sunny disposition seems almost permanent and can be relied upon even on the rainiest of days.

Women born under this sign are almost never malicious. If ever they seem to be, it is only seeming. Sagittarians are often a little short on tact and say literally anything that comes into their pretty little heads no matter what the occasion. Sometimes the words that tumble out of their mouths seem downright cutting and cruel. Still, no matter what she says, she means well. The Sagittarius woman is quite capable of losing some of her friends—and perhaps even some of yours—through a careless slip of the lip.

On the other hand, you are liable to appreciate her honesty and good intentions. To you, qualities of this sort play an important part in life. With a little patience and practice, you can probably help cure your Sagittarian of her loose tongue; in most cases, she'll give in to your better judgement and try to follow your advice to the letter.

Chances are she'll be the outdoors type of girl friend. Long hikes, fishing trips, and white-water canoeing will most likely appeal to her. She's a busy person; no one could ever call her a slouch. She sets great store in mobility. Her feet are itchy and she won't sit still for a minute if she doesn't have to.

She is great company most of the time and, generally, lots of fun. Even if your buddies drop by for poker and beer, she won't have any trouble fitting in.

On the whole, she is a very kind and sympathetic woman. If she feels she's made a mistake, she'll be the first to call your attention to it. She's not afraid to own up to her faults and shortcomings.

You might lose your patience with her once or twice. After she's seen how upset her shortsightedness or tendency to be a blabbermouth has made you, she'll do her best to straighten up.

The Sagittarian woman is not the kind who will pry into your business affairs. But she'll always be there, ready to offer advice if you need it. If you come home with red stains on your collar and you say it's paint and not lipstick, she'll believe you.

She'll seldom be suspicious; your word will almost always be good enough for her.

She is a wonderful and loving friend to her children.

AQUARIUS MAN
CAPRICORN WOMAN

If you are not a successful businessman or, at least, on your way to success, it's quite possible that a Capricorn woman will have no interest in entering your life. Generally speaking, she is a very security-minded female; she'll see to it that she invests her time only in sure things. Men who whittle away their time with one unsuccessful scheme or another, seldom attract a Capricorn. Men who are interested in getting somewhere in life and keep their noses close to the grindstone quite often have a Capricorn woman behind them, helping them to get ahead.

Although she is a kind of "climber," she is not what you could call cruel or hard-hearted. Beneath that cool, seemingly calculating, exterior, there's a warm and desirable woman. She just happens to think that it is as easy to fall in love with a rich or ambitious man as it is with a poor or lazy one. She's practical.

The Capricorn woman may be keenly interested in rising to the top, but she'll never be aggressive about it. She'll seldom step on someone's feet or nudge competitors away with her elbows. She's quiet about her desires. She sits, waits, and watches. When an opening or opportunity does appear, she'll latch onto it lickety-split. For an on-the-move man, an ambitious Capricorn wife or girl friend can be quite an asset. She can probably give you some very good advice about business matters. When you invite the boss and his wife for dinner, she'll charm them both right off the ground.

The Capricorn woman is thorough in whatever she does: cooking, cleaning, making a success out of life. Capricorns make excellent hostesses as well as guests. Generally, they are very well mannered and gracious, no matter what their backgrounds are. They seem to have a built-in sense of what is right. Crude behavior or a careless faux-pas can offend them no end.

If you should marry a woman born under Capricorn you need never worry about her going on a wild shopping spree. Capricorns are careful with every cent that comes into their hands. They understand the value of money better than most women and have no room in their lives for careless spending.

Capricorn girls are usually very fond of family—their own, that is. With them, family ties run very deep. Don't make jokes about her relatives; she won't stand for it. You'd better check her family out before you get down on bended knee; after your marriage you'll undoubtedly be seeing lots of them.

Capricorn mothers train their children to be polite and kind.

AQUARIUS MAN
AQUARIUS WOMAN

If you find that you've fallen head over heels for a woman born under the sign of the Water Bearer, you'd better fasten your safety belt. It may take you quite a while to actually discover what this girl is like—and even then, you may have nothing to go on but a string of vague hunches. The Aquarian is like a rainbow, full of bright and shining hues; she's like no other girl you've ever known. There is something elusive about her—something delightfully mysterious. You'll most likely never be able to put your finger on it. It's nothing calculated, either; Aquarians don't believe in phony charm.

There will never be a dull moment in your life with this Water Bearing woman; she seems to radiate adventure and magic. She'll most likely be the most open-minded and tolerant woman you've ever met. She has a strong dislike for injustice and prejudice. Narrow-mindedness runs against her grain.

She is very independent by nature and quite capable of shifting for herself if necessary. She may receive many proposals for marriage from all sorts of people without ever really taking them seriously. Marriage is a very big step for her; she wants to be sure she knows what she's getting into. If she thinks that it will seriously curb her independence and love of freedom, she's liable to shake her head and give the man his engagement ring back—if indeed she's let the romance get that far.

The line between friendship and romance is a pretty fuzzy one for an Aquarian. It's not difficult for her to remain buddy-buddy with an ex-lover. She's tolerant, remember? So, if you should see her on the arm of an old love, don't jump to any hasty conclusions.

She's not a jealous person herself and doesn't expect you to be either. You'll find her pretty much of a free spirit most of the time. Just when you think you know her inside-out, you'll discover that you don't really know her at all.

She's a very sympathetic and warm person; she can be helpful to people in need of assistance and advice.

She'll seldom be suspicious even if she has every right to be. If she loves a man, she'll forgive him just about anything. If he allows himself a little fling, chances are she'll just turn her head the other way. Her tolerance does have its limits, however, and her man should never press his luck at hanky-panky.

She makes a big-hearted mother; her good qualities rub off on her children.

AQUARIUS MAN
PISCES WOMAN

Many a man dreams of a Piscean kind of a girl. You're perhaps no exception. She's soft and cuddly—very domestic. She'll let you be the brains of the family; she's contented to just lean on your shoulder and let you be the master of the household.

She can be very ladylike and proper. Your business associates and friends will be dazzled by her warmth and femininity. Although she's a charmer, there is a lot more to her than just a pretty face. There is a brain ticking away behind that soft, womanly facade. You may never become aware of it—that is, until you're married to her. It's no cause for alarm, however; she'll most likely never use it against you.

If she feels you're botching up your married life through careless behavior or if she feels you could be earning more money than you do, she'll tell you about it. But any wife would, really. She will never try to usurp your position as head of the family.

No one had better dare say one uncomplimentary word about you in her presence. It's liable to cause her to break into tears. Pisces women are usually very sensitive beings. Their reaction to adversity, frustration, or anger is just a plain, good, old-fashioned cry. They can weep buckets when inclined.

She'll have an extra-special dinner waiting for you when you come home from an important business meeting. Don't bother to go into any of the details about the meeting, though, at the dinner table; she doesn't have much of a head for business matters usually, and is only too happy to leave that up to you.

She can do wonders with a house. She is very fond of soft and beautiful things. There will always be plenty of fresh-cut flowers around the house. She'll see that you always have plenty of socks and underwear in that top drawer of your dresser.

Treat her with tenderness and your relationship will be an enjoyable one. She's most likely fond of chocolates. A bunch of beautiful roses will never fail to make her eyes light up. See to it that you never forget her birthday or your anniversary. She won't. If you are patient and kind, you can keep a Pisces woman happy for a lifetime. She is, however, not without her faults. Her "sensitivity" may get on your nerves after a while. You may find her lacking in imagination and zest. You may even feel that she only uses her tears as a method of getting her own way.

She makes a strong, self-sacrificing mother. She'll find it difficult to refuse her children anything.

<u>PISCES</u>
February 19 — March 20

CHARACTER ANALYSIS

Quite often people born under the sign of Pisces are rather dreamy in their ways. Generally speaking, they are responsive and impressionable. Theirs is a sensitive nature. They usually approach life in serious, yet somewhat unrealistic way. The sign of Pisces—the two fish—indicates a double nature. Indeed, there often seems to be more to someone born under this twelfth sign of the zodiac than meets the eye. His behavior is often a riddle to others. He may seem secretive about the smallest, most unimportant things, yet open in important matters when perhaps he should not be. Chances are he is a gentle and kind person He would never do anything that would injure someone's feelings.

People generally like the person born under Pisces. He can be trusted; he is conscientious in all that he undertakes. Others can depend on him no matter what the situation. His word is usually his bond. Likeable and pleasant, others usually feel comfortable when in his company. He is a person who likes peace and quiet. His personality is usually such that others feel calm and even-tempered when in his presence. Because he is so easy-going, opportunists usually try to take advantage of his good nature.

The person born under the sign of Pisces is usually methodical in his work. He may seem a bit lazy to others; but; in fact, he will live up to his responsibilities at home or at work if he sees that it is necessary for keeping peace and order. He usually takes life as it comes. He doesn't generally complain. He adapts himself

The Piscean is not afraid of changes. In fact, he welcomes them, especially if others can benefit from them. Anything that he feels will make the world a better place in which to live is something he will support.

The Piscean is a person who sympathizes readily with people who are in dire straights. He is always prepared to help someone in need if he can. In a rather uncanny way, he seems to know how other people are feeling before they say anything. He is very perceptive and is familiar with the problems of the world. He is generally imaginative, and his thoughts are usually concerned with bettering the world situation. However, he tends to be too much of a dreamer to put his plans and hopes into action. He lacks that driving force to turn plans into reality.

When he does go about finishing up his work and completing his plans, he can usually make an important contribution to others. He is generous, sometimes to a fault. He thinks more of others, at times, than he does of himself. He can be quite self-sacrificing. In general, though, he seldom gets around to realizing his plans. He's too much of a dreamer, and is afraid of encountering frustration once he commits himself to action

The person born under this sign is usually interested in the arts. In the world of music, painting, or poetry, he can lose himself to his heart's content and forget about the hard realities of life. Mysterious things attract him. Unknown realms seem to lure him on, at the same time this sort of interest clashes with his basic personality, making it rather difficult for him to adjust to the facts of life. He is the kind of a person who when he takes up something goes all the way. He is very susceptible. Subjects that interest him have a complete hold on him until he knows them inside-out. Theories, beliefs, and the like interest him greatly. While he may know a great deal about them, he may be somewhat saddened, for he feels that his knowledge cuts him off from others. Some Piceans feel superior in their intellectual isolation.

The person born under this sign is sometimes moody. He can go from feeling high to low in a remarkably short time if he isn't careful. At times he feels rather sorry for himself; he feels that his talents are not really appreciated. The strong Piscean, however, knows how to put such thoughts out of his mind and to forge ahead. Sometimes he can inspire others better than he can inspire himself. He is somewhat afraid of conflict and frustration and will do his best to avoid them. When forced to face harsh reality, he sometimes finds himself at loose ends. It is too much for him. He would rather hear a pleasant lie than the cold, hard truth. If things become too difficult to manage, he may try to neglect his responsibilities. He feels good when he is in the company of strong, purposeful people. He is not the kind of person who does very well alone. When others encourage him, he may try harder to realize his plans.

Health

The average Piscean may not look very strong or healthy. However, his constitution is usually quite good and he can recover from an illness fairly quickly. In general, his health is good; the great out of doors is likely to be good for him. He needs plenty of sunshine and fresh air in order to feel fit. He should also see to it that he gets plenty of exercise; on the other hand, he should not do anything that might cause him to strain himself. Quite often the person born under the sign of Pisces looks younger than he really is.

The average Piscean is rather slim and delicate. Many of the world's best dancers are born under this sign. His eyes and his feet are usually the weak points of his anatomy. He should do what he can to guard against chills and cold.

It is important that the Piscean be moderate in his behavior. Overindulgence is apt to be bad for his constitution. A well-balanced diet should help him to keep in shape. Plenty of green vegetables and fresh fruit are necessary. The person born under this sign may have a weakness for anything that stimulated him physically. He will have to watch out that he does not abuse his good health through the use of alcohol or drugs. The Piscean who knows what is good for him will live to a ripe old age, generally. Some Pisceans are rather stubborn, however, and do the things that please them most without giving much thought to the consequences. If he does become addicted to drugs or to alcohol, he may have a difficult time trying to break the habit. His will is often not very strong. Sometimes he likes others to feel sorry for him, so he does his best to appear pitiful and vicitimized.

Occupation

The Piscean does well in any kind of work that involves helping others. This is his main interest in life. He likes doing what he can for others. The sick and needy can always depend on him for help. Quite often Pisces people make good doctors, psychiatrists, teachers, and accountants. Social work is another profession that often attracts someone born under this sign. On the whole, he is a sympathetic person. He often knows what is wrong with someone before the person knows it himself. Others often turn to him when in trouble and in need of advice. He can easily put himself in someone else's place. He has a certain charm, generally, and may do well in diplomatic work.

The Piscean's strong point is his ability to understand others—his insight into the problems of others. When choosing a job or career, he should try to make use of this gift that he has.

The average Piscean is generally quite flexible. He can take on many different roles if need be. There are two sides to his nature; he usually has many interests. He can move in any direction with equal skill. Sometimes he does well in the world of film or theater. He often has remarkable dramatic talents. This is usually because of his flexible personality. He understands others and knows how to express himself as if he is the character he portrays. Sometimes he does well as a playwright.

Whatever he does, the Piscean is happiest if he has a chance to exercise his many interests. He likes a lot of variety in his work. If he finds the position that is cut out for his talents, he is usually a very happy person. In the right job, he is not afraid of encountering frustration or opposition for he is well equipped to deal with it.

Work that requires a great deal of concentration and bother about small details seldom interests him. However, he can apply himself to anything that completely absorbs his imagination and spirit. He is the kind of worker who can always be depended on to do his best. He is methodical and industrious. At times, he is clever enough to think up a way of cutting his work time in half, much to the surprise of those who work with him. He is generally well liked by his co-workers. He is easy to get along with and always ready to listen to another's problems or troubles.

The weaker sort of Piscean can be quite lazy at times. As soon as he meets with the slightest upset he is ready to call it quits. He does not have much faith in himself or what he can do. Confusion completely ruins him—he can become disorganized when confronted with frustration. He may have difficulty in putting his thoughts in order.

The Piscean is a bit of a sensualist. He likes to pamper himself. He likes his comfort. He is fond of material things which make him feel good. Money does not interest him for what it is but for what it can do. He is fond of the security that money can bring. Many Pisceans are a bit afraid of growing old, and they want to see to it that they have a nest-egg they can draw on when they become senior citizens. If he does not have as much money as he thinks he needs, he may worry about it constantly. In fact, he may worry about it so much that it prevents him from making the headway he so desperately desires. When he becomes involved with others and tries to help them solve their problems he may become more generous than he should. He sometimes spends money to help others when he should really save it to help himself. Chances are that the average Piscean will never become a millionaire. However, this does not bother him, as long as he has enough money to adequately provide for himself and those he cares for. If he does come into a lot of money unexpectedly, opportunists will probably find a way to take it away from him. He is the kind of person who finds it difficult to say no, especially if someone is in dire need.

Sometimes the average Piscean does not really know what he wants in life. He may find it difficult to direct himself toward any one particular goal. However, once he finds his niche in life, he can go far on sheer will and determination. The strong Piscean has a good sense of direction and will work hard to attain those things he desires. Some people born under this sign are rather lucky and attain financial success without working hard for it. The well-heeled Piscean would be wise to invest his money in real estate or something secure. He should avoid risks as much as possible.

Some Pisceans make good businessmen, even though they may not have a very competitive nature. Somehow or other, they manage to hold their own through determination. In a partnership situation the Piscean can do well, if his partner has those business qualities he lacks.

Home and Family

The Piscean is very susceptible to his environment. If he is to succeed, he has to be in an environment that encourages success. He likes a home where he can relax in comfort—a place where he can let his imagination roam. Home and family are important to the Piscean who wants to get far in life. It gives him the kind of stability he needs.

The Pisces person is a home-lover by nature. Nothing pleases him as much as the warm and peaceful atmosphere of home. His tastes are generally simple and plain. Comfort is important. His home may contain some art objects that mean a lot to him. Art plays an important part in his life. At times it means more to him than so-called practical things. He likes a home that is neat and tidy. A home in the country would please him very much. He likes the wide open spaces—a place where he can wander about freely without having to worry about traffic or crowds. The countryside gives him a chance to relax and to let his imagination run free.

People enjoy visiting the Pisces man or woman because he or she knows how to make guests feel at home. The Piscean is a good conversationalist. When others talk about themselves, he is never bored, but listens to them carefully, interrupting every now and again to make a helpful suggestion.

He is a romantic kind of person. Marriage appeals to him in that it gives him a chance to explore the romantic side of his nature. Both men and women born under this sign are rather fond of domestic life and do what they can to have a happy home.

Social Relationships

The Piscean is perhaps the most sensitive kind of person in existence. He is very gentle, considerate, and kind. He does not want to hurt others and does what he can to avoid injury to himself. Romance and love mean a great deal to him. In general, he is open and sincere. He does not like people who are mean or petty. He is earnest in expressing his affections.

Most of the time, his standards are pretty high. He is looking for someone who is well-groomed and intelligent; someone who probably has as great an interest in the arts as he does. When he has found the person of his dreams, he may become rather possessive. He is the kind of person who may suspect his loved one of infidelity when he really has no grounds. He easily becomes jealous and this could emotionally destroy him if he is not careful. The happy Piscean is someone who can take a person for what he or she is and not long for perfection; someone who is realistic when looking for a friend or a mate.

Naturally affectionate himself, the average Piscean man likes a woman who is free in expressing herself as far as her affection for him is concerned. He has to be reassured that his loved one really loves him. He likes to be complimented—to be told what a good lover he is. Flattery is music to his ears. His feelings are too sensitive at times, and this may cause him to end an affair. He may imagine he has been slighted when that is not the case at all. The strong Piscean guards against becoming a victim to this sort of illusion. He does what he can to keep his romance alive and healthy.

The weak Piscean does not really know what he wants in romance, and he may stumble from one affair to an other not knowing how to make up his mind.

The dreamy Pisces person often has very high ideals. If he has the right person behind him he is bound to go far. He needs someone who understands his weaknesses as well as his strengths. The Piscean needs love. If he does not have it, his life may seem useless and empty to him.

He can be the dreamy sort of lover, thinking more about the kind of romance he would like to have and doing very little to make this a reality. Alone, he is not very strong, He has little confidence in his thoughts, whims, or fancies. They amuse him and make him feel safe. He is not a strong-willed person as far as character is concerned. He does best when in company of strong people—people who know their own minds; their self-confidence seems to rub off on him. He is an adaptable person and can easily take on the character of the people he associates with. Therefore, it is very important that he mix with the right people. When looking for a mate, he should try to find someone who has those qualities he lacks—someone who is positive-thinking with a firm grip on reality.

LOVE AND MARRIAGE

The Piscean feels deeply. When he gives his love, it usually is for good. He doesn't believe in playing with the affections of others; love is too important to him for that. He must watch out for stronger people. If someone is in love with him and makes definite advances, he may be too weak to resist; he then finds himself in a love affair he neither wished nor willed. At times, the average Piscean may shuttle from one mood to another without warning and this is apt to puzzle his loved one. It is possible for him to be passionate one moment and cool the next—and for no apparent reason. Someone who loves him must learn to accept this. Another thing; it is sometimes difficult for even his most intimate friend to really know how he feels. His lover may feel she has reason to doubt his love even when he professes it. Others find it difficult to know whether or not the Piscean really means what he says, at times.

The intelligent Pisces person takes stock of himself and tries to do something about his weak points. He tries to correct his personality faults and quirks. He may even try to appear tougher than he really is as a sort of protection against people who would like to take advantage of his kind nature. He may fool many—but not the people who really know him. While exhibiting a hard-bitten exterior, he is likely to be as soft as cotton candy inside. The person who loves him will accept him for his faults and good qualities. She will not be put off by his mask of toughness and hard-boiledness.

Home means a lot to the person born under the sign of Pisces. It is a place where he can relax in comfort and be himself without fear of being taken advantage of. The Pisces woman generally makes a good housewife; she likes the domestic life. She keeps things in order. Romance after marriage also means a lot to the average Piscean. He or she is affectionate and warm and likes love to be returned. Pisces makes a very considerate mate—someone who will do all he can to see to it that his partner is comfortable and well-provided for. He is easy to get along with most of the time. The Pisces woman cries readily if she has a disagreement or argument.

Romance and the Pisces Woman

Of all the women of the Zodiac, the Piscean is the most sensitive and the most loving. She is very giving by nature and does what she can to make those she loves happy and content. Marriage means a lot to her. She is sincere and affectionate. The man who wins her is a lucky fellow.

She is usually interested in a sensitive sort of man. Someone who is intelligent and has an understanding and appreciation of the arts. She cannot abide a man who is mean or petty. She likes someone who is expansive and strong, someone she can depend on at all times. She may find it difficult to make up her own mind at times, so it is important for her to have someone who knows what he wants in life, someone she can lean upon and ask for advice when she needs it.

Some Pisces women really don't know what they want in a man and may drift from one romance to another, somewhat in a daze. She is a romantic and may spend her waking hours day-dreaming about the kind of love life she would like to have; but then she may just keep it a dream, a bit afraid to go out and do something about it. She likes her loved one to make a fuss over her; to tell her how lovely and desirable she is. She has to be assured that her man really loves her. Small gifts from time to time and compliments tend to keep her spirits up.

The Pisces woman is rather sensitive and may imagine that someone has insulted her when she has no real reason for thinking so. She can become very jealous at times. If she suspects her lover of being unfaithful, it could mean the end of the relationship. Although her lover may be innocent of the accusation, he may find it impossible to convince his Piscean sweetheart that this is so. The strong Pisces woman acknowledges this weakness she has and does her best to brush imagined jealousy out of her mind.

She is a good wife and likes taking care of things at home. She may not have a good head for figures; she may spend more money than is really necessary. A practical husband can bring her to reason as far as this is concerned.

She loves children and makes a tender and permissive mother. Her tendency is to spoil children. She may give them too much love and attention when a firmer hand is needed. There is always a strong tie between a Pisces mother and her child.

Romance and the Pisces Man

The Pisces man is a romantic. He is sincere in his affections and does not tend to move from one romance to another. He believes in being true to just one woman. He likes an artistic and intelligent woman—someone with whom he can discuss his interests as an equal. He likes a woman who is apt to fuss over him. He likes being flattered even if there is not a grain of truth in what is said. He has to be constantly reassured. He has to have a woman who is kind and considerate, someone who is able to put up with his changing moods.

A woman who has a strong character is well-suited to the Piscean man. He must not have someone who is weaker than himself. He is the kind of a man who has to be in love. Without love, he is apt to feel lonely and unwanted. He may try to make up for this by drinking rather heavily or abusing his health in other ways. However, too strong or forceful a woman may be too much for him. He may find it impossible to avoid her advances and may later find himself involved with someone he does not really love.

He likes to know where his loved one is every moment of the day. He can be rather possessive even before marriage. His loved one may find some of his demands rather excessive at times. Jealousy could easily destroy him and his romance. The wise Pisces man knows how to put foolish thoughts out of his head and to trust the woman he loves when he has no reason to do otherwise.

His love is deep. When he marries and settles down, it's usually for good. He makes a faithful husband. He does what he can to provide for his family. A happy, well-run home is important to him and he does what he can to make his wife and children feel loved and needed. Security is also important to him, and he will always do what he can to keep his home together.

Children love him. He may be too easy-going as a father, letting his children do as they please. It is fine if his wife is a bit firmer in handling the offspring, for then they have a chance of turning out well.

Woman—Man

PISCES WOMAN
ARIES MAN

Although it's possible that a Pisces woman could find happiness with a man born under the sign of the Ram, it's uncertain as to how long that happiness would last.

An Arien who has made his mark in the world and is somewhat steadfast in his outlook and attitude could be quite a catch for you. On the other hand, men under this sign are often swift-footed and quick-minded; their industrious mannerisms may fail to impress you, especially if you feel that much of their get-up-and-go often leads nowhere.

When it comes to a fine romance, you want someone with a nice, broad shoulder to lean on. You are likely to find a relationship with someone who doesn't like to stay put for too long somewhat upsetting.

The Arien may have a little trouble in understanding you, too—at least, in the beginning of the relationship. He may find you a bit too shy and moody. Ariens tend to speak their minds; he's liable to criticize you at the drop of a hat.

You may find a man born under this sign too demanding. He may give you the impression that he expects you to be at his constant beck and call. You have a lot of patience at your disposal, and he may try every last bit of it. He is apt to be not as thorough as you in everything he does. In order to achieve success or a goal quickly, he is liable to overlook small but important details—and regret it when it is far too late.

Being married to an Arien does not mean that you'll have a secure and safe life as far as finances are concerned. Not all Ariens are rash with cash, but they lack the sound head you perhaps have for putting away something for that inevitable rainy day. He'll do his best, however, to see that you're adequately provided for—even though his efforts may leave something to be desired as far as you're concerned.

With an Aries man for a mate, you'll find yourself constantly among people. Ariens generally have many friends—and you may not heartily approve of them all. People born under this sign are often more interested in "interesting" people than they are in influential ones. Although there may be a family squabble from time to time, you are stable enough to be able to take it in your stride.

Aries men love children. They make wonderful fathers. Kids take to them like ducks to water. Their quick minds and behavior appeal to the young.

PISCES WOMAN
TAURUS MAN

Some Taurus men are strong and silent. They do all they can to protect and provide for the women they love. The Taurus man will never let you down. He's steady, sturdy, and reliable. He's pretty honest and practical, too. He says what he means and means what he says. He never indulges in deceit and will always put his cards on the table.

The Taurean is a very affectionate man. Being loved, appreciated and understood are very important for his well-being. Like you, he is also looking for peace and security in his life. If you both work toward these goals together, you'll find that they are easily attained.

If you should marry a Taurus man, you can be sure that the wolf will never darken your door. They are notoriously good providers, and do everything they can to make their families comfortable and happy.

He'll appreciate the way you have of making a home warm and inviting. Slippers and pipe, and the evening papers are essential ingredients in making your Taurus husband happy at the end of the workday. Although he may be a big lug of a guy, you'll find that he's pretty fond of gentleness and soft things, If you puff up his pillow and tuck him in at night, he won't complain. He'll eat it up and ask for more.

You probably won't complain about his friends. The Taurean tends to seek out friends who are successful or prominent. You admire people, too, who work hard and achieve what they set out for. It helps to reassure your way of life and the way you look at things.

The Taurus man doesn't care too much for change. He's a stay-at-home of the first-order. Chances are that the house you move into after you're married will be the house you'll live in for the rest of your life.

You'll find that the man born under this sign is easy to get along with. It's unlikely that you'll have many quarrels or arguments.

Although he'll be gentle and tender with you, your Taurus man is far from being a sensitive type. He's a man's man. Chances are he loves sports like fishing and football. He can be earthy, as well as down-to-earth.

Taureans love their children very much but do everything they can not to spoil them. They believe in children staying in their places. They make excellent disciplinarians. Your children will be polite and respectful.

PISCES WOMAN
GEMINI MAN

The Gemini man is quite a catch. Many a woman has set her cap for him and failed to bag him. Generally, Gemini men are intelligent, witty, and outgoing. Many of them tend to be versatile.

On the other hand, some of them seem to lack that sort of common sense that you set so much store in. Their tendencies to start a half-dozen projects, then toss them up in the air out of boredom may do nothing more than exasperate you.

One thing that causes a Twin's mind and affection to wander is a bore, and it is unlikely that an active woman like you would ever allow herself to be accused of being that. The Gemini man who has caught your heart will admire you for your ideas and intellect—perhaps even more than for your home-making talents and good looks.

A strong-willed woman could easily fill the role of rudder for her Gemini's ship-without-a-sail. The intelligent Gemini is often aware of his shortcomings and doesn't mind if someone with better bearings gives him a shove in the right direction—when it's needed. The average Gemini doesn't have serious ego-hangups and will even accept a well-deserved chewing out from his mate or girl friend gracefully.

A successful and serious-minded Gemini could make you a very happy woman, perhaps, if you gave him half the chance. Although he may give you the impression that he has a hole in his head, the Gemini man generally has a good head on his shoulders and can make efficient use of it when he wants. Some of them, who have learned the art of being steadfast, have risen to great heights in their professions. President John F. Kennedy was a Gemini, as was writer Thomas Mann and poet William Butler Yeats.

Once you convince yourself that not all people born under the sign of the Twins are witless grasshoppers, you won't mind dating a few—to test your newborn conviction. If you do wind up walking down the aisle with one, accept the fact that married life with him will mean your taking the bitter with the sweet.

Life with a Gemini man can be more fun than a barrel of clowns. You'll never be allowed to experience a dull moment. Don't leave money matters to him or you'll both wind up behind the eight ball.

Gemini men are always attractive to the opposite sex. You'll perhaps have to allow him an occasional harmless flirt—it will seldom amount to more than that if you're his proper mate.

The Gemini father is a pushover for children. See to it that you keep them in line; otherwise they'll be running the house.

PISCES WOMAN
CANCER MAN

The man born under the sign of Cancer may very well be the man after your own heart. Generally, Cancerians are steady people. They are interested in security and practicality. Despite their seemingly grouchy exterior sometimes, men born under the sign of the Crab are rather sensitive and kind individuals. They are almost always hard workers and are very interested in making successes of themselves in business as well as socially. You'll find that his conservative outlook on many things often agrees with yours. He'll be a man on whom you can depend come rain or come shine. He'll never shirk his responsibilities as a provider, and he'll always see to it that his wife and family never want.

Your patience will come in handy if you decide it's a Cancerian you want for a mate. He isn't the type that rushes headlong into romance. He wants to be as sure about love as you do. If after the first couple of months of dating, he suggests that you take a walk with him down lovers' lane, don't jump to the conclusion that he's about to make his "great play." Chances are he'll only hold your hand and seriously observe the stars. Don't let his coolness fool you, though. Beneath his starched reserve lies a very warm heart. He's just not interested in showing off as far as affection is concerned. Don't think his interest is wandering if he doesn't kiss you goodnight at the front door; that just isn't his style. For him, affection should only be displayed for two sets of eyes—yours and his. He's passionate only in private.

He will never step out of line. He's too much of a gentleman for that. When you're all alone with him and there's no chance of you being disturbed or spied upon, he'll pull out an engagement ring (that used to belong to his grandmother) and slip it on your trembling finger.

Speaking of relatives, you'll have to get pretty much used to the fact that Cancerians are overly fond of their mothers. When he says his mother's the most wonderful woman in the world, you'd·better agree with him—that is, if you want to become his wife.

He'll always be a faithful husband; Cancerians never pussyfoot around after they've taken that marriage vow. They don't take marriage responsibilities lightly. He'll see to it that everything in the house runs smoothly and that bills are paid promptly—never put aside. He's liable to take all kinds of insurance polices out on his family and property. He'll arrange it so that when retirement time rolls around, you'll both be very well off.

Men under this sign make patient and understanding fathers.

PISCES WOMAN
LEO MAN

To know a man born under the sign of the Lion is not necessarily to love him—even though the temptation may be great. When he fixes most girls with his leonine double-whammy, it causes their hearts to pitter-pat and their minds to cloud over.

You are a little too sensible to allow yourself to be bowled over by a regal strut and a roar. Still, there's no denying that Leo has a way with women—even sensible women like yourself. Once he's swept a girl off her feet, it may be hard for her to scramble upright again. Still, you are no pushover for romantic charm—especially if you feel it's all show.

He'll wine you and dine you in the fanciest places. He'll croon to you under the moon and shower you with diamonds if he can get a hold of them. Still, it would be wise to find out just how long that shower is going to last before consenting to be his wife.

Lions in love are hard to ignore, let alone brush off. Your no's will have a way of nudging him on until he feels he has you completely under his spell. Once mesmerized by this romantic powerhouse, you will most likely find yourself doing things you never dreamed of. Leos can be like vain pussycats when involved romantically. They like to be cuddled, curried, and tickled under the chin. This may not be your cup of tea exactly, still when you're romantically dealing with a man born under the sign of Leo, you'll find yourself doing all kinds of things to make him purr.

Although he may be big and magnanimous while trying to win you, he'll let out a blood-curdling roar if he thinks he's not getting the tender love and care he feels is his due. If you keep him well supplied with affection, you can be sure his eyes will never look for someone else and his heart will never wander.

Leo men often tend to be authoritarian—they are bound to lord it over others in one way or another it seems. If he is the top banana at his firm, he'll most likely do everything he can to stay on top. If he's not number one, he's most likely working on it and will be sitting on the throne before long.

You'll have more security than you can use if he is in a position to support you in the manner to which he feels you should be accustomed. He is apt to be too lavish, though—at least, by your standards.

You'll always have plenty of friends when you have a Leo for a mate. He's a natural-born friend-maker and entertainer. He just loves to let his hair down at parties.

As fathers, Leos tend to spoil their children no end.

PISCES WOMAN
VIRGO MAN

Although the Virgo man may be a bit of a fuss-budget at times, his seriousness and dedication to common sense may help you to overlook his tendency to sometimes be overly critical about minor things.

Virgo men are often quiet, respectable types who set great store in conservative behavior and level-headedness. He'll admire you for your practicality and tenacity, perhaps even more than for your good looks. He's seldom bowled over by a glamour-puss. When he gets his courage up, he turns to a serious and reliable girl for romance. He'll be far from a Valentino while dating. In fact, you may wind up making all the passes. Once he does get his motor running, however, he can be a warm and wonderful fellow—to the right girl.

He's gradual about love. Chances are your romance with him will most likely start out looking like an ordinary friendship. Once he's sure you're no fly-by-night flirt and have no plans of taking him for a ride, he'll open up and spread sunshine all over your heart.

Virgo men tend to marry late in life. He believes in holding out until he's met the right girl. He may not have many names in his little black book; in fact, he may not even have a black book. He's not interested in playing the field, leaving that to men of the more flamboyant signs. The Virgo man is so particular that he may remain romantically inactive for a long period. His girl has to be perfect or it's no go. If you find yourself feeling weak-kneed for a Virgo, do your best to convince him that perfection is not so important when it comes to love; help him to realize that he's missing out on a great deal by not considering the near-perfect or whatever it is you consider yourself to be. With your sure-fire perseverance, you will most likely be able to make him listen to reason and he'll wind up reciprocating your romantic interests.

The Virgo man is no block of ice. He'll respond to what he feels to be the right feminine flame. Once your love-life with a Virgo man starts to bubble, don't give it a chance to fall flat. You may never have a second chance at winning his heart.

If you should ever have a falling out with him, forget about patching it up. He'd prefer to let the pieces lie scattered. Once married, though, he'll stay that way—even if it hurts. He's too conscientious to try to back out of a legal deal of any sort.

The Virgo man is as neat as a pin. He's thumbs down on sloppy housekeeping. Keep everything bright, neat, and shiny, and that goes for the children, too, at least by the time he gets home from work. Chocolate-coated kisses from Daddy's little girl go over like a lead balloon with him.

PISCES WOMAN
LIBRA MAN

You are apt to find men born under the sign of Libra too wrapped up in their own private dreams to be really interesting as far as love and romance are concerned. Quite often, he is a difficult person to bring back down to earth; it is hard for him to face reality at times. Although he may be very cautious about weighing both sides of an argument, he may never really come to a reasonable decision about anything. Decision-making is something that often makes the Libra man uncomfortable; he'd rather leave that job to someone else. Don't ask him why for he probably doesn't know himself.

Qualities such as permanence and constancy are important to you in a love relationship. The Libra man may be quite a puzzlement for you. One moment he comes on hard and strong with declarations of his love; the next moment you find he's left you like yesterday's mashed potatoes. It does no good to wonder what went wrong. Chances are nothing, really. It's just one of Libra's strange ways.

He is not exactly what you would call an ambitious person; you are perhaps looking for a mate or friend with more drive and fidelity. You are the sort of person who is interested in getting ahead—in making some headway in the areas that interest you; the Libran is often contented just to drift along. He does have drive, however, but it's not the long-range kind. It is not that he's shiftless or lazy. He's interested in material things; he appreciates luxuries and the like, but he may not be willing to work hard enough to obtain them. Beauty and harmony interest him. He'll dedicate a lot of time to arranging things so that they are aesthetically pleasing. It would be difficult to accuse the Libra man of being practical; nine times out of ten, he isn't.

If you do begin a relationship with a man born under this sign, you will have to coax him now and again to face various situations in a realistic manner. You'll have your hands full, that's for sure. But if you love him, you'll undoubtedly do your best to understand him—no matter how difficult this may be.

If you take up with a Libra man, either temporarily or permanently, you'd better take over the task of managing his money. Often he has little understanding of financial matters; he tends to spend without thinking, following his whims.

PISCES WOMAN
SCORPIO MAN

Some people have a hard time understanding the man born under the sign of Scorpio; few, however, are able to resist his fiery charm. When angered, he can act like an overturned wasps' nest; his sting can leave an almost permanent mark. If you find yourself interested in the Scorpio man, you'd better learn how to keep on his good side.

The Scorpio man can be quite blunt when he chooses; at times, he may seem rather hard-hearted. He can be touchy every now and then, and this is apt to get on your nerves after a while. When you feel like you can't take it anymore, you'd better tiptoe away from the scene rather than chance an explosive confrontation. He's capable of giving you a sounding-out that will make you pack your bags and go back to Mother—for good.

If he finds fault with you, he'll let you know. He's liable to misinterpret your patience and think it a sign of indifference. Still and all, you are the kind of woman who can adapt to almost any sort of relationship or circumstance if you put your heart and mind to it.

Scorpio men are all quite perceptive and intelligent. In some respects, they know how to use their brains more effectively than most. They believe in winning, in whatever they do; second place holds no interest for them. In business, they usually achieve the position they want through drive and use of intellect.

Your interest in home-life is not likely to be shared by him. No matter how comfortable you've managed to make the house, it will have very little influence on him with regard to making him aware of his family responsibilities. He does not like to be tied down, generally, and would rather be out on the battlefield of life, belting away at what he feels to be a just and worthy cause. Don't try to keep the homefires burning too brightly while you wait for him to come home from work—you may just run out of firewood.

The Scorpio man is passionate in all things—including love. Most women are easily attracted to him, and you are perhaps no exception. Those who allow themselves to be swept off their feet by a Scorpio man, shortly find that they're dealing with a carton of romantic fireworks. The Scorpio man is passionate with a capital

P, make no mistake about that. Some women may find that he's just too love-happy, but that's their problem.

Scorpio men are straight to the point. They can be as sharp as a razor blade and just as cutting to anyone that crosses them.

Scorpio fathers like large families, generally.

PISCES WOMAN
SAGITTARIUS MAN

The woman who has set her cap for a man born under the sign of Sagittarius may have to apply an awful amount of strategy before she can get him to drop down on bended knee. Although some Sagittarians may be marriage-shy, they're not ones to skitter away from romance. A high-spirited woman may find a relationship with a Sagittarian—whether a fling or "the real thing"—a very enjoyable experience.

As a rule, Sagittarians are bright, happy, and healthy people. They have a strong sense of fair play. Often they're a source of inspiration to others. They're full of ideas and drive.

You'll be taken by the Sagittarian's infectious grin and his light-hearted, friendly nature. If you do wind up being the woman in his life, you'll find that he's apt to treat you more like a buddy than the love of his life. It's just his way. Sagittarians are often chummy instead of romantic.

You'll admire his broadmindedness in most matters—including those of the heart. If, while dating you, he claims that he still wants to play the field, he'll expect you to enjoy the same liberty. Once he's promised to love, honor, and obey, however, he does just that. Marriage for him, once he's taken that big step, is very serious business.

A woman who has a keen imagination and a great love of freedom will not be disappointed if she does tie up with a Sagittarian. The Sagittarius man is often quick-witted. Men of this sign have a genuine interest in equality. They hate prejudice and injustice.

If he does insist on a night out with the boys once a week, he won't scowl if you decide to let him shift for himself in the kitchen once a week while you pursue some of your own interests. He believes in fairness.

He's not much of a homebody. Quite often he's occupied with far away places either in his dreams or in reality. He enjoys—just as you do—being on the go or on the move. He's got ants in his pants and refuses to sit still for long stretches at a time. Humdrum routine—especially at home—bores him. At the drop of a hat, he may ask you to whip off your apron and dine out for a change. He likes surprising people. He'll take great pride in showing you off to his friends. He'll always be a considerate mate; he will never embarrass or disappoint you intentionally.

He's very tolerant when it comes to friends, and you'll most likely spend a lot of time entertaining people.

Sagittarians become interested in their children when they're out of the baby stage.

PISCES WOMAN
CAPRICORN MAN

A with-it girl like you is likely to find the average Capricorn man a bit of a drag. The man born under the sign of the Goat is often a closed person and difficult to get to know. Even if you do get to know him, you may not find him very interesting.

In romance, Capricorn men are a little on the rusty side. You'll probably have to make all the passes.

You may find his plodding manner irritating and his conservative, traditional ways downright maddening. He's not one to take chances on anything. "If it was good enough for my father, it's good enough for me" may be his motto. He follows a way that is tried and true. Whenever adventure rears its tantalizing head, the Goat will turn the other way; he's just not interested.

He may be just as ambitious as you are—perhaps even more so—but his ways of accomplishing his aims are more subterranean or, at least, seem so. He operates from the background a good deal of the time. At a gathering you may never even notice him, but he's there, taking in everything, sizing everyone up, planning his next careful move.

Although Capricorns may be intellectual to a degree, it is not generally the kind of intelligence you appreciate. He may not be as quick or as bright as you; it may take him ages to understand a simple joke.

If you do decide to take up with a man born under this sign, you should be pretty good in the "cheering up" department. The Capricorn man often acts as though he's constantly being followed by a cloud of gloom.

The Capricorn man is most at ease when in the comfort and privacy of his own home. The security possible within four walls can make him a happy man. He'll spend as much time as he can at home. If he is loaded down with extra work, he'll bring it home instead of working overtime at the office.

You'll most likely find yourself frequently confronted by his relatives. Family is very important to the Capricorn—his family, that is. They had better have a pretty important place in your life, too, if you want to keep your home a happy one.

Although his caution in most matters may all but drive you up the wall, you'll find that his concerned way with money is justified most of the time. He'll plan everything right down to the last penny.

He can be quite a scold with children. You'll have to step in and smooth things out.

PISCES WOMAN
AQUARIUS MAN

You are liable to find the Aquarius man the most broadminded man you have ever met; on the other hand, you are also liable to find him the most impractical. Often he's more of a dreamer than a doer. If you don't mind putting up with a man whose heart and mind are as wide as the Missouri but whose head is almost always up in the clouds, then start dating that Aquarian who has somehow captured your fancy. Maybe you, with your good sense, can bring him back down to earth when he gets too starry-eyed.

He's no dumb bell; make no mistake about that. He can be busy making some very complicated and idealistic plans when he's got that out-to-lunch look in his eyes. But more than likely, he'll never execute them. After he's shared one or two of his progressive ideas with you, you are liable to ask yourself, "Who is this nut?" But don't go jumping to conclusions. There's a saying that Aquarians are a half-century ahead of everybody else in the thinking department.

If you decide to answer "Yes" to his "Will you marry me?" you'll find out how right his zany whims are on or about your 50th anniversary. Maybe the waiting will be worth it. Could be that you have an Einstein on your hands—and heart.

Life with an Aquarian won't be one of total despair if you can learn to temper his airiness with your down-to-earth practicality. He won't gripe if you do. The Aquarian always maintains an open mind; he'll entertain the ideas and opinions of everybody. He may not agree with all of them.

Don't go tearing your hair out when you find that it's almost impossible to hold a normal conversation with your Aquarius friend at times. He's capable of answering your "how-are-you-feeling" with a run down on the price of Arizona sugar beets. Always try to keep in mind that he means well.

His broadmindedness doesn't stop when it comes to you and your personal freedom. You won't have to give up any of your hobbies or projects after you're married; he'll encourage you to continue in your interests.

He'll be a kind and generous husband. He'll never quibble over petty things. Keep track of the money you both spend. He can't. Money burns a hole in his pocket.

At times, you may feel like calling it quits. Chances are, though, that you'll always give him another chance.

He's a good family man. He understands children as much as he loves them.

PISCES WOMAN
PISCES MAN

The man born under Pisces is quite a dreamer. Sometimes he's so wrapped up in his dreams that he's difficult to reach. To the average, active woman, he may seem a little sluggish.

He's easy-going most of the time. He seems to take things in his stride. He'll entertain all kinds of views and opinions from just about everyone, nodding or smiling vaguely, giving the impression that he's with them one hundred percent while that may not be the case at all. His attitude may be "why bother" when he's confronted with someone wrong who thinks he's right. The Pisces man will seldom speak his mind if he thinks he'll be rigidly opposed.

The Pisces man is oversensitive at times—he's afraid of getting his feelings hurt. He'll sometimes imagine a personal affront when none's been made. Chances are you'll find this complex of his maddening; at times you may feel like giving him a swift kick where it hurts the most. It wouldn't do any good, though. It would just add fuel to the fire of his complex.

One thing you'll admire about this man is his concern for people who are sickly or troubled. He'll make his shoulder available to anyone in the mood for a good cry. He can listen to one hard-luck story after another without seeming to tire. When his advice is asked, he is capable of coming across with some words of wisdom. He often knows what is bugging someone before that person is aware of it himself. It's almost intuitive with Pisceans, it seems. Still, at the end of the day, this man will want some peace and quiet. If you've got a problem when he comes home, don't unload it in his lap. If you do, you are liable to find him short-tempered. He's a good listener but he can only take so much.

Pisceans are not aimless although they may seem so at times. The positive sort of Pisces man is quite often successful in his profession and is likely to wind up rich and influential. Material gain, however, is never a direct goal for a man born under this sign.

The weaker Pisces are usually content to stay on the level where they find themselves. They won't complain too much if the roof leaks or if the fence is in need of repair.

Because of their seemingly laissez-faire manner, people under this sign—needless to say—are immensely popular with children. For tots they play the double role of confidant and playmate. It will never enter his mind to discipline a child, no matter how spoiled or incorrigible that child becomes.

Man—Woman

PISCES MAN
ARIES WOMAN

The Aries woman may be a little too bossy and busy for you. Generally speaking, Ariens are ambitious creatures. They can become a little impatient with people who are more thorough and deliberate than they are—especially if they feel they're taking too much time. The Aries woman is a fast worker. Sometimes she's so fast she forgets to look where she's going. When she stumbles or falls, it would be nice if you were there to catch her. Ariens are proud women. They don't like to be told "I told you so" when they err. Tongue lashings can turn them into blocks of ice. Don't begin to think that the Aries woman frequently gets tripped up in her plans. Quite often they are capable of taking aim and hitting the bull's-eye. You'll be flabbergasted at times by their accuracy as well as by their ambition. On the other hand, you're apt to spot a flaw in your Arien's plans before she does.

You are perhaps somewhat slower than the Arien in attaining your goals. Still, you are not apt to make mistakes along the way; you're almost always well-prepared.

The Aries woman is rather sensitive at times. She likes to be handled with gentleness and respect. Let her know that you love her for her brains as well as for her good looks. Never give her cause to become jealous. When your Aries date sees green, you'd better forget about sharing a rosy future together. Handle her with tender loving care and she's yours.

The Aries woman can be giving if she feels her partner is deserving. She is no iceberg; she responds to the proper masculine flame. She needs a man she can look up to and feel proud of. If the shoe fits, put it on. If not, better put your sneakers back on and quietly tiptoe out of her sight. She can cause you plenty of heartache if you've made up your mind about her but she hasn't made up hers about you. Aries women are very demanding at times.

Some of them tend to be high-strung; they can be difficult if they feel their independence is being hampered.

The cultivated Aries woman makes a wonderful homemaker and hostess. You'll find she's very clever in decorating and using color. Your house will be tastefully furnished; she'll see to it that it radiates harmony. The Aries wife knows how to make guests feel at home.

Although the Aries woman may not be keen on burdensome responsibilities, she is fond of children and the joy they bring.

PISCES MAN
TAURUS WOMAN

A Taurus woman could perhaps understand you better than most women. She is very considerate and loving. She is thorough and methodical in whatever she does. She knows how to take her time in doing things; she is anxious to avoid mistakes. She is a careful person. She never skips over things that may seem unimportant; she goes over everything with a fine-tooth comb.

Home is very important to the Taurus woman. She is an excellent homemaker. Although your home may not be a palace, it will become, under her care, a comfortable and happy abode. She'll love it when friends drop by for the evening. She is a good cook and enjoys feeding people well. No one will ever go away from your house with an empty stomach.

The Taurus woman is serious about love and affection. When she has taken a tumble for someone, she'll stay by him—for good, if possible. She will try to be practical in romance, to some extent. When she sets her cap for a man, she keeps after him until he's won her. Generally, the Taurus woman is a passionate lover, even though she may appear otherwise at first glance. She is on the look-out for someone who can return her affection fully. Taureans are sometimes given to fits of jealousy and possessiveness. They expect fair play in the area of marriage; when it doesn't come about, they can be bitingly sarcastic and mean.

The Taurus woman is generally an easy-going person. She's fond of keeping peace. She won't argue unless she has to. She'll do her best to keep your love relationship on an even keel.

Marriage is generally a one-time thing for Taureans. Once they've made the serious step, they seldom try to back out of it. Marriage is for keeps. They are fond of love and warmth. With the right man, they turn out to be ideal wives.

The Taurus woman will respect you for your steady ways; she'll have confidence in your common sense.

Taurus women seldom put up with nonsense from their children. They are not so much strict as concerned. They like their children to be well-behaved and dutiful. Nothing pleases a Taurus mother more than a compliment from a neighbor or teacher about her child's behavior. Although some children may inwardly resent the iron hand of a Taurus mother, in later life they are often thankful that they were brought up in such an orderly and conscientious way.

PISCES MAN
GEMINI WOMAN

You may find a romance with a woman born under the sign of the Twins a many-splendored thing. In her you can find the intellectual companionship you often look for in a friend or mate. A Gemini girl friend can appreciate your aims and desires because she travels pretty much the same road as you do intellectually. that is, at least part of the way. She may share your interests but she will lack your tenacity.

She suffers from itchy feet. She can be here, there, all over the place and at the same time, or so it would seem. Her eagerness to move about may make you dizzy; still you'll enjoy and appreciate her liveliness and mental agility.

Geminians often have sparkling personalities; you'll be attracted by her warmth and grace. While she's on your arm you'll probably notice that many male eyes are drawn to her—she may even return a gaze or two, but don't let that worry you. All women born under this sign have nothing against a harmless flirt once in a while. They enjoy this sort of attention; if she feels she is already spoken for, however, she will never let it get out of hand.

Although she may not be as handy as you'd like in the kitchen, you'll never go hungry for a filling and tasty meal. The Gemini girl is always in a rush; she won't feel like she's cheating by breaking out the instant mashed potatoes or the frozen peas. She may not be much of a good cook but she is clever; with a dash of this and a suggestion of that, she can make an uninteresting TV dinner taste like something out of a James Beard cookbook. Then, again, maybe you've struck it rich and have a Gemini girl friend who finds complicated recipes a challenge to her intellect. If so, you'll find every meal a tantalizing and mouth-watering surprise.

When you're beating your brains out over the Sunday crossword puzzle and find yourself stuck, just ask your Gemini girlie; she'll give you all the right answers without batting an eyelash.

Like you, she loves all kinds of people. You may even find that you're a bit more particular than she. Often all that a Geminian requires is that her friends be interesting—and stay interesting.

One thing she's not able to abide is a dullard.

Leave the party-organizing to your Gemini sweetheart or mate, and you'll never have a chance to know what a dull moment is. She'll bring out the swinger in you if you give her half the chance.

A Gemini mother enjoys her children. Like them, she's often restless, adventurous, and easily bored.

PISCES MAN
CANCER WOMAN

The girl born under the sign of Cancer needs to be protected from the cold, cruel world. She'll love you for your masculine, yet gentle manner; you make her feel safe and secure. You don't have to pull any he-man or heroic stunts to win her heart; that's not what interests her. She's more likely to be impressed by your sure, steady ways—that way you have of putting your arm around her and making her feel that she's the only girl in the world. When she's feeling glum and tears begin to well up in her eyes, you have that knack of saying just the right thing—you know how to calm her fears, no matter how silly some of them may seem.

The girl born under this sign is inclined to have her ups and downs. You have that talent, for smoothing out the ruffles in her sea of life. She'll most likely worship the ground you walk on or put you on a terribly high pedestal. Don't disappoint her if you can help it. She'll never disappoint you. This is the kind of woman who will take great pleasure in devoting the rest of her natural life to you. She'll darn your socks, mend your overalls, scrub floors, wash windows, shop, cook, and do just about anything short of murder in order to please you and to let you know that she loves you. Sounds like that legendary good old-fashioned girl, doesn't it? Contrary to popular belief, there are still a good number of them around—and many of them are Cancerians.

Of all the signs of the zodiac, the women under the Cancer sign are the most maternal. In caring for and bringing up children, they know just how to combine the right amount of tenderness with the proper dash of discipline. A child couldn't ask for a better mother. Cancer women are sympathetic, affectionate, and patient with their children.

While we're on the subject of motherhood, there's one thing you should be warned about: never be unkind to your mother-in-law. It will be the only golden rule your Cancerian wife will probably expect you to live up to. No mother-in-law jokes in the presence of your Mrs., please. With her, they'll go over like a lead balloon. Mother is something pretty special for her. She may be the crankiest, nosiest old bat this side of the Great Divide, still she's your wife's mother; you'd better treat her like she's one of the landed gentry. Sometimes this may be difficult to swallow, but if you want to keep your home together and your wife happy, you'd better learn to grin and bear it.

Treat your Cancer wife like a queen, and she'll treat you royally.

PISCES MAN
LEO WOMAN

The Leo woman can make most men roar like lions. If any woman in the zodiac has that indefinable something that can make men lose their heads and find their hearts, it's the Leo woman.

She's got more than a fair share of charm and glamour and she knows how to make the most of her assets, especially when she's in the company of the opposite sex. Jealous men are apt to lose their cool or their sanity when trying to woo a woman born under the sign of the Lion. She likes to kick up her heels quite often and doesn't care who knows it. She often makes heads turn and tongues wag. You don't necessarily have to believe any of what you hear—it's most likely jealous gossip or wishful thinking. Needless to say, other women in her vicinity turn green with envy and will try anything short of shoving her into the nearest lake in order to put her out of the running.

Although this vamp makes the blood rush to your head and makes you momentarily forget all the things you thought were important and necessary in your life, you may feel differently when you come back down to earth and the stars are out of your eyes. You may feel that she isn't the kind of girl you planned to bring home to Mother. Not that your mother might disapprove of your choice—but you might after the shoes and rice are a thing of the past. Although the Leo woman may do her best to be a good wife for you, chances are she'll fall short of your idea of what a good wife should be like.

If you're planning on not going as far as the altar with that Leo woman who has you flipping your lid, you'd better be financially equipped for some very expensive dating. Be prepared to shower her with expensive gifts and to take her dining and dancing to the smartest spots in town. Promise her the moon if you're in a position to go that far. Luxury and glamour are two things that are bound to lower a Leo's resistance. She's got expensive tastes, and you'd better cater to them if you expect to get to first base with this femme.

If you've got an important business deal to clinch and you have doubts as to whether you can swing it or not, bring your Leo girlie along to the business luncheon. Chances are that with her on your arm, you'll be able to win any business battle with both hands tied. She won't have to say or do anything—just being there at your side is enough. The grouchiest oil magnate can be transformed into a gushing, obedient schoolboy if there's a charming Leo woman in the room.

Leo mothers are blind to the faults of their children. They make very loving and affectionate parents and tend to spoil their offspring.

PISCES MAN
VIRGO WOMAN

The Virgo woman may be a little too difficult for you to understand at first. Her waters run deep. Even when you think you know her, don't take any bets on it. She's capable of keeping things hidden in the deep recesses of her womanly soul—things she'll only release when she's sure that you're the man she's been looking for. It may take her some time to come around to this decision. Virgo girls are finicky about almost everything; everything has to be letter-perfect before they're satisfied. Many of them have the idea that the only people who can do things right are Virgos.

Nothing offends a Virgo woman more than slovenly dress, sloppy character, or a careless display of affection. Make sure your tie is not crooked and your shoes sport a bright shine before you go calling on this lady. Keep your off-color jokes for the locker-room; she'll have none of that. Take her arm when crossing the street. Don't rush the romance. Trying to corner her in the back of a cab may be one way of striking out. Never criticize the way she looks—in fact, the best policy would be to agree with her as much as possible. Still, there's just so much a man can take; all those dos and don'ts you'll have to observe if you want to get to first base with a virgo may be just a little too much to ask of you. After a few dates, you may come to the conclusion that she just isn't worth all that trouble. However, the Virgo woman is mysterious enough, generally speaking, to keep her men running back for more. Chances are you'll be intrigued by her airs and graces.

If lovemaking means a lot to you, you'll be disappointed at first in the cool ways of your Virgo girlie. However, under her glacial facade there lies a hot cauldron of seething excitement. If you're patient and artful in your romantic approach, you'll find that all that caution was well worth the trouble. When Virgos love, they don't stint. It's all or nothing as far as they're concerned. once they're convinced that they love you, they go all the way, right off the bat, tossing all cares to the wind.

One thing a Virgo woman can't stand in love is hypocrisy. They don't give a hoot about what the neighbors say, if their hearts tell them "Go ahead!" They're very concerned with human truths—so much so that if their hearts stumble upon another fancy, they're liable to be true to that new heart-throb and leave you standing in the rain. She's honest to her heart and will be as true to you are you are with her, generally. Do her wrong once, however, and it's farewell.

Both strict and tender, she tries to bring out the best in her children.

PISCES MAN
LIBRA WOMAN

As the song goes, it's a woman's prerogative to change her mind. The lyricist must have had the Libra woman in his thoughts when he jotted this ditty out. Her changeability, in spite of its undeniable charm (sometimes) could actually drive even a man of your patience up the wall. She's capable of smothering you with love and kisses one day and on the next, avoid you like the plague. If you think you're a man of steel nerves then perhaps you can tolerate her sometimey-ness without suffering too much. However, if you own up to the fact that you're only a mere mortal who can only take so much, then you'd better fasten your attention on a girl who's somewhat more constant.

But don't get the wrong idea: a love affair with a Libran is not bad at all. In fact, it can have an awful lot of plusses to it. Libra women are soft, very feminine, and warm. She doesn't have to vamp all over the place in order to gain a man's attention. Her delicate presence is enough to warm the cockles of any man's heart. One smile and you're like a piece of putty in the palm of her hand.

She can be fluffy and affectionate—things you like in a girl. On the other hand, her indecision about which dress to wear, what to cook for dinner, or whether to redo the rumpus room or not could make you tear your hair out. What will perhaps be more exasperating is her flat denial to the accusation that she cannot make even the simplest decision. The trouble is that she wants to be fair or just in all matters; she'll spend hours weighing pros and cons. Don't make her rush into a decision; that will only irritate her.

The Libra woman likes to be surrounded by beautiful things. Money is no object when beauty is concerned. There will always be plenty of flowers in the house. She'll know how to arrange them tastefully, too. Women under this sign are fond of beautiful clothes and furnishings. They will run up bills without batting an eye—if given the chance.

Once she's cottoned to you, the Libra woman will do everything in her power to make you happy. She'll wait on you hand and foot when you're sick and bring you breakfast in bed on Sundays. She'll be very thoughtful and devoted. If anyone dares suggest you're not the grandest man in the world, your Libra wife will give that person a good sounding-out.

Librans work wonders with children. Gentle persuasion and affection are all she uses in bringing them up, and it works.

PISCES MAN
SCORPIO WOMAN

When the Scorpio woman chooses to be sweet, she's apt to give the impression that butter wouldn't melt in her mouth . . . but, of course, it would. When her temper flies, so will everything else that isn't bolted down. She can be as hot as a *tamale* or as cool as a cucumber when she wants. Whatever mood she's in, you can be sure it's for real. She doesn't believe in poses or hypocrisy.

The Scorpio woman is often seductive and sultry. Her femme fatale charm can pierce through the hardest of hearts like a laser ray. She doesn't have to look like Mata Hari (many of them resemble the tomboy next door), but once you've looked into those tantalizing eyes, you're a goner.

The Scorpio woman can be a whirlwind of passion. Life with a girl born under this sign will not be all smiles and smooth-sailing. If you think you can handle a woman who can purr like a pussycat when handled correctly but spit bullets once her fur is ruffled, then try your luck. Your stable and steady nature will most likely have a calming effect on her. You're the kind of man she can trust and rely on. But never cross her—even on the smallest thing; if you do, you'd better tell Fido to make room for you in the doghouse —you'll be his guest for the next couple of days.

Generally, the Scorpio woman will keep family battles within the walls of your home. When company visits, she's apt to give the impression that married life with you is one big joy-ride. It's just her way of expressing her loyalty to you—at least, in front of others. She believes that family matters are and should stay private. She'll certainly see to it that others have a high opinion of you both. She'll be right behind you whatever it is you want to do. Although she's an individualist, after she has married, she'll put her own interests aside for those of the man she loves. With a woman like this behind, you can't help but go far. She'll never try to take over your role as boss of the family. She'll give you all the support you need in order to fulfill that role. She won't complain if the going gets rough. She is a courageous woman. She's as anxious as you to find that place in the sun for you both. She's as determined a person as you are.

Although she may love her children, she may not be very affectionate toward them. She'll make a devoted mother, though. She'll be anxious to see them develop their talents. She'll teach the children to be courageous and steadfast.

PISCES MAN
SAGITTARIUS WOMAN

You'll most likely never come across a more good-natured girl than the one born under the sign of Sagittarius. Generally, they're full of bounce and good cheer. Their sunny dispositions seem almost permanent and can be relied upon even on the rainiest of days.

Women born under this sign are almost never malicious. If ever they seem to be, it is only seeming. Sagittarians are often a little short on tact and say literally anything that comes into their pretty little heads—no matter what the occasion. Sometimes the words that tumble out of their mouths seem downright cutting and cruel. Still, no matter what she says, she means well. The Sagittarius woman is quite capable of losing some of her friends—and perhaps even some of yours—through a careless slip of the lip.

On the other hand, you are liable to appreciate her honesty and good intentions. To you, qualities of this sort play an important part in life. With a little patience and practice, you can probably help cure your Sagittarian of her loose tongue; in most cases, she'll give in to your better judgement and try to follow your advice to letter.

Chances are, she'll be the outdoor-type of girl friend. Long hikes, fishing trips, and white-water canoeing will most likely appeal to her. She's a busy person; no one could ever·call her a slouch. She sets great store in mobility. She won't sit still for one minute if she doesn't have to.

She is great company most of the time and, generally, lots of fun. Even if your buddies drop by for poker and beer, she won't have any trouble fitting in.

On the whole, she is a very kind and sympathetic woman. If she feels she's made a mistake, she'll be the first to call your attention to it. She's not afraid to own up to her own faults and shortcomings.

You might lose your patience with her once or twice. After she's seen how upset her shortsightedness or tendency to blabbermouth has made you, she'll do her best to straighten up.

The Sagittarius woman is not the kind who will pry into your business affairs. But she'll always be there, ready to offer advice if you need it.

The Sagittarius woman is seldom suspicious. Your word will almost always be good enough for her.

She is a wonderful and loving friend to her children.

PISCES MAN
CAPRICORN WOMAN

The Capricorn woman may not be the most romantic of the zodiac, but she's far from frigid when she meets the right man. She believes in true love; she doesn't appreciate getting involved in flings. To her, they're just a waste of time. She's looking for a man who means "business"—in life as well as in love. Although she can be very affectionate with her boy friend or mate, she tends to let her head govern her heart. That is not to say she is a cool, calculating cucumber. On the contrary, she just feels she can be more honest about love if she consults her brain first. She wants to size up the situation before throwing her heart in the ring. She wants to make sure it won't get stepped on.

The Capricorn woman is faithful, dependable, and systematic in just about everything she undertakes. She is quite concerned with security and sees to it that every penny she spends is spent wisely. She is very economical about using her time, too. She does not believe in whittling away her energy on a scheme that is bound not to pay off.

Ambitious themselves, Capricorns are quite often attracted to ambitious men—men who are interested in getting somewhere in life. If a man of this sort wins her heart, she'll stick by him and do all she can to help him get to the top.

The Capricorn woman is almost always diplomatic. She makes an excellent hostess. She can be very influential when your business acquaintances come to dinner.

The Capricorn woman is likely to be very concerned, if not downright proud, about her family tree. Relatives are pretty important to her, particularly if they're socially prominent. Never say a cross word about her family members. That can really go against her grain, and she'll punish you by not talking to you for days.

She's generally thorough in whatever she does. Capricorn women are well-mannered and gracious, no matter what their backgrounds. They seem to have it in their natures to always behave properly.

If you should marry a woman born under this sign, you need

never worry about her going on a wild shopping spree. They understand the value of money better than most women. If you turn over your paycheck to her at the end of the week, you can be sure that a good hunk of it will wind up in the bank.

The Capricorn mother is loving and correct.

PISCES MAN
AQUARIUS WOMAN

If you find that you've fallen head over heels for a woman born under the sign of the Water Bearer, you'd better fasten your safety belt. It may take you quite a while to actually discover what this girl is like—and even then, you may have nothing to go on but a string of vague hunches. The Aquarian is like a rainbow, full of bright and shining hues; she's like no other girl you've ever known. There is something elusive about her, something difficult to put your finger on.

The Aquarius woman can be pretty odd and eccentric at times. Some say this is the source of her mysterious charm. You are liable to think she's just a plain screwball; you may be 50 percent right.

Aquarius women often have their heads full of dreams. By nature, they're often unconventional; they have their own ideas about how the world should be run. Sometimes their ideas may seem pretty weird—chances are they're just a little bit too progressive. There is a saying that runs "The way the Aquarian thinks, so will the world in 50 years." She'll most likely be the most tolerant and open-minded woman you've ever encountered.

If you find that she's too much mystery and charm for you to handle, just talk it out with her and say that you think it would be better to call it quits. She'll most likely give you a peck on the cheek and say, "Okay, but let's still be friends." Aquarius women are like that. Perhaps you'll both find it easier to get along in a friendship than in a romance.

It is not difficult for her to remain buddy-buddy with an ex-lover. For many Aquarians, the line between friendship and romance is a pretty fuzzy one.

She is not a jealous person and, while you're romancing her, she won't expect you to be, either. You'll find her a pretty free spirit most of the time. Just when you think you know her inside-out, you'll discover that you don't really know her at all.

She's a very sympathetic and warm person; she is often helpful to those in need of assistance and advice.

She'll seldom be suspicious, even when she has every right to be. If the man she loves makes a little slip, she's liable to forgive and forget it.

She makes a fine mother. Her positive and big-hearted qualities are easily transmitted to her offspring.

PISCES MAN
PISCES WOMAN

Many a man dreams of a Piscean kind of girl. You're perhaps no exception. She's soft and cuddly and very domestic. She'll let you be the brains of the family; she's contented to just lean on your shoulder and let you be the master of the household.

She can be very ladylike and proper. Your business associates and friends will be dazzled by her warmth and femininity. Although she's a charmer, there is a lot more to her than just a pretty exterior. There is a brain ticking away behind that soft, womanly facade. You may never become aware of it—that is, until you're married to her. It's no cause for alarm, however; she'll most likely never use it against you.

If she feels you're botching up your married life through careless behavior or if she feels you could be earning more money than you do, she'll tell you about it. But any wife would, really. She will never try to usurp your positon as head and breadwinner of the family.

No one had better dare say one uncomplimentary word about you in her presence. It's liable to cause her to break into tears. Pisces women are usually very sensitive beings. Their reaction to adversity, frustration , or anger is just a plain, good, old-fashioned cry. They can weep buckets when inclined.

She'll have an extra-special dinner prepared for you when you make a new conquest in your profession. Don't bother to go into details, though, at the dinner table; she doesn't have much of a head for business matters, usually, and is only too happy to leave that up to you.

She can do wonders with a house. She is very fond of soft and beautiful things. There will always be plenty of fresh-cut flowers around the house. She'll see that you always have plenty of clean socks and underwear in that top drawer of your dresser.

Treat her with tenderness, and your relationship will be an enjoyable one. She's most likely fond of chocolates. A bunch of beautiful flowers will never fail to make her eyes light up. See to it that you never forget her birthday or your anniversary. These things are very important to her. If you let them slip your mind, you'll send her into a crying fit that could last a considerable length of time. If you are patient and kind, you can keep a Pisces woman happy for a lifetime. She, however, is not without her faults. Her "sensitivity" may get on your nerves after a while; you may find her lacking in imagination and zest; you may even feel that she uses her tears as a method of getting her own way. She makes a strong, self-sacrificing mother.